GREG DYKE was born in 1947 and educated at Hayes Grammar School and York University. Before becoming Director-General of the BBC in January 2000, he had enjoyed spells as Editor-in-Chief at TV-am, Director of Programmes at TVS and LWT (where he was Chief Executive from 1990 to 1994), a Director of Channel Four Television, and Chairman and Chief Executive of Pearson Television (1995–9).

He lives with his partner Sue Howes in Twickenham, Middlesex, and has four children.

For automatic updates on GREG DYKE visit harperperennial.co.uk and register for AuthorTracker.

From the reviews of *Inside Story*:

'A must-read for anyone interested in the history of British broadcasting. The once famous names of great programmes ... float past as he spiritedly recreates the intensity of the wars over franchises and breakfast television ... A good read and an historical contribution'

BRENDA MADDOX, *Literary Review*

'There is more to *Inside Story* than Hutton. It is a fascinating account of a long journey ... to the hallowed portals of Broadcasting House. The book demonstrates the energy, passion, intelligence and commitment that made Dyke an exceptional director-general'

CHRISTOPHER BLAND, *New Statesman*

'*Inside Story* is a pacy romp ... Dyke's book is far greater than the episode about the BBC and Iraq ... His robust dissection of t̶h̶̶ ̶J̶o̶h̶n̶ ̶B̶i̶̶... ̶a̶t̶ ̶t̶h̶e̶ ̶B̶B̶C̶ is a balanced

D0293798

account ... Should be required reading for anyone seeking to understand the complex relationship between the viewer, the television industry and the flexing muscles of the State'
Observer

'The most accessible of all books written by those who have held high office in the BBC. Its clarity is in its style ... Greg Dyke's book contains considerable and valuable material on the Gilligan affair and the various moves within and without the BBC as to how this was progressed ... An important documentary account'
Irish Times

GREG DYKE

Inside Story

HARPER PERENNIAL
London, New York, Toronto and Sydney

Harper Perennial
An imprint of HarperCollins*Publishers*
77–85 Fulham Palace Road
Hammersmith
London W6 8JB

www.harperperennial.co.uk

This edition published by Harper Perennial 2005
1

First published by HarperCollins*Publishers* 2004

A catalogue record for this book
is available from the British Library

ISBN 0 00 719364 5

Set in Sabon by
Rowland Phototypesetting Ltd, Bury St Edmunds, Suffolk

Printed and bound in Great Britain by
Clays Ltd, St Ives plc

Contents

Illustrations   vii

Acknowledgements   ix

1   Three Days in January   1

2   The First Thirty Years   34

3   Into Television   55

4   A Year at TV-am   69

5   TVS and Back to LWT   92

6   Running and Losing LWT   109

7   Joining the BBC   135

8   The BBC Years (1)   155

9   The BBC Years (2)   180

10 Why Did They Cry?   198

11 Television and Sport   221

12 Gilligan, Kelly, and Hutton   250

13 Why Hutton Was Wrong   287

14 Some Final Thoughts   318

    Index   331

To Sue

And to Matthew, Christine, Alice, and Joe

Illustrations

My mum and dad on their wedding day in 1939.
In the back garden of our hourse in Cerne Close, Hayes.
Aged seven, a pupil at Yeading Primary School in Hayes.
Form 1b at Hayes Grammar School in 1958.
The Hayes Grammar 'upper sixth' in 1965.
In my last year at school.
My leaving party at the *Hillingdon Mirror*, 1969.
Outside 1, Briggs Street, York. © *Jeffrey Wright*
With my dog Jake on the North Yorkshire moors, 1972. © *Jeffrey Wright*
The Six O'Clock Show team at LWT, 1982.
My leaving card from LWT: illustration by Carlo Roberto.
My family in 1989.
My message to LWT staff.
With Christopher Bland. © *Topfoto/UPPA*
The great match at Wembley in 1987.
Steve Cram chops me from behind.
The LWT joke poster.
LWT's top management and stars on the day we retained the franchise.
Celebrating Labour's victory, 1997. © *Justin Williams/The Sunday Times*
Sue and me on election night, May 1997. © *Andrew Shaw/The Daily Telegraph*
Outside Old Trafford, 1997. © *Tom Jenkins*.
With Alex Ferguson and other directors of Manchester United.

Directors and officials of Manchester United before the match in
  Barcelona.
Dr Dyke. © *Guzelian*
At Thora Hird's memorial service. © *Tim Rooke/Rex Features*
The BBC Board of Governors, July 2003. © *BBC Photo Library*
Outside Television Centre on the day I left the BBC. © *Fiona Hanson/
  PA Photos*
Taking out tea to the television crews. © *Stephen Lock/The Daily
  Telegraph*

Cartoons: Newman/NI Syndication; Franklin/NI Syndication; Richard
  Willson/NI Syndication; Heath/NI Syndication.

Acknowledgements

I've always believed that autobiographies are ridiculously self-serving and, as such, shouldn't be taken too seriously. That was before I had written one. I suspect in writing this book I've fallen into all the traps of self-justification that have made me laugh when I have read others' accounts of their lives. If I have, please forgive me. My dad always taught me that being pompous and self-important was just about the greatest sin of all; at least I hope I've avoided that in this book.

I started this book the weekend after I was fired from the BBC when my friend Melvyn Bragg rang me and told me that I had better write a book because if I didn't do something I'd drive my friends and my family mad. Melvyn is normally right about most things but on this occasion he got it wrong: I've driven my family mad anyway while writing this account of my life. They are almost as bored with Lord Hutton as I am.

But I sincerely believe we are living through something profound; that we are in the midst of a great political scandal; and if this book helps in a small way to expose that scandal, then I'll be happy.

There are people to thank. At HarperCollins there are Caroline Michel and Richard Johnson, whose enthusiasm has kept me going; there's my agent, Vivien Green (I've never had an agent before and she seems terribly nice); there's James Hogan, who suggested the title of the book; there are Jeff Wright, John Morrison, Alice Pearman, Trevor East, David Fairbairn, Clive Jones, Tony Cohen, Susan Spindler, Carolyn Fairbairn, Gavyn Davies and others who have helped me with different parts of the book. Then there's Christopher Bland, who read it all, corrected some facts, and tried to make some sense of my grammar; and finally there was

Melvyn Bragg, who gave me the confidence to start and has given invaluable advice chapter by chapter (not that he's agreed with all the sentiments in them).

I'll end by thanking my mum for just about everything but in particular for the wonderful words of advice she gave me when I rang and told her I was writing a book. She thought for a moment and said, 'I hope you're not going to cause trouble, dear.' I sincerely hope I am.

CHAPTER ONE

Three Days in January

As I left home on the morning of Tuesday 27 January 2004, I had no idea that within thirty-six hours my career as Director-General of the BBC would be over. I didn't even see it as a remote possibility that I would be fired by a board of BBC Governors behaving like frightened rabbits caught in the headlights – a board unnerved by a combination of the resignation of their Chairman, Lord Hutton's infamous report, and the prospect of the revenge the Government might seek to take against the BBC.

Of course very few people knew then that Lord Hutton's report, due to be published the following day, would so damn the BBC and would so totally exonerate the Government of any mistakes or wrongdoing. It was our view that the BBC had made some mistakes and was likely to be criticized but that the Government would deservedly suffer at least as much. Nor could anyone have known that within forty-eight hours the acting Chairman of the BBC would do lasting damage to the BBC's reputation at home and abroad by issuing the most grovelling of apologies to a vitriolic Government.

And who could possibly have foreseen that thousands of BBC employees, in all parts of the United Kingdom, would have taken to the streets to support me, or that they would have clubbed together to pay for a full-page advertisement in the *Daily Telegraph* backing me and challenging the Governors to defend the independence of the BBC? And how could anyone have known on that Tuesday morning that by the end of the week Lord Hutton's report would have been so comprehensively ridiculed by media and public alike, its findings dismissed as a crude

1

whitewash of the Government and yet another example of Number Ten spin?

Nevertheless, as I left home that morning I certainly knew that it was going to be a lively week.

With the publication of the Hutton Report imminent, the photographers and reporters were already camped outside my house in Twickenham, so even the most innocent of passers-by would have known that something was up. My partner Sue was away in Suffolk for the week, real evidence that we didn't expect a major crisis: if we had, then there was no way she would have gone. Only Joe and I were there that morning. Joe was sixteen at the time, the youngest of our four children and the only one at home. He was used to journalists and camera crews turning up outside our house and we both smiled when we saw them there that morning.

Our house backs onto nine acres of parkland that we share with forty or so other houses. This gives us numerous choices for getting in and out, making it virtually impossible for any reporter, photographer, or camera crew to catch me. We saw avoiding them as a game that we had been playing, on and off, for the four years I'd been Director-General. On some occasions Joe or my daughter Alice, who in January was away building a school in Africa, used to take pity on them and would tell them that I'd already left, but the journalists never believed them. Joe, Alice, and I quite enjoyed the game. Sue, on the other hand, hated these people intruding into our privacy in this way.

Because I had expected the press to arrive, I had already arranged for Joe to spend the next couple of days at a friend's house, so on that Tuesday morning we left together through the back door, with Joe pushing his bike and carrying a bagful of clothes. We got onto the road through the garden of Number 10a and when we got there I rang Bill, my driver, and he drove around the corner and picked me up. Meanwhile, Joe cycled off to college. An easy win that morning. The next time Joe and I were to meet was on Thursday evening, when I was no longer the Director-General and he had already started making jokes about leaving home if I was going to be there full time.

That Tuesday was Hutton publication day minus one, the day when all of those involved in the inquiry were to get an advanced copy of the report. We were to receive it exactly twenty-four hours before Hutton pronounced, which meant we would get it around lunchtime. A total of twenty-two of us at the BBC had signed confidentiality agreements and we had agreed a timetable for the day. I was going to read the report alone in my office. Richard Sambrook, the Director of BBC News, and his deputy Mark Damazer would read it in the meeting room next door, along with Magnus Brooke, my acting business manager. Magnus was a lawyer whom I had picked from relative obscurity within the BBC for this job, and he was brilliant. During the summer he had gone back to the legal division for a period to help out on Hutton. The rest of the people entitled to read the report that day would be in rooms nearby. Andrew Gilligan, the journalist at the centre of the row, and his legal team also had a room allocated in the building.

We had all set aside four hours to read the report knowing that it was likely to be nearly 700 pages long; but as it turned out, we didn't need anything like as long as that. Halfway down page three I knew we were in trouble. It was on that page that Lord Hutton explained that he had decided to limit the scope of his inquiry and completely ignore the crucial question of what sort of weapons of mass destruction the Government was warning us about in the dossier they had published in September 2002. With this one inexplicable decision Lord Hutton had wiped out key parts of the BBC's evidence and a critical foundation of our case. The following week we were to discover perhaps the most damning fact of all: that the Prime Minister himself had no idea what sort of weapons of mass destruction he had referred to, even though he'd used the so-called evidence of their existence as the central theme of his own introduction to the dossier and a reason for going to war.

There was a crumb of comfort for everyone at the BBC at the bottom of page three when Hutton said he was satisfied that no one involved in the row, including the BBC, could possibly have realized that Dr David Kelly, the Government expert on weapons of mass destruction who had been the BBC's source for its original story, might take his own life. But these were virtually the only kind words about the BBC in the whole report, and even that reference was far kinder to those in 10 Downing Street and the Ministry of Defence than it was to the BBC. It was Number Ten and the MOD who had hounded Dr Kelly, not the BBC: we had gone to great lengths to keep his identity secret.

I tried to plough on through the report but rapidly discovered it was a cut and paste job. It felt like Hutton, late in life, had learnt how to use Microsoft Word: the report was largely made up of tracts of evidence given to the inquiry with Hutton's opinion simply tacked on at the end, often without any explanation as to how or why he had reached his conclusions. When writing about the report later, the former editor of *The Times*, Lord Rees-Mogg, agreed. He called it a defective document in which the conclusions did not follow from the evidence.

I began to skim the document at about the same time as Mark Damazer stuck his head round the door to tell me that I only had to read the seven pages that made up Chapter 12 because the guts of the report was all there. This was the summary of Hutton's conclusions and I read them in total disbelief. This man wasn't on the same planet as the rest of us. Hadn't he listened to the evidence? Hadn't he listened to his own QC during the inquiry? How could he possibly have reached these conclusions?

Forty minutes after I started reading the report I walked into the adjoining meeting room where Sambrook, Damazer, and young Magnus Brooke were all sitting looking shell shocked. They tell me I said something like, 'Well, boys, we've been fucked, so what are we going to do about it?'

In the week or two before publication we had worked on a whole range of scenarios for what Hutton might say and how we should respond. The problem was that none of our scenarios was as bad as the reality. In our scenario planning it had only crossed our minds once, and then only fleetingly, that Hutton might find that the dossier had not been 'sexed up' at all. We all laughed and dismissed it, as the evidence was so clear cut. But that was exactly what Hutton had decided. There had been no sexing up; even worse, he had found against the BBC and for the Government on virtually every single count.

The four of us rapidly and prophetically agreed that this report was so one-sided we didn't believe it would turn out to be such good news for the Government as initially appeared to be the case. It was so much in their favour people would find it hard to believe. After all, dozens of journalists had sat through the inquiry and listened to the evidence. Surely they would see Hutton's findings as completely inconsistent with the evidence? And what about the wider public? They had followed the inquiry in large numbers and would surely see the same inconsistencies. Interestingly, over at *The Sun* newspaper, which, unbeknown to any of us, had illicitly obtained a copy of the report, the reaction was very similar. There the paper's editor, Rebekah Wade, and her team immediately saw that the report might be seen as a complete whitewash.

The problem we faced on that Tuesday was: how long would it take before this happened, and what would our defence be in the meantime? We discussed a strategy and decided to stick to the plan we had developed in advance. We would say that most of the criticisms of the BBC had been acknowledged during the inquiry; that, as a result, we had taken steps to improve our procedures; and that we would soon announce changes to the BBC's editorial guidelines. However, I did add a new line. We would also say, on the crucial issue of reporting a confidential source, that we had real doubts whether Lord Hutton had got it right, that he had misunderstood the law, and that his conclusions were a threat to free journalism in the UK.

Around 2.30 p.m. we went down one flight of stairs to see the BBC Chairman Gavyn Davies. He was with the two other BBC Governors who had been allowed to read the report in advance – Pauline Neville-Jones and the Vice-Chairman, Lord Ryder. Both were very Establishment figures. Richard Ryder had been Chief Whip in the last Conservative Government and Neville-Jones had been a career civil servant at the Foreign Office and was a former Chair of the Joint Intelligence Committee (JIC). She had left the Foreign Office when she was not appointed Britain's Ambassador in Paris.

I can't say I liked Pauline Neville-Jones, but I did have some respect for her. She was one of a number of Governors who had fought against my appointment as Director-General four years earlier and was still a powerful voice on the current Board, which was a bit short of people with authority. She certainly worked harder than any other Governor in my time at the BBC, was obviously very clever in a manipulative Foreign Office sort of way, and had successfully sustained the BBC's close relationship with the Foreign Office. This mattered because it was the Foreign Office who funded the BBC World Service.

But neither I nor the two BBC chairmen I worked with, Christopher Bland and Gavyn Davies, ever totally trusted Pauline. She applied to be Deputy Chairman of the BBC when Lord Ryder was recruited and was turned down. She was incredibly ambitious but I always suspected she had not been as successful in life as she had wished or expected.

On the other hand, I did like Richard Ryder. I first met him at the Conservative Party Conference a decade or so earlier when I was Chief Executive of London Weekend Television and found him quiet and thoughtful, unlike most politicians. He had been one of the people who had worked with the public relations guru Gordon Rees back in the late 1970s transforming Margaret Thatcher's image, so he'd been around the fringes of politics for a long time. When he became Deputy Chairman of the BBC he was still on the Board of Ipswich Town Football Club, and as a former Director of Manchester United I had plenty to chat with him about. The problem with Richard was that he had been recruited as Deputy Chairman to help build a relationship with the Conservative Party but quite clearly disliked many of the people now leading it. He had failed to make a single speech since he was elevated to the House of Lords in 1997 and seemed reluctant even to attend, let alone host, lunches and dinners in the Lords in support of the BBC. People in both Public Affairs and the Secretary's office at the BBC complained all the time that he didn't work hard enough to be the Deputy Chairman.

When we met up with Gavyn, Pauline, and Richard they, too, seemed shocked. Pauline said she was horrified by the report; Richard said very little. Gavyn told us that he had been told by a close friend that we had made a mistake co-operating with Hutton in the first place and that from the moment this particular judge had been appointed the result was a foregone conclusion. Our only hope, according to Gavyn's friend, had been to attack the way Hutton ran the whole inquiry at every available opportunity: that way we would have been able to demonstrate that he had been appointed by the Government to deliver a verdict that would favour them. It was an interesting perspective but hardly relevant to the position we were now in. In the middle of this discussion Tara Conlan, a journalist on the *Daily Mail*, rang Gavyn on his mobile phone and asked him openly what was in the report. We all laughed as he gave her a very polite brush-off.

By late afternoon we moved to a bigger room, where we were joined by our legal and press teams. Our QC, Andrew Caldecott, turned up with a comprehensive argument detailing how Hutton had completely misunderstood the law on 'qualified privilege', which covered the rights journalistic organizations now possessed. In the end we split into two groups, one to plan strategy and the other practicalities.

I worked on a comparatively aggressive statement, which we would put out the following day and which we'd all agreed Gavyn was to deliver. Together we watched the result of the parliamentary vote on tuition fees, which took place around 7.00 p.m. We got even more depressed when the Government narrowly won, thanks to Gordon Brown delivering his supporters at the last minute. Our reaction was nothing to do with the pros and cons of the issue; we simply thought we'd get an easier time the following day if the Government had another crisis on its hands.

The whole team then had dinner together. I remember being pleased that someone had ordered something other than sandwiches. At the time I was on the Atkins diet, and January is also one of the two months in the year when I don't drink alcohol, so as I munched through two or three pieces of chicken, and drank my bottled water, I was feeling very virtuous.

By now Gavyn had begun to talk privately about resigning. I was strongly against it, but I thought it had to be his decision. As the hours went by he became more and more convinced it was the right and honourable thing for him to do. I certainly had no intention of resigning. We discussed the position briefly with Richard Ryder before he disappeared for the evening and we talked over the whole strategy with Pauline Neville-Jones later in the evening after she had returned from a drinks party.

The three of us – Gavyn, Pauline, and I – sat privately in a room together and weighed up the options, a conversation that was to take on greater importance later given what happened the following day. Gavyn said he believed it was right for him to resign because the Governors had been criticized for the actions they had taken. I disagreed and said that if someone had to go, then we should discuss whether it should be him or me, given that Lord Hutton had also criticized the management. I didn't believe it was necessary for either of us to go. I didn't believe then, and still don't believe today, that the BBC had done enough wrong to merit such a drastic response.

My view was that if Lord Hutton's criticisms required resignations, then the Chairman, all the Governors, the Director-General, and several senior people in BBC News should all go at once. Since I also knew that Tony Blair had told Gavyn in a private telephone conversation that, whatever happened, Number Ten would not be calling on either Gavyn or me to go, I was of the view we should all sit out the coming storm.

While Gavyn hadn't finally made up his mind he was of the view that at least one resignation was essential. As he says now: 'I was willing to resign in preference to apologizing for doing nothing wrong, indeed for telling the British people the truth about the September dossier. I was never going to grovel but I am not sure that a strategy of "no apology and no resignation" was ever viable after Hutton.'

Once Pauline realized that Gavyn was likely to go she turned to me and said it would be impossible for both of us to go at the same time. I agreed. Given what she did the following day, this was an interesting position, one that both Gavyn and I clearly remember her taking. I said that, in those circumstances, I would need the Governors to make it clear they supported me, and she agreed with that.

During the evening, Richard Sambrook took a call from the BBC's political editor, Andy Marr, who told us that *The Sun* had got a comprehensive leak of the report that made it very clear that Downing Street had been cleared and that the BBC had got the blame. It was a good scoop and the BBC's Ten O'Clock News reported the story in full. Tuition fees were now yesterday's news and, a day earlier than expected, Hutton was now the big story.

But where had the leak come from? I and a million others immediately assumed it was Alastair Campbell, that it was payback time for *The Sun* in recognition of the support they had given Tony Blair and the Government during the Iraq war. During his time in Downing Street Campbell had regularly given exclusives to *The Sun*, sometimes when they were other people's stories. As Alastair was no longer on the staff at Number Ten, my view at the time was that he had little to lose by leaking the document even if he was caught, and there wasn't much chance of that. Despite having spun his exit brilliantly we knew that Campbell had been pushed out. I had absolutely no evidence to support the view that Campbell leaked the story, and I now believe my immediate response was wrong. What I do know is that Downing Street was very scared that it would be blamed for the leak and that evening demanded that Rebekah Wade, *The Sun*'s editor, put out a statement making it clear that it wasn't Downing Street or Campbell who had leaked it.

Since then, it has been suggested to me that the leak might have come from someone on our side who was playing a very Machiavellian game to make it look like it originated with Campbell. I don't buy that because it would have taken such a peculiar sort of mind to think that way, and what would have been the point? Another theory is that *The Sun* got the report from the printers. Lord Hutton set up an inquiry to try to discover who leaked his report, but I suspect we'll never know who actually did it.

At around 11 p.m. we all decided it was time to pack up and go home. I took the back way out of Broadcasting House to avoid any journalists but I did notice that Tara Conlan was still in reception. She rang me in the car about twenty minutes later, still digging.

I've always had a love–hate relationship with Tara, the *Daily Mail*'s TV editor. She was my bête noire when the *Daily Mail* was attacking me and the BBC virtually every day. She used to ask ridiculous questions at press conferences. I once replied to her by saying that her paper had already run the story in question on at least three separate occasions and yet she was now asking about it for the fourth time. Her answer was wonderful. 'Yes, I know,' she said, 'but my editor likes the story.' Later, when our relationship with the *Mail* improved, I grew to respect her. She worked incredibly hard, and when other journalists gave up she was always there.

On that Tuesday night I told her very politely that I was still bound by the confidentiality agreement we'd all signed and that I wouldn't break it (even though by then someone had broken it quite spectacularly). The only unauthorized person I had told about the contents of the report was Sue when I rang her in Suffolk. She asked what it was like. I answered in one word, 'Grim', and that was all I told her.

The next morning saw the same pattern as the day before. I left home early, escaping from my house via the back door and walking down to 10a, where Bill picked me up. There were even more journalists and crews outside my house than the previous day. I was glad that Sue was away and that I'd arranged for Joe to stay with a friend. Why should they have to put up with all this hassle simply because I was a public figure? I'd chosen that life, they hadn't.

It was an odd morning in the office. My PA for the past sixteen years, Fiona Hillary, arrived back from a holiday in Cuba not knowing that both our days at the BBC were numbered. By that evening she was in tears – not something I've seen from Fiona during the years we've worked together. She was also in a particularly difficult position: she is a close

GREG DYKE: INSIDE STORY

friend of Tony and Cherie Blair (her husband, Barry Cox, the Deputy Chairman of Channel Four, had previously been their next-door neighbour).

I didn't really have enough to do on that Wednesday morning and yet I couldn't concentrate on anything else. So I hung around chatting to various people. Sally Osman, our ever smiling Head of Communications, wandered through. For me, one of the joys of working at the BBC was working with Sally: we managed to laugh our way through almost every crisis – and you get a lot at the BBC. Mark Damazer also joined us and, at one point during that morning, all three of us were in with Gavyn Davies trying to persuade him not to resign or, at the very least, to wait until later in the day. I did get him to agree that he wouldn't announce anything until after Hutton had made his public statement at lunchtime. Gavyn also made it clear that, as he was likely to resign, he would not now be able to be the person who responded to Hutton on behalf of the BBC. I would have to do that instead.

I had arranged for most of the members of my seventeen-strong executive team, which was known around the BBC as Exco, to watch Lord Hutton deliver his findings in a room in Broadcasting House where my office was based. We had arranged for lunch to be delivered and once again the Atkins dieters, of whom there were at least two others on Exco, were well provided for. So far Atkins had survived the crisis, and so had my abstinence from alcohol.

I warned my team it was bad news and on a confidential basis told them that Gavyn was seriously considering resignation. We all watched Hutton and then the statements in the House of Commons from the party leaders. I marvelled at how good Blair was. It is a great shame that his skills at people management and strategic leadership have never matched his skills as an orator or in public relations. If they had, he would have been a great Prime Minister.

The new Conservative leader, Michael Howard, had an impossible task, having only had the report for four hours; but I believe he made a crucial mistake in accepting Hutton's findings immediately. If he had delayed and given himself another forty-eight hours I believe he would have taken a different approach. In particular, he accepted Hutton's view that Blair had said nothing inappropriate to journalists about the naming of David Kelly when he was on the plane from Shanghai to Hong Kong.

THREE DAYS IN JANUARY

Anyone who had followed the inquiry would have known that Hutton never questioned a single witness on that issue.

My own team were pretty badly shaken. I remember John Smith, the Director of Finance, saying something about resignations being needed (though I don't think he was referring to me) and Jenny Abramsky, the Director of Radio, sitting looking terribly serious in the corner, in the way that Jenny did. We all discussed the proposed statement I and the team had written. Virtually everyone wanted me to take out the more aggressive paragraphs, one of which said: 'We do have serious reservations about one aspect of the report which we believe could have significant implications for British journalism.' In effect I let them water down the proposed response. In retrospect I wish I hadn't because I believed then, as I do today, that the BBC had got the story largely right and that Downing Street's behaviour had been unacceptable. I was also convinced, as were our legal team, that Hutton had got the law wrong.

At 3.30 p.m. I recorded the statement and made it available to all news outlets. On BBC News 24 it was immediately interpreted as 'a robust response' from the BBC. Personally I thought it was conciliatory, but then being conciliatory is not necessarily one of my stronger points so perhaps I wasn't the best person to judge. I certainly wasn't going to roll over in the way Lord Ryder did the following day. Like Gavyn, I'd rather have resigned. I remember thinking at the time that it was a good job News 24 hadn't seen my original draft.

What did make me and the BBC look foolish later in the afternoon was the final paragraph of my statement, which said: 'The BBC Governors will be meeting formally tomorrow and will consider Lord Hutton's report. No further comment will be made until after that meeting.' Everyone had agreed that paragraph, but within half an hour of the statement being broadcast Andy Marr was back on the screens saying that he had it on very good authority that Gavyn Davies had resigned. Of course he only had a single unattributable source for his story, so under Lord Hutton's rules of journalism one wonders whether he should have broadcast it without corroboration. His source was a pretty good one though. It was Gavyn himself.

Gavyn was taking advice from his wife Sue, one of Gordon Brown's inner circle. Sue was very much of the view that it is better to resign on principle after being criticized than to be forced out later. As a strategy it only made sense if you believed you would be forced out in the end, which Gavyn now did.

Gavyn believed that by resigning quickly it would be contrasted with the Government's 'awful' behaviour and help turn the tables on Hutton, which in many ways it did. And as he had made clear the night before, he was not going to apologize because he still believed the BBC had largely been right. Some people believe Gavyn's early resignation cost me my job and that he should have done a deal with the Governors that I should stay before making his resignation public. That may or may not be true, but he took his decision for the best and most honourable of reasons.

It was by complete chance that the Governors were due to meet that evening in a private session starting at 5 p.m. The meeting had been set up some time in 2003 when the annual BBC calendar was drawn up; when I discovered, a week or two earlier, that the meeting coincided with the publication of the Hutton report I urged Gavyn to cancel it. I told him I feared the Governors would rush around and make rash decisions, which is exactly what they did. Gavyn was against moving it and so was Simon Milner, the BBC Secretary who organized the Governors' meetings. Simon should have had the political nous to understand the dangers but unfortunately, while Simon had many talents, he lacked political judgement. Despite my efforts, the meeting stayed in the diary and I continued to tell them both it was a mistake.

The Governors started their meeting at 5 p.m. and virtually never left the room until the early hours of the following day. They didn't see Jon Snow on Channel Four News at 7 p.m. raising the question of whether Hutton was a whitewash. This was significant because throughout the inquiry we thought that Channel Four's news coverage of Hutton was the most authoritative, better than the BBC's Six O'Clock News. The Governors didn't see the same theme continued on *Newsnight*; they didn't see the BBC's former chairman Christopher Bland saying that one resignation was enough; and they didn't see the early edition of *The Independent* with its blank front page simply saying 'Whitewash'.

The Governors didn't want to see anyone. They wouldn't even meet Andrew Caldecott, the BBC's own QC, who sat outside all evening waiting to be called in to give his detailed and informed legal opinion on Hutton, which was very critical of the report. Andrew knew more about Hutton than all the Governors put together, but they never saw him. After waiting for five hours he went home. At Andrew's hourly rate, keeping him waiting outside the meeting was criminal.

Later in the evening the Governors did agree to see the BBC's Director of Policy, Caroline Thomson, so she could give them a briefing: she had spent all evening gathering intelligence at Westminster. The BBC's Director of Human Resources, Stephen Dando, demanded to be seen and was allowed in. He told the Governors that getting rid of me would be a terrible blow to the staff and the BBC. But by then it was too late. The Governors had already made up their minds before speaking to either of them. They did what people under pressure often do: they turned inwards, talked to each other, and panicked.

I was there for the first forty minutes of the meeting. When they arrived, the Governors knew that Gavyn was going and some turned up with the view that they too should resign. In retrospect I should have let them. Instead I argued what I believed to be right: that the BBC couldn't be left without a Chairman and Governors because, in those circumstances, it would have no effective constitution. They agreed to stay.

When it came to discussing what should happen to members of the management team who had been criticized I offered to leave the meeting. I leant across to Simon Milner, who was sitting next to me, and reminded him what Gavyn and I had told him of our conversation the night before. It was his job to tell the Governors that if I was to continue I needed them to support me publicly. Gavyn and I then left the meeting for what I expected to be a half-hour discussion. As it turned out, I never went back that evening, and I will never have to go to another meeting of the BBC Governors again. There are some upsides in the whole affair.

As I walked down the corridor with Gavyn I saw Sarah Hogg scampering down the corridor the other way. She was late for the Governors' meeting. Sarah was never my favourite Governor. She had been Head of the Downing Street Policy Unit in John Major's Conservative Government and was the person who had invented 'Back to Basics' – one of the most disastrous policy initiatives introduced by any prime minister in the post-war years. She was recruited as a BBC Governor as a Tory, the view being that we were short of Conservative supporters on the Board. The irony was that by the end of my time at the BBC the Governors were dominated by people from the political Right. Virtually all the powerful players were Conservatives, with the exception of Gavyn, who in his capacity as Chairman bent over backwards to hold the ring by being politically neutral. It was so typical of Blair's New Labour. They were so worried about newspaper charges of 'Tony's cronies' that they allowed the BBC's Board of Governors to be dominated by the Right. Could anyone have imagined Margaret Thatcher allowing the Board to be dominated by Labour supporters?

While being a strong supporter of the BBC, Sarah Hogg never left her politics or prejudices at the door of Governors' meetings, not that there was anything wrong with that. She was married to a patrician, landowning Tory MP, Douglas Hogg, and lived in a political world. When we tried to change our political coverage to make it more appropriate for the twenty-first century it was Sarah who led the opposition on the grounds that we shouldn't upset the politicians. She was also upset by the lack of coverage of the Countryside March in September 2002 (probably the only march she'd ever been on). She insisted that the BBC was not covering rural affairs properly and demanded a full Governors' investigation, which she got – at the cost of many thousands of pounds. It always struck me as a classic case of special pleading from a Governor who lived on the family estate in rural Lincolnshire.

Sarah always gave the appearance that she was superior to most other people at Governors' meetings, sitting nodding in obvious support when she agreed with another Governor and shaking her head when she didn't, as if her opinion was the one that mattered most. Given that some of the other Governors were not as confident as Sarah, and didn't give the impression that they were born to rule, her opinions probably did matter a lot. Sarah and Pauline Neville-Jones were by far the most vocal Governors and I nicknamed them 'the posh ladies'. It was always clear to me that neither liked me much and Sarah, I now know, actively disliked me. The feeling was mutual.

Sarah's term as a Governor was due to finish at the end of January and she didn't want it renewed, which was just as well because neither did Gavyn or I. We both believed the right-wing bias of the Governors was unhealthy and that we needed more Governors without strong political views. So as Sarah ran past us in the corridor that night she only had a couple of days left as a Governor. It was her last chance to settle old scores. I now know that she came to the meeting determined to get rid of me.

I had been sitting in my office for maybe an hour and a half when

Simon Milner came in and said that Pauline and the Deputy Chairman wanted to see me downstairs. I'd thought their meeting was taking a long time, but it never crossed my mind that they would want me out. When I met them, Richard Ryder was pretty blunt. He said that the Governors had discussed the position and that they had decided I should go: if I stayed I'd be a lame-duck Director-General. It was a ridiculous argument: anyone who knew me well would know that there was never a chance of me being a lame-duck anything. I asked if this was the view of all the Governors. Typically, Richard told me he hadn't expressed a view but was reporting the views of the rest. Pauline said nothing.

Of course I should have seen it coming, but I hadn't. I was completely shocked. I had absolutely no idea what to say. I pointed out that I had a contract that they would have to honour, but I made it clear that if they didn't want me I wouldn't stay. It all took about five minutes and I said I needed to talk to Stephen Dando, the Head of Human Resources.

I went back to my office and sat there stunned. I had worked flat out for four years to try and turn round a deeply unhappy and troubled organization and was now being thrown out by the people I respected least in the whole place, the BBC Governors. I sat there in disbelief. Fancy being fired by a bunch of the great and the good, people whose contribution to the BBC was minimal to say the least, and who, in recent months, had become more and more obsessed about the survival of the Governors as an institution.

I asked Fiona to come into my room. We'd been together a long time at LWT, Pearson, and now the BBC. She'd arrived later than me at the BBC because Christopher Bland believed that her friendship with the Blairs would be a political liability for me and the BBC. That night I got up and gave her a hug and told her it was over, that the Governors wanted me out, and that I was going to resign.

Over the next hour or so I talked to Stephen Dando at some length. When he learnt what was happening he told the Governors that they were making a disastrous decision and warned them how the staff would react. Pat Loughrey, the Director of Nations and Regions, came in and told me not to go. He too went downstairs to demand to see the Governors, but they wouldn't let him in. Several members of my immediate team also came in and urged me not to resign.

Around 9 p.m. I changed my mind. I decided I wouldn't give the

Governors the satisfaction of getting rid of me without a fight. I asked Simon Milner to come and see me. He looked horrified when I told him that I didn't intend to resign and that they would have to sack me.

Ten minutes later I was back in a meeting with Ryder and Neville-Jones. I told them I wasn't going willingly and that I had never intended to resign, a veiled reference to the discussion Gavyn, Pauline, and I had had the night before. Richard Ryder got angry and slightly threatening, the sort of approach he must have adopted almost daily as a Chief Whip. I stayed firm and told them they must inform the other Governors that I wasn't resigning. I then went back to my office.

During that evening I talked on the phone with the three people who probably have more influence over me than anyone else. Firstly I reached Sue and told her what was happening. Her response was predictable: 'Fight the bastards, and if it means you get sacked, get sacked. Who cares?' That's my girl. She summed up the very reason why we've been together for twenty years. Sue was never very fond of my being at the BBC anyway. She thought the job was too time consuming, and she didn't like some of the senior people she met there. She thought they were lacking in fun, highly political, and falsely sycophantic.

I also phoned Christopher Bland, my former Chairman at LWT who'd gone on to become Chairman of the BBC and who, in turn, had persuaded me to join the organization in the first place. He had given up being Chairman two years earlier after he became the Chairman of BT, but before he did so he put his future in my hands. He told me: 'I brought you here so if you want me to stay I'll turn down BT and stay.' I thought he was right to take the BT job: he was in his sixties and he obviously fancied one last big challenge, so I advised him to go.

Christopher and I had been in battles together before. Some we'd won and some we'd lost, but he was great to have on your side. He never lost his nerve and I've known times when he supported me even though it was not in his personal interests to do so. I'd like to think I'd do the same for him. I loved working for him over the years, and he was always one of my two mentors. When I rang him and told him what was happening he couldn't believe that the Governors were trying to get me out and promised to do all he could. He appeared on *Newsnight* later in the evening. He also agreed with Sue and told me that I should tell them to 'fuck off'.

The third person I rang that evening was Melvyn Bragg, a close friend and my other mentor. Melvyn is probably the cleverest person I know; he knows so much about so many subjects. I first met him many years earlier when I was a young researcher at LWT and he was the famous Melvyn Bragg, editor and presenter of the *South Bank Show*. I remember being very flattered when he even remembered my name, but as a boy from a working-class background Melvyn had never lost the ability to relate to all around him, no matter what job they did. Much later, when I was Director of Programmes at LWT, I elevated the Arts Department into full departmental status just so that I could have Melvyn on my immediate team.

Melvyn was also one of the people who had encouraged me to join the BBC and had supported what I was trying to do there, although not uncritically. During those last three days at the BBC, he gave me all the support you could ask for from a friend, including writing a wonderful appraisal of what I had achieved in four years in that weekend's *Observer*. I got hold of him late on the Wednesday night, by which time I had had a further meeting with Ryder and Neville-Jones. They told me that the Board was adamant: I either resigned or was fired that night. Melvyn recognized that I was terribly upset and asked me how would I want it to be seen in six months' time: would I rather be seen to have resigned or to have been sacked? I answered 'Resigned'.

Normally when top executives leave or lose their posts these sorts of decisions are about pay-offs. But money was largely irrelevant in this case. The BBC would have had to pay up on my contract either way.

While all this was happening, Emma Scott – a feisty project manager who had worked with me from the first day I joined the BBC – decided she was going to rally my supporters by ringing around members of the executive team to get them to come in and support me. She persuaded Caroline Thomson to come back and talk to the Governors, Pat Loughrey stayed around for the whole evening, Andy Duncan, the BBC's outstanding Director of Marketing and now Chief Executive of Channel Four, turned up to support me, and Peter Salmon, the Director of Sport, phoned in to tell me to hang on in there.

Meanwhile Mark Byford, my recently appointed deputy, had been sitting outside the Governors' meeting for several hours, like the schoolboy summoned to the headmaster's study. Mark and I have always got on well and I've always liked and respected him as a professional broadcaster, but I still wonder why he didn't just wander up one flight of stairs for a chat that evening. Instead, he just sat there on his own for hour after hour. I suspect he was under instructions from the Governors not to talk to me, which would explain it.

I always saw Mark as a possible successor to me within the BBC, but that evening, and in the days that followed, his chances of becoming Director-General were wiped out. It was clear to me that, with Gavyn and me both gone, any new Chairman would want his or her own Director-General, not someone tainted by the events of that night and the weeks that followed. To be fair to Mark, he was put in a terrible position by the Governors, a position that wasn't of his own making. I have no doubt he did what he thought was his duty: he is that sort of man.

The pressures of that day finally told and I succumbed. I abandoned both the Atkins diet and abstinence from alcohol and ate a whole pizza and drank at least half a bottle of wine while all sorts of people were coming in and out of my office. I'm not sure I can ever forgive a combination of Lord Hutton and the Governors for forcing me to break my diet.

Gavyn Davies, who had been out of the loop since we left the Governors' meeting together earlier that evening, decided at about 11 p.m. to go home. I had already told him that the Governors wanted me out, but we'd agreed there was little he could do about it. Before he left, he decided to say a final goodbye to his former colleagues, but when he walked into the room he found the atmosphere had changed completely in five hours. It was a very hostile environment, with the aggression mainly coming from Sarah Hogg, who, according to him, was 'seething'.

I've since discovered that Sarah had told Gavyn the day before that he shouldn't resign but that I should go. Gavyn had told her then that there were no circumstances in which he'd let me go while he stayed, and I genuinely think that that was one of the reasons Gavyn resigned. Gavyn and I had worked very closely together, particularly on Hutton, and we both believed we were right. I think his view was that if one of us should go it should be him and that way he would protect me. According to others at that meeting, when Gavyn walked in Sarah launched a ferocious attack on him, accusing him of 'cowardice under fire' .

In the end I announced at about one in the morning that I wasn't negotiating or discussing any more. I was going home. The Governors were still downstairs, but by then I'd had enough. I would decide whether to resign or be fired in the morning. Either way I knew I'd be leaving the BBC.

Outside there was thick snow everywhere and I remember thinking how sad that I'd hardly noticed it falling. I got into the car and told my driver Bill that I was leaving. He, too, got upset. He told me later that neither he nor his wife Ann slept a wink all night.

The following morning I took the usual precautions to avoid the journalists and the camera crews outside my house. In the car I got a call from John Smith, the BBC's Finance Director, wanting to know what was happening. I told him and he decided to set about working on some of the Governors. He was confident he could get them to change their minds. But I knew it was too late. Overnight I hadn't slept a lot, but I had taken a decision. I would resign, but over the next few days I would make it very clear I had been given little option by a bunch of intransigent Governors.

So why did I choose that path? Looking back now I am not sure I know. With the benefit of hindsight, I think I should have stayed and dared them to fire me. But at the time I felt isolated. I also felt hurt and had a deep sense of injustice. I didn't believe that I had done anything to justify resignation, nor did I believe the BBC had done anything seriously wrong. I wasn't to know then that the staff would react in the way they did and that Hutton would be dismissed so quickly and comprehensively. What I do remember thinking was that if I was to go, I wanted to do so with some dignity.

If the Governors had only waited another day or two there would have been no need for me to leave: by then, it was Blair's people who were on the run. By the weekend Number Ten couldn't understand what had happened. The report had exonerated them and yet the public hadn't. They had no concept then, and still don't have, of how fast Blair had lost the trust of the people in Britain, of how quickly he'd gone from being seen as an honest and open man to being regarded as a public relations manipulator, a man without real principles. Iraq and spin had destroyed his reputation.

I got into the office about ten past eight on that Thursday morning and immediately started rewriting a couple of draft statements I'd prepared the night before. The first was the public announcement I would make. The second, much more important to me, was the e-mail I would send to all the staff telling them I was going. I was determined that the staff would learn the news from me and that the e-mail would go out before any press or public announcement.

That morning all feels a blur now. I remember lots of people coming in and out, and lots of people crying. Most of my immediate support staff were either crying or trying to stop. I remember Carolyn Fairbairn, the BBC's Head of Strategy with whom I'd worked so closely over four years, turning up looking as if she'd been crying all the way from Winchester, where she lived. Melvyn Bragg had been presenting his Radio Four programme *In Our Time* that morning and he too came up to my office and was there for at least an hour, talking to me, advising me, and reassuring my staff. They loved him for showing so much care. In the end even he got upset.

All morning the e-mails had been pouring in from staff urging me not to resign, but at around 1.30 p.m. I sent out my e-mail statement to the staff. It was typical of my all-staff e-mails. I had started sending them almost as soon as I joined the BBC and found it an incredibly effective way for a Chief Executive to communicate with every member of staff. During my four years I refused to send out long, boring e-mails; I wanted people to read them, so they had to be short, to the point, and interesting. This one would certainly have an impact. It was only a few paragraphs long, free of jargon, and in a language everyone could understand. It said:

This is the hardest e mail I've ever written. In a few moments I'll be announcing to the outside world that I'm leaving after four years as Director General. I don't want to go and I'll miss everyone here hugely. However the management of the BBC was heavily criticised in the Hutton Report and as the Director General I am responsible for the management.

I accept that the BBC made errors of judgement and I've sadly come to the conclusion that it will be hard to draw a line under this whole affair while I am still here. We need closure. We need closure to protect the future of the BBC, not for you or me but for the benefit of everyone out there. It might sound pompous but I believe the BBC really matters. Throughout this affair my sole aim as Director General of the BBC has been to defend our editorial independence and to act in the public interest.

In four years we've achieved a lot between us. I believe we've changed the place fundamentally and I hope those changes will last beyond me. The BBC has always been a great organization but I hope that, over the last four years, I've helped to make it a more human place where everyone who works here feels appreciated. If that's anywhere near true I leave contented if sad.

Thank you all for the help and support you've given me. This might sound schmaltzy but I really will miss you all.

Greg

As soon as the e-mail had gone I went downstairs to the entrance of Broadcasting House in Langham Place, where there was a massive, totally disorganized media scrum right on the BBC's own doorstep. I walked out through the revolving door, realized I was in danger of being crushed, stepped back into the drum, and revolved back into the building. After a couple of minutes there was enough room for me to move outside and, live on BBC News 24, Sky News, and the ITV News Channel, I announced I was leaving. The irony was that BBC News 24 almost missed the whole event because their crew was stuck at the back of the scrum and couldn't get a decent shot of me making the statement.

Then it was back upstairs and lots of drink and food with friends and colleagues. By then all thoughts of Atkins and abstinence had totally disappeared. Mark Damazer, whom I first worked with at TV-am twenty years earlier, made a short but funny speech talking about my strengths and weaknesses. I replied by telling everyone that this was not a day for bandstanding. I was going and they should protect their careers. I also told them to support Mark Byford, who was to be acting Director-General; he was a good bloke and had played no part in my demise.

Oddly, it was about that time that Mark was making a terrible mistake. He had agreed to stand with Lord Ryder while the acting Chairman recorded a statement. When asked to do this, Mark should have declined.

Instead, he stood by while Ryder made the most grovelling of apologies in which he said sorry for any mistake the BBC might have made, without actually defining what the mistakes were. He apologized 'unreservedly'. It was as if he had apologized for anything anyone in Government could accuse the BBC of. It was the style of delivery that made the apology seem so grovelling. The two of them looked like the leaders of an old Eastern European government: grey, boring, and frightened.

The statement was on the news bulletins all day and was seen throughout the world. Without realizing it, Lord Ryder had done enormous damage to the reputation of the BBC, and to himself.

When, that afternoon, Lord Ryder was asked at a special meeting of the BBC's executive committee whether his statement would be enough to satisfy the Government, he replied that he had been assured it would, leaving a number of members of the committee with the clear impression that he had discussed and cleared the statement with Downing Street before delivering it.

I have since had it confirmed by the BBC that, before he made his statement, Lord Ryder had been in contact with Number Ten telling them both of the content of the statement he planned to make and that I was going. The BBC now say this was only a matter of 'courtesy', but it has serious implications. The whole independence of the BBC is based on its separation from Government, and yet here was its acting Chairman effectively clearing a statement before he made it. We don't know if they asked for changes. What would he have done if they had?

It also brings into question whether or not Downing Street wanted my head. Gavyn had reached an agreement with Blair, in one of the many phone calls they had between June and December, that no matter what Hutton said the Government would not call for either of us to go. When he watched Blair in the House of Commons immediately after Hutton's press conference Gavyn realized the Prime Minister had gone back on his word. He told me: 'Blair skilfully piled the pressure on, and did nothing to discharge his promise that there should be no resignations at the BBC. I assumed he had reneged. Then I saw Campbell calling us liars, and demanding that heads should roll. I assumed that Blair had deliberately unleashed the dogs against us, and that there would be no peace with the Government until we either resigned or apologized.'

I, too, had been assured in advance, in discussions between myself and

22

Campbell's successor, Dave Hill – a more rational and reasonable man than Campbell – that when the Hutton report was published Number Ten would not criticize the BBC if we agreed not to criticize them. Hill had also assured me that they would be able to control Campbell, that he would be back inside Number Ten for the publication of the Hutton Report and would take orders. So on that Wednesday Blair could have stopped Campbell from calling for heads. He chose not to. And on the Thursday morning Downing Street was told what was happening at the BBC but Blair did nothing to prevent my 'resignation'. Since then, he has let it be known through friends that he didn't want either Gavyn or me to go and has even invited me to meet with him informally. I refused. I no longer regard Tony Blair as someone to be trusted.

Ryder's 'unreserved' apology had other repercussions. From that moment onwards the BBC stopped publicly arguing the case it had argued throughout the Hutton inquiry: that while it had made some mistakes, it had been right to broadcast Dr Kelly's claims that Downing Street had 'sexed up' the dossier to make a more convincing case for war. From that moment onwards no one from within the BBC was allowed to make that argument, and yet it is what I still believe happened and I will argue the case passionately in this book.

The real irony came several weeks later when *The Guardian* ran a story that said that Lord Hutton was 'shocked' by the reaction to his report and hadn't expected any heads to roll at the BBC. If this is true, he is a remarkably naive man.

My day and my time at the BBC were rapidly coming to an end. I was preparing to leave my office for the last time when I got a phone call from Peter Salmon at Television Centre. He told me that there were remarkable scenes happening and that I ought to come over. He said that hundreds of members of staff had taken to the streets with 'Bring Back Greg' posters and that the demonstration was getting bigger by the minute. I turned to Magnus and Emma and said we ought to go. Andrew Harvey, a friend and talented journalist whom I had brought in to edit *Ariel*, the BBC's in-house magazine, was with me at the time, so he came along too.

In all there were five of us in the car. It was a fifteen-minute drive and no one said anything. When we got to White City and drove down towards Television Centre we found the roads outside the BBC buildings thronged with chanting staff holding up placards. The scenes were amazing. As I got out of the car people were applauding and trying to shake my hand. There were news crews everywhere trying to interview me. For a brief period of my life I suddenly found out what it was like to be an American presidential candidate or Madonna. It was frightening.

Someone thrust a megaphone into my hand and I made an impromptu speech. We were all a bit scared for our safety and Magnus and Emma tried to guide me through the crowd. We lost Andrew Harvey somewhere and didn't see him again that day. At one stage Emma even thumped a news cameraman who was getting a bit rough; but, inch by inch, we gradually moved towards the entrance to Stage Six, the home of BBC News.

Inside the building there were people everywhere shouting and applauding. I stopped for a quick but hassled interview with Kirsty Wark, the *Newsnight* presenter, whom I admired a lot. I then decided to go up to the BBC News room. As I walked in people started applauding and eventually I climbed onto a desk and spoke to them all. I told them that our journalism had to be fair but not to lose their nerve, unaware that it was being broadcast live to the nation on BBC News 24. I told the staff in the newsroom, and the rest of the world live on television, that all we had been trying to do was to defend the 'integrity and independence of the BBC'. I later discovered that this really upset Downing Street, but in truth it was exactly what the whole thing had been about. We were defending the BBC from a wholesale attack on its journalism by Alastair Campbell, a man whom some in the Labour Government are only now beginning to understand was a complete maverick and who had been given unprecedented power by Tony Blair.

I also went to visit the staff of the *Today* programme, on which Andrew Gilligan had worked. There was a more sombre mood amongst the *Today* staff.

We went quickly to others parts of the building and the response was overwhelming. I then decided it was time to go. We went outside and were surrounded yet again. Someone had written 'We love you Greg' on my car windscreen in lipstick, and if my driver Bill and a policeman hadn't stopped them they would have written all over the car. We drove out with hundreds of people still cheering and waving their placards.

Eventually I got back to my office at Broadcasting House to discover that what had happened at Television Centre was not a one-off. All over the country the staff had taken to the streets to protest that their boss was leaving. In Cardiff, Glasgow, Belfast, Manchester, Newcastle, and Birmingham hundreds had walked out to protest. But it wasn't only in the big centres. The staff of local radio stations had also left their offices. At BBC Radio Shropshire in Shrewsbury all the staff had walked out, including the presenter who was on air. He had gone outside to express solidarity, whilst rightly continuing to broadcast live to the people of Shropshire.

In the next few days more than six thousand staff replied to my e-mail wishing me luck, thanking me for what I had done during my time at the BBC, and telling me how much they would miss me. I have chosen two examples – one from a producer in the World Service, and one from News; but there were thousands like them. The first said:

> Your greatest achievement was giving the kiss of life to a body of people who'd been systematically throttled, castrated and lobotomised. To leave us all very much alive and kicking, loving the BBC and respecting the role of Director General again, is a fantastic legacy.

And the second:

> The only way I can come to terms with the extraordinary events of the last 48 hours is to pay testimony to the vision and energy you have brought to the BBC. Men and women, even journalists, cried today. People came together and talked about their emotions, their fears, their frustrations all because the man who had embodied the hope, the vision, the pride they had begun to feel about the future of the organization had gone.

They came from all parts of the BBC and at all levels, all thanking me for changing the BBC. Well, all bar one. Amongst this great pile of e-mails my staff sifted out the only negative communication. It simply said:

> Fuck off Dyke, I'm glad you are going, I never liked you anyway.

That same night some of the staff in Factual Programmes and Current Affairs began collecting money to pay for an advertisement in the *Daily*

Telegraph to express their support. In twenty-four hours they collected twice as much as they needed, with all sorts of people contributing right across the BBC, from the lowest paid to the highest. Even people in the canteen who didn't work for the BBC, and who earned very little money, contributed. The spare money, nearly £10,000, was given to a charity of my choice. The *Telegraph* carried a full-page advertisement with a heading 'The Independence of the BBC' followed by a paragraph explaining that it had been paid for by BBC staff. It then said:

> Greg Dyke stood for brave, independent and rigorous BBC journalism that was fearless in its search for the truth. We are resolute that the BBC should not step back from its determination to investigate the facts in pursuit of the truth.
>
> Through his passion and integrity Greg inspired us to make programmes of the highest quality and creativity.
>
> We are dismayed by Greg's departure, but we are determined to maintain his achievements and his vision for an independent organization that serves the public above all else.

The page included just some of the thousands of names of BBC staff who had paid for the advertisement. They couldn't get all the names on the page. When I read it, I think it was the only time during the whole saga that I broke down and cried.

As I left Broadcasting House for the final time it seemed like everyone working there had come down to cheer me off. My own office staff all came out to the car: Fiona, Emma, Magnus, Orla, and Cheryl were all there to wave me goodbye, plus virtually the whole of the marketing department. I did a couple more quick interviews and in the middle of being interviewed live on Sky News my mobile phone rang. I answered it to find David Frost on the other end, so I offered him the opportunity to speak live to the world on Sky News. I don't think he quite understood what was happening.

And then I was gone. Four years to the very day that I had become Director-General I was driven away for the last time.

That evening Sue (who had driven back from Suffolk just for the night), Joe, and I went out for dinner. I think we were all on a strange high, laughing and joking. We ended up round the corner with our good friends John Stapleton and Lynn Faulds Wood, where I promised to do a live phone interview for John's early morning programme on GMTV the following day. I decided then that I would only do three interviews: with John, because he's a good friend; with the *Today* programme the following morning, when I could put on record what I was feeling; and with David Frost on Sunday, again repaying the support and friendship that he and his wife Carina had shown Sue and me over the years.

For the *Today* interview, which I fixed up at about four in the morning, I suggested they send the radio car round to my house. When they turned up a BBC News television crew was already there so I thought I'd make everyone a cup of tea. It is ironic that, after three days of avoiding journalists and news crews outside the house, the pictures of me carrying out the tea for the crews is one of the memorable shots of the whole affair. Virtually everyone I know saw it and mentions it when we meet. I also know that the pictures caused great consternation inside 10 Downing Street. Who says there's no such thing as news management?

It was three days before I began to realize that perhaps all was not as it had seemed to be. The idea came to me when I was talking to someone from within the BBC who told me that she believed some of the Governors had been out to get me regardless of Hutton. It got me thinking: did some of the Governors have another agenda?

By then I knew that three of the eleven Governors had supported me in the crunch vote: the ballet dancer Deborah Bull, the Oxford academic Ruth Deech and voluntary sector consultant Angela Sarkis were all against my leaving. They were the three Governors who had most recently joined the Board. The 'posh ladies' had both been against me and Sarah Hogg, in particular, had led the charge. She had told the Board that she had never liked me.

I was surprised when I discovered that I had not received any support from the Governors representing Scotland, Wales, Northern Ireland, and the English regions. If I had achieved one thing in my time at the BBC it was to increase investment and improve morale outside of London, and yet when the crunch came the Governors with particular responsibility for the Nations and Regions had all voted against me.

Not that they were ever the strongest of Governors. Three of them –

Ranjit Sondhi, Fabian Monds, and Merfyn Jones – had said very little over the years. It always seemed to me that they were intimidated by the posh ladies. In the case of Ranjit, I understand he was in real trouble when he got home. His wife, Anita Bhalla, who works for the BBC as Head of Political and Community Affairs for the English Regions, was a big Dyke supporter and, reportedly, tore him to shreds for going along with the decision. Ranjit was a really likeable, incredibly hard-working Governor, but he was never likely to rock the boat about anything.

Only Robert Smith, an accountant and business leader from Scotland, had played a significant role at Governors' meetings in my time, and it was always difficult to judge where he was coming from. At that time we all knew he was after a big new job as chairman of a major public company, and like so many accountants he loved to look tough if the opportunity presented itself.

I began to think about the conversation Gavyn, Pauline Neville-Jones, and I had had the night before Hutton was published. Surely if Pauline had said that she thought it was impossible for Gavyn and me to leave at the same time, shouldn't she have been arguing on my behalf, given that Gavyn had already gone? And yet she hadn't stood up for me and had in fact voted the other way. I began to think some more.

Pauline Neville-Jones had always been a big supporter of Mark Byford. As the Governor with special responsibility for the World Service she had worked closely with him and clearly rated him highly. I suspect she also liked him because, like most of the BBC lifers, he was better at the politics of dealing with the Governors, better at playing the game of being respectful. It was a game that I refused to play. I saw no reason why I should treat the Governors any differently from the way I treated everyone else. I certainly wasn't going to regard the earth they walked on as if it was somehow holy ground. This wasn't a wilful decision. It was just the way I am.

After I had left the BBC one senior executive said to me that if I had been a bit more servile in my attitude to the Governors I would still be there today. I have no doubt that's true. Certainly both chairmen in my time at the BBC, Christopher Bland and Gavyn Davies, suggested on occasions that I ought to be more respectful and make fewer jokes at Governors' meetings, but in truth I was never going to do that. I have never been one to respect position for its own sake and I was hardly likely to start in my fifties, particularly when dealing with a group of people most of whom knew absolutely nothing about the media, and who would have struggled to get a senior job at the BBC. In my time there were some excellent Governors, people like Richard Eyre and Barbara Young who had been on the Board when I joined, but I was not a fan of the system and made that obvious at times.

Whether this attitude to life is a weakness or a strength (and I suspect it is a bit of both) is largely irrelevant. That's the way my DNA is. I'm not particularly good at watching my back, and never have been. If you employ me you have to take me for what I am. In the commercial world that's not a problem because you are largely judged on the numbers. In the public sector, where accountability has become an obsession, you are judged on the strangest things, including how well you get on with the great and the good.

So why hadn't Pauline Neville-Jones supported me as I thought she would? Again I thought back a few months. One day in early December 2003, at our regular weekly meeting, Gavyn Davies told me that Pauline and Sarah Hogg had been to see him and were demanding that he call a meeting of the Governors without me being present so that they could appoint Mark Byford as my deputy and put him in charge of all the BBC's news output. I would then be told it was a *fait accompli.*

I laughed and told him that if they did that, then I would resign immediately. Gavyn told me that they were serious and were demanding he call the meeting. He asked me what he should do about it. I started by telling him that it was his problem but later said I'd think about it.

I'm certain Mark Byford didn't know anything about this move; in his time working for me Mark was always loyal and supportive. In many ways the proposal for Mark to become my deputy was a good idea. I had never had an official number two but Mark acted as my deputy, if he was around, when I was away and in fact I had suggested the move to Gavyn myself earlier that year. Mark had real strengths, many of which complemented mine. I tended to be broad brush, he was into detail. I was into big decisions and taking risks, whilst Mark, like many of the senior people who had worked their whole life at the BBC, tended to be cautious and process driven. We would have been a good fit. Gavyn was against it at that stage because it would have indicated that Mark was the Board's chosen successor to me when the time came for me to leave in three years' time when I reached the age of sixty.

My objection to the proposal from the posh ladies was, firstly, the way they were going about it by going behind my back; secondly, that it was nothing to do with them, that I was the DG and would suggest who my deputy should be, not them; and, thirdly, that they wanted to put Mark in charge of all the BBC's news output, thus effectively demoting the Director of News, Richard Sambrook. I was having none of that. However, with the Hutton report pending, even someone as naturally combative as me recognized that this was not a time for a big bust-up with the Governors and I had reached the conclusion we needed a change to the organization.

As Hutton had progressed, I had come to the view that our systems of compliance prior to and post broadcast needed to be brought together under one person, so I suggested to Gavyn that, as a way of appeasing the posh ladies, we should appoint Mark as my deputy and allow him to remain in charge of Global News but also take over all our compliance systems.

Gavyn took this proposal to the Governors and they agreed. The posh ladies seemed satisfied. On 1 January 2004, Mark Byford officially became my deputy. A month later I was gone and he was acting Director-General.

In the week after leaving I also discovered more about what had happened at that private Governors' meeting on the previous Wednesday. When I had left the meeting with Gavyn I had asked the Secretary, Simon Milner, to tell the Governors that I wanted their support if I was to stay. I later discovered he told them that I had resigned, a subtle but crucial difference. Of course Pauline Neville-Jones knew that wasn't what we had discussed the night before, so why didn't she question it? I also discovered that, later in the meeting, when they were discussing whether or not they should change their position on my going, Simon had intervened to say that it was a bad idea because they'd never be able to control me if that happened.

The week after my departure I discovered the Governors were having a secret meeting to review what had happened the week before. Sitting at home unemployed, I decided that there were things I wanted them to know. I phoned Simon Milner and told him I wanted to e-mail the Governors to tell them about the conversation Pauline Neville-Jones, Gavyn, and I had had the night before the crucial meeting. I suggested they might consider it odd that Pauline had neither mentioned the conversation to them nor carried out what was agreed. I told them they should consult Gavyn for corroboration. It seemed to me important that they should understand the background to Gavyn's rapid departure and my surprise at the Governors' lack of support. Simon asked me what I wanted. Tongue in cheek, I told him I wanted my job back. What I really wanted was to make sure they all knew exactly how Pauline Neville-Jones had behaved.

The nature of my departure hit a nerve with the public. For a few weeks I became something of a hero in many people's eyes. They thought I had been badly treated and yet I must be a good bloke because why else would so many of the BBC's employees come out on my side? Of course I was helped by Alastair Campbell's performance on the day the Hutton report was published.

Standing on the stairs at the Foreign Press Association, Campbell gave about as pompous a performance as it's possible to imagine. For a man who was known to be economical with the truth, and who had certainly deliberately misled the House of Commons Foreign Affairs Select Committee during their Iraq hearings, he said that the Government had told the truth and that the BBC, from the Chairman and Director-General down, had not. He then called for heads to roll at the BBC.

Campbell is a man who has the ability to delude himself. He didn't realize how much he was disliked and distrusted by the British public, who saw him as Blair's Svengali. He believed throughout that he was right, and he now believed Hutton was right. The British public didn't. In attacking Gavyn and me he helped to put the public even further on our side. When asked about his response on the *Today* programme I said I thought that Campbell was 'remarkably graceless'. What I really felt was that he was a deranged, vindictive bastard, but I couldn't possibly say that on the radio.

The emotional response to my dismissal was not only from the staff. I received letters from all over Britain and all over the world – from people I'd never met, from people I'd met only occasionally, and from good friends. Everywhere I went people wanted to shake my hand: in the pub, in the supermarket, walking down the street, even at football matches. Sue and I went for dinner with Melvyn and his wife Cate in the House of Lords the following week and all sorts of people wanted to say hello and that they were sorry about what had happened. One Liberal

Democrat peer, an eminent lawyer, offered to take up my case against Hutton, whilst a prominent Tory peer offered to help pay for me to go to law. So many peers from all parties came up that Melvyn described it as 'a royal procession'.

I even got a message from my architect friend Chris Henderson, with whom I go riding every weekend, to say that the Hursley and Hambledon Hunt was 100 per cent behind me. I was eternally grateful – not that it will change my views about fox hunting. Even Ian, who cuts my hair, told me all his clients were on my side, with the exception of one. He also cuts the hair of the former Director-General of the BBC, John Birt.

Two weeks after I left the BBC we went with the Stapleton family to South Africa for a holiday and I met the same reaction there. Dozens of British tourists recognized me and wanted to shake my hand and say they thought I'd been treated badly and 'well done' for standing up to the Government. The funniest moment came when I was standing in the sea and a large tattooed man came up to me. 'Well done, mate,' he said. 'They're all fucking bastards.' And off he wandered into the deep.

Inside the television industry the reaction was the same. At the Royal Television Society's annual awards ceremony I was given a long standing ovation when I was presented with the annual judges' award for my contribution to television. The same happened a month later at the annual BAFTA awards, which were televised on ITV. First Paul Abbott, the brilliant writer of *Clocking Off* and *State of Play*, attacked the BBC Governors for getting rid of me, then I was given a standing ovation when I went up to present the award for best current affairs programme. I used the opportunity to have my first public dig at the BBC Governors.

Months after I had left the BBC all sorts of people I didn't know were still coming up to me saying they were sorry that 'they' had got me. So what was all this about, and who did they mean by 'they'? I can only presume they were talking about Blair, Campbell, and those around them, combined in their minds with Lord Hutton and the BBC Governors. To all these well-wishers, I was someone prepared to stand up against 'them'.

I even became a phenomenon amongst the business community. People from business schools all over the world were in contact. Every leader of an organization would like to think that if they were fired their people would take to the streets to support them, but most knew they wouldn't, so they were intrigued to know what had happened and why. It was best summed up for me by a wonderful old man called Herb Schlosser, who was once President and CEO of NBC in the United States. He wrote, 'I saw on the internet BBC employees marching in support of a CEO. This is a first in the history of the Western World.'

And that was about the end of it. From the most powerful media job in the UK to unemployed in just three days. It was a remarkable period, but what were those crazy three days all about? Why did the Governors do what they did?

When you combine the unpredicted savagery of the Hutton Report towards the BBC, the whitewashing of Number Ten, Gavyn's early resignation, Pauline Neville-Jones's astonishing behaviour, the posh ladies' hostility towards me, their influence on a relatively weak Board, Richard Ryder's ineffectiveness as a leader, and my natural assumption that the majority of the Governors would want me to stay, you can understand what happened and why. Of course I was not without blame. I had made mistakes in how we dealt with the whole affair, and in those dying days I shouldn't have said I needed the Governors' support to stay. I certainly shouldn't have believed I would get it. I trusted certain people who were not to be trusted. In many ways it was a very British coup in which the Establishment figures got their opportunity to get rid of the upstart.

There are still questions to be answered. Why did Hutton write the report he wrote? Why did the British people reject Hutton out of hand, and so quickly? Why did it damage the Government instead of helping it? And why did people in the wider world sympathize so strongly with my position?

Why did my leaving create such a response inside the BBC? Why wasn't I perceived as just another suit, as most managers are? What had we done to the culture of the BBC in such a short period of time that provoked such emotion and such loyalty?

As one letter I received from within the BBC said so profoundly, 'How did a short, bald man with a speech impediment have such an impact?' I hope this book will go some way towards answering that question.

CHAPTER TWO

The First Thirty Years

Every so often I try to explain to my own kids what life was like growing up in a small West London suburban street in the 1950s, but I only get mocked for my efforts. I think they laugh because I make it sound too much like the Hovis advertisement where everyone was poor but happy, and the luxuries we aspired to were very simple.

We lived, for the first nine years of my life, in a very ordinary cul-de-sac on the borders between Hayes and Southall in Middlesex. My parents Joseph and Denise bought the house, a new, small suburban semi in a street called Cerne Close, in 1946 for £650. Today it would sell for close to £250,000. They moved there with my brothers Ian, then aged five, and Howard, who was only a few months old. I was born the following year in 1947, a year when there were more births in Britain than in any other year in history. It was the peak of the post-war baby boom with a million children born compared with an average of 600,000 a year today.

The reality was that most people did live very simple lives, compared with today. It's when I tell my kids that the milk was still delivered by horse and cart that they laugh. We walked to school in a big crowd – just kids, without any parents to escort us – and we all played football in the street with a tennis ball. No one in the street was divorced, and virtually all the children lived with two parents in a classic nuclear family, often with a grandparent in tow. Dad went out to work and Mum stayed behind to look after the children and the home. It was as simple as that.

My dad's job was selling insurance; as a result we were one of only two families in the street with a car, owned by his company, so we were seen as quite affluent. We also had a telephone for the same reason and neighbours used regularly to knock on the door to ask if they could come in and use the phone.

We were luckier than most of the people in our street as we had at least three holidays each year. Every summer we stayed in a bungalow on the beach at Pevensey Bay in East Sussex, where the big treat of the week was a trip on a boat called the *William Olchorn*, which took holidaymakers out on trips around Beachy Head lighthouse. On the way back to the bungalow we would all have fish and chips, which we saw as something special. Every Easter we stayed for a week with my parents' best friends, Uncle Frank and Auntie Vi, in Bridgend in South Wales, and at Whitsun we stayed with 'Auntie' Edna and 'Uncle' Bill in Emneth near Wisbech in Cambridgeshire, where my Auntie Doreen was evacuated during the war; she was joined by my mum and my brother Ian towards the end of the war after their house in Bromley, Kent, had been bombed.

The years we lived in that little street in Hayes were happy times. No one was well off, but neither were they poor. We all had food and clothes, and life was uncomplicated by the choices that greater affluence has brought. I suspect it was also pretty dull, but as a child you didn't know that.

The Middlesex suburbs have never had a very good press and were widely looked down upon, particularly by the English upper-middle classes, but the criticism was, and is, unfair. These areas were largely populated by the aspiring English working class; most of the people who lived in this area of West London had moved there from pretty awful conditions in inner London. They wanted something better for themselves and, in particular, they wanted something better for their children. In most cases they achieved it.

My parents were typical. They had both been brought up in Hackney in East London. On my mother's side her father had been a soldier who had fought in the Boer War. He fell in love with South Africa and wanted to stay but his fiancée, my grandmother, refused to leave London and join him. Instead he came back to England, got married, and went to live on the Isle of Dogs, where he became a docker like the rest of his family. He was later injured in an accident at the docks and, after a long battle, won some compensation from the dock owners. With it he bought a small newsagent's and tobacconist's shop in Morning Lane, Hackney. My grandmother ran the shop while my grandfather spent the takings at the local dog track. Whenever he had a big win he would come home in a taxi with his bike on the top.

My mum's mother, my gran, was one of six children who had been brought up by their grandparents in Farnham, Surrey, after both their parents had died when they were young. She always told how the local villagers were supposed to doff their caps to the gentry as they went by, but her grandfather wouldn't let them. He used to tell them 'You're as good as they are.' My grandmother went into 'service' at a young age and worked her way up from the scullery to become a ladies' maid at a big house in Sloane Square in London. Her life was tinged with tragedy. She never really got over the loss of all three of her brothers in the First World War. All were much younger than her, and she had helped to bring them up. During the war they lived with her in the shop in Hackney when they were home on leave. One by one they all died. Their loss was enormous. Right up until she died, in 1973, you could call in to see her and find her in tears thinking of her brothers and the waste of their lives.

My paternal grandfather came from a family of publicans in North London. They owned a series of pubs in Islington and Dalston and my father was born in one of these, the Trafalgar. They were a fairly affluent North London family and there is a Dyke family vault in the Abney Park Cemetery in Stoke Newington, near where Christine, my eldest daughter, now lives with her partner Martin. My grandfather died in his early thirties in the 1919 flu epidemic, which worldwide claimed more victims than the First World War. My dad was seven at the time.

His mother, my paternal grandmother, left home at the age of fourteen when her widowed mother took up with another man – known only in the family as Mr Sadgrove – and had an illegitimate child, Horace James. Years later, at her ninetieth birthday party, everyone kept pointing out Horace and saying, in very loud whispers, 'He's the illegitimate one, but don't mention it.' When she left home my grandmother got a job as a barmaid at one of the Dyke pubs and married out of her class when she became the wife of the publican's son, Leonard Dyke. He left my grandmother penniless when he died; any money he had he left in trust for my dad and his brother Leonard. My grandmother wasn't even allowed to continue running their pub because, as a woman, she couldn't hold a licence. Instead, the brewery offered her an off-licence and general grocer's shop in Tresham Avenue, Hackney, where my father and his brother Len were brought up.

My grandmother Lil came from a big Walthamstow family that was dominated for more than half a century by four powerful sisters: Lil, Beat, Flo, and Ruby. They were known in the family as the big four, and all dominated their husbands. They all lived long lives; two of them received telegrams from the Queen on their hundredth birthdays. My grandmother died at the age of 101. She and I never really got on: according to the rest of the family we were too alike. We were both very competitive and hated losing (as a young boy I regularly beat her at cards). One of her brothers, Albert Silverton, worked as a commissionaire at Broadcasting House in Portland Place in the 1930s. When I joined the BBC it became a family joke – commissionaire to Director-General in only two generations.

My parents met at St John's Church in Hackney and got married in 1939, living first in Birmingham and later in Bromley. They moved to Hayes soon after the end of the war. As a family we weren't poor but we never had any money. Like most of those around us, we never went abroad for a family holiday – my first visit overseas came when I was sixteen on a school trip to Paris. And we certainly never ate in restaurants. The first time we ever ate out together as a family was at the Swan and Bottle, a Berni Inn steak bar in Uxbridge: I was 14 or 15 at the time.

Some things are memorable from that time. I vividly remember being told by my mother that King George VI had died: it was the same day in February 1952 that my brother Ian took the 11-plus exam. For my parents, the King represented something special because of the symbolic role he had played in the East End of London during the Second World War. People in the East End respected the King and Queen because they had stayed in London during the Blitz and had regularly visited the parts of East London that were badly bombed.

On the day of the King's funeral they both went to stand by the railway bridge in nearby Southall as the train carrying the King's body passed by on its way to Windsor. They thought it important that they pay their respects and I can remember to this day my dad leaving in his best suit and trilby hat and my mother in her best dress. They were dressed to the nines just to stand by a railway bridge. This was still the age of respect.

None of my memories of living in Cerne Close is as exciting as those of the street party my mother helped organize to celebrate the coronation of Queen Elizabeth the following year. My brother Ian took part in a sketch put on by the older kids and I sang a song, pretending that the tennis racket I was holding was a guitar. We all had jellies and sandwiches in the street – it was a magical day for a six-year-old. Nearly fifty years later I sat in the royal box in the grounds of Buckingham Palace as the BBC put on two spectacular concerts to celebrate the fiftieth anniversary of the Queen's accession, and afterwards I wandered around the Palace meeting members of the Royal Family. It was a lifetime away from Cerne Close.

I remember the coming of television vividly. My early childhood was spent with *Listen with Mother* on the Home Service. Then television arrived. Initially, only two people in our street had television sets, the Riches at Number 21 and Mrs Unstead, who lived in the corner house, and all the kids in the street used to pile into one or other house to watch children's television. And then, in 1953, came the great day when Howard and I, walking home from school, were, by complete coincidence, counting the number of houses that had television aerials. Life in Hayes wasn't exactly exciting in those days and this was the sort of thing you did as a kid. We turned the corner and, lo and behold, there was an aerial on the roof of our house. We rushed in to find a television set, which my dad had bought so my mother could watch the Coronation and he could watch the Cup Final. We were really excited until about a week later when it stopped working. My dad called out the TV repair man, who came and plugged it back in. Dad was never a practical man, and I've followed in his footsteps.

Our set only received BBC and when ITV started in 1955 my dad refused to change the set, which meant that my brothers and I missed all those early ITV programmes like *The Invisible Man*, *Robin Hood*, *Take Your Pick*, and *Double Your Money*. I remember we felt very deprived that we couldn't join in the conversations at school about these programmes. My dad was always of the view that the BBC was 'proper' television and that advertiser-funded television was inevitably inferior. He believed this until the day he died in 1990.

In our last years in Hayes, in the late Fifties, the area began to change rapidly. Southall became a massive centre for Indian immigrants and changed beyond recognition in just a few years. For those original residents who remained in the area the speed of change must have been traumatic. One moment you knew all your neighbours; the next, most of them were strangers from an entirely different culture who didn't speak your language.

After we had moved from our street some residents clubbed together to try to prevent Asian families from buying houses in the road. Of course they were branded as racist by some, but that was unfair. They weren't being unkind or reactionary – quite the opposite. They were simply scared by the pace and scale of change all around them and didn't understand its causes. They had seen the centre of Southall change beyond recognition and they didn't want to see the same happen to their street.

A couple of years ago I went back to the area when, as Director-General, I was invited to open the new hall at Yeading Junior school, where I was a pupil between 1954 and 1958. In 1958 the school was entirely populated by white working-class and lower-middle-class kids. Forty years later it was 80 per cent non-white, with children from dozens of different ethnic backgrounds. If a sociologist had moved into our house when we moved out in 1956, and had stayed to study Cerne Close and the surrounding area over the next forty years, he or she would have had a brilliant case study of the impact of immigration on a small community.

These were the days when the 11-plus dominated life for parents in streets like ours. If you were one of the 20 per cent who passed the exam you went to the local grammar school; if you didn't, you went to the secondary modern and, educationally, were effectively written off. No one we knew went to private school. I don't think anyone considered it an option: it wasn't on their radar screen even if they could have afforded it, which they couldn't.

One of the most traumatic memories I have of my childhood was when my eldest brother Ian failed the 11-plus. It was a family tragedy, and my parents were distraught. I took the exam six years later when there were four or five boys from our street taking it. Only one failed but his parents were broken hearted. My hatred of the 11-plus, and the whole concept of selection at the age of eleven, is rooted in those experiences. This was one of the main reasons why, later in life, I joined the Labour Party and Sue and I sent all our kids to comprehensive schools.

We left Hayes in 1957 to move to a bigger house three miles away in Hillingdon. My parents paid £4,500 for it: today it would be worth somewhere between £350,000 and £400,000. We moved there when I was nine and it was certainly a move up market. We had a detached three-bedroomed house with a large garden where my father spent most Saturdays and Sundays tending his vegetables, when he wasn't fishing at a gravel pit in nearby Harefield.

Unlike Ian, both Howard and I passed the 11-plus and consequently went to Hayes Grammar School; neither of us was notably academic and one year I came bottom of the whole year – 132nd out of 132 pupils. Another year I remember Howard getting 7 per cent in his maths exam and his teacher saying in his school report that 'He thoroughly deserves this mark.' I also remember walking into a chemistry exam and the teacher saying to me 'Not a lot of point you coming in, Dyke.'

Our school was dominated by the headmaster, Ralph Scurfield. When I look back I think he was a really good headmaster, a great character, and a real leader, but we all lived in fear of him. After I left school I had no contact with him for nearly twenty years until I first hit the headlines at TV-am. One day Jane Tatnall, my secretary at the time, told me there was a Mr Scurfield on the phone. I picked it up and he said 'Is that you, Dyke?' My answer was entirely predictable. I said 'Yes, sir', as if nothing had changed over the intervening years. I was even tempted to stand up when I said it. Mr Scurfield had retired by then but was phoning on behalf of the new head teacher to ask me to give the prizes at speech day.

I went, and so did Mr Scurfield, who confided in me that day that he wished he had never used the cane while a headmaster. As I had been beaten by him on a couple of occasions, his conversion to non-violence didn't impress me. I wasn't ready for truth and reconciliation yet. Mr Scurfield is still alive and living in Sheffield and we write to each other once or twice a year.

Soon after I became Director-General I invited a few of my old teachers to dinner at the BBC, along with my brother Howard. I suppose I invited them so I could say to them 'OK, I didn't do so badly after all, did I?' All the teachers were retired and seemed to enjoy their evening, especially the red wine. After a few bottles one of them said to me that on the way there they had discussed my progress in life. 'We would like to say we spotted your potential,' he said, 'but in truth we all agreed you were one of the least likely pupils to succeed.' It's amazing how teachers can still wound, even after nearly forty years.

In Hillingdon we lived in a road called Cedars Drive, where I really enjoyed my teenage years. The street was full of boys (there were very few girls, except for my friend Val Clifton), and we did all the things boys did. Some of us became paper boys at the local newsagent's, which was run by a retired army officer, John Kane, known to us as Major John. We all liked working there, but he drove us all mad. He smoked like a chimney and would regularly leave his cigarette on the pile of newspapers he was marking up, which would then catch fire. But what really annoyed us about Major John was his habit of sleeping in so that when we turned up to collect our papers for delivery they were never ready for us. My first experience of being an 'activist' came at the age of fourteen or fifteen when I organized industrial action amongst the paper boys. We weren't bold enough to strike, but we decided that it was time we frightened Major John, so none of us turned up for our rounds until an hour after the normal time. I think he was a bit shocked but he quickly found out I was the ringleader and took me to task. He told me that if I didn't want to work on his terms and conditions I should leave. Forty years later I can understand what he was getting at, but at the time I thought he was being extremely unreasonable. My greatest success as a paper boy came when my friend Mick Higgins and I decided to go round to all our customers at Christmas, knock on their door, and wish them the compliments of the season. I think we got twice as many Christmas tips as anyone else.

Until girls came along, sport dominated the lives of all the boys on our estate and over the years we set up two football teams. The first, called Cedarwood Rangers, played in Newcastle United's black and white shirts; then, when we were older, we started Vine Athletic, who played in blue. The team was named after the local pub, the Vine, where we did most of our training. It was one of those pubs where you could be a regular at sixteen.

I've often wanted to make a documentary about kids from a typical street and tell the story of what happened to them in later life. In our street, the boys went on to do a whole range of things. Roger Weller became a teacher while his brother Keith was a senior civil servant in the Department of Education and ended up with an OBE. Mick Higgins went to work as a sales rep in the food industry, and Peter Hinley became a hairdresser but sadly died young. John Hayes did well in finance, while

Martin Webb worked for British Airways before joining his dad's business. Peter Bowden became an estate agent and Robin Cameron went into interior design. My brother Howard is currently a professor at the top university in South Korea while my brother Ian, after a life in the insurance industry, was the first to retire and was very proud of it.

I suppose I became the most famous by becoming Director-General of the BBC, but Christopher Barrett-Jolly came a close second. He came from the poshest family on our estate – at least we all thought they were posh because they had a double-barrelled name – and went off to be an airline pilot. At one time he ran a company flying live animals in and out of Birmingham Airport, which brought him a lot of flak from the animal rights lobby. Later, Chris hit bad times and received a good deal of publicity when he was sentenced to twenty years in jail for trying to smuggle £22 million worth of cocaine into the country. He had been caught flying a plane full of the drugs into Southend Airport. When he realized the police were waiting for him at the airport, he and his colleagues decided to try throwing the drugs out of the back of the plane, littering the runway with cocaine.

My best friend, then and now, is Richard Webb, who also lived on our estate. He had TB as a kid and as a result has a shortened left leg, which means he has had to wear a raised boot for most of his life – although you'd never have known it as you watched him playing football, cricket, or, in later life, in business. When people accuse me of being a competitive human being I always tell them they ought to meet my friend Richard. This was a man who impounded an easyJet plane, when it was full of passengers and just about to leave Stansted Airport for Nice, because he was owed £520 by the company. They refused to pay, so he went to the local County Court, representing himself, and got a court order. EasyJet still refused to pay so he got the bailiffs out and seized the plane. When an anxious easyJet executive rang and agreed to pay up, Richard made him send the money in cash by bike before he would release the plane.

Richard left school at sixteen and trained to become a chartered accountant. He's been my financial adviser for most of my life and in recent years has been involved in virtually all the business ventures I've undertaken. The only reason I've got lots of money today is because Richard has looked after it for me. I've only ever paid him for his advice once. When we all made a lot of money out of London Weekend Television in the early Nineties I gave him a pile of my shares, explaining that it was his payment for life: twenty years in arrears and twenty years in advance. I'm a bit worried that the second twenty years ends in 2012.

I trust Richard more than anyone else I've ever met in my life. We've always argued and disagreed about all sorts of things, but we go back so far that it would never occur to either of us not to act in the other's best interests. Richard has access to every bank account I possess and he could completely clean me out if he wanted to, but of course it would never happen. That's what friendship is. When I was running the BBC and was criticized for retaining certain private business interests – on the grounds that I couldn't do more than one job at once – I tried to explain that they took up very little of my time because my friend Richard looked after my business interests for me. Of course for the journalists that spoiled a good story, so they ignored it.

I had a very happy childhood; as the third son in the family I had few of the battles with my parents that my elder brothers had had. In those days the vast majority of school leavers didn't go on to higher education; sadly, many of the brightest kids at my school left at sixteen because their families either couldn't afford, or didn't have the aspiration, for them to stay on. Although I had not done well at school my results picked up a bit in the last year or two and I passed six GCE O-levels. It was just about enough for me to stay on for the sixth form, but going on to university or college was never a realistic prospect.

I had a great time in my last two years at school. I played rugby for the First XV, was the school 440 yards running champion, was in all the school plays, and even sang in the choir. That's a slight exaggeration. I used to stand next to my good friend Dave Hornby, who had a great bass voice. He sang and I mimed. In fact we were together in the choir at the Royal Albert Hall on the night President Kennedy was assassinated. When people ask me where I was when JFK died, I always tell them I was miming at the Albert Hall.

I was enthusiastic about everything in those last two years, except academic work. I took A-levels in economics, and pure and applied maths, but didn't understand any of it. When I achieved a grade E in my combined maths A-level, which meant I had just passed, I was amazed – as was my maths teacher. When I met him in a pub about ten years after I left school he told me he still used me as an example of why pupils shouldn't give up at the mocks 'because miracles could happen'.

On Saturdays I used to work in a shoe shop, first in Ealing and later in Acton. My greatest claim to fame at that time was that I sold Roger Daltrey a pair of plimsolls. We sold cheap shoes but it didn't stop people complaining. I'll always remember someone coming back unhappy, not unreasonably, because on getting home and opening the bag they'd found I'd sold them odd shoes – one was a size six, the other a size ten. What was strange was that we never found the matching pair.

While selling shoes, I learnt a lot about how salesmen con the public. If the shoes we were trying to sell were too big we'd explain that it was cool in our basement and that the customer's feet would expand when they got outside. If they were too small we'd say that they had been walking a lot and that their feet had expanded but that the shoes would be fine once they got home. The biggest scam was selling the shoes for which we got extra commission – the shoes people didn't want to buy. The trick was to bring the customer the wrong-sized shoes, and then miraculously pull out a pair that fitted perfectly, which just happened to be the pair on which we earned the largest commission.

When it came to leaving school and getting a proper job my mother had always warned me that I would have to 'buckle down' and that life wouldn't be as much fun any more. She was so right; in my first venture into the world of full-time work I became a trainee manager at Marks & Spencer, at the Watford branch in Hertfordshire. I got the job largely because my dad's brother, my Uncle Len, was a manager at M&S for more than thirty years and he put a word in for me. I started in September 1965, and hated every minute of it; it was purgatory.

In those days, M&S stores were largely managed by cautious public-school boys. Most of the bright people worked in head office, where they controlled almost everything. It was obvious to me that people in the stores were not encouraged to use their own initiative. When, many years later, M&S was in financial difficulties and the company decided to change the way they ran things, they announced that they wanted their managers to act as if they were franchisees. When I read this I nearly wrote to them to tell them that they had no chance of making this work. The people they now wanted to run their stores had either been sacked or had left in desperation over the years. The people they'd retained were those who did what they were told and kept their noses clean. They didn't seem to understand that you can't change the fundamental culture of a company merely by announcing that you've done so. It's rather more complicated than that.

I remember being constantly in trouble, almost from the day I arrived at M&S. I set up the all-time broken biscuit record when I worked in the stockroom, got told off for not having my hair cut short enough, was told to stop chatting up the attractive shop girls, and was asked by the manager if I'd had any elocution lessons when I was at school. As a joke, I told him I'd gone to school in Hayes, where no one could even spell elocution, let alone take lessons in it. He didn't think it was at all funny.

After four months I got the sack. Because I was a management trainee they sent down some bigwig from head office to give me the news. With him came the latest of the Sieff family, who ran M&S. He was learning about human resources as he was fast tracked through the organization. I was shocked to be fired, but also absolutely delighted. They even gave me three months' money to leave. Years later, when I got a lot of publicity at TV-am, I was interviewed by one journalist and asked if I regretted not going into television earlier in life. My answer was that everyone should start their working life at Marks & Spencer, because it could only get better after that. Soon after the interview, David Frost bumped into Marcus Sieff, the then boss of M&S. Sieff said to him, 'I see you are employing one of our boys now,' so clearly someone had noticed.

The four months I spent at M&S had a profound influence on my future direction in life. It certainly prejudiced my views against public-school boys for many years, which, in turn, pushed my political views further in the direction of Labour. It also convinced me that my mother had been wrong. I decided there and then that I would never do a job and be miserable again; if I didn't like a job in the future I would leave. My dad, horrified that I was out of work, then tried to persuade me to follow him and my eldest brother into the insurance industry, or else try for a job in the local solicitor's office. I was having none of it. I'd tried work their way. Now it was my turn.

I was determined to find something exciting through which I could express myself. One day, when I was still unemployed, I wandered into the office of a fairly new local newspaper based in Uxbridge called the *Hillingdon Mirror* and met the editor, Brian Cummins. The paper was a tabloid with a colour picture on the front page; the office was a complete tip. I had a long chat with Brian and told him why I wanted to be a journalist; as I left I remember thinking that I could enjoy life there. A few months later, while I was working in a temporary job, he rang me and offered me a job as a reporter.

Brian was 27 at the time but he seemed old to us youngsters in the office. Not only was he the boss, he had also spent two years in the RAF doing national service. We always used to joke that he'd spent his time learning to fly Sopwith Camels. He was a great man to work for and let us all get on with it. The paper was manned by indentured junior reporters, young kids who had signed up for three years at very little money to learn the business. It was Brian's job, along with his deputy, Peter Hurst, to teach us.

The newspaper group we all worked for, King & Hutchings of Uxbridge, was so mean they didn't even supply typewriters; you had to buy your own. I've still got mine. Expenses were virtually unheard of, although at a stretch they would pay bus fares, and the entertaining policy was straightforward: don't, and if you do you won't be reimbursed. I was always someone who challenged everything and after a couple of years I decided this was exploitation, particularly when we found out that the tele-ad girls earned more money than the indentured journalists. I organized a demonstration of junior reporters. Ray Snoddy, later to be an eminent media journalist on the *Financial Times* and *The Times*, was one of those who joined the protest. We demanded to see the top man.

We clearly got the company worried because in the end Mr Larriman agreed to meet us. Now everyone at King & Hutchings believed Mr Larriman was a mythical figure. No one knew him but when middle management talked about him it was in hushed tones. He was only ever known as Mr Larriman: no one knew his first name, let alone used it. He ran the whole newspaper group, ten or twelve prosperous papers stretching right across West London. When we met him we tried to explain that all the indentured juniors, and there must have been forty of us in all, were short of money and needed more. I can remember his reply to this day. He told us there was no point in increasing our wages because we were young and would only spend the money on things like records and portable radios. I think the Sixties youth revolution must have passed Mr Larriman by.

We all pretended we were proper big shot journalists and joined the National Union of Journalists so that we could flash the big NUJ membership card around. Having failed to impress Mr Larriman by organizing the junior journalists, I decided on a different approach and got myself elected as Father of the Chapel – the shop steward for all the journalists working in Uxbridge. I spent the next year or so trying to be a pain to the management.

On the *Hillingdon Mirror* we were trying to break the mould of local journalism. We didn't report the local court proceedings much, and we certainly didn't cover weddings and funerals. As a result we struggled to find enough to fill the paper, and consequently didn't sell that many copies. We'd spend our days on the road making 'contact calls', as Brian Cummins used to call them – trying to find stories. My best friend as a reporter was a tall, good-looking boy called Roy Eldridge, who ended up in the pop music industry. His version of contact calls was different from the rest of us – he ended up having a torrid affair with the woman who ran one of the local residents' associations. My girlfriend at the time was another reporter on the paper, Christine Webb. One day I was called in by Brian Cummins and told that his boss, the editor-in-chief, had seen us 'making contact' in the office one evening and that this wasn't appreciated.

I've always enjoyed working hard, so in my days on the *Hillingdon Mirror* I had a second job at the weekends to earn a bit more money. I worked for a news agency in Guildford called Cassidy and Leigh. If you talk to anyone who has run the newsdesk of a popular national paper they'll know about Cassidy and Leigh. Our job was to sell stories to them. Cassidy and Leigh were good, hard newsmen, but they also provided frothy stories for the tabloids. Not all these stories had to be 100 per cent true, just as long as the people you were writing about agreed they were. I remember, in particular, that we sold a whole string of stories about a Roman Catholic convent in Godalming whose nuns were terribly publicity conscious and getting headlines like 'Officiating at the Morning Service' – with a picture of a nun lying under a car wielding an enormous spanner.

My interest in politics really dates back to that time working on the *Hillingdon Mirror*. I became the paper's part-time political reporter and spent a lot of time with local councillors, MPs, and the like. I left the paper in 1969, initially to run the Staines regional office of the *Evening*

Mail, a brand-new evening paper that was being started in Slough, but within a few months I had become its full-time political reporter. I was now a specialist. At that time I shared a flat in Windsor with a photographer called Jeff Wright, whom I had first met at King & Hutchings and who had made the move to the *Evening Mail* a few months before me. Jeff and I are still close friends.

In my second year at the *Evening Mail* I began to think about going to university. Although I was told I didn't need a degree to have a good future as a journalist, I began to become conscious that I hadn't had much of an education. Someone I knew had got a place at university without the normal qualifications and I began to think about applying myself. I suppose I felt intellectually inferior to those who had been to university and needed to prove to myself, and to others, that I wasn't. I was also getting more and more interested in politics and wanted to study the subject.

I persuaded the editor of the Slough *Evening Mail*, John Rees, to give me a reference and set about filling in the appropriate university entrance forms. Much to my surprise I was offered interviews at Lancaster, East Anglia, and York, and then was offered places at all three. Although I only had my one maths A-level, all three were willing to take a chance on me. I chose to go to York because it was a beautiful campus and the people I met at the interview were both challenging and friendly. Twenty years later, after I had made a great deal of money, I decided that the risk the university had taken by offering me a place deserved to be rewarded. As a way of saying thank you, I gave them a quarter of a million pounds, which they used to build an all-weather sports pitch.

Changing from being a reporter on popular newspapers to studying politics required an enormous adjustment that took me at least a year to achieve. For the first time in my life I had to understand what academic study was all about. I remember vividly the first essay I wrote at York. I was asked to 'Discuss the causes of the English industrial revolution'. I remember reading one chapter of one book, thinking 'That's it, cracked that', and then just repeating what I'd read. It was pointed out to me by my tutor that academia was about collecting a range of opinion and assessing the strengths of different ideas, not just taking the first available option. I was no longer a pop journalist.

Gradually I grew to understand what it was all about and, as an older student who had made a positive decision to go to university, I worked pretty hard compared to most of those around me. In my politics course I tended to specialize in three areas. I wrote my dissertation on the origins of the Cuban revolution, and grew fascinated by the history of the Soviet Union; but the most exciting period came in my final year, 1974, when I was studying American politics. It coincided with the unfolding of the Watergate scandal – Richard Nixon resigned as President just after I had finished the course. The American Politics lecturers decided to abandon their usual course and rearrange the whole year around Watergate, which was a brilliant move as it meant you could study the theoretical base of US politics through what was actually happening during that year. The separation of powers between President, the Senate, and the Congress really meant something when the President was in the process of being impeached. I have been a Watergate groupie ever since, although even now I still don't fully understand why Nixon's people decided to burgle the Watergate building in the first place, and I'm not sure anyone else does.

I had long been interested in US politics and at the end of my first year at York spent the entire summer wandering around the United States. I went to the Democratic Party convention in Miami, where I worked briefly on the campaign for George McGovern, the US senator who was to stand for the Democrats in the 1972 presidential election. I then wandered off to find out about the USA. I hitched my way around the country, covering some eight thousand miles. I was on my own, which enabled me to discover America in a way I couldn't have done by any other means. From Europe we tend to see the USA as California and the Eastern seaboard. By hitching through the Midwest you discover another America.

The Vietnam War was still raging and in town after town in the Midwest there were very few young men in evidence – they were all away at the war. I also travelled down to El Paso in Texas to meet members of our extended family. Both my US cousins had fought in Vietnam, and both had been screwed up by the experience.

Being at York University in the early Seventies was an interesting experience. These were the days of sit-ins and radical action. Having gone to university from a job in which I'd been seen as a bit of a leftie, at York I was seen as a revisionist because I was a Labour Party supporter. The Socialist Workers Party and their like saw me as dangerous because, although I was of the Left, I didn't agree with them that the true path to change was through revolution. I distinctly remember the leader of the hard Left at York walking into a meeting and apologizing for being late by explaining that he had 'been out working for the revolution'. All his fans applauded. His name was Peter Hitchens, now a right-wing columnist on the *Mail on Sunday*. I'm amazed when I discover that there are still Trotskyist organizations active in British universities, egged on by the last of the Trotskyist academics.

Unlike most students I did pretty well financially while at university. As I was 24 I got a full local authority grant and when I arrived at York decided I didn't want to live on campus but would rent my own house instead. I then rapidly came to the conclusion that it would be cheaper to buy than rent. My dad had just retired and one of his insurance policies had paid out, so I borrowed the lot, paying him a decent rate of interest, and bought a small terraced house in Briggs Street, near the Rowntree factory. I paid the princely sum of £1,200 for the house, got a local authority grant to add on a bathroom, and sold it for £5,000 when I left. When I was in York recently I was fascinated to see similar houses are now selling for £120,000. I wonder where the poor of York can now afford to live.

But my most memorable financial experience at university was my libel action against the local evening paper, the *York Evening Press*. They had run an article saying that a local printer wouldn't print a student news-paper because of an article written by me that was claimed to be obscene. While it was true that the printer wouldn't print the paper it had nothing to do with my article, which was about the California marijuana initiative (an attempt to make the drug legal on the West Coast of the United States). I asked for an apology but the editor of the *Evening Press*, unaware that he was dealing with a student who had trained as a journalist, refused. So I decided to sue. In the end I got a full apology, all my legal costs, and £250 as an out of court settlement. Given that a full grant in 1974 was just £420, this was a good day: my girlfriend at the time, later my wife, Christine Taylor and I had a good summer in France on the *York Evening Press*.

There is a postscript to the story. In 2003 I was invited as Director-General of the BBC to be the guest speaker and present the awards at the *York Evening Press* Annual Business Awards. As DG you get hundreds of similar invites, but this was one I couldn't resist. Clearly no one at the paper was aware of the history; in my speech I told the whole story. I ended by thanking the *Evening Press* for making my life at York more comfortable.

Going to York as a mature student completely changed my life; it's why I've always been keen to encourage as many people as possible to go to university, particularly those who are older and who may have missed out on formal education the first time round. After I had left York I convinced Jeff Wright, my flatmate in Windsor, that although he didn't have a single O-level he was certainly clever enough to go to university. He ended up with a very good degree from Swansea University and went on to get a Masters. He was just another kid whose education was screwed up by the 11-plus.

In late 2003 I was appointed Chancellor elect of York University, which the *Sunday Times* recently named as University of the Year. For someone who went as a student with one A-level and caused a fair amount of trouble when I was there, I was both amazed and flattered to be asked to take on the role.

Unlike most students I haven't remained in close contact with many of my friends at York, with the exception of Marianne Geary, a girl from Northern Ireland. We've always enjoyed each other's company and she's very perceptive about me and what drives me. Just a few days after I left the BBC, I received an e-mail from Marianne telling me that Keith, her husband, had cancer and was about to have a kidney removed. At a time when I was feeling pretty sorry for myself it was a real awakening. By comparison, what was I making such a fuss about? Thankfully, it looks like Keith will make a full recovery.

When I left York after three incredibly stimulating years I wasn't sure what to do, so I went back to work in regional newspapers. My girlfriend Christine, who became my wife in 1975, was going to Newcastle University to do a one-year course to train as a probation officer, and it so happened that John Rees, my former editor on the Slough *Evening Mail*, was now the editor of the *Journal* in Newcastle. I wrote to him and he immediately offered me a job.

Going back to local journalism was a terrible mistake. Just as I had had to unlearn being a pop journalist when I went to university, so I was expected to forget all I had learnt while there and be a pop journalist

once again. I hated the experience. I wasn't the slightest bit interested in
what some jumped-up councillor thought, nor was I prepared to create
stories simply because someone said they were true when it was quite
clear they were bullshit. The only good thing about the six months I spent
on the *Journal* was that I met some people there who were to play a
significant part in my future life. One was Peter McHugh, the industrial
correspondent on the paper at the time, who later worked with me at
TV-am and is now in charge of GMTV. The second was Nick Evans,
who was doing a similar job to me on the regional evening paper, the
Evening Chronicle.

Nick is a very close friend who always claims that he was the better
reporter of the two of us, and it is certainly true that his shorthand was
better than mine. Much later in life, Nick became famous when he wrote
his first book, *The Horse Whisperer*, which became an international best-
seller and was turned into a film starring Robert Redford. Nick played a
big part in getting me my first job in television and later we worked
together running a programme at London Weekend Television.

While in Newcastle I decided I didn't want to be a journalist any more
– I wanted to do something more useful in society; so I got a job as a
campaign organizer for Wandsworth Council for Community Relations.
This meant Christine and me leaving Newcastle, which we both liked
(even though I disliked my job), and moving to London, where she became
a probation officer, also in Wandsworth. One day I was at home decorating our flat when she brought home a fellow probation officer, a very
attractive girl called Sue Howes. Seven years later, after both our marriages
had failed, Sue and I became an item, and still are.

My job involved organizing campaigns in the field of race relations.
The Borough of Wandsworth had been a centre for both Asian and West
Indian immigration in the 1960s and 1970s and the Community Relations
Council was an organization that sought to bring representatives of the
different ethnic minority communities together. I'm not sure anyone was
really quite sure what a Community Relations Council was supposed to
do, but my boss there, a man called Charles Boxer, believed that we should
be a campaigning organization influencing local and national policy in
the field of race. He employed me to set up campaigns and to get him,
the organization, and the campaigns plenty of press publicity, which is
exactly what I did.

I worked at WCCR for close on two years and discovered something profound: that no one, at any level, had solutions to some of the problems we identified. Worse still, neither did we – although of course we pretended we did by blaming the Government or the local council or claiming that more money would sort out all the problems. I had given up regional journalism because I thought it was superficial. Now I had found exactly the same thing in another area.

From this I began to recognize what I still believe today to be a fundamental difficulty in the relationship between pressure groups, media, and politics. Politicians are incapable of saying 'We don't know the solution to this', or even 'We don't think there is a solution'. If they did, they would be portrayed as weak or incompetent by the media. Pressure groups and opposition politicians play the same game by demanding that 'Something *must* be done', while politicians in power resort to saying 'Something *is* being done'. The whole process is damaging to media, politics, and the public understanding of the issues of the day.

Not that this growing understanding of the limitations of politics deterred me from following an ambition of mine that had developed in the years in Slough and afterwards: to be a politician. While I was at WCCR the opportunity arose for me to become the Labour Party's candidate for the Greater London Council election in Putney, one of four constituencies in the Borough of Wandsworth. The GLC was elected through the same constituencies as local MPs, so being the GLC candidate for Putney was quite a big deal.

I was nominated by one of the Labour branches in Battersea, where I was a member of the Party and where my friend Mark Mildred was also a member. I knew Mark, a successful lawyer who had worked on personal injury cases like Thalidomide, because his wife Sarah Rackham worked with me at WCCR. He put my name forward. Quite why Putney Labour Party wanted me I was never sure, but I was selected as their candidate for the 1977 GLC election. At that time Putney was a Labour seat both in Parliament and the GLC, but it was always going to be difficult to hang on to it.

The problem was that the Labour Government at the time, led by Jim Callaghan, was incredibly unpopular, so my chances of holding the seat seemed slim. And so it proved. I turned a Labour majority of 4,000 into a Conservative majority of 7,000, a massive 17 per cent swing to the

Conservatives. At the General Election two years later David Mellor, whom I had met and liked while I was active in Putney, also won the parliamentary seat for the Conservatives. During the GLC election I had met Ken Livingstone, who was organizing a left-wing grouping of potential GLC councillors. I joined his group, as he never ceases to remind me, but it was all in vain as very few of us won. Four years later he did the same thing again and became the Labour leader of the GLC, but by then my political ambitions had disappeared.

I often think how different my life might have been if I had won in April 1977. I would have become a full-time GLC councillor, and probably gone on to be a Labour MP, and would never have gone into the television industry. I have to say I am eternally grateful that I lost that election. I've seen too many people I really like go into politics only to find it frustrating and unrewarding.

A couple of months before the election I had resigned from WCCR, frustrated by all I had found in the race relations industry, which in those days was racked by the politics of race. On 20 May 1977 I celebrated my thirtieth birthday unemployed, having just turned a reasonably good Labour seat into a safe Conservative one. I was depressed and unsure of the future. I had always been ambitious and believed I would be a success in life, yet here I was with very little to show. I spent my birthday sitting on a log on Wandsworth Common asking myself 'Whatever happened to me?'

And then, just four months later, my life changed for ever.

CHAPTER THREE

Into Television

It was my friend from Newcastle, Nick Evans, who told me that there was a researcher's job going at London Weekend Television on *Weekend World*, ITV's prestigious but little watched current affairs show that was broadcast on Sunday lunchtimes. Nick had left Newcastle soon after me to become a researcher on *Weekend World* and had rapidly been promoted to become a producer. He told me if I applied for the job he would make sure the least I got was an interview; as I was unemployed at the time I didn't take much persuading.

I was interviewed by a whole range of people on the programme, including one who was very much against me. At that time Jane Hewland was a senior producer who was later to become Head of Features and Current Affairs at LWT. Today she runs a successful independent production company, Hewland International, which makes a lot of programmes for BSkyB. After meeting me, Jane decided I wasn't the right sort for LWT, although I only discovered this years later when, as Director of Programmes at LWT, I got access to my old file, and was able to read what Jane initially thought about me. By then Jane was working for me, so I included her comments about me in the speech I made at her leaving party. She's never forgiven me. I have her original report framed and hanging in my office. She said of me:

> He was so glib, fast talking and sure of himself and so contemptuous of all the TV people he has met so far I fear we would never be able to break his spirit and bring him to see the light as we see it. I think he would just turn out to be a pain in the arse, get disgruntled with us and leave.

At the final interview for the *Weekend World* job I had been told by Nick Evans that the most important person on the Board was John Birt, who was then head of Features and Current Affairs and was all powerful. At the interview I thought I did pretty well, answering most of the questions intelligently, and getting a few laughs at the same time. In particular John Birt laughed quite a lot – or so I thought.

I discovered afterwards that I had muddled up the people on the Board and that the man who was laughing was actually Barry Cox, the head of Current Affairs. The only person on the Board I didn't take to was the person to my left, who kept asking me really awkward questions and didn't laugh once. When Nick Evans called to ask me how I had got on I described this man to him and discovered it had been John Birt.

I didn't get the job on *Weekend World,* but I must have done all right because I was asked to apply for another LWT job as a reporter on their regional current affairs programme, called *The London Programme.* I went in to meet the editor, Julian Norridge, and we ended up talking about the Cuban revolution, the subject of my thesis at university three years earlier. Quite what Cuba had to do with London I had no idea, but I got the job.

Suddenly one of the blackest periods in my life was over: I had got the job in television I'd always dreamed of having. There are three periods of my life that had a profound influence on me, on my career, and on the way I think. The first was the three years I spent at York University. The second was about to begin – the six years from 1977 to 1983 that I spent in the current affairs department at LWT. The third wouldn't come until 1989, when I went to the Harvard Business School.

When I joined LWT in the autumn of 1977 it was a really exciting place. The company had won its ITV franchise in 1968. After a disastrous start, when it nearly went broke, it had recovered and was looking for ways to ensure it got its franchise renewed by the Independent Broadcasting Authority in 1980. The Current Affairs and Features Department under John Birt was expanding fast. *Weekend World* had introduced a new, more intellectual form of current affairs on British television, and two well-funded local programmes had changed regional programming. The first was the *London Weekend Show*, a programme for teenagers presented by Janet Street-Porter. The second was the programme I was joining, *The London Programme.*

The LWT style of journalism had been pioneered by John Birt, who had developed the whole approach when editing *Weekend World*. Many in television, then and now, have mocked his philosophy, but I would defend it to this day. What John argued was that understanding the issue or story was more important than necessarily getting the right pictures, and that if you couldn't get the pictures it didn't mean you had to abandon the whole programme. But the approach went further. Birt argued that demonstrating there was a problem wasn't enough: you also had to explain what could be done about it. His thesis, known as 'The Bias Against Understanding', was first outlined in an article written by Birt and Peter Jay in *The Times* in 1975. What this analytical approach to television current affairs meant was that, first, you were able to tackle difficult subjects that weren't necessarily televisual, and, second, you couldn't get away with just saying that something was an outrage: you had to show that there was something the policy makers could do about it.

The programme I joined, *The London Programme*, had been the idea of Barry Cox when he was a producer at Granada. He'd had the idea of producing a weekly, well-resourced current affairs programme, in the style of *World in Action* but only about London stories and London issues, and taken it to John Birt. I joined for the third series.

It is difficult to explain how exciting working on a programme like that was for me at that time. It was intellectually satisfying compared to the other jobs I had had since leaving York. You had six weeks to make a single half-hour film about a particular issue, which meant you had four weeks to research it. In that time you could get to know a subject well. You were helped because you were from 'television', so you could get access to the experts in the field you were examining: television opens doors. But the real challenge was to understand the subject. In many ways it was more like being at university than being in the media. In those days people joked about the LWT current affairs department being 'Balliol on Thames', a place where programme makers spent weeks constructing theses and made programmes that no one except other programme makers, MPs, and Whitehall mandarins watched. It also kept up the tradition of the long summer vacation when the current affairs department would empty for weeks on end.

My first ever television programme was a story I had discovered while working in community relations and was about landlords harassing tenants. This was followed by one about the chances of London flooding, and here I had an amazing piece of luck. The programme was made to commemorate the twenty-fifth anniversary of the great London flood of 1952. The Thames barrier was then being built and the programme asked what the chance was of London being flooded again before it was finished.

Three days after the programme was broadcast in the autumn of 1977 there was a surge tide, with the wind in the right direction, and London was inches from being under water. The Labour Government of the day was terrified and asked LWT to repeat the programme so that people would understand the danger and what they should do if the worst happened. Michael Grade, then the Director of Programmes at LWT, repeated it at 10.30 p.m. on the Friday night and we got an enormous rating, the largest for any *London Programme* that series.

I read recently that, according to some academic study or other, people born in May, like me, are the luckiest, and it's certainly been true in my case. My old managing director at LWT, Brian Tesler, once told me he would invest in any company I ran – not because I was brilliant, but because I had 'the luck' on my side. Most things I touched worked. When I was at TV-am in 1984 the astrologer Marjorie Orr did my chart and told me I could expect twenty wonderful years when all would go right. The trouble was, the twenty years ended in 2004. I must ask her some time if it was just coincidence that I was fired from the BBC the very moment the twenty years was up.

I had a pretty good first year at LWT and, at the end of it, was asked to join *Weekend World* as junior producer, progressing during the year to become a full producer. The programme I was most proud of while at *Weekend World* was one I made on the European Common Agricultural Policy, a system that only about six people in the world seemed to understand. I became the seventh and tried to explain it to the nation on this intellectual programme by telling a joke.

I told the story of a German cow. We saw it milked and then followed the cow's milk to the dairy, where it was made into powdered milk. The powdered milk was then bought by the EEC intervention board, who stored it in enormous sheds as part of the EEC milk mountain. Eventually it was sold back to the same farmer to be fed to the same cow who had produced the milk in the first place. When I finished the programme I was convinced that the Common Agricultural Policy was doomed. It was so inefficient and made so little economic sense. How wrong I was. It's still going strong today, costing the average family of four in Britain something like £1,000 a year.

My year on *Weekend World* was not a happy time – not because of the work, but because of what happened in my private life. On getting a job in television I had thrown myself into it full time and in the process my marriage fell apart. Christine felt neglected and found another life without me. It was without doubt the worst time of my life, culminating in my sitting in the office one day trying to work with tears rolling down my face. I am forever grateful to a lovely PA called Julie Shaw, who, seeing how distressed I was, came up to me and said 'Why don't we go for a walk?' I also went in to see the editor of *Weekend World*, the brilliant but mad David Cox, and told him I needed a few days off because my marriage was collapsing. He just looked up and said, 'So is mine.'

Ever since then I've always tried either to talk or write to the people working for me when their life is in crisis because of a marriage breakdown, a family tragedy, or some other major problem. A small gesture from the boss at a time of crisis can really mean something. I also learnt from that time onwards how important it was to keep a decent balance between work and the rest of your life, although I haven't always managed to achieve it. These were the days in television when you weren't seen as a 'proper' producer if you didn't sleep on the cutting room floor and ignore the rest of your life. It was complete nonsense.

In later years, when people came to see me and said their marriage was breaking down, I always told them to try again. Marriages and relationships inevitably go through difficult times, but sometimes they recover. And I've always insisted people take their holidays despite whatever crisis might be happening at work, because holidays matter in family life. I've only ever had to cancel two, the first when Granada launched a takeover bid for LWT in late 1993 and the other in the summer of 2003 after Dr Kelly committed suicide.

Thankfully, Christine and I had not had children so our break-up was relatively uncomplicated. We simply split what we owned and went our own ways. Some years later, when we were both with other people and Christine wanted to get married again, we discovered that, due to a mistake of our own making, we weren't actually divorced. We both had to turn up in court to affirm that we no longer wanted to be married to each other – a very odd experience. We hadn't seen each other for some years and it was like meeting someone you were at university with, rather than meeting your ex-wife.

Much later, more than twenty years after we had split up and when I was Director-General of the BBC, the *Mail on Sunday* went in search of Christine with the obvious intent of getting her to dish the dirt on me. They found her at her home in Yorkshire, but when she said there was no animosity between us and that, although we no longer saw each other, we were still fond of one another, the reporter gave up and went back to London. No story there.

At the end of my year on *Weekend World* Nick Evans and I were asked to become a team to run *The London Programme*. He would be the editor and, after just two years in television, I would be his deputy. We had two small adjoining offices, the states of which reflected our differing personalities. His was always neat and tidy, with a completely clear desk at the end of the day. Mine was always a tip, with piles of paper everywhere. My problem was that I really wanted a desk like his but could never quite achieve it; so on the nights when I was working late and he'd gone home, I used to sneak into his office and work at his desk. It was bliss.

Nick and his wife Jenny were great friends to me during this time. As anyone knows who has got divorced, or has seen a long-term relationship split up, these are times when the emotional swings are enormous. The highs are higher but the lows are much lower. Nick and Jenny helped me through so many of the low times. Sadly, much later, their own marriage split up as well and Nick has recently remarried.

Running a weekly current affairs show with one of your best friends was a lot of fun. What I discovered was the importance, in a creative business, of people with good ideas. In my relatively brief time in television I had always worked on stories that I had found myself, or on issue-based programmes I had suggested, so I had always assumed most producers worked on their own ideas. When I became an editor I discovered it wasn't true. There are brilliant producers who have few ideas themselves, but they can take an idea and make it into an outstanding programme.

What I discovered in the two years I was doing that job was that people with good ideas are worth their weight in gold. I discovered later that the same applies in business. When I was at the Harvard Business School some years later, one of the professors came up with a great description of this when he said 'Man can live for three weeks without food, four days without water and five minutes without oxygen; but some men can live a lifetime without a good idea.'

The point is that in programme making you can screw up a good idea and make a bad programme, but you can never make a good programme out of a lousy idea. Whenever I've talked to people coming new into television I've always told them that you can learn the process of making programmes relatively easily; what really matters is the originality and quality of your ideas.

Nick and I ran *The London Programme* for two years. We had a good team with us and tried to make it a fun and exciting place to work. As always, we made some good programmes and some bad ones. The hardest job of being a programme editor is having to 'save' a programme – to try to turn a potentially disastrous programme into one that is at least average. I always remember Nick trying to do this with a programme on local government finance. The end product was totally incomprehensible, but at least Nick had made it look stylish: a week earlier it had both been incomprehensible and looked terrible. It is exactly the same in news. Producing a programme on a good news day is ten times easier than when there is nothing happening. The latter is the test of a good editor, as I was to discover later at TV-am.

In January 1982 LWT began another ten years as the weekend ITV broadcaster in London, which was good news for the company, although the renewal of the franchise wasn't unexpected. LWT's only challenger was from a consortium led by quizmaster Hughie Green. Even better news was that, instead of taking over – as usual – from Thames Television at 7 p.m. on Friday nights, LWT would in future start at 5.30. LWT had another hour and a half to fill each weekend, and another hour and a half's worth of advertising to sell.

I was given the job of filling some of that extra time – the hour between six and seven every Friday night. After just four years in television I was given my own programme. I was to be the editor of what became a mould-breaking programme called *The Six O'Clock Show*, which was due to launch in January 1982. It was only called that because we didn't have a name to put on the door of the office when we first brought the team together in September 1981. In the next three months we came up with about twenty different names and put them all forward to Michael Grade, LWT's Director of Programmes at the time, for him to choose. In the end he chose the name on the door. The name of programmes doesn't really matter; it's the content that is important. Who in their right mind would call a situation comedy about a couple of wide boys from East London *Only Fools and Horses*, and yet it is one of the great television comedies of all time.

LWT in 1982 was a company with enormous confidence. It had won back its franchise and had a series of big hits on its hands. Cilla Black's *Surprise! Surprise!* was hugely popular and that year it launched another entertainment show called *Game for a Laugh*, which became Britain's Number One show in a matter of weeks. A new LWT drama called *Dempsey and Makepeace* became another big hit while *Weekend World* and *The South Bank Show* were there to prove that the company had an intellectual heart. Into this mix came *The Six O'Clock Show*.

The Six O'Clock Show broke the mould for a number of reasons. We were the first programme to use single-camera tape: up until then it had only been used for news. LWT had just got a union agreement allowing the company to use electronic news gathering (ENG) and we decided to see if we could use this new technology in an original and more creative way. We pre-planned every three- or four-minute item we were to shoot as if it were a thirty-minute documentary. We had a budget that people in television would dream about today, which meant we had a producer, a director, and a researcher on every short item. Because tape was so much cheaper than film, we shot masses of it on every item and only used a tiny proportion of it. As a result, we got some gems at times.

The aim of *The Six O'Clock Show* was to create a different feeling: that this was Friday night and Friday night was the beginning of the weekend. In fact, I wanted to call the show *Thank God it's Friday* and commissioned research to demonstrate that the public wouldn't be offended by the use of the word 'God' in this way. Unfortunately, the research showed exactly the opposite: it turned out that large numbers of people *would* be offended, so I had to drop the idea.

One of my complaints about most news and current affairs programmes is that they never deal with the good things in life, only problems and issues. If you had watched LWT's regional output at that time you wouldn't have known that anyone in London ever actually enjoyed living there. I decided *The Six O'Clock Show* would counter that. Its aim would be to tell the funnier side of life in London, to put on the eccentrics, and to tell the sort of stories people told each other in the pub, in the shop, or at work – the stories that would never have found their way onto a news programme. My hunch was that these were the stories that people really wanted to hear.

For instance, we once found a small cutting in a local paper about an eccentric man who had spent ten years building a model of the *Titanic* out of matchsticks. When it was finally completed he had launched it on the pond on Wimbledon Common and, true to form, it had sunk on its maiden voyage. We decided that *The Six O'Clock Show* would raise the *Titanic*. We hired a frogman, put Janet Street-Porter into a rubber dinghy, and sent them, plus a camera crew, out to find the sunken model. Unfortunately, the pond was too shallow for our frogman to dive under the water so he could only walk up and down in his diving gear, with the boat's proud owner telling him roughly where his pride and joy had sunk. Sadly, our diver found the boat by treading on it and the *Titanic* ended up being raised in two pieces.

We made three pilots for *The Six O'Clock Show*. All three were bad, but the final one was spectacularly awful. The problem was we had a monkey on the show that escaped in the studio and ended up swinging around on the lighting rig. The poor director, Danny Wiles, had no idea whether to use his cameras to follow the monkey or concentrate on what was left of the show. I was very keen to shoot the monkey, but not with the cameras. At the drinks party afterwards I was downcast. I could see my career as an editor disappearing even before it had started. I cheered up when one of the team, Tony Cohen, who was then a researcher but who became my alter ego for many years and now runs one of the world's largest independent production companies, Fremantle Media, turned up with his wife Alison and their new-born baby.

After the drinks I was sitting with the show's executive producer, Barry Cox, discussing what we could do to save it when I got an agitated phone call from Tony. He explained that he was at the hospital because the monkey, which he claimed had got drunk in hospitality, had scratched his baby and the doctors were demanding to see it. I told the story to Barry who then uttered the immortal words, 'Did this happen on London

Weekend property?' All turned out OK in the end. We never found the monkey, but Tony's son Ben suffered no unpleasant after-effects and is now a strapping, six-foot-tall 22-year-old.

Despite the pilots, and to everyone's surprise, including mine, *The Six O'Clock Show* was a smash hit and became the most watched regional programme in Britain. One week we even got into the top ten programmes in London and were sent a case of champagne by the management. Looking back now I think its success was rooted in our ability to reflect the social, economic, and political changes that were happening in London at the time and talk about them in an entertaining way. It was a time when London was experiencing a massive change in social habits, when yuppies, cocktail bars, and crêperies were replacing traditional life in the working-class areas of the capital.

Every week we did three or four stories like the *Titanic* item, stories about another side of London. Michael Aspel presented the show. He was not Michael Grade's first choice – he wanted Terry Wogan to leave the BBC to do the show – but Michael turned out to be a great success. He was very witty and managed to stand above the chaos that was sometimes around him in the studio. The show sounded very London, with a cast of character reporters on the road and in the studio that included Janet Street-Porter, the former *Mastermind* winner and London cabbie Fred Housego, and the brilliant Danny Baker, all of whom had strong London accents. The team was completed by a small, wonderfully mad, rather posh man called Andy Price, who was an on-the-road reporter.

I decided that we should capitalize on Janet's accent and turn her into a working-class heroine. The problem was that Janet wanted to be seen as being cultured. It was fine to begin with, but one evening, after she had spent all day shooting an item about pigeon fancying, she burst into my office to tell me she'd had enough of being covered in pigeon shit and didn't want to be seen that way any more. She told me she wanted the audience to know she liked 'fucking opera', as she put it. I explained that that wasn't her role, that Michael was the cultured one in the team. As a result, Janet decided to leave and we replaced her with Paula Yates.

In many ways it was the juxtaposition between Michael Aspel and Danny Baker that made the show work. One represented suave London of the Sixties and Seventies, the other uppity London of the Eighties. Remember, this was the London of Ken Livingstone 'mark one', when he was both dangerous and very funny and was hated by the Thatcher Government of the day. *The Six O'Clock Show* was also dangerous – and live. That's why it worked. Things went wrong. One week Tony Cohen fixed up for part of the show to come live from the beach at Southend but he mixed up the tide tables and halfway through the show the tide came in and wrecked the whole thing. On another occasion a live outside link went completely wrong when it was invaded by a bunch of kids. It was only saved as a piece of television when Andy Price, who was presenting, lost his temper and picked up one of the kids and threw him across the street. This was live on television.

For me, *The Six O'Clock Show* was the first programme that was completely mine, and totally under my control. From running it I learnt much about teamwork and leadership. I learnt about encouraging everyone, from the most junior to the most senior, to be part of the team and come up with ideas, and about the importance of celebrating success – and mourning failure – together as a team. And I learnt how important the leader was to the team. These were all themes that I developed further over the next twenty years as I went on to run larger and larger groups of people. I also learnt how important it was constantly to push the system and to defy the rules, because that way you got a better end result. But taking on the rules at LWT meant fighting both the management and the unions.

These were the days when the unions ran television. Earlier in my time at LWT I had been the trade union representative for the producers and directors; in fact when I became Managing Director of the company in 1990 I had to renegotiate some of the ridiculous deals that I had won from the management when I was a union negotiator. I learned just how ridiculous the whole thing was when, on my first ever shoot at LWT, a man turned up driving a car with no one and nothing in it. I asked who he was and was told he was the electrician's driver. So where was the electrician? I asked. I was told he liked to bring his own car as well so he could claim the mileage allowance on top of having a driver. In those days all the crews demanded expensive lunches every day in fairly upmarket restaurants. If they didn't get them they made your life a misery as a researcher or a producer.

The LWT management were feeble when it came to standing up to the unions. When another friend, Andy Forrester, and I were the union negotiators for the producers and directors we demanded a 20 per cent wage increase. We nearly fell off our chairs when the management's second offer was 18 per cent – we couldn't get out of the room fast enough. We always called it the 'pop-up toaster deal' because on top of the 18 per cent we got everything else we had asked for, including company televisions and video recorders for all our members. We reckoned if we'd asked for a pop-up toaster we would have got that as well.

It is difficult to believe now, when there are so many outstanding women working in television, but in those days there was not a single woman director working in the Current Affairs and Features Department at LWT, and very few female producers. I was determined to break this and be the first to employ a female director. I had always been a strong supporter of the women's movement and wanted to put my beliefs into practice.

I found a great director for *The Six O'Clock Show* called Vikki Barras, who went on to invent *What Not to Wear* for the BBC. She applied for the job of director and got it, but the union objected as she hadn't got the right sort of union card. The LWT management immediately folded and agreed with the union that we couldn't employ her. I thought they were gutless bastards and decided to fight.

I was on holiday in Aberdovey in West Wales at the time and was fully dressed in a wet suit and about to go windsurfing when the phone rang. It was Roy Van Gelder, LWT's Director of Human Resources, who had called to tell me that the union had said 'No' to Vikki. Luckily Gavyn Waddell, the chairman of the shop stewards' committee, was with Roy. Gavyn was the cleverest, most articulate trade unionist I have ever met. He was a natural leader of men and would have made a great senior manager. Like many of the union people at LWT he was also a hardline Tory and he eventually resigned from the union, the ACTT, when they gave money to support the 1984 miners' strike.

Fully dressed in my wet suit I demanded to talk to Gavyn. Everyone at LWT knew that, where the union was concerned, Gavyn was the person you had to get on side. After ten minutes' discussion he agreed it was time we had a woman director and that he would withdraw the objection to my employing Vikki – which meant he would tell the activists in the union to back off. So when Vikki became our first woman director it was no thanks to the management.

In general the LWT management gave in to almost every demand from the unions. This was the company that, in the mid Seventies, paid a videotape engineer £150,000 a year, resulting in the joke 'What's the difference between an Arab oil sheikh and an LWT video engineer?' Answer: 'The engineer gets London weighting.' And it was the same management who, in the ITV national strike in 1979, allowed us to picket inside the building in case it rained – no cold nights and braziers for us. As usual we won the strike when the ITV managements around Britain folded and we all went back to work with another large increase in our wages.

The television unions of those days stifled creativity and good programme making by their obsession with restrictive practices. I decided to take them on whenever I could. Sometimes I did it as an editor, and thus as part of the management; but on other occasions a few of us did it as members of the union. When the management decided that crews would have first-class travel on flights to the USA the programme makers reversed the policy at the union meeting. We argued that the effect would be no more foreign shoots, and that the losers would be the viewers.

On *The Six O'Clock Show* we were 'advised' by management not to do single-camera live links into the programme because, although the unions had agreed we could do them, the management feared they wouldn't like it. Today these happen in almost every live programme, but in 1982 they were virtually unheard of. I did them from day one. Eventually the union demanded we had a floor manager on these shoots. I simply refused.

We were also told by the management that we had to have props people on location if we wanted to use any props at all. Again, we just ignored it. When we wanted a rubber boat for Janet to use on Wimbledon Common I sent a researcher out to buy one; and when we needed some golf balls sewn into the back of a pyjama jacket for an item on snoring, Tony Cohen persuaded his reluctant wife to do the job. We ignored the union's rules whenever and wherever we could, and more often than not we got away with it. It was a lesson I have applied in every job I have had since. As I learnt later at Harvard Business School, 'No one ever succeeded in an organization by following the rules.'

In the years since Christine and I had broken up I had, as a single man in his thirties in the television business, played the field quite a lot. But in my last year on *The Six O'Clock Show* I had struck up a new relationship with the woman who had admired my decorating all those years earlier when Christine had brought her round to our flat in Wandsworth. The relationship was based on false pretences; because she'd seen me decorating she thought I was a handyman, whereas the truth was that this was the only time in my whole life I'd ever decorated a room. By then Sue had split from her husband and had taken her two children to live in Bradford upon Avon in Somerset. I began to go down for weekends after the show ended, and Sue and I quickly decided to set up home together.

I wanted Sue to come and live in Clapham, where I was then living, but an afternoon she spent wandering across Clapham Common soon put paid to that idea. The wonderful thing about the Common was that all of life was there – including people playing chess with enormous pieces, people with model boats, and lots of sportsmen. Unfortunately there were also a lot of drug dealers, pimps, and police and Sue absolutely refused to bring her children to live there. I think she was influenced by the fact that too many of her old clients as a probation officer lived nearby.

Instead we bought a house together further west in London, in Barnes. Matthew was five and Christine four when Sue and I set up home together, and overnight I became a family man – although like most people who haven't had kids of their own I had no idea what it meant. I think Sue's sister Anne summed it up best when she described visiting us as visiting Sue, her family, and her rather strange live-in lover. And then there was Jeff.

Jeff Wright, my old friend from my early newspaper days, had been living with me in Clapham when I sold up. He had nowhere else to go, and didn't have a job at the time, so he came too. Our neighbours in Barnes must have wondered what sort of people had moved in next door. Sue always joked that between Jeff and me she had just about got one decent partner, although he wasn't much good at decorating either.

Sue went back to work as a probation officer at Wandsworth Prison. She drove there early every morning, and I agreed to drop the kids at school before going into LWT on the train. My life as a family man was beginning to take shape. And then one day I got a phone call from a Conservative MP called Jonathan Aitken, and the world changed again.

CHAPTER FOUR

A Year at TV-am

TV-am was Britain's first ever venture into commercial breakfast television. Launched in February 1983, it was an instant failure with the audience, which in turn resulted in a bloodbath on the Board and the organization plunging into a deep financial crisis. All this happened in just a matter of weeks during which 'ailing' TV-am dominated the headlines. And then I was appointed to the job of Editor-in-Chief and was told I had one task and one task only: to save the station. An interesting challenge for a 35-year-old who had been unemployed just five years earlier.

I was originally asked to join TV-am six or seven months before it was due to be launched when Michael Deakin, TV-am's Director of Programmes, rang me and asked me to go along for a chat. At the time I was still running *The Six O'Clock Show* and had no intention of giving that up. I went along out of curiosity.

Michael was a flamboyant programme maker who had had a brilliant career in documentary making at Yorkshire Television. He had made some wonderful programmes and was a great raconteur, but he knew very little about news and magazine programming, the staple diet of breakfast television. In fact, he was never intended for the role of Director of Programmes at TV-am at all and had got the job by default.

When David Frost created his consortium to bid for Britain's first ever breakfast television franchise he brought together an odd bunch of high-profile people, most of whom were either too grand, or unsuitable, to do the jobs they were allocated. David mainly concentrated on building a team of five of the most famous presenters of the day. He recruited the king of the chat show, Michael Parkinson; the two most famous female newsreaders of their day, Angela Rippon from the BBC and Anna Ford from ITN; and, as a real political heavyweight, Robert Kee from BBC Current Affairs. David believed that this combination would wow the viewers with their talent and sexual chemistry. The problem with this strategy was that the people who make or break television programmes are not the on-screen talent but the production teams. A great presenter has never saved a lousy show, while there have been many successful programmes with very average presenters.

Frost's group of presenters became known as the 'Famous Five', and although they never convinced the viewers of their combined talents they certainly convinced the members of the Independent Broadcasting Authority, who, to everyone's surprise, gave the franchise to their consortium. Frost persuaded Peter Jay, the former British Ambassador to Washington, to run the whole company as Chairman and Chief Executive, completely ignoring the fact that, although he was both a former *Times* economics editor and the former presenter of the prestigious LWT current affairs programme *Weekend World*, he had no experience of being in charge of a business. Like many economists, Jay was good at writing and talking about business but was not impressive when it came to running one. In putting his production team together, Frost tended to opt for programme executives whose track records in television would impress the 'great and the good' of the IBA, rather than people who had the proven skills to deliver three and a half hours of good television every morning, week in and week out.

When the Frost group won the breakfast franchise the Director of Programmes designate was another LWT man, Nick Elliot, a former Editor of *Weekend World*. But Nick, who has spent the past ten years as a highly successful head of drama for ITV, changed his mind after the franchise was won and decided that instead of 5 a.m. starts he would stick with LWT, where he had been offered a new job as Controller of Drama and Arts. History was to show that he made a very wise decision. Michael Deakin, who was in the original Frost consortium in charge of features, was instead promoted to the top programming job, despite his total lack of experience in this area of television.

My own meeting with Deakin convinced me that my instinct to stay with LWT was the right one. Michael said he wanted me to be number three or four in the programme hierarchy but didn't seem to be able to describe what that hierarchy was, or who was doing what. Even more worrying was that he didn't seem to know what was going to be in the programme; he appeared to believe that filling three and a half hours of television a morning was going to happen by some sort of process of osmosis. Michael only became really animated when he talked about the building in Camden in North London that TV-am was planning to occupy, a building used today by MTV but known for years as Eggcup Towers. Designed by a young Terry Farrell, who went on to become one of Britain's top post-war architects, it was clear to me that Michael loved the building a lot more than he loved the prospect of breakfast television.

With Jay as Chairman and Chief Executive and Deakin as Director of Programmes TV-am had people in the two most important jobs in the company who were peculiarly unqualified for their particular roles. But it got worse. They had also promised the Independent Broadcasting Authority that they would produce a new and intellectual approach to news and current affairs because they had a 'mission to inform'. This completely ignored the fact that the most likely viewers to be attracted to breakfast television would be heavy television watchers, disproportionately women with children. Neither group was likely to be interested in the bill of goods the Frost consortium had sold to the IBA.

With the wrong Chief Executive, the wrong Director of Programmes, and a completely unrealistic remit, you could argue that TV-am's fate was sealed long before it went on air. Turning down Michael Deakin's offer of a job was one of the best decisions I ever made.

TV-am finally went live on Tuesday 1 February 1983 and was an instant disaster. Two weeks earlier, on Monday 17 January, the BBC had launched *Breakfast Time*, their first foray into early-morning television. It was unashamedly populist and was clearly a spoiler. TV-am had won their franchise promising to bring serious news and analysis to the early morning. The BBC had arrived with keep fit, horoscopes, and cookery. But it also had a very competent production team led by Ron Neill, an inspirational editor, and two very good presenters in Frank Bough and Selina Scott. Selina certainly brought sexual chemistry to breakfast television.

Within weeks TV-am turned from a disaster into a bloodbath. Peter Jay was ousted in a boardroom coup led by the Aitken cousins, Jonathan and Tim. Michael Deakin only survived because he supported the Aitkens, but by then he was largely discredited. The programme had gone from bad to worse and David Frost had been replaced as the main presenter by a young sports presenter called Nick Owen. Ratings barely registered and there was virtually no advertising, partly due to the lack of ratings and partly to industrial action from the actors' union Equity, who wanted a new deal for their members for breakfast television. Most serious of all – although not publicly known at the time – was that TV-am Ltd was running out of money. The company had been under-capitalized from the beginning so that all the founders could have significant shareholdings without putting up a lot of cash. The problem was that the business plan required it to be a financial success from day one or it would have to raise more cash from the shareholders. In normal circumstances that would not have been an insurmountable problem, but the particular circumstances of TV-am made it very difficult. City institutions didn't like to be publicly associated with mayhem and failure, particularly when it was all over the front pages of the newspapers day after day. And the press, smelling blood, began to stalk the wounded station.

To raise more money TV-am had to convince institutional investors that they could get the programme right, and do it quickly. They needed a new programme head, and that was where I came in. It was around this time that I got my second approach to join TV-am; this time the phone call came from Jonathan Aitken, who, although he was still the Conservative MP for Thanet, had taken over from Jay as acting Chief Executive of TV-am, while former British Railways boss Dick Marsh, an ex-Labour MP, had become Chairman.

Aitken invited me to lunch at his grand house in Lord North Street in Westminster – the very same house his bankruptcy trustees sold eighteen years later to help pay off his debts after he lost his libel case against *The Guardian* and Granada Television (he was later sentenced to eighteen months in jail after pleading guilty to perjury and perverting the course of justice during the case). I remember the lunch very well. Most of all I remember the incredibly camp butler who served the lunch Kenneth Williams style. Julian and Sandy, the outrageously camp characters from *Round the Horne*, the popular radio programme of the 1960s, had nothing on Jonathan's butler.

While I sat intrigued by the butler, Jonathan set about trying to persuade me to join TV-am as Editor-in-Chief. He had approached me at just the right time. Despite the success of *The Six O'Clock Show* I was looking for a change after running the programme for eighteen months. And I was particularly incensed that LWT had refused to give me a company car whilst giving one to the Editor of *Weekend World*, a programme I had previously worked on as a producer. After all, *The Six O'Clock Show* added ratings while *Weekend World* lost them. My programme made money for the company, his lost it. Wasn't this supposed to be commercial television? Looking back now it is ridiculous that I decided my whole future on something as trivial as a company car; but I've never been a believer in grand career plans. My view has always been that you take the opportunities as they come and they either work for you or they don't.

I was intrigued by the challenge that the chaos at TV-am offered. It never crossed my mind that I wouldn't succeed in turning it around. As the novelist Maeve Haran, a former colleague on *The Six O'Clock Show*, always said about me, the only reason I had turned out to be successful in life was that I didn't have enough imagination to contemplate failure. I suspect there's some truth in that.

With all the confidence of a brash 35-year-old, and despite the fact that I was a relative newcomer to the television industry, I had no doubt I could make TV-am into a success. My view was that what was needed was, firstly, a programme vision that appealed to the sort of audience likely to watch breakfast television and, secondly, a programme team who could deliver it. In turn that meant I would need to bring in new people while also trying to convince a disillusioned staff that, together, we could succeed. As it turned out, the job was harder than that – but not a lot harder.

What I thought was a lunchtime chat with Jonathan Aitken was actually an interview, job offer, and negotiation all in one. He offered to double my current salary, buy out my pension, put me on a ratings-based bonus scheme, and, importantly in the circumstances, give me a smart company car. If everything worked out I would, by my standards in 1983, be comparatively well off for the first time in my life. Of course what I didn't know that day was that TV-am was rapidly running out of cash and that for me to get everything Jonathan was offering would be a long and hard fight.

Towards the end of the lunch Michael Deakin turned up and pretended that I would be working for him. I made it very clear that if I was to take the job I would have to have complete charge of all the programming. He was effectively redundant. I found out later that Jonathan was determined he wouldn't let me leave his house that day without my signing some sort of letter committing myself to TV-am. I think he was pretty desperate to get someone who knew about magazine programming, and the BBC's Ron Neill had already turned him down. Jonathan succeeded and I signed a letter, although I suspect what I actually signed had no legal value whatsoever. Jonathan was nervous that I would go home and change my mind so as I left the lunch he invited Sue and me for dinner on the following Sunday evening so we could cement the deal. This was clearly his attempt to persuade Sue that I should join TV-am. I persuaded her to come to the dinner, if only to meet the butler.

We duly turned up and were introduced to Jonathan's now famous wife Lolicia, the blonde who didn't pay the Paris hotel bill in his notorious libel case against Granada Television and *The Guardian*. She clearly had no interest in us and obviously didn't want to be there. It was a dull evening but two things happened that have had a profound effect on my life since then.

Firstly I met Clive Jones at the dinner. Today Clive is Chief Executive of ITV News; back then he had just been appointed Editor of TV-am by Jonathan and would work directly to me as Editor-in-Chief. It was the combination of Clive and myself that was to turn the whole place around, a combination of my ideas and leadership and his capabilities as a producer. Clive had an amazing capacity for work. A few weeks after I joined TV-am I reckoned the programme was still pretty awful. I said to him that it was only going to get better if one of us got in there at five every morning and drove the show from the gallery five days a week. I added that I thought it should be him, and that's what he did – week in and week out until it had improved. Over the years Clive and I have worked together on many occasions and he has turned out to be a good and trusted friend. In life there are some people whom you can be certain will always be there for you. Clive is one of those people.

But the more important event that night came when Sue and I left the house in Lord North Street. We'd only been living together for a few months and we were still learning about each other. As the butler shut the front door she turned to me and said that if I wanted the job I should take it but that whatever I did I should never trust those people, referring to Jonathan and Lolicia.

In the years since I've learnt on many occasions that Sue's judgement of people is better than mine. I regularly, and naively, take people at face value. She doesn't. She knew instinctively that night that these were not our sort of people, that they came from different backgrounds, had different values, and played in a different world, one in which friendship and trust were commodities that were bought and sold. According to Sue, what Jonathan said and promised were not to be believed – a fact well and truly established at the Old Bailey sixteen years later.

I went back to LWT and told everyone I was leaving. As a result I was summoned to a meeting with LWT's then Director of Programmes John Birt, who had been promoted into the job when Michael Grade left to go to America in 1981. John told me that if I left there would be no way back into the company, ironic given that seven years later I became its Chief Executive. However, I stuck to my guns and told him I was definitely going, and after that we had a pleasant chat.

John asked me who was going to be the Chief Executive of TV-am. I told him exactly what Jonathan had told me: that he, Jonathan, was going to give up his parliamentary seat and become the full-time CEO. A few days later the story appeared in *The Guardian*; Jonathan immediately announced that it wasn't true and that if the paper didn't withdraw the article he would sue. Months later a sheepish John Birt rang me at TV-am to tell me he was helping *The Guardian* in their battle with Jonathan over the story and asked if I recollected what I had told him. I suddenly realized that he had been *The Guardian*'s source.

I had the usual LWT send-off with speeches and videos that were characteristically rude – no prisoners were ever taken at LWT leaving events. Danny Baker, one of the presenters on *The Six O'Clock Show*, ended the video sitting in a trap in a public toilet reading a limerick that went: 'There was a young fellow called Dyke/Largely did what he liked/Went to TV-am/Never heard of again/Fucking well served him right'. When I read my leaving card I also discovered that my immediate boss, David Cox, LWT's head of Current Affairs, had written in it 'Fuck off Dyke and good riddance'. When I returned to LWT just four years later as his boss I didn't need to remind him of this friendly message. He remembered it.

By the time I turned up for work at TV-am in May 1983 Jonathan Aitken had stepped down as Chief Executive and his cousin Timothy had taken on the job part time while continuing to run the family's merchant bank, Aitken Hume. Ratings and advertising were still non-existent and if anything the programme had got worse. I'll never forget watching it at home the week before I joined when Yehudi Menuhin was brought on to play the violin live. I sat there amazed. What producer in their right mind could possibly have believed that people rushing to work or struggling to get the kids to school had the time or the inclination to watch a classical violinist for five minutes in the morning?

When I was appointed Editor-in-Chief, TV-am had announced that I was to be its saviour and, for the first time in my life, I was all over the newspapers. My appointment even made the television news, much to my mother's excitement. TV-am had also announced that I would re-launch the whole weekday programme three weeks after joining. So what the previous management had got wrong in eighteen months of planning I was expected to fix in just three weeks!

On my first day at TV-am I had arranged to take Michael Parkinson out to lunch. Michael was one of the few successes at the station, largely because he had himself taken charge of the programming at the weekends as well as presenting the shows with his wife Mary. Michael is a rare breed in television: a great interviewer and presenter who is also a very good producer and motivator of the team around him. Melvyn Bragg is another. We had a pleasant lunch discussing the shambles that was TV-am and what could be done about it.

I went back to the office only to discover later in the afternoon that Tim Aitken had sacked two of the Famous Five without telling me. Both Angela Rippon and Anna Ford had been summarily dismissed for something they had done on the programme on the day Peter Jay left. They had said that 'treachery' was happening at TV-am and this had understandably upset the Aitkens because it implied that they were the perpetrators. Tim decided to get his revenge on the two women on my very first day by firing both of them. His nickname of Pol Pot was born that day. But both women got their revenge. First Anna very publicly threw a glass of red wine over Jonathan at a smart cocktail party and made sure it was in all the papers; and later both of them threatened to sue the company for breach of contract and were paid off.

My eventful first day ended when I went into the TV-am car park to collect my first company car only to find a battered BMW that had quite clearly been in a recent pile-up. I drove it home but got stopped by the police on the way on suspicion of driving an unroadworthy vehicle. So much for company cars! Luckily I didn't keep that car for long as one of the games we played at TV-am was executive car swap. Every time Tim fired another executive I would pinch his car and pass mine on to Clive Jones. We both ended up with very smart cars.

After the turmoil of my first day I already knew that the car wasn't the only thing that wasn't living up to Jonathan Aitken's promises. On the second day things only got worse. Overnight Michael Parkinson had decided he would go into battle to defend Anna Ford and Angela Rippon and had announced to the world that if they went he would go too.

Given that Michael produced and presented the only vaguely successful part of TV-am, it would not have been good news if he had left. My job was to persuade him not to go. But like so much at TV-am, even this descended into black comedy. I sat in my office with Michael, his wife Mary, and their agent John Webber trying to persuade him to stay. We were joined by the new Chairman, Dick Marsh, who had come in to help out. The trouble was that Dick had had a vasectomy that morning and every time he leaned forward to emphasize to Michael how important he was to TV-am he would end up clutching his crotch in agony.

Distracted by Dick Marsh's discomfort I didn't make much progress with Michael; in the end it was Tim Aitken who persuaded him to stay by the classic combination of flattery and bribery. He offered Michael a seat on the TV-am Board. It had clearly annoyed the other four members of the Famous Five that David Frost was the only one of their number who had a board seat. Now Michael was to join him. So Anna and Angela were forgotten and Michael announced to the scrum of reporters and photographers outside Eggcup Towers that he was to stay after all.

After the chaotic events of my first two days I had to get down to the programme relaunch itself. The problem I faced was that not only was it the wrong programme, as the appetite for a serious news and current affairs programme at that time in the morning was very limited, it was also badly produced. The news didn't start on time, the items were too long, and frankly it was boring. It had no character, no humour, and there was no team feeling amongst the presenters.

By then Clive Jones was in charge and was desperate to make changes to improve things. I told him his job was not to make the programme better but, if possible, to make it even worse, so that when we did unveil the much promised relaunch the contrast would be that much greater. I think those were the worst three weeks of his life in television.

The problem we both faced was the staff. There were some very talented young researchers and producers being led by much less talented people who were being paid far more money; but the one thing that virtually all of them shared was that they were shattered. They had joined with such high hopes: TV-am had advertised for staff with a picture of the Famous Five saying 'Join us and make history'. They had worked ridiculously hard only to find themselves and their programme publicly ridiculed. Four months into 'making history', most of them were desperate. They were trying to leave in their droves; many were very emotional. It was certainly different from LWT, which was full of smart, funny, and flamboyant people. In the end, Clive and I sat down together and worked out which members of staff we thought we could save and which were either so hopeless or so damaged by the experience of TV-am that they ought to leave. We settled on a list of sixty-odd people who had to go, and by one means or another we managed to lose all but two over the next six months.

The great thing about crisis – and TV-am was a very public crisis – is that while most people collapse, a few blossom. Lynn Faulds Wood, the consumer editor, turned up smiling in my office very proud of what she'd achieved. I agreed with her and doubled the number of slots she had in the schedule. Mark Damazer, then a young producer and now Deputy Head of News at the BBC, and Adam Boulton, now a great success at Sky News, had managed to produce some decent political coverage so I invented a morning political slot for them called 'Spotlight', edited by a talented producer called Andy Webb. I also brought in some people from outside. We desperately needed people who understood popular journalism and what the audience actually cared about, as opposed to what Peter Jay and Michael Deakin thought they ought to care about. I had known Peter McHugh since we worked together on the Newcastle *Journal* in the mid Seventies. He was, and still is, one of the best judges of a popular story I've ever met. He was working on the *Daily Mail* and hating it, so it wasn't difficult to persuade him to come. He's been a very successful

Director of Programmes at GMTV for the past decade. I also persuaded Eve Pollard – another journalist who understood the target audience – to leave her job as Assistant Editor of the *Sunday People* and join the features department at TV-am, promising her two on-screen gossip slots a week and that we'd teach her about television. She ended up as Features Editor before going back to Fleet Street, where she was editor of the *Sunday Mirror* between 1987 and 1991 and of the *Sunday Express* from 1991 to 1995.

Clive and I also put together a completely new team of on-screen presenters in a remarkably short period of time. Nick Owen had already become the male anchor, and we poached Anne Diamond from BBC's *Nationwide* to be the female lead. Clive had spotted a female weather presenter on Tyne Tees Television called Wincy Willis, so I phoned her and she joined us within a week. We brought former ITN newsreader Gordon Honeycombe out of semi-retirement to read the news and later we were joined by Lynn Faulds Wood's husband John Stapleton, who left *Newsnight* to do our serious political interviewing and a few bits beside. He's never forgiven me for asking him to read out the newspaper bingo numbers every morning.

I remember taking the new team of presenters out to lunch one day. I explained the scale of the problem we faced but how exciting it would be if we succeeded. I also warned them that if it worked they would become famous and at least one of them would become a monster. Of course it's not for me to say if that is what happened to any of them.

The relaunch went fairly well and we managed to increase our peak quarter-hour ratings in the first week from the pathetically small 0.2 (i.e. 0.2 per cent of the whole potential TV audience) to a not quite so pathetically small 0.3. We claimed a 50 per cent increase in ratings in the press and, for just about the first time, 'ailing' TV-am got some positive responses. We never mentioned that these figures were so small that, taking into account the margin for error in the research process, it was still quite possible we had no viewers at all.

It was around this time that we introduced Diana Dors and her diet on TV-am. Every Friday she would turn up and weigh in; over sixteen weeks she managed to lose 5 stone. One of my better ideas was that one Friday we should pull onto the set the amount of weight she had lost in lard. Seeing a pallet full of animal fat next to Diana had a dramatic effect.

Whether Diana actually lost all that weight I was never too sure. Clive and I always suspected she'd started her first weigh-in with a lead belt around her stomach and had then taken off one of the weights week by week. Either way, it was our most successful item and Fridays became our best day in terms of ratings, thanks to Diana.

When the diet was coming to an end Diana kept promising to tell the viewers the secret of how she had lost so much weight. We were all worried that she was intending to plug a commercial product, which would get us into real trouble with the Independent Broadcasting Authority; given that we already had enough problems with the IBA I was determined to stop her. So on the day of her final slot I told Clive that under no circumstances was she to take anything onto the set that could resemble a commercial product. Clive duly did the check, but I'm afraid Diana was far too smart for all of us.

As she sat down with John Stapleton for her usual Friday diet chat on the sofa she suddenly reached into her bra, which in Diana's case was pretty large, as her bosom had always been her trademark, and pulled out a cheap-looking calculator. She then announced that this Diana Dors Calorie Counter was the secret of her diet and that it was available for only £5.99 if people wrote directly to her at TV-am. Over the next week we received at least ten thousand letters from people wanting to buy the calculator, but I was so angry I refused to give them to Diana, arguing that they belonged to TV-am, not to her. She even took us to court to try to get them. She didn't win, she never got the letters, and the viewers didn't get their personally signed Diana Dors Calorie Counter.

Of course Diana had been a big star in the 1950s and 1960s, Britain's answer to Marilyn Monroe according to the tabloids. Although her best days were long gone she was still a massive personality and the public were still very much interested in her. I asked her agent once if she would be willing to present a show for TV-am on Sunday mornings. He came back and said that, being a Roman Catholic, her Sunday morning mass was very important to her, to which I said I assumed that meant she wouldn't do it. He replied, 'No, what it means is that it is going to cost you a lot of money.' Instead I asked David Frost to do the programme, thus bringing about the birth of *Frost on Sunday*, a programme that was still running (though on the BBC) twenty years later.

Diana died of cancer within a few months and because she was a

TV-am star we decided to do a special programme about her on the Saturday morning, the day after she had died. We invited on her friend, the singer Jess Conrad, who decided to use the opportunity to plug his latest record, and Barbara Windsor, who, like Diana, had also been a busty blonde film star. She was delightful about Diana on the set but when she came off she turned to me and said: 'You know I hated her, don't you?'

But while Diana made a difference to TV-am it was children's programming that proved to be the turning point for the station. In the June half-term week we ran half an hour of children's programming every day at 9 a.m. It was made by a very talented producer, Anne Wood, who later went on to fame and fortune by creating the Teletubbies. At this time Anne had discovered a talented puppeteer called David Claridge, who played a series of characters, the most important of whom was called Roland Rat. Little did I know then that the rat would haunt me for the next twenty years, with *The Sun* describing me as 'Roland Rat's dad' on more than one occasion. In this one half-term week our peak quarter-hour ratings increased by two points, and it happened when Roland was on. I decided there and then that our big chance for turning everything around would come in the school holidays in the summer.

It is important to understand the difference between David Claridge and Roland. David was a miserable, rather dull man who only came alive when he put his hand up this puppet's rear end. He then suddenly became clever and witty. As with so many puppeteers, I am not at all sure which was the real David, himself or the character he played. I certainly preferred the latter.

As David, he came to me one day to complain that Roland and his mate Kevin the Gerbil hadn't got an office. I looked at him as if he was mad and tried to explain that they weren't real and that, being puppets, they didn't need an office. David was having none of it: to him, they were real. In the end I relented, had the broom cupboard cleared out, and handed it over to Roland and Kevin.

On another occasion, when we were making Roland Rat in Switzerland, David fell on the ski slopes and as a result took to his hotel room. Later that day the floor manager looked in to see if he was OK only to find David, Roland, and Kevin snuggled up in bed together. David was fast asleep, with Roland on one side of him and Kevin on the other.

But the funniest experience dealing with David Claridge came after the rat had saved TV-am – an event that led to the famous joke that it was the first time a rat had saved a sinking ship. By then Roland was our biggest star, so it clearly mattered when we got a call to the press office one Friday telling us that the *Daily Star* planned to run a story on their front page the following day in which they would claim that Claridge had hosted a Soho club called 'Skin Two' for rubber and latex fetishists. Almost anywhere else I've worked this would have led to a great crisis; but TV-am was in permanent crisis, and when Tim Aitken, Clive Jones, and I met to discuss this prospective story we couldn't stop laughing. Imagine it: the saviour of the station, the man behind the most popular children's characters of the day, involved in a sexual fetishists' club.

In the end we got lucky. I was deputed to phone the programme department of the Independent Broadcasting Authority to give them the news, but it was the day their Director was leaving and everyone had been out for a rather long leaving lunch at which the alcohol had clearly flowed generously. When I got through and explained the problem all I got from the other end was someone shouting rather loudly at me saying that he wasn't bothered about that sort of thing, and then the phone went dead.

Our luck held. The *Daily Star* didn't run the story on their front page after all; it was replaced by a story about Billy Connolly's divorce instead, and Claridge, Roland, and the rubber story were relegated to page seven or nine, where they duly disappeared.

In planning the TV-am schedule for the summer of 1983 Clive Jones and I decided to send the Rat out on the road. Anne Wood bought a 1957 Ford Anglia, which we painted bright pink, and off they went to produce a half-hour show every morning for six weeks. The difficult question was what to do with the other three hours in a period notoriously short of news.

Here we had the idea of doing the programme live from the seaside beaches of Britain. In fact it was the idea of a woman called Juliet Blake, who came looking for a job. We took her idea and gave her a job as compensation. Juliet now lives in Los Angeles but is still a good friend. We were lucky that it turned out to be a scorching summer, but that also had its downside as Eggcup Towers had no air conditioning and we were all dying from the heat. The story going the rounds at TV-am that boiling summer was that the Board had had to choose between air conditioning and an executive flat when planning the building and they'd chosen the latter.

To produce *By the Seaside*, as I imaginatively called the idea, we needed an outside broadcast (OB) unit, a star, a producer, a director, and a union agreement in a matter of just a few weeks. In most organizations that would have been difficult to deliver, but at TV-am anything was always possible. In a matter of weeks we had them all.

We found an old OB unit sitting unused outside Ewart's studio complex in Wandsworth. The trouble was that Keith Ewart, who owned the studios, wanted £12,000 for it and TV-am was out of cash. I went to the finance director, who refused to sanction it; so instead I rang Tim Aitken, who was on holiday in the South of France. He was wonderfully pragmatic when I told him the finance director's view. 'Silly bastard. We're going bust anyway.' So I agreed to buy the OB unit and sent someone over to collect it. Luckily we managed to get it out of the yard, towing it because the engine didn't work, without actually handing over any cash. I think it was some years before Mr Ewart's cheque actually cleared.

Now a £12,000 OB unit isn't exactly television professionalism at its best. As John Stapleton always reminds me, it looked more like a Mr Whippy van than a traditional OB vehicle; in winter months you could only get the antenna up to broadcast the signal if you thawed it out with an electric fire first. But for *By the Seaside* it was fine.

For a presenter I turned to Chris Tarrant, whom I'd seen on *Tiswas*, the outrageous and brilliant ITV children's show, on Saturday mornings. I loved Tarrant's anarchic style. I met him and his agent Paul Vaughan one night for dinner and as I sat down at the table Chris just looked at me and said, 'Oh, so you're Mr TV fucking wonderman.' He was great to work with and became a good friend; I even appeared on his *This is Your Life*.

Chris's great advantage as a presenter is that he actually likes and admires ordinary people, the people so many television presenters dismiss. My friends John Stapleton and Lynn Faulds Wood are the same. Go on holiday with them and they never tire of signing autographs or chatting to the people who come up to them. They don't see it as a chore.

Tarrant was brilliant on *By the Seaside*, whether it was dancing with the local mayor and with someone dressed up as a gorilla on the beach at Blackpool, or jokingly throwing fish back at the audience on the beach in Great Yarmouth after they'd started throwing them at him. In Brighton a rather strange man carrying a plastic bag wandered onto the set and stayed there. We later discovered he was a patient at a local institution, but Chris treated him as just another member of the team. This sort of television seemed a long way from Peter Jay's 'mission to inform', but it was original and funny and the audiences watched in large numbers.

When *By the Seaside* was over Chris came in to Eggcup Towers one day to fill in his expenses. I saw him from my office and told him to cancel everything he'd planned for the day because we needed him for our 'Stub it out with TV-am' anti-smoking campaign. We sent him straight out round the streets of London with a pair of scissors and a bucket of water: his job was to cut people's cigarettes in half and to threaten them with the bucket of water if they resisted. Not only did he agree, he actually soaked a couple of people, which they didn't regard as at all funny.

To produce *By the Seaside* we used one of our existing producers, Sally Bruce Lockhart, combined with Juliet Blake, whose idea it had been in the first place. For a director I got an Irishman called John McColgan, who has since become one of the richest men I know after he and his girlfriend, Moya Doherty, helped to create *Riverdance*. The trouble was that because McColgan was coming straight from Ireland he didn't have the relevant union ticket, and these were the days when the trade unions controlled commercial television. They blacked him for weeks.

I was so desperate to find a director that in the end I persuaded Noel Green, a friend from LWT, to moonlight for us. For one week he did *By the Seaside* in the mornings and worked for LWT Entertainment in the afternoons and evenings. Later Bob Merrilees, another person I brought from LWT, took over.

The combination of Roland Rat and Chris Tarrant live from the seaside turned the ratings around. After about three weeks of the summer holidays I was in Florida on vacation when I got a phone call from Clive Jones. He was so excited he just shouted down the phone: 'Our ratings have passed the BBC!' In three months we'd created a new show, done something totally different for the summer, reinvigorated the staff, and now we'd sailed past the BBC. I never doubted we could do it.

So we turned the ratings round, but soon we discovered that these weren't our only problem. We were always running out of money. On at least three occasions we sent out little notes to the staff saying 'Due to computer error your salary won't be in the bank this Friday'. Everyone knew that this meant that there was another financial crisis. In fact for a long period we paid no bills at all and ended up with a pile of writs in one corner of the finance department. We didn't mind writs because we could ignore them for twenty-eight days, and at a place like TV-am twenty-eight days was a long time.

The failure to pay bills did give us some problems. Our newsagent refused to deliver papers, something of a problem for a news organization, and the taxi firm refused to deliver guests for the morning show, which made producing three and a half hours of television difficult. However, we managed to find alternative suppliers for both. Worst of all was the day the London Electricity Board turned up while we were live on air one morning and said they would cut us off if we didn't pay their bill within half an hour. Breakfast television without newspapers and guests was one thing; breakfast television without electricity was impossible. We managed to persuade them to postpone the decision for twenty-four hours and someone managed to find some cash from somewhere.

Running a television station without cash sounds funny today, but at the time it made life very difficult for everyone at TV-am. Researchers who had signed for hotel bills found bailiffs coming round to their houses to claim their possessions; regional correspondents were forced to use public phone boxes because the office phone had been cut off; and crews would turn up at hotels to find TV-am had no credit because the last bill hadn't been paid. One day John Stapleton asked Jonathan Aitken if things were getting better. He replied 'Let's face it, we're still one step ahead of the sheriff.'

For those of us who lived through those days it was ridiculous but exciting, an experience we were unlikely to have again. My favourite moment came when our advertising agency said they would stop producing our promotions unless we paid up. I pointed out to them that would mean they would be moved out of one creditors' pile and into another. They asked what I meant. I explained that while one pile might, just might, get paid there was no chance of our paying the people who had withdrawn their services. They carried on making the promotions, and in the end everyone got paid.

It was around this time that we decided to open the mysterious filing cabinet that Tim Aitken had found in his office. There were no keys so no one had bothered with it for months, but in the end curiosity got the better of us and we forced it open with a crowbar. Inside there were just bottles and bottles and bottles of pink champagne. We never found out who had bought them.

And then there were the mornings when the overnight editors used to come in to complain that Jonathan Aitken had been on the phone again in the middle of the night demanding that some unknown Arab should be interviewed on the show the following day. Once or twice they even got on. Much later we discovered why. The Arabs had put up all the money for the Aitken shares in TV-am and thus were, in effect, major shareholders, even though that was illegal at the time. Jonathan hadn't even told Timothy where the money had come from.

Summer moved into the autumn and on to the winter of 1984. The use of Roland Rat and Chris Tarrant had worked, the viewers who had found TV-am in the summer had stayed with us, and our ratings continued to rise. We consistently beat the BBC, which then did what the BBC always did. When they were winning they crowed about ratings, when they were losing they decided ratings didn't matter and we were too downmarket. It was a theme I was to come across on many occasions in my life in television.

But although the ratings were good the amount of advertising was still pitiful. I recollect that at one time we only had three regular advertisers, Ponds Cold Cream, Edam cheese, and Wall's pork sausages. In those circumstances I was concerned when Lynn Faulds Wood wanted to use her consumer slot to expose Wall's sausages for containing too much water. We both agreed that perhaps that was a story we should put into the drawer for a few months.

In early 1984 Tim Aitken asked me to become a member of the Board of TV-am Ltd. Today I would have declined and pointed out that, by my reckoning, we were close to trading insolvently. Back then I didn't know what trading insolvently meant, so I joined.

Unlike his cousin Jonathan, I grew to like and trust Tim Aitken. The grandson of Lord Beaverbrook, he was short, aggressive, and a lot of fun. He was also prepared to take risks. Anyone who knows me could see why I liked him. But there were problems – he spent most of his time at the

My mum and dad on their wedding day in 1939. They got married at their local church – St John's in Morning Lane, Hackney, which was opposite the newsagents run by my grandparents.

My mum with my two brothers (Ian and Howard) and me (bottom left) in the back garden of our house in Cerne Close, Hayes, in the summer of 1948. My parents bought the house for £650 in 1945; today it would sell for £250,000.

Aged seven, a pupil at Yeading Primary School in Hayes. Nearly fifty years later I was invited back to open the new school hall.

Top: Form 1b at Hayes Grammar School in 1958 (back row, fourth from right). I once came bottom of the whole year in the end-of-term exams.

Above: The Hayes Grammar 'upper sixth' in 1965 (sixth from right, second row from top). I left there to become a trainee manager at Marks & Spencer but was fired after three horrible months.

Left: In my last year at school.

Above: My leaving party when I left the *Hillingdon Mirror* in 1969. The paper itself was closed down in the 1970s.

Left: Outside 1, Briggs Street, York – the house I bought for £1,200 when I went to university. By then the beard and hair were getting longer.

Below: With my dog Jake on the North Yorkshire moors in 1972. By then I was a politics student at York University. In my time there I sued the local evening paper for libel.

Above: The Six O'Clock Show team at LWT in 1982: I'm standing behind Janet Street-Porter and Michael Aspel. This was my first job running my own show, and the programme was ground-breaking in many ways.

Left: The cartoon from my leaving card when I left LWT in 1983 to spend a bizarre year at TV-am. My team gave me the characteristic LWT send-off with very rude speeches.

Aitken Hume Bank, knew absolutely nothing about running a television company, and had a pathological hatred of the trade unions. He relished being known as Pol Pot, and by and large he was unpopular with the staff, although those who got to know him grew to respect his qualities as a fighter. He had been brought up in North America and, despite his background, no more liked the British Establishment than I did.

The financial crisis at TV-am came to a head early in 1984 when we went back to our shareholders, including our two big new investors, Fleet Holdings, who owned the Express Group, and the Australian broadcasting magnate Kerry Packer, to ask for more investment because we'd run out of cash again. Tim decided we needed to demonstrate to the shareholders that we were a strong management team; we could do that by changing all the staff rosters, which would both save money and show we could stand up to the unions. That way, he believed, the shareholders would back us.

Clive and I agreed with the strategy and set about trying to deliver it. We cajoled and persuaded dozens of union members that it was necessary if we were to survive. In the end it all came down to one union meeting at which most of the staff would have a vote. The proposition was simple. If they voted in favour of the changes we would get the extra money and survive; if they voted against we would go into liquidation.

Tim Aitken decided he wanted to talk to the staff to warn them of the consequences of voting against. Given that he was so disliked by the union members, Clive and I reckoned this would probably lose us the vote. So as Tim's secretary, Jane Stanton, went round putting up the notices announcing Tim's address to the staff we had people going round taking them down. In the end Tim backed down but accused Clive and me of 'hooligan management'.

On the day of the vote all the management parked their cars outside the building in case the vote went against and the company went into liquidation. At least they could get home if that happened. Tim Aitken cleared his office, packed up all his pictures, and invited the union shop steward in to see what he was doing. I worked out that TV-am still owed me about £30,000 so I looked around for something I could take and then sell to get my money if all went wrong. I reckoned the only thing the company actually owned was the barge at the back of Eggcup Towers on the Grand Union Canal, so I pinched the keys. I somehow had this mad idea that, as the company went into liquidation, I would chug away down the canal with its only saleable asset.

In the end the vote went our way and TV-am was saved yet again. This time, as it turned out, it was saved for the longer term. The shareholders put in the extra few million that was needed; I even put in the £10,000 that TV-am had finally paid me to buy out my LWT pension fund. I thought that as I'd never had that much money in my life I'd gamble it. I was the only person who had not taken part in the earlier financing exercises who was allowed to invest at this stage. Just a few years later that £10,000 was worth £360,000 when the company was floated on the stock exchange.

In early 1984, soon after the latest refinancing, Kerry Packer turned up to visit the station. Rumour had it that he was under investigation for something or other in Australia and had decided to spend some time in the UK. He brought with him the man who was his nominee on the TV-am Board, Bruce Gyngell. Packer was a legendary media figure in Australia and was known as one of the world's top gamblers. I once asked Packer why he'd invested in TV-am. He replied that for him it was just a punt and that he regularly won and lost more than the two million pounds he'd invested in TV-am at the race track or in the casino on a single day.

One day he came into my office, told me how impressed he was by what I had achieved, and asked me what was needed to really finish the job. He assured me that anything I said would be confidential; naively I believed him. I explained that, much as I liked and admired Tim, we needed a full-time Chief Executive, not one who spent half his time running a merchant bank. He thanked me and then, as I found out later, went straight in to see Tim Aitken to tell him that 'Dyke says I should sack you.' So much for a confidential conversation.

In the end it was agreed that Tim Aitken would go, but only if he was promoted to Chairman and if Bruce Gyngell stayed in the UK to run the business as Chief Executive. The trouble was that when the shareholder representatives came to carry out this plan at the board meeting no one had told the current Chairman, Dick Marsh, that he was on his way out. In a story I have heard David Frost tell on numerous occasions, the senior members of the Board whispered to each other at the meeting, asking each other very politely if they had had a word with Dick. When they discovered no one had done so, Ian Irvine of Fleet had to tell him in front of the whole Board that his services were no longer required and that Tim, who was sitting opposite him, would be taking his job. David Frost, in a way that only David could, then proposed a vote of thanks to Dick for all he'd done for TV-am. An unusual way for a company to change its chairman.

The arrival of Bruce Gyngell was the beginning of the end for me. He was a delightful man but had odd hobbies like numerology, walking on hot coals, and encouraging everyone to wear pink. Bruce, although technically a married man when he arrived in Britain, was very much into women. I remember him distinctly clapping his arm around Adrian Moore, the Director of Production, and saying that he was relying on him to tell him which of the many attractive women at TV-am were an easy lay. Not that Adrian, a happily married man who didn't play around, would have known. This same man later became very friendly with Mrs Thatcher, married Kathy Rowan, one of the producers at TV-am who had earlier been at LWT, and within five years was lecturing Britain on its public morals.

Bruce and I went out to lunch on his first day and he insisted on applying numerology to our respective birth dates. He assured me that the result confirmed that we were going to get on wonderfully well together. I was gone within a month.

We fell out when he started telling me what should go in the programme. I pointed out to him that the programme was fine and doing well; when I had agreed to join TV-am Jonathan Aitken had assured me that I would have complete control over the station's output. I also pointed out that the problems of TV-am were no longer to do with ratings but were business difficulties and that it was his job to sort them out. What I didn't know was that Bruce wasn't a particularly smart businessman. His reputation in Australia was based on the fact that he had been the first ever presenter on Australian television.

To emphasize the point that I was in charge of the programme I called a meeting of my senior team, who told Bruce the same thing. We had turned TV-am's ratings around and we weren't having this upstart Australian telling us what to do. Within a year most of the people at that meeting had gone. People like John Stapleton, Lynn Faulds Wood, Clive Jones, Peter McHugh, Andy Webb and others were all out, and over the next few years we were all systematically airbrushed out of the history of TV-am by Bruce. It was like being part of Stalin's Politburo when the political winds changed.

I left because Gyngell wanted me out and I couldn't be bothered to fight him. We'd achieved what I went to TV-am to achieve. Ratings and staff morale were unrecognizable compared with twelve months earlier, and I had been offered the role of Director of Programmes at TVS, another of the new ITV companies that had launched in 1982. Clive Jones joined me there within a couple of months as Controller of News, Current Affairs and Sport.

The twelve months I spent at TV-am were the most bizarre, the most stimulating, and the funniest of my life. I have never laughed so much. I made more good friends in that extraordinary period than at any other time. I learnt an enormous amount – not much about television but a lot about business for the first time, about leadership, and about life in a pressure cooker. I learnt that most people hated crisis but that I relished it. Most of all I learnt two things that were to influence what I did and how I did it for the next twenty years.

Firstly, I learnt that in crisis people would follow you if you led from the front and communicated openly and honestly with them. This I did instinctively, but up until TV-am I had only been able to see it work with small programme teams. Now I had tried it with a bigger organization and it had worked again.

Secondly, I learnt that if you demand, and are given, the whole train set to play with, it doesn't last for ever. In the end, someone will always want their train set back, or someone else will want to play with it.

Seven years later, in 1991, I organized the revenge of those who had turned TV-am around only to be thrown out of the company for their troubles. As Chief Executive of LWT, I put together the Sunrise consortium made up of LWT, Disney, the Guardian Group, and Scottish Television to bid for, and win, the ITV breakfast franchise for GMTV.

On 31 December 1992, TV-am closed down. Game set and match to us.

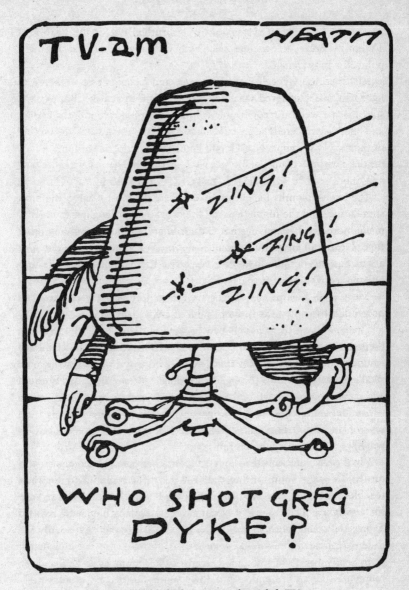

A cartoon published in 1984 after I left TV-am.
The same cartoon with the words changed could have been used
in 1994 when I left LWT and in 2004 when I left the BBC.

CHAPTER FIVE

TVS and Back to LWT

If you believed the tabloid press, TV-am was saved by a combination of Roland Rat and me, in that order, so my departure from TV-am got quite a lot of publicity, although not as much as Roland when he left a year later to join the BBC.

I was now unemployed, because my next job wasn't yet vacant. By this time Michael Grade, my old boss at LWT, had announced that he was coming back from the USA to become Controller of BBC One and he rang a few times asking me to join him to make some shows for the BBC. I had decided by then that I wanted to stay in management and didn't want to go back to being a producer. When I look back now I think that was a mistake and that I stopped producing too early in my career. Whenever I go back and get involved in a production, as I did when I presented *Have I Got News For You* three months after leaving the BBC, I realize how much I miss it.

I had been approached to join TVS, another new ITV company, this one based in the South of England. The man who had asked me to join was the Managing Director, James Gatward, who was planning to oust the incumbent Director of Programmes and replace him with me. He hadn't quite succeeded in this when he and I first met. Eventually the deed was done and my predecessor left.

In September 1984 I became Director of Programmes at TVS and the family moved out of London and down south. Sue was six months pregnant so it was not exactly an ideal moment to move, but we found a big Victorian house that we thought, with a bit of work, we could make into a home. I remember the move well because Sue booked the removal firm

92

from an advert she'd found in *Time Out*; while the removers were quite effective they were unlike any other removal people I'd met. They were true 'heads', with very long hair, and they kept adding the word 'man' to the end of every sentence. When we got to the house, in a village called Swanmore, about ten miles out of Southampton, I went off for a wander around the large garden while the removers unloaded the van. In the greenhouse I found nothing but cannabis plants, the smallest of which was about five foot tall. I went to find Sue to tell her the news. She was talking to the removal men and one of them turned to me and asked, 'Is that a problem, man?' I explained that it wasn't a career-enhancing move for the Director of Programmes of the regional ITV station to have enough cannabis in his greenhouse to get half of Southampton stoned.

'Don't worry, man, we'll take it,' replied the removal man, and they did. They cleared most of the plants out of the greenhouse, piled them in the cabin of their removal van, and drove back to London, up to their waists in cannabis plants. I've often wondered how they would have explained this if they'd been stopped by the police on the M3. The following weekend I made a bonfire of the remainder of the plants, which probably had unintended effects on the state of the elderly couple who lived next door.

My period at TVS was, by the standards of most of my time in television, fairly uneventful. In my early days there I fell out with James Gatward because I believed I had joined on the basis that my job carried a place on the Board of TVS Ltd, the holding company for TVS, and he disagreed. Eventually he gave in, but only after I had threatened to leave the company. After that, he and I got on well together. When, some years later, he was fired from the company he had founded, I sent him a big bunch of flowers with a note that said, 'Don't let the bastards get to you.' We still see each other occasionally.

The irony of the ITV system in those days was that the company with the smallest share of viewers in its region, TVS, could charge the most for its advertising. I've spent years trying to explain this to people but they don't easily understand. It's all about supply and demand.

TVS was an incredibly successful company because of the region it covered. The South of England is the richest part of Britain, outside of London, and the people who live there watch more BBC programmes and fewer ITV programmes than the country as a whole does. It is very much the BBC's heartland. This means that in the south people watch less advertiser-funded programming than in areas like Yorkshire, where ITV is very popular. But advertisers need the people in the south to see their adverts for cars or financial services because that's where the money is; this in turn means that advertisers have to buy more advertising spots in the south to have the same impact as they would in, say, Yorkshire. With the number of adverts allowed on ITV limited by the regulators, you had a classic case of demand outstripping supply, which led to higher prices. So the less successful TVS was in attracting an audience, the more money it made. It defied all normal business logic but, financially, it made TVS a very successful company.

In those days ITV was divided into two sorts of companies: the major companies, Thames, Granada, Yorkshire, Central, and LWT, that made most of the programmes for the ITV network, and the regional companies that largely made programmes for their particular areas and bought their network programming from the big five. But there was a growing problem. In terms of advertising revenue, TVS was now considerably bigger than Yorkshire and was fast catching up with both Granada and LWT. The reality was that, in terms of revenue, there was no longer a big five but a big six.

James Gatward and I decided to launch a campaign to persuade the Independent Broadcasting Authority to turn TVS into the sixth major ITV company. I wanted it because it would mean TVS making more network programming; James was in favour because he wanted TVS to be seen as a 'big' player. By nature both of us were the sort of people who hated being seen as 'junior partners'. We were supported in our campaign to change the system by Gus – now Lord – Macdonald, who was doing the same job as me at Scottish Television, and he wanted the system changed to suit his company.

The five major companies all opposed the move. They believed they should make all the programmes that mattered for ITV. But we persisted and although we didn't win the battle we did win the war. The whole system of majors and regionals was dismantled the next time the ITV franchises were advertised, in 1991, largely as a result of our campaign. Instead an ITV Network Centre was established and it commissioned all network programmes for ITV from the best ideas, wherever they came from.

There were some very good programme makers at TVS. Some were there when I joined, others we attracted to the region. My deputy was Anna Home, who was in charge of children's output and eventually became Controller of Children's Programming at the BBC. When she left I appointed Nigel Pickard to take on her children's role at TVS. Today Nigel is in charge of the whole ITV network.

My close friend from TV-am, Clive Jones, joined to run news, current affairs, and sport. Working for him in the sports department at TVS were Vic Wakeling and Mark Sharman, who later became big players in television when they ran Sky Sports. In fact Vic is still probably the most powerful man in television sport as he controls the purse strings at Sky for sports contracts. Factual programmes were run by Peter Williams, who had a real eye for popular documentaries. It was Peter and his crew who were with Robert Ballard when he first found and explored the submerged wreck of the *Titanic*.

Graham Benson joined to run drama and hit on a rich stream when he produced *The Ruth Rendell Mysteries* with George Baker as Inspector Wexford. An ex-LWT man, John Kaye Cooper, came to run entertainment for a very successful three years. In that time John and I discovered that we had both been born within a few hours of each other on the same day in 1947, so we celebrated our fortieth birthdays together. John later joined me back at LWT as Controller of Entertainment.

Although it was a new ITV company, TVS was no different from LWT in terms of the trade unions and cautious management, so we continued my policy of trying to break the rules wherever possible. At one time John and I wanted to launch a new network game show called *Catchphrase* with Roy Walker as the host. To make the pilot for the show we needed to buy some very expensive computer-generated graphics equipment, but if the show failed we would not get our money back. Someone, somewhere in facilities management refused to sanction the cost. We bought it anyway without telling them.

We bonded pretty well together as a team and most of us still meet up for dinner once a year to discuss old times. But you had to be very careful in a place like the South of England when recruiting staff. Too many people wanted to move there to live in the country and do as little real work as possible. When interviewing people I always asked if they enjoyed riding or sailing. If the answer was yes, I invariably didn't give them the job. I was determined TVS was not going to be a refuge for the semi-retired.

In my time at TVS we regularly covered opera at Glyndebourne, which was broadcast on Channel Four; so, as a company, we used Glyndebourne to entertain people we already either regarded as friends of the company or people we wanted to be our friends. The first time Sue and I went we took the Director of Television at the Independent Broadcasting Authority, David Glencross, and his wife Liz. Glyndebourne is where the South of England upper classes go to play, and some of the accents you hear as you wander around the beautiful grounds are remarkably cut-glass. In fact one right-wing merchant banker friend of mine, Anthony Fry, says Glyndebourne is the only place in Britain that could turn him into a Marxist. Not that it stops him going.

On our first visit, Sue and I had no idea what the protocol was, but our driver at the time – a wonderful man called Michael Davies, now sadly dead – showed us what we had to do. I was dressed up in a dinner suit, we took the champagne and the picnic, and we had a wonderful evening, although I've no idea what opera we actually saw. As we were being driven home, sitting in the back of the car finishing off the champagne, Sue turned to me and said, 'You do know we've become the sort of people we wanted to blow up twenty years ago.'

For me it was during the years spent at TVS that I first learnt about being a family man. Sue and I had no sooner got together in Barnes than I was off to TV-am, and was hardly seen for a year. It was only in Hampshire that we became a proper family, helped by the fact that three months after we moved Alice was born on 28 November 1984. Sue had had her two other children in hospital and had hated the experience. This time she was determined that her baby would be born at home. I was terrified; what happened if anything went wrong? But Sue was adamant, and my views were irrelevant. After all, I was only the father. So Alice was born in our bedroom in the house in Swanmore.

Sue was right, of course, and Alice's being born at home was a magical experience. Within an hour of the birth we were all sitting on the bed very excited, Sue, me, Matthew, Christine, the dog, and of course the new baby. One of the lasting memories of my life is sitting on the rocking chair in the bedroom that night, when everyone else had gone to sleep, holding my first-born and singing 'Summertime' to her. As I am completely tone deaf, I don't suppose it helped her much. It's probably the reason she cried non-stop for the next three months.

Two and a half years later Joe, too, was born in that same room, much to the annoyance of his older sister, who kept asking questions like 'When is that baby going home?' and 'Where have its parents gone?' – referring to the midwife and the doctor. As one who comes from a family of three sons, who in their fifties still raced each other on the beach to see who was the fastest, and even today still kick hell out of each other in our annual family football match, I understand all about sibling rivalry.

One morning while I was still in bed, about three years after I had joined TVS, I got a call from Brian Tesler, the Managing Director of LWT. He wanted to know if I could go up to London that afternoon to meet him and LWT's Chairman, Christopher Bland. I didn't ask what it was about, I just said yes, which I later discovered had puzzled Brian. He wanted to know why I hadn't asked him about the purpose of the meeting. I explained that if the Managing Director of LWT rings you at 7.30 a.m. and asks you to meet him, it's got to be worth saying yes.

Brian had been running LWT for thirteen years. He was not a great businessman, and would never have claimed to be; but he was as good a judge of programmes as I've ever met. His analysis of what was right and what was wrong about a programme was brilliant. He was also a pretty good judge of people: in his time as MD he appointed to the role of Director of Programmes at LWT three of the people who were to dominate British television management for the next twenty years, Michael Grade, John Birt, and then me.

When I got to the LWT offices on the South Bank I was shown into Brian's room, where Brian and Christopher were waiting. John Birt was with them. Of course I knew John well, and I knew Brian Tesler a bit at that time, but I had only met Christopher on a couple of occasions. They explained that Birt, who had been lined up to replace Brian Tesler as MD, was instead leaving to become Deputy Director-General of the BBC in charge of all news and current affairs programming. John looked a bit awkward and obviously wanted to know what I thought. I remember congratulating him but I was puzzled as to why he wanted to do the job. I thought he would have a lot more fun running LWT, and would certainly make more money.

John had been asked to look after the BBC's journalism by Michael

Checkland, an accountant who was formerly in charge of finance at BBC Television and who had recently been made Director-General. Checkland was the compromise candidate chosen by the BBC's Board of Governors after his predecessor, Alasdair Milne, had been fired by the BBC's new chairman, Duke Hussey. Hussey went on to fire Checkland six years later, replacing him with John Birt. When his autobiography was published, Hussey said he regretted not firing Birt as well. I often wondered whether Hussey ever thought that he himself might be the problem.

Brian Tesler and Christopher Bland told me that they wanted me to replace John as Director of Programmes. I had recently made the short list for the same job at Thames Television, which went to David Elstein instead, and John Birt had already hinted to me that when he became Managing Director of LWT he wanted me to be his Director of Programmes; so the offer wasn't completely out of the blue, although the timing was sooner than I had expected.

I knew immediately that I would take the job, but said I had to go back and discuss it with Sue. I realized it would mean dragging the whole family back up to London and I knew that wouldn't be popular, for by this time Sue had started lecturing in sociology at the local college and the older kids were settled in school. When we discussed it Sue agreed to the move, but with conditions. The first was that wherever we moved next we had to stay for at least ten years: she made the point that Matthew was only nine but had already been to three different schools. Now I'd be moving him to a fourth. I agreed.

The second condition was harder to deliver. She said she'd only move back to London if we could buy one of just six houses in a particular road in Barnes. Given that all six were occupied I wasn't sure I could meet this demand, but disingenuously I assured her I'd do my best. Amazingly, I discovered one of the six was for sale and we went to see it, taking our architect Chris Henderson, who is today also my horse-riding partner. It was the perfect house, but there were two problems. First, we'd have to spend another year with builders, having only just got rid of them from our existing house; second, Chris reckoned the whole back wall was about to fall off.

In the end, Sue relented and I was allowed to look further afield. We eventually found our present house, between Richmond and Twickenham, which had the great advantage of being in wonderful condition – not that it stopped us knocking a few walls down here and there. I always remember the builder whom we'd asked to demolish a wall in the kitchen saying to me, 'Funny old world, isn't it, mate? I only built this wall last year.' I thought then that it was an unknowingly profound statement that could have been applied to the whole process of Western capitalism.

My appointment at LWT took some time to finalize as Brian and Christopher felt obliged to interview some internal candidates who also wanted the job. The internal runners were the Head of Entertainment, Alan Boyd, who went on to replace me at TVS, the Head of Drama and Arts, Nick Elliot, and my former boss at LWT, Barry Cox, who was Head of Current Affairs and Features. In the end, Brian and Christopher stuck with their original choice and gave the job to me. To take it I gave up some quite valuable stock options at TVS, which in the end didn't matter because their value evaporated a year or two later when TVS decided to expand in America and buy a large US production company called MTM, named after its founder, the actress Mary Tyler Moore. It was a disastrous buy and virtually bankrupted the company.

Instead I was awarded stock options in LWT and the traditional Dyke luck came into play yet again. The price of the options was to be based on the average price of the shares over a short period of time in October 1987. The lower the price the better it was for me, so I was one of the few big gainers on Black Monday, 19 October 1987, when the world's stock exchanges crashed. LWT's share price fell by a third in a week and my options were set at the new, lower price. As the share price recovered over the next year the value of my options went up with it.

In May 1987, soon after I had agreed to return to LWT, I took a call from David Frost, who offered me the most frightening experience of my life. Would I play in his football team against Jimmy Tarbuck's XI in a charity match? No problem with that. The scary bit was that the match was to be played at Wembley, in front of 80,000 people, just before the 1987 FA Cup Final between Coventry and Tottenham. I was to be in a Tottenham shirt and John Birt, who was also playing, would be in Coventry colours.

The rest of the teams were genuine celebrities, with people like Daley Thompson, Dennis Waterman, Steve Cram, Nick Berry, and Steve Davis all playing. I don't think the football fans in the stadium had any idea who John and I were when we ran out onto the pitch. I always reckoned that David had invited us so he could maintain a good relationship with both ITV and the BBC, and make sure he had plenty of work over the next decade. Either way, I was scared to death. I was a park footballer, terrified of making a complete fool of myself in front of all these people. Late in the game I did one good sliding tackle and 40,000 Spurs fans cheered. At that moment I knew what it was like to be David Beckham.

The match was televised live on ITV and Jimmy Greaves, the former Tottenham and England forward, picked me out as the man of the match, which was flattering until he admitted he had done so because I was his new boss at LWT: it had nothing to do with my footballing abilities. I have always kept a picture of me being tackled by the World Championship winning runner Steve Cram on the wall in my study, and when he was little my son Joe always referred to it as 'when you were a footballer, Dad'. If only. Every couple of years I watch the video of the match to remind me of what might have been.

Returning to LWT was like going back to my spiritual home. I probably spent the happiest days of my working life there and made many good friends. To this day I still love that area along the South Bank of the Thames where the LWT building is based. I had left as a programme editor being told by my boss that if I went I would never be allowed back. Four years later I was back in the elevated position of Director of Programmes, a job that had two distinct roles at LWT. Firstly, I decided which programmes LWT made, both for the network and for the London region; secondly, I was responsible for scheduling the weekend for the whole of the ITV network, which meant deciding which network programmes went where.

I inherited a good team, the most important of whom was Nick Elliot, LWT's Head of Drama, a truly wonderful man who tended even then towards the eccentric. Every so often Nick would get so annoyed that a 'Nick Elliot memo' would turn up on my desk attacking everyone and everything. The trick with Nick was to wait forty-eight hours and then ask him to come up. By then he was usually deeply ashamed of the memo he'd sent and would crawl into the office like Uriah Heep. The letter Nick sent me when I left the BBC sums up his writing style:

I just wanted to say how sad and angry I am about what has happened – an appalling combination of all the people I hate in life – politicians, regulators, journalists, wankers. Our TV world is united behind you. Whenever you want me to join in a revenge attack just say.

As a head of drama Nick was, and still is, second to none in Britain. This really mattered because when I got to LWT I decided that we had to take the weekend schedule upmarket, particularly on Sunday nights, and the way to do that was to play more drama.

In those days, deciding to take ITV upmarket was a pretty radical decision. It meant getting rid of a lot of the cheap game shows that were in the schedule and using the money elsewhere. We did it because it was clear that the very nature of advertising was changing. The big growth area of the decade was financial services advertising – banks, building societies, and the like – aimed at more affluent and aspirational viewers.

An hour of drama is probably the most expensive hour you get on television, so if we were to run more drama I had to save money elsewhere. I scrapped *Weekend World* and replaced it with *Walden*, a show in which the former Labour MP interviewed major politicians of the day, as it seemed to me that the Brian Walden interview had become the most important part of the programme and the new format was significantly cheaper. I also scrapped the big Sunday night variety show *Live from the Palladium* starring Jimmy Tarbuck. I even scrapped my beloved *Six O'Clock Show*, which I thought looked tired and was too expensive. I used all the money I saved from such cuts to introduce double drama on a Sunday night, with an hour of family drama at eight and an hour of more adult drama at nine. It's a pattern that ITV still follows to this day and, more than fifteen years later, it continues to win Sunday nights for ITV.

We produced some of this drama ourselves at LWT – shows like *Poirot* and *London's Burning* – but were helped enormously by Yorkshire Television and their Director of Programmes, John Fairley. John is one of the most talented people I've met in the television business, but he's never been keen to work a full week. At Yorkshire he was known as 'rarely, therely, Fairley'. A few years later, when I was Chairman of ITV, I offered him the job of running the whole ITV network. He told me he would take it if I could make it a Tuesdays-, Wednesdays- and Thursdays-only job. I didn't have the nerve to do that, but John could probably have managed it in just three days of the week. He was a brilliant creative executive.

I was once invited by the Royal Television Society to make a speech to their branch in Leeds and I decided to use it to pay tribute to what John had achieved. I praised the programme making department John had built and ended by saying, 'For John to have done all this is a great achievement in any circumstances, but to have done it all from a box at York races is quite remarkable.' John has now got his ideal job, running all the racing coverage for Channel Four as an independent producer.

John and Yorkshire Television decided to support my vision for a more upmarket Sunday night and they delivered all the David Jason programmes for Sundays, including *Frost*, plus a remarkable success story called *Heartbeat*. Initially we played *Heartbeat* on Fridays in the summer because we had been told by Yorkshire that they thought it was a 'dog' and they asked us to bury it somewhere. The ratings were low, but they grew over the series and, more importantly, the appreciation figures were enormous.

My Head of Planning, Warren Breach, and I realized that *Heartbeat* had real potential, so we moved it to Sunday nights; the rest is television history. Within a year it was pulling in over seventeen million viewers every week. *Heartbeat* was a classic example of what any commissioner or scheduler knows: that on many crucial calls you don't know anything. You can think something is going to be a big hit and then be proved spectacularly wrong. And exactly the same can happen the other way, as it did with *Heartbeat*.

My upmarket Sunday night was a big success with the sales team. The Director of Sales at LWT was one of the great figures of the whole industry, Ron Miller. An East End boy, Ron was a genius as a sales-man. He understood that selling was about relationships, and Ron knew everyone and everyone knew Ron. He somehow managed to persuade the advertisers that an AB male watching television on a Sunday night was much more valuable than the same AB male watching television on a Monday night, when it just happened that Thames, and not LWT, were selling the advertising in London. It was complete bullshit, but all the buyers went along with it because they liked Ron and they didn't much like his opposite number at Thames Television, a man called Jonathan Shier. He later went on to run, and create chaos at, ABC in Australia. Ron Miller believes to this day that ITV never had a better or classier Sunday night than my upmarket Sunday, with a line-up of *Heartbeat*, *Poirot*, *Hale and Pace*, the News, and the *South Bank Show*.

The combination of the new drama programming, our scheduling, and Ron's selling gave LWT a few really profitable years. We competed with our big rival, Thames Television, quite aggressively and we markedly increased our share of the London market in both ratings and advertising revenue.

In the area of entertainment – LWT had traditionally been an entertainment company – I was lucky; I had inherited *Blind Date*, which had been running for a couple of seasons when I became Director of Programmes. *Blind Date* was a clever format but it was made into a great show by Cilla Black – a considerable star whom I predict will return to her former glory. When I arrived back at LWT the actual dates, when the couple went out together, were covered by stills photographers but I soon decided to spend more money on the show and we sent a video crew on every date – a definite improvement.

The hardest thing for LWT to control was the after-show *Blind Date* party, where all the contestants met together and all sorts of people got off with each other. Quite often a contestant would decide that he or she had picked the wrong person and would make a play for one of the others. In the end, the producers used separate hotels for the boys and girls in a bid to keep them apart, largely to no avail.

Marcus Plantin was Head of Entertainment, a strange person to be in that role. While he picked good shows and was a very good producer, he didn't have much of a sense of humour. It was Marcus who spotted *Gladiators* on American television and introduced it into the UK, where it was a much bigger hit than it had been in the USA.

In those days Michael Barrymore was an exclusive artist at LWT. I'll always remember meeting Michael when Sue and I went to see Billy Connolly's one-man show. We chatted for a while and then Sue turned to him and asked him what he did. I didn't know whether to laugh or look embarrassed. Sue didn't bat an eyelid when I explained he was one of Britain's top comedians.

Michael was brilliant, but like a number of great comedians he was incredibly difficult to manage, and he surrounded himself with people who constantly pandered to him. These were the days when he was still married to Cheryl, although we all knew he was gay. There were times when he disappeared for days on end when he should have been making a show. His behaviour drove John K. Cooper, Marcus Plantin's successor as Head of Entertainment at LWT, completely mad. And yet he was the best popular comedian of his generation by a long way. Though he has recently been through some difficult times I hope he recovers because anyone with his talent should be working on British television.

Not everything I did as Director of Programmes at LWT was successful. One area where Marcus and I failed was situation comedy. We scrapped one comedy, called *Me and My Girl*, that was getting good ratings on a Friday night because neither of us liked the show and found the production company difficult. It was run by a man we used to call 'fucking Al Mitchell', whom I had never met. The following year I went over to introduce myself to a new neighbour in Twickenham and the man explained he too was in the television business and that his name was Al Mitchell. I looked at him and said, 'You're not "fucking Al Mitchell", are you?' It was the very same. We ended up good friends and he still sends me e-mails signed 'fucking Al Mitchell'.

We cancelled *Me and My Girl* because, despite its popularity with viewers, we were sure we could do better. But over the next seven years we didn't produce one new comedy that got the sort of ratings it used to attract.

Situation comedy is an incredibly valuable genre if you can get it right. It's cheaper than most drama to produce and it repeats well. Look how often *Dad's Army*, *Only Fools and Horses*, and *Fawlty Towers*, to name but three, have been successfully repeated. But situation comedy is probably the hardest thing to produce on television. Everyone struggles with it, but over the years the BBC has been the master and ITV an also-ran. That is still the case.

Another area where I tried to make changes and failed was religion. These were the days when ITV and BBC One were required to play religious programming at the same time on a Sunday evening. The God slot ran for thirty-five minutes between six and seven every Sunday evening. I regarded this requirement as deeply illiberal as it effectively forced viewers to watch religious programmes regardless of whether they were believers or not. I proposed that the God slot should be scrapped, but naturally the idea did not go down well in religious circles. I even spoke at a religious conference at which I was heckled by members of the clergy. In the end a body called CRAC, the Central Religious Advisory Council, which was chaired by a bishop, not surprisingly voted against the proposal and the Independent Broadcasting Authority, as well as the BBC Governors, supported them.

This was less than twenty years ago but it demonstrates how much the world has changed since then. The idea of an enforced God slot on ITV and BBC One at the same time would now be seen as ridiculous. As it turned out, I was only slightly ahead of my time: the 1990 Broadcast Act effectively ended the enforced God slot. By the time the Act came into force in 1992 I was Chief Executive of LWT and scrapped the God slot on the first day it was legally possible to do so.

I've no doubt the religious lobby would describe it as dumbing down. I disagree. Religious programming is still there for those who want it, but is not being forced on those who don't. The recent Ofcom report, which asked people what sort of public service programming they valued most, had religious programming very near the bottom of the list.

As Director of Programmes at LWT I had a good team. My business manager was Sydney Perry, whom I inherited from John Birt, who, in turn, had inherited him from Michael Grade. Sydney was quite a lot older than the rest of us and over the years we changed his name from Sydney, to Syd, to old Syd, and finally to poor old Syd. Luckily he had a good sense of humour and gave us as good as he got. We eventually promoted him to run LWT International, which he did very successfully.

I replaced him with Mike Southgate, who had worked with me in several different organizations. Then there was Tony Cohen, who, since first working for me as a researcher on *The Six O'Clock Show*, had spent a year at the London Business School. He became my strategist. A few years later, when I joined Pearson Television, I explained that I didn't come alone: Tony Cohen came with me. I remember Frank Barlow, Managing Director of Pearson, asking what Tony did that I didn't do. I explained that Tony was the brains and that I did the PR. 'So why don't we just employ Tony?' he asked. 'Brains don't work without the PR,' I replied.

In 1989 Brian Tesler decided he would relinquish the role of Managing Director of LWT. Head hunters were brought in and eventually recommended that a man who sold bikes in the Midlands should get the job. Brian was unhappy, as he wanted the job to go to me, but Christopher Bland took some convincing: he didn't believe I had enough business experience. But in the end they offered me the job. So thirteen years after I had first joined LWT as a reporter I was to be its Managing Director.

To satisfy Christopher's concerns about my business skills we agreed that I would spend the autumn of 1989 on the Advanced Management Programme at the Harvard Business School and would take over as Managing Director of LWT early the following year. I was probably the first leader of an ITV company to go to business school. Many people in British television ridiculed me for it, but it was the first sign that British television was turning into a real business run by people who took business seriously. I later sent the top echelon of LWT to business school and introduced serious management training for many in senior and middle management.

Those twelve weeks I spent at Harvard were as exciting a period as I've spent anywhere. Sue advised me not to go. Knowing that I'm not a natural academic she said that I was an instinctive leader and that if I tried to intellectualize the process I could well screw it up. With that ringing endorsement in my ears I went anyway.

I was very nervous. I knew that I was a jumped-up television producer who worked in a monopoly industry. What the hell did I know about real business? There were 160 of us on the course, including half a dozen from Britain. Unlike the rest of the students we were required to wear business attire as we were on the most senior programme there. On occasions I insisted on wearing a white suit just to show that I wasn't from a 'normal' business. One day I remember a bunch of us walking along in our suits when we passed a group of MBA students coming the other way. They were half our age and as we walked by I heard one turn to another and say 'Jesus, is that what we're aspiring to be?'

Half way through the course, when all the natural competitiveness had died away and we had become mates, I discovered that I wasn't the only one who had been anxious about the programme. One of the great advantages age and experience give you is a better understanding of the human psyche. When I was first in the television business I used to respect those in high places in television because I thought 'they must know'. Having now done those jobs myself I realize my confidence in them was misplaced. No one knows: you just pretend to know. The great myth of management is that somehow you know more than those you are leading, whereas the only real advantage you've got is the position and the power.

What that period at Harvard gave me was an intellectual rationale for running businesses and organizations the way I ran them instinctively. I came across a brilliant American professor called John Kotter, who was the first person I'd met who talked about the difference between being a manager and being a leader. This was 1989, the height of Thatcherism, when everyone in Britain still believed that successful management was all about being tough with your staff, the unions, your competitors, and virtually everyone else. I had never believed that, and Kotter reinforced my view of the world. When I turned up at the BBC a decade later I was amazed to find that the old view of management still persisted.

The biggest revelation through being at Harvard and listening to John Kotter was, for me, the discovery that the most successful organizations in the world were those that treated their staff properly. I believed in that concept but was surprised to discover it also led to competitive advantage and business success. The days when capital treated labour as if it was a commodity to be bought and sold increasingly didn't work. If you wanted a successful company you had to treat your people well.

When I came back from Harvard I rang up Peter Mandelson, whom I knew from when he was a producer at LWT and who was at that time in charge of communications for the Labour Party, to ask him to lunch. I explained that my experience at Harvard had given me a new vision for the Labour Party. The most successful companies in the world were treating their staff in the way that we, on the Left, had always argued people should be treated. The mistake we'd made was believing that state-owned organizations would be better at doing that than the private sector. Modern capitalism required an enthusiastic and fulfilled workforce if a company was to be successful; we could thus achieve what we had always aimed for within a mixed economy. Peter listened, and I think he took it in.

As a result of going to Harvard I decided to rejoin the Labour Party, which I don't think was the intention of Christopher Bland when he laid out $30,000 for me to go there. Christopher was a Tory and had been chairman of the liberal Tory pressure group, the Bow Group. I became an early supporter of what New Labour was to stand for.

Later, in 1994, when Gail Rebuck, the head of the publishers Random House in the UK, asked me to write a book on management and leadership I told her that I didn't know enough to fill a pamphlet, let alone a book. I didn't feel I could do it, but I knew what the title should be: *Management Without Fear.*

I ended my time at Harvard by taking part in the sketch show that is put on at the end of every course. This was entertainment so I knew more about it than the bankers and industrial managers who made up most of the people on the course. I had great fun playing a thick, uneducated Texan who mocked the whole Harvard Business School experience by saying that it was impossible to fail so long as you had paid your $30,000 fee: after all, even he'd got a certificate saying he'd passed.

I came back to Britain with the task of running LWT and trying to put some of these ideas into practice.

CHAPTER SIX

Running and Losing LWT

On my first day in charge at LWT I put up an enormous picture of me in reception at our building on the South Bank with a notice saying that I was taking over the organization that day, that I would be spending the day wandering around trying to meet as many people as possible, and that everyone was invited to have a drink on me in the LWT bar at lunchtime. My aim was obvious: as a Managing Director I wanted to be seen as accessible, open, and friendly.

In that first year, 1990, I introduced a couple of policies that I hoped would demonstrate we were a 'caring' management. I started sending a bunch of flowers from the company to everyone who had a new baby. I had learnt from my own recent experience how important a day this was in your life and wanted people on the staff to know we recognized that. And at Christmas each year I put on an enormous party for the children and grandchildren of the people who worked for LWT. People in television worked very long hours, and this was a small way of thanking their families. That first year I played Father Christmas and gave out the presents to all the children, including my own. The cost of doing all this was pathetically small compared with the goodwill it fostered.

I discovered that it didn't take more than a small gesture to get people on-side. When we completely redesigned the monthly presentation of the accounts, which took an enormous effort from the finance department, I turned up with a few bottles of champagne to thank the people who had done the work. They never forgot it.

I also started a weekly breakfast meeting for the top forty people in the company at which, as well as discussing what was happening inside

LWT and in the industry generally, we'd have a lot of laughs. The meetings were key to the management spirit I was trying to engender. With humour, wit, speed, confidence, and fun we tried to give the place a sense of purpose.

Within days of my taking over at LWT my father died. He had had an operation for cancer of the colon three years earlier but the disease had reappeared in his lungs and we'd watched him getting worse month by month for the past year. I had been with him when he was told by the specialist, a wonderful man at Hammersmith Hospital called Karol Sikora, that he had a maximum of two years to live. My dad was not one who showed emotion, but that week he was devastated.

His own father had died when he was young. He had no role model as a father; yet to my brothers and me he was very special. Both he and my mother were always supportive of us, no matter what we did. When I was seventeen I bought a bubble car against his wishes. In fact I didn't tell him and he thought the car parked outside our house had been dumped there until my mother told him it was mine. It turned out to be a disastrous buy and was a hopeless vehicle, but he never said 'I told you so'. He just helped me try to make it work. He was a very conservative man who did a job he hated in the insurance industry, but he had a serene quality about him. He hated pompous people and was the only person I knew who would regularly stop and talk to the road sweeper, to make him feel like a real human being rather than someone doing a lowly job in society. That was my dad, and that was the way he brought us up.

My mother was wonderful looking after him in those last months but eventually we decided it would be best if he went into the local hospice. I remember that last weekend as if it was yesterday. It was 1990 and Manchester United were playing Crystal Palace in the FA Cup Final. I had tickets to take my son Matthew but in the end I decided to stay with my dad, who by then was no longer conscious. My brothers and I watched the match in the hospice.

On the Monday morning he was still alive and I made one of those inexplicable decisions that you have to live with for the rest of your life. I had my first big network meeting as Managing Director of LWT on that Monday and instead of staying with my dad I went to the meeting, promising to come back that afternoon. He died around midday and I wasn't there. Even as I write this now there are tears streaming down my cheeks. Why did I go? It was only a bloody meeting. I'll never be able to justify that decision to myself and I shall always feel I let him down at the end.

In some ways it was a relief when he died: he had been so ill and the withered old man in that hospice bed bore no relation to the man who had brought us up and been such a great father. It was some months before it really hit me that he had gone, that he wouldn't see my kids growing up, that he wouldn't be there with that quiet word of support. Now, fourteen years later, not a week goes by when I don't think about him or tell my kids stories about him. My brothers and I were so lucky to have had the parents we did.

The problem I faced taking over LWT in 1990 was that its future was far from certain. The Thatcher Government had decided that ITV needed to be reformed. It was partly the fault of LWT. When Brian Walden had gone along to interview Mrs Thatcher several years earlier we had sent some forty-odd people to do a two-camera interview. Someone in Downing Street had counted them all in and counted them all out and had decided, quite rightly, that this was a ridiculous number of people to do just one interview. In those days the unions still effectively ran the ITV companies and Mrs Thatcher hated the unions, so it followed she hated ITV.

In 1985 she had set up a committee to look into the funding of television chaired by Professor Alan Peacock, an economist who had been teaching at York University when I was there. In fact the students had occupied his department for a while demanding that he should teach Marxist as well as market economics. In 1985 he was the Director of Edinburgh's David Hume Institute and had been asked by Mrs Thatcher to look into the whole question of putting advertisements on the BBC. To Mrs Thatcher's disappointment his report came out against the idea: there simply wasn't enough advertising revenue around to finance the BBC as well as ITV. As an afterthought he suggested that next time the ITV franchises were to be awarded they should be auctioned to the highest bidder. Everyone laughed at the suggestion, with the exception of Mrs Thatcher, who decided to implement it. So my job in 1990 was to prepare LWT for the auction of the ITV franchises that was to take place in 1991, with the new franchises due to begin in January 1993.

What I knew was that LWT had no chance of winning a franchise in its current state. We had to reduce the size of the company and get rid of the excesses that we all knew were deeply embedded in the organization. This was a company where, like the rest of the ITV companies, the unions had been allowed to run riot for at least three decades. This had happened partly because over many years there had been a special tax on the profits of the commercial television companies – at one time they were paying something in excess of 90 per cent tax on any profits they made. As a result, no one in management worried too much about how much was spent as the taxpayer picked up the tab for almost all of it so long as the ITV companies stayed profitable. There was no incentive to be efficient, which was why the trade unions effectively ran ITV, and it was never financially worthwhile for the managements of the ITV companies to take them on.

On a couple of occasions Christopher Bland had prevented the management from taking on a small group of workers who could then have shut down the whole of LWT, leaving the company to continue paying the wages of the vast majority of the workforce with no advertising income coming in. Christopher's view was that if we were to take on the unions we had to take everyone on at the same time. If there was to be a bust-up, it had to be a big one. He was quite right.

The threat of an auction and the likelihood of your franchise going to the highest bidder changed the world. It meant that you had to become efficient as a company and fast. We were all helped in achieving this by what had happened at TV-am in 1987 when Bruce Gyngell sacked all his technicians after their union had called them out on strike. Initially the management had taken over all their jobs, but in the end Bruce employed non-union labour. The strikers never returned to TV-am.

I knew for the first time that change was possible at LWT when I went to a meeting with the unions while I was Director of Programmes. For years they had threatened to go on strike if management didn't give in to their demands. This time they were the exact opposite and accused us of trying to create a situation in which, as at TV-am, they would be locked out. I knew then that their many years of power were coming to an end. We got rid of scams like paying ridiculous multiples for overtime, paying enormous expenses, and employing technicians who often didn't turn up but still got paid, and we did it without a single day being lost through strike action.

The threat of a franchise auction coincided with the coming of independent producers, another of Mrs Thatcher's changes, which meant that ITV and the BBC would have to give 25 per cent of their commissions each year to the independent sector. As far as negotiating with the unions was concerned, this strengthened our hand enormously.

In fact when I first returned to LWT I had had a major confrontation with the unions over a drama production called *Betty* that was to star Twiggy. The set had been built at Shepperton Studios and shooting was about to get under way when the unions demanded that, even though it was an independent production, it should be made under ITV union agreements. For us this would have been a disaster as our union agreements were terrible and far too expensive. I decided to take a stand, cancelled the whole production, wrote off more than a million pounds, and publicly announced that I wouldn't be blackmailed by the trade unions.

This had three consequences. Firstly, the unions got the blame for the cancellation of *Betty*, which was never made, much to Twiggy's annoyance. As a result, all future independent productions for ITV were made under a different agreement. Secondly, at LWT we used this opportunity to tell our own people that if we didn't change our agreements all our drama in the future would be made by independent producers. They changed. Thirdly, my stand was obviously noticed in Downing Street. That was the only year I received a Christmas card from Margaret and Denis Thatcher.

If your political sympathies were on the Left, it was always difficult to explain why it was necessary to take on the trade unions in the television industry. My view was that most of the leaders of these unions, just like Fleet Street, were not the slightest bit interested in anything that resembled socialism. They didn't want a more egalitarian society in which opportunities were open to all, and they certainly didn't believe in efficiency. Worst of all I never saw any sign in those days that they were interested in making the best possible programmes for the audiences. They were only interested in their own power and in enriching themselves and their members. To round it off many of the union leaders at LWT at the time were hardline Thatcherites.

All this happened before I became Managing Director, but when I took over I decided I had to explain to the staff why we needed more change. In those days we employed about fifteen hundred people; by the time I left that had been nearly halved to some eight hundred. I decided to talk to everyone in the company in groups of about twenty to explain what we were trying to achieve, and why we had to make more cuts to the organization to survive.

At that time we had a senior non-executive director on the Board of LWT called Roger Harrison, who was Deputy Chairman of Capital Radio but had formerly been Managing Director of *The Observer*. He was a very wise old bird and I always listened carefully to his advice. He told me that what he had discovered from the restructuring of Fleet Street was that you could afford to be very generous to the people you were making redundant as the savings were potentially massive. I followed his advice and did everything I could to help people to leave the organization feeling they had been well treated.

One day I went to the leaving party of some videotape engineers who had earned fortunes in their time at LWT but who didn't want to stay on in the new world when their wages, and in particular their overtime, would be cut dramatically. They had decided to take redundancy instead. One of them summed up the past when he said quite openly to me, 'You can't blame us, Governor. If the management were fools enough to give it, we were going to take it.' Who can disagree?

We decided to convert our resources division into a proper profit-and-loss company and put Mike Southgate in charge of it. We called the new company the London Studios and it proved to be a great and continuing success. I was back at the London Studios, on the South Bank, only months after I left the BBC when I was the guest presenter on *Have I Got News for You*, which, although a BBC show, has been made at the London Studios for many years for the independent producer Hat Trick.

Turning an old facilities business into a profit-and-loss operation meant that – for the first time – LWT programme makers had to negotiate prices for the studios and crews they used. In doing so we discovered the London Studios was losing £16 million a year. Mike's task was to make it a break-even business by the time the new franchises started in 1993, which he pretty much achieved by a combination of bringing in outside clients, a lot of restructuring, and a great many redundancies.

While I was trying to get the operating business right Christopher Bland, as the Chairman of LWT, began to think about the financing of the organization. Christopher's view was that, as a television company, we should 'stick to our knitting': he therefore sold the company's two subsidiary businesses, the travel company Page & Moy and the publishers Hutchinson. He got good prices for both, which meant that LWT was sitting on a pile of cash. Then one morning in early 1989 he suggested to Brian Tesler and me that we undertake a management buyout. By using the cash we had in the business, plus borrowing, he reckoned the management could buy the whole of LWT.

In the end we didn't go for the total buyout, but a variation of it. We gave all the shareholders back a good deal of money, much of which we had borrowed, reduced the market capitalization of the business, and gave massive incentives to the management. Christopher's view was that by doing this we improved our chances in the franchise auction. We would have tied in a talented management who might otherwise have been attracted to rival bids; we would all be massively incentivized to make the company as efficient as possible; and we would have replaced much of the equity base of the company with cheaper debt, which meant we could bid more in the franchise round.

I was given the job of deciding who should qualify to be in the management scheme and I was determined we would include a wide range of people. In the end we had forty-four people who stood to make real money if we could increase the share price significantly over the coming years. As management we all put in our own money. Some had to mortgage their houses; others, like me, had enough valuable existing share options or shares in LWT that they didn't need to find any more cash. But we all took a risk, so it wasn't like a normal share option scheme. The idea was that if the share price rose from 83p to 240p over the next three years the number of shares we owned in the company would quadruple and the forty-four of us would end up owning 15 per cent of LWT. The details of the scheme were drawn up by Neil Canetty-Clarke, a young merchant banker who happened to be on a placement with LWT. He later became Finance Director.

There was some opposition to the scheme in the City, particularly from the Pearl, Eagle Star, and Scottish Amicable, but we got the 75 per cent of the shareholders we needed to vote in favour. When we launched the scheme the share price actually went down. We had paid 83p a share and now they were trading at 76p. Later, when people criticized the scheme for being too generous to the management, I regularly asked them why,

*Christopher Bland dreamt up a scheme whereby the LWT
management ended up owning 15 per cent of the company.
Becoming rich didn't make us universally popular in ITV.*

if it was that easy to predict how successful we would be, they hadn't invested when the shares were at 76p. That normally shut them up.

For the management there was no doubt it was a massive success. Having invested at 83p a share in 1990 we got back the equivalent of £30 a share just four years later. I ended up making £7 million, as did Brian Tesler and Ron Miller. Christopher, I think, made more, but then it was his idea in the first place. I had ensured that the scheme went down quite a long way in the management so people who had never imagined making a lot of money became comparatively rich. For instance, Peter Coppock, who ran the press office, made £1 million, which really upset the Fleet Street journalists. Not that the ordinary shareholders had anything to complain about: if they had invested in 1990 at 76p, or even 83p, they would have been able to sell out at £7.50p four years later.

When we finally cashed out I decided we should all share some of our gains with the staff at LWT who had worked for the company since the scheme was set up in 1990. I suggested to the forty-four participants in the scheme that we should all contribute on a sliding scale, depending on how much we'd made. It was a voluntary scheme but forty-three of the forty-four who had made money contributed to the pot. I think my share was about £220,000. The one member of the scheme who didn't put any money in criticized me in the newspapers for suggesting we should share some of our gains with the rest of the staff. He said I was a 'funny bloke' with socialist inclinations. I suppose I'd suggested giving some money to the rest of the staff because I'd never envisaged that we would all make so much and felt a degree of guilt that we hadn't included more of the people at LWT.

One of the reasons we made so much money was that we won back our franchise at a much smaller figure than we had estimated. Mrs Thatcher's original plan was a straight auction in which the highest bidder automatically won. As the Bill went through Parliament it was amended to add a quality threshold to the scheme. This clause was slipped into the Act by David Mellor, then a junior minister in the Home Office. I always suspected that David disliked the whole idea of the auction and did all he could to ensure that the good ITV companies survived. Under his clause any bidder had to satisfy the Independent Television Commission that they could both sustain the ITV system financially and deliver programmes of sufficient quality.

It was a mad system and by the mid Nineties it was very hard to find a Conservative MP who admitted to having voted for it, let alone proposing it in the first place. By then Margaret Thatcher had gone and she was blamed for the whole debacle. Two companies who discovered they had no opposition, Central and Scottish, bid just £2,000 a year for their franchises and won them, while others like TVS and Television South West bid £59 million and £16 million respectively and were ruled out by the ITC for having bid too much.

At LWT we thought long and hard about how much to bid. We knew we had only one competitor, London Independent Broadcasting, a franchise fronted by the music company Polygram and put together by a friend of mine, Tom Gutteridge, who had run York University TV while I was a student, after which he founded and ran a successful independent production company in the UK called Mentorn; he now runs Fremantle Television's operation in the United States. Tom is still a friend and, having forgiven him for bidding against us at LWT, Sue and I went to his wedding in 2003 when he married the wonderful Rosetta. The wedding was a classic Gutteridge production – no expense spared. There was even a bishop at the service: Tom and Rosetta had persuaded their local vicar that, although both of them were divorced, he should marry them in the local church. Tom always had that ability to sell anything to anyone. I think the bishop came along out of curiosity.

We didn't think much of the Polygram consortium and I dedicated a fortnight of my life to finding out everything I could about them. In that time I spoke to people who had been offered the job of Managing Director, to people who had been approached about finance, and to programme makers. I came to the conclusion that, no matter how much they bid, they couldn't win because they weren't properly financed. Unlike for his wedding, Tom hadn't raised enough money to pay for the project. He told me years later that if we'd offered him a couple of million pounds' worth of programming every year for Mentorn he would have pulled out. We'd guessed that might be the case at the time but we didn't dare risk it. If we'd been caught doing it there was a risk that we'd be ruled unfit to hold an ITV franchise. It didn't stop Gus Macdonald up in Scotland who gave programme deals to virtually every independent possible. Looking back now he was probably right to do so.

Having established Polygram's cash situation I was in favour of a lowish bid, but it was Christopher's idea that we should bid a really low figure, one that was just enough to be respectable. We hit on the figure of £7.58 million and won. The Polygram consortium bid £35 million and lost. It was a truly ridiculous system.

The whole process leading up to the bids and afterwards was a cloak and dagger affair. One Friday I got a letter from someone saying he knew how much Polygram were going to bid and that if I paid him £5,000 he would tell me. He said that if I wanted to contact him I had to put an advert in the *Evening Standard* headed 'Something for the Weekend'. We didn't bother because we knew by then that our bid was going to be much lower than Polygram's. The funniest story I heard was about Yorkshire Television and Mersey Television getting together secretly to bid for the Granada franchise. They were due to have a confidential meeting at a hotel in Leeds but arrived to find that the hotel manager, in his enthusiasm, had put up a sign in the lobby saying that the hotel welcomed 'Yorkshire Television and Mersey Television'.

Ray Snoddy, the *Financial Times* media editor at the time and my former colleague in Uxbridge, managed to discover most of the bids for the different franchises around the UK, but not LWT's. He even tried exploiting our old friendship to try and persuade me to give him a hint, but I refused. When everyone discovered that we'd only bid £7 million, even though we had a serious competitor, they were all shocked, and that included members of the LWT Board. When I told our Director of Broadcasting, Robin Paxton, on the morning the results were expected, that we'd bid that low he went a deathly white. We'd taken a calculated gamble and it had come off; if it hadn't, I shudder to think what the staff's reaction would have been.

We also put together a bid for the ITV breakfast television franchise held by my old company TV-am. The rules only allowed us to own 20 per cent of the station, but because we'd put the bid together we managed to sell to the consortium an unused studio in our building, LWT crews, and the LWT transmission facilities. We bid too much for the franchise, £34.61 million a year, and it was a decade before GMTV started making a decent profit. But LWT made money from day one. It was a good deal for us.

Many conspiracy stories surround the size of our bid for the breakfast franchise. It has been suggested that we knew what our biggest rival, an

ITN-backed consortium, was likely to bid. This was perfectly true. I had found out the size of their bid and had told the members of our consortium how much extra we had to bid to win. We agreed to do it, upped our bid, and won. I've never revealed who told me the size of the ITN bid, and I never will, but I have said on many occasions that it wasn't Michael Green, whose company, Carlton, was part of the ITN consortium. After we had won he took up the last 20 per cent in our group and that started all the rumours that he'd doubled-crossed his group. But it wasn't true.

So on the day the results of the franchise auction were announced we had two things to celebrate at LWT: we'd won back our franchise and our consortium had also won the breakfast franchise. At lunchtime Christopher Bland, Brian Tesler, and I got a standing ovation from our staff in the LWT bar and that evening we had a great staff party that went on most of the night. I had prepared a speech I would make to the staff if we won the franchise battle and I duly delivered it that night; but I had never prepared for losing. I had asked Tony Cohen to draft me a losing speech because I couldn't face doing it, but he only admitted to me years later that he couldn't do it either. Thankfully, it wasn't needed.

There were still bodies lying around the building the morning after the party, people who were just too drunk or too tired to go home. I had been pretty confident of winning and had arranged for a lot of posters to go up all over London with the LWT comedians Hale and Pace saying 'LWT done the business'. My only fear was that I wouldn't be able to stop them going up if we'd lost. This nearly happened to Granada, who had arranged for a small bottle of champagne to be delivered to the home of everyone who worked for the company if they won. The trouble was the company commissioned to deliver the bottles started delivering them before the result was known. Luckily for them Granada had won.

It was a sad day at some ITV companies and I rang the managing directors of Thames, TVS, and TSW to say how sorry I was. I didn't ring Bruce Gyngell at TV-am – it was hardly appropriate, given that we had outbid him for his franchise. In truth, TV-am had never had much chance of winning. We'd calculated it was always going to be cheaper to run a breakfast service off the back of another broadcasting organization than run it as a stand-alone business, which meant we, or the ITN consortium that was also bidding, could always bid more than TV-am.

Losing still came as a shock to Bruce Gyngell. In his years in Britain, he had become a favourite of Margaret Thatcher, particularly after he'd taken on the television unions and beaten them, and she was distraught when his company lost its franchise as a result of legislation pushed through by her own Government. She wrote to Bruce to tell him how much she regretted it. Bruce clearly didn't feel the same way about her and he read her private letter out at a press conference at Eggcup Towers. Part of her letter ran:

> When I see how some of the other licences have been awarded I am mystified that you did not receive yours, and heartbroken. You of all people have done so much for the whole of television – there seems to have been no attention to that. I am only too painfully aware that I was responsible for the legislation.

It was typical of Margaret Thatcher that she automatically thought her friends would be immune to the impact of a really terrible piece of legislation, which her Government had pushed through. At that same press conference Bruce also said that GMTV would be dead inside two years. Twelve years later it is a profitable, thriving business.

I felt particularly sad for my friend Richard Dunn, who was in charge of Thames, the biggest of the ITV companies. He'd had a really strong bidder against him in Michael Green's Carlton and I'd always feared he might lose because he hadn't done enough cost cutting at Thames to allow him to make a knockout bid. I think he believed the Independent Television Commission would invoke the special circumstances clause, a discretionary power the legislation had given them, to save Thames. But Thames was very unpopular with the Government because of a programme called *Death on the Rock* about the killing by British soldiers of IRA terrorists in Gibraltar. Mrs Thatcher had attacked the programme and it would have taken a brave ITC to have treated Thames as a special case and not Mrs Thatcher's friend Bruce Gyngell. In the end they didn't use the special circumstances clause at all.

Richard Dunn and I had agreed some months earlier that we wouldn't bid for each other's franchise as second choice. It was a deal that suited LWT as we had decided to bid low, but I was never quite sure why it suited Richard. Losing Thames was a terrible blow to him, but he recovered and was successfully rebuilding his career when, tragically, he was found dead at the bottom of his swimming pool in August 1998 having suffered a heart attack.

The results of the auction were announced in October 1991 but didn't take effect until fifteen months later, in January 1993. Guiding ITV through the interregnum was going to be difficult but interesting, and I decided I would try to do it by becoming the Chairman of ITV for a two-year period. At times we had representatives of twenty companies sitting around the table, twelve of whom had retained their franchises, four who had lost, and the four new franchise holders. The losers hated the winners and the winners didn't want to have anything to do with the losers. We even had to persuade Carlton that it was in their interests, and in the interests of ITV, to buy some of the Thames programmes like *The Bill*; but we made a mistake in not buying *Men Behaving Badly*, which later became a big hit on the BBC.

Overall, we managed the process and towards the end of 1992 the old ITV companies held a dinner for the losers. I made a speech praising Bruce Gyngell, eight years after he had fired me from TV-am. I no longer felt animosity towards him and told him how much a colourful character like him would be missed in ITV. Just over a year later I would join him on the outside.

It was June 1993 and, along with Mike Southgate and John K. Cooper, I had gone to Hilversum in Holland on business. We were sitting by a canal having lunch when the owner of the restaurant asked if there was a Mr Dyke in our party. He told me there was a phone call for me. It was Christopher Bland, who told me that it wasn't a good day to be out of the country as that morning Granada had gone into the market and bought 14.99 per cent of LWT at £5 a share. This cost Granada a total of £67.9 million and they had paid 30 per cent more per share than the closing price on the London Stock Exchange the day before. A week later they bought another 5 per cent, taking them up to 19.9 per cent, the maximum they were allowed to own.

On the plane home that day I was very down. I had made several million pounds that morning and yet I realized what it could mean. We were in danger of losing the company we loved.

There was much speculation at the time that the Government was going to change the ownership rules on ITV to allow any one company to own two large franchises. Gerry Robinson and Charles Allen, two people from the catering industry who were now running Granada, had clearly decided that they wanted to own LWT if the opportunity arose and had made a pre-emptive strike.

A month earlier, in May 1993, LWT had bought a 14 per cent stake in Yorkshire/Tyne Tees Television in a friendly deal I did with the company's Chairman and Managing Director Clive Leach. As part of the deal we had taken over responsibility for selling Yorkshire's advertising time. In September of that year we found out that Yorkshire had been overstating its total advertising revenue. The company was about to declare a decent profit when in fact it had made a significant loss.

Ron Miller, LWT's Sales Director, had discovered this and as LWT's director on the Board of Yorkshire/Tyne Tees I had been the whistle blower. I had to go direct to the Chairman of the Audit Committee and tell him what we had found. As a result, Clive Leach resigned from the company and a Tyne Tees man, Ward Thomas, took over as Chairman. A couple of years later Bruce Gyngell became Managing Director of the company and stayed until it was sold to Granada in 1997.

Granada finally made their bid for LWT in December 1993. We knew it was coming and were ready. We had an alternative proposal to put to the shareholders. Instead of Granada buying LWT we, along with Anglia Television, would buy the whole of Yorkshire/Tyne Tees. We would own 80 per cent of the Yorkshire licence and 20 per cent of the Tyne Tees, while Anglia would own 80 per cent of Tyne Tees and 20 per cent of Yorkshire. Eventually, when the rules allowed it, we would merge all four companies to create a single ITV company to cover London and the East of England.

It was a brilliant plan and I believe to this day that it would have worked and that we could have seen off the Granada bid. We had an agreement to buy Yorkshire/Tyne Tees at £4 a share, which turned out to be a great price (it was eventually bought by Granada in June 1997 at £7 a share). But the directors of Anglia lost their nerve. Their merchant bank told them that the Granada takeover of LWT would happen and that Anglia would be left stranded. Gutlessly, they pulled out.

It was then a straight battle between Granada and LWT. We put up a spirited fight and forced Granada to increase their bid for the company on two occasions before 57 per cent of our shareholders finally accepted the bid. We were a very successful management team with a brilliant track record – I believe we had been the fourth most successful company in Britain over the previous four years in terms of the increase in our stock price – and yet our shareholders sold us out. The real villain was a woman called Carol Galley who worked for Mercury Asset Management. When you met her she was charming but her nickname in the City was 'the ice maiden'. Mercury owned about 14 per cent of Granada and 14 per cent of LWT, and she decided to go against us even though we believed we had the better management. From that moment on I always described her as 'the witch'. She did exactly the same thing a couple of years later when Granada bought Forte: she sold out Forte. She was wrong both times. Carol Galley's reputation was bruised some years later when Unilever took Mercury to court claiming that they had mismanaged the Unilever pension fund. In the end Mercury had to pay £130 million into the fund. I opened a bottle of champagne that night and toasted a great result.

On the last day of the battle for LWT Christopher Bland and I considered doing something rather brave, if not reckless, to try to save the company. Christopher had been phoned that morning by an arbitrager (someone who buys in one market for immediate resale in another) who had built up a 3 per cent stake in the company. He was just about to sell out to Granada but told Christopher that if he offered a higher bid he could have the shares.

We knew the result of the takeover bid was going to be close, with shareholders like Warburg Pincus (an American venture capital business) and Fidelity supporting us, and when I got into the office Christopher suggested that he and I between us bought the shares we were being offered by the arbitrager. It would have cost us some £23 million. As neither of us had that sort of money we set about trying to raise it by borrowing it. After about an hour we both realized this could be madness: we could both lose an awful lot of money -- as much as we'd made from the whole LWT scheme. I looked up at Christopher and said, 'If I go home tonight and we've lost I won't have a job. If we do this I might be penniless as well.' In the end the arbitrager's shares had gone before we could do it, which was just as well as we would still have lost the bid and we would have overpaid for the shares. But it certainly kept us busy for a couple of hours in a day that turned out to be our last in control of LWT.

Late in the afternoon of Friday 25 February 1994 Gerry Robinson rang Christopher and told him that Granada now had 57 per cent acceptances and owned LWT. That night we had another big party in the LWT bar, although it was more like a wake.

LWT and Granada had never been on friendly terms so it was ironic that we had been bought by the ITV company we disliked the most. In a speech to the Royal Television Society biennial symposium in Cambridge in September 1993, Christopher had explained how great the animosity was between the two companies when he said of John Birt: 'While at LWT he tried desperately to persuade Granada to act in the interests of the ITV system as a whole. In the end he left LWT and took on the much easier task of trying to modernize the BBC.'

The following week I met Gerry Robinson, who tried to persuade me to stay as Chief Executive of LWT. During the bid Granada had tried to split Christopher and me by making it clear that there was a good job for me in Granada if they won. I was having none of it during the bid and I was having none of it now. As far as I was concerned, Christopher was my friend and Granada was the enemy. There were no circumstances in which I would work for them, so I turned down the offer to stay, took the two years' pay my contract stipulated, and left LWT.

There was something about LWT at that time that was lost with the Granada takeover. It was a cocky, confident place where programme makers liked to work. As a result they made some extraordinary programmes. It was one big family, but with the takeover that came to an end. Over the next few years most of my team left, and when they did many of them rang me to tell me they were going, as if they wanted my approval.

It is difficult to explain today how devastated I felt then. Only a couple of things in my life – the failure of my marriage and the death of my father – had been as bad. I was 47 and my world had disappeared. I no longer knew what I was or who I was. I remember going to pick the kids up from school thinking everyone was watching me, seeing me as a has-been. Without the power, the title, the staff, the driver, the personal assistant, what was left? What was I?

That I was now rich didn't make any difference to how I felt. I remember going for lunch with a mate, the pop music promoter Harvey Goldsmith, and I started by telling him what we had done wrong. He looked up and said, 'Greg, you've just walked away with £7 million. You didn't do anything wrong.' That wasn't how I saw it. I'd lost my job, my company, and my colleagues. Living through that period made what happened ten years later at the BBC so much easier to bear.

It was a truly miserable time and I made life at home truly miserable. When Clive Jones, by then an executive with Carlton, rang one day Alice answered the phone. Aged nine, she asked him if he could get me a job because I was driving everyone mad. That old line that politicians use so often when they are fired, that they wanted to 'spend more time with their family', didn't apply to me. I discovered that my family didn't want to spend that much more time with me.

I learnt a lot from the LWT experience, but it took me some time to understand it. I learned about money and City institutions and how it didn't matter how well you had done – they would still sell you out if it suited them. I learnt that, emotionally, you shouldn't get too tied into an organization because, just as had happened at TV-am ten years earlier, someone could take it away and there would be nothing you could do about it. And finally I had learnt that as the boss you could make a difference, that you could take a company through difficult times and still treat people properly and with respect.

I also learnt to live with suddenly being rich. Both Sue and I worried about the effect it would have on our life, our kids, and our attitude to

I left LWT when it was taken over by Granada. I was asked to stay on to carry on running the company but I didn't want to work for people I saw as 'the enemy'.

the world. We set up a charitable trust fund and gave quite a lot of money away: in particular we looked for opportunities to help individuals change their lives by helping with their education.

But we also enjoyed the money. We renovated a beautiful set of derelict barns near Stockbridge in Hampshire, which we turned into a place to relax and play. In one barn we built an indoor swimming pool and I insisted on having a chute from the floor above so you could get out of bed, wander along to the chute and go straight into the pool. We built our own football pitch, a tennis court, and some stables. At the age of 50, I took up horse riding, which I discovered could be quite dangerous. One day, when I'd come off yet again and my horse (appropriately named Big Horse) had arrived home without me, I asked Sue if she'd been worried when the horse had returned riderless. She replied that her only thought was, 'I'm rich.'

I found out later that becoming rich also turned you into a different sort of employee. Once you've got what is known as 'fuck-off money' you take more risks and become more cavalier in your attitude: if money is plentiful you don't have to take crap from your employer. In many ways you become more creative and more likely to succeed, but also more dangerous.

During this period I also began to make other investments with the money I'd made. It was in the middle of the recession and a lot of businesses were in trouble; there were bargains to be picked up. I bought a golf club and a number of cottages in Dartmouth in Devon from the receiver. After a few difficult years at the beginning it is now a very successful business. I also bought a restaurant, which taught me never to buy another one; and I began developing properties in the West Country. (When I joined the BBC I was allowed to keep these businesses, which meant that the newspapers were to crawl all over these activities a few years later.)

I was out of full-time work for most of the year. I was offered a few jobs I didn't fancy as I wanted to stay in the television business. Early on I was asked by the US media company Time Warner to get involved in a bid for Channel Five and I became a consultant for them, working a couple of days a week. Their partners were the media groups Pearson, who had recently bought the remnants of Thames Television, and United News and Media, who owned most of Meridian Television, which had won the old TVS franchise. The idea was that I would become the Chief Executive if we won the Channel Five franchise.

After a few months Frank Barlow, the Managing Director of Pearson, decided that he would rather I was running his fledgling television business than be Chief Executive of a Channel Five bid that might, or might not, succeed. He offered me the job of Chairman and Chief Executive of Pearson Television and I decided to accept. I joined Pearson in January 1995.

I immediately asked Tony Cohen to leave the Granada-owned LWT and come and join me to help plan a strategy to build a significant television business. Pearson had already bought Thames Television from Thorn EMI at what turned out to be a ridiculously low price of £99 million. In the years to come we sold the Thames shares in SAS, the European satellite business, for £130 million and made a lot of money out of continuing to sell *The Bill* to ITV. On top of that there was a £30 million surplus in the Thames pension fund that was merged into the Pearson fund. By any standards Frank Barlow had done a great deal and Colin Southgate, Chairman of Thorn EMI, a terrible one.

Tony Cohen and I decided that the only way to expand was to go international. At the time Reg Grundy's business was for sale and we decided to try to buy it. Grundy Worldwide had started as an Australian business making game shows and soaps. Its greatest success was *Neighbours*, a big hit for the BBC that was making Grundy a lot of money. As a result he'd moved the business out of Australia to Bermuda. He had one of the most complicated tax structures I'd ever seen. Reg had made tax avoidance an art form.

A few years earlier he had decided to expand in Europe and by the time we were interested in buying the company he had three successful daily soaps running in Germany – *Gute Zeiten, Schlechte Zeiten* (Good Times Bad Times), *Unter Uns* (Among Us), and *Verbotene Liebe* (Forbidden Love). Reg, who owned the vast bulk of the business, was in the process of floating the company on the New York Stock Exchange when we intervened. He was interested in selling to us but needed to be assured that we would care for his company.

We arranged to meet at JFK Airport in New York in March 1995 and I flew out on Concorde for a four-hour meeting before flying back the same night. I met Reg and his wife Joy in a room at the airport and took a tough American merchant banker with me, Nancy Peretsman. Reg and

Joy were very emotional. Joy explained that the company was their baby: they had never had children, and losing it was terribly sad for them. At one time they were both crying.

Nancy looked at me as if to ask, 'What the hell is this?' But I understood how they both felt and tried to look and sound sympathetic. In the end they agreed to sell the company for $386 million and I then had the job of convincing Frank Barlow and the Board of Pearson that it was a good deal. Eventually they too agreed and we announced the deal, much to the surprise of the people working for Grundy and of their merchant bankers, who were in the middle of the US flotation.

It turned out to be a brilliant deal. Thanks to Mike Murphy, Grundy's head of drama in Europe, within two years we had two extra soaps running in Germany, a soap and a weekly serial in Italy, and a soap in Hungary. We doubled Grundy's profits and also opened up production companies right across Europe.

With the success of Grundy I had got the acquisition bug and with the help of Tony Cohen and a brilliant young French strategist called Cecile Frot Coutaz we set about buying some more companies. We next acquired SelecTV, the makers of *Birds of a Feather*, who also owned 15 per cent of the Meridian franchise. Buying it was difficult because it was a publicly quoted company, although the Managing Director, Alan McKeon, who was married to the comedienne Tracey Ullman, ran it more like a private business.

Eventually the deal went through, in February 1996, for £46 million and we immediately sold the shares in Meridian to Clive Hollick, the Chief Executive of Meridian's parent company United News and Media, for £27 million. He bought the broadcasting assets and we bought the production company and the programme library, which included a deal with the situation comedy writers Laurence Marks and Maurice Gran. In retrospect Clive got the better deal; sadly, in the time Marks and Gran were writing for Pearson they never produced the equivalent of *Birds of a Feather*.

After SelecTV we acquired a US movie distribution company called ACI, which we bought from a range of producers who made television movies for the US networks. Initially it was a good buy but in recent years the US networks have put more and more of their work in-house, squeezing out the independent producers.

Finally we bought All American, a big US production company that made *Baywatch* and, for the CBS network, *The Price is Right*. It also had a big library of game show formats, which was one of the businesses we were in across Europe. We bought it from an American of Italian descent called Tony Scotti and after acquiring it we heard some odd stories about the company. It seemed that a prostitute used to turn up in the Los Angeles offices every afternoon to satisfy one of the staff (not, I might add, Tony Scotti).

In four years we built Pearson Television into one of the biggest independent production companies in the world, with operations in twenty-five countries. We had also expanded our broadcasting business by being part of the consortium that won the Channel Five franchise in the UK. Our partners in Channel Five were Clive Hollick's United News and Media, RTL (the Luxembourg-based broadcasting company), and Warburg Pincus, who had been a shareholder in LWT and whose director, Dominic Shorthouse, I much admired. I also admired the way they had supported management all the way through the LWT takeover when it would have been much easier not to do so. When we needed a fourth shareholder I phoned Dominic.

The bidding process for Channel Five was comparatively simple. It was what happened soon after the bids were submitted that made it interesting. The Independent Television Commission had decided that they weren't going to let Ray Snoddy reveal the sizes of all the bids this time. Instead they were going to announce how much people had bid on the day they received them.

There were four bids. The highest was from UKTV, a consortium led by a Canadian Company called Can West, who owned broadcasters in Canada and Australia. While legally they met the ownership requirements, it was quite clear it was a foreign bid. They also bid a figure of £36 million, to be paid annually to the Treasury, which we all believed the ITC would decide was too high.

Amazingly the next two bidders, our group and a Virgin consortium, had both bid the identical sum, exactly £22 million and two thousand pounds a year. No one believed this was a coincidence and the press naturally portrayed it as a conspiracy. The only problem was that no one could explain why we would have chosen to have bid the same amount. If we had known the exact size of the Virgin bid we would have gone higher; if Virgin had known ours, they would surely have bid higher too.

The strange thing was that on the morning the bids were submitted Clive Hollick and I had changed our bid. The bid had to be multiples of a thousand pounds and we had a long discussion about whether or not one thousand was a multiple of a thousand or not. In the end we decided to increase our bid by one thousand pounds without consulting our partners in the consortium. That one decision made the two bids identical. To this day I still don't know whether it was a bizarre coincidence or whether there was indeed some sort of conspiracy. While writing this book I've had a 'Come on, now, tell me the truth' conversation with Clive, but he denies that there was a plot, and I certainly wasn't involved in one, so maybe it was just a coincidence.

In the end it didn't matter because neither the Can West Consortium nor Virgin passed the quality threshold and, rather surprisingly, we were left the winner. The only other bidder to get through the quality threshold was a consortium involving BSkyB headed up by David Elstein. They were planning to bid £25 million and would have won, but at the last minute Rupert Murdoch dramatically reduced the bid to just £2 million. His partners in the consortium were furious with him because they knew that, at that level, it effectively meant they were dropping out. So why did he do this?

There had certainly been a campaign run in the non-Murdoch press against the BSkyB bid and Michael Grade, then Chief Executive at Channel Four, had written a very strong article arguing against his gaining control of Channel Five; but none of this would have been enough to stop the Murdoch bid. I've always suspected that he was told by the Prime Minister, John Major, or by one of his senior people, that for him to be in effective control of Channel Five, as well as BSkyB and all his national newspapers, was a step too far. Why else would he pull out when all the work had been done?

At Channel Five we set about doing the preparatory work for launching the channel. We changed our Chief Executive after a few months because we couldn't get it through to the management that, as the shareholders, we wanted preferential treatment in things like programme supply. We brought in David Elstein, who had been working for BSkyB since leaving Thames some years earlier. Soon afterwards I replaced Frank Barlow as Chairman of the company, a position I held until I joined the BBC in 1999.

The biggest task Channel Five faced was the retuning of about two-thirds of the nation's video recorders, which was no small challenge. We recruited an army of retuners and set about the task. We met a million problems, including the eccentricities of some of the residents of Britain. In one house the retuner found a sausage stuck in the back of the video. When asked why it was there the householder explained that he could only get his video to work when he had his finger in the same place. This had naturally proved tiring, so he had used a sausage instead.

The cost of retuning ended up being £165 million – about three times what we had set aside in our business plan. I am still not convinced it was necessary. In the few areas where we should have retuned, but didn't, it didn't seem to make any difference.

Our second major problem was that when we launched the channel the signal in London wasn't strong enough and the picture in many homes in the London area was awful. We only solved this problem when the ITC agreed that we could change our position on the mast at Crystal Palace, which broadcasts to the whole of the London area. By moving to a higher position on the transmitter the picture quality improved markedly.

In Dawn Airey, Channel Five had a charismatic Director of Programmes who was an outstanding leader of her team. Some time after I had left, the Board decided to replace David Elstein as Chief Executive with Dawn. She has since joined BSkyB and is now one of James Murdoch's main lieutenants, but I know she desperately misses running her own show.

Today, Channel Five gets between a 6 and 7 per cent share of all viewing in the UK and is now profitable. I doubt it has a long-term future as a stand-alone channel and believe it needs to be part of a bigger family of channels. Clive Hollick and I always envisaged the time when Channel Five and ITV would merge and Five would become an effective ITV2. Whether it ever happens time will tell, but it would be to the benefit of both organizations if it did.

Soon after Labour came to power I received a very curious call from Peter Mandelson asking if I had half an hour to spare for a chat. I duly went to meet him and he offered me the job of finishing and running the Millennium Dome at Greenwich. I couldn't think of anything I wanted to do less, but I was polite and told him I was happy at Pearson and didn't want to move. He looked up at me and said, in that sort of threatening way that Mandelson has adopted, that if I didn't take the job the Prime Minister would be 'very disappointed'. Given what happened later to the Dome it was a pretty good decision on my part.

Later, when the Dome was opened, just a month before I became Director-General of the BBC, I was one of many people who were invited to the opening on Millennium night. Sue and I, plus Joe and one of his friends, went to Stratford Railway Station as instructed where we waited for close on three hours to get on a train to the Dome. I, to say the least, got very annoyed at the wait. At one time a policeman told me to calm down because I might start a riot. I said that was exactly what I was trying to do. I've always hated the way the British are happy to stand in a queue for hours on end.

When we finally got to the Dome I confronted Peter Mandelson and told him there were thousands of people stuck at Stratford. Many of them were not VIPs but ordinary people who had won competitions and the like and for them it was supposed to be the best night of their lives. Mandelson was dismissive. He said, 'It won't happen again.' That night killed the Dome because most of the editors of the national newspapers were standing in that queue and they never forgot.

In many ways the Dome saga tells you a great deal about New Labour. Tony Blair decided to go ahead with the project despite the opposition of the relevant Minister, Chris Smith, and most of the Cabinet. They discussed it and voted against, but Blair did it anyway. And of course although it was quite a good idea, it cost more than planned and didn't work very well. It was an early sign that New Labour wasn't great on delivery.

In my last year at Pearson it was clear to me that it didn't make sense for the television business to stay part of the wider Pearson Group. There were no synergies to be gained by Pearson owning a television business alongside an educational publisher, Penguin Books, and the *Financial Times*. I believed the television business needed to be in a group with European-wide broadcasting interests. The problem was that Marjorie Scardino, the colourful American Chief Executive of Pearson, liked the television business and wanted to keep it in her group. A few months after I left she merged Pearson's TV business with RTL, which was part of the deal I had been urging for months. It was a true case of Sod's Law.

It was Marjorie who really got me interested in joining the BBC. One day she said she had read an article in which my name had been mentioned as a possible candidate to run the BBC. She looked up and in her delightful Texan drawl said, 'You know, if you get offered it you've got to do it. It really matters.'

So I did it.

CHAPTER SEVEN

Joining the BBC

It was about ten past six on the morning of 2 June 1999 when the phone rang. We are not early risers in our house and we regard ten past six as the middle of the night, so we were all fast asleep. I struggled to find the phone and when I eventually picked it up John Fallon, the head of public relations for the Pearson Group, was on the other end.

'Greg, did you hear the six o'clock news on Radio Four?' he asked. I remember thinking, 'This guy doesn't have to get into work until nine. What was he doing getting up at this unearthly hour, let alone listening to the radio?' There is some irony here as it was a broadcast at seven minutes past six on Radio Four that eventually led to my demise at the BBC.

I told John that I hadn't heard the six o'clock news and was only just awake. He told me I'd better wake up pretty fast and listen to the six-thirty bulletin.

What I learnt was that William Hague, the leader of the Conservative Opposition, had issued a statement overnight announcing that he had written to the Chairman of the BBC saying that I was an unsuitable person to become Director-General. He argued that I should be ruled out of the reckoning because I was a supporter of the Labour Party, to which I had given money over a number of years. BBC News had decided that this was the number one story of the day and were headlining it.

The argument William Hague was putting forward wasn't new. Peter Ainsworth, the Opposition spokesman on Culture, Media and Sport, had said similar things already, as had *The Times* and other newspapers. In particular they had pointed out that I had helped to fund Tony Blair's challenge for the Labour leadership back in 1994. But with this move the Conservatives were really upping the ante. William Hague was the leader of Her Majesty's official Opposition. A real political heavyweight weighing in.

By the time Hague joined the game I was quite close to getting the job of Director-General and I've always suspected that this was a last-ditch attempt by the Conservative Party to stop me. As it turned out it had the opposite effect. I've also always believed that by coming out against me William Hague actually secured the job for me. That's not to say that Hague was my only opponent. The six months leading up to my appointment had been a lively time, but he put the BBC Governors in a difficult position. His intervention galvanized the Labour supporters on the BBC Board behind me and meant that if the BBC Governors rejected me they would be accused of bowing to political pressure. This, in turn, would have called into question the political independence of the whole of the BBC.

Once I had got the job I had to try to make my peace with William Hague, so along with the BBC Chairman Christopher Bland and the outgoing Director-General John Birt, I went to meet him to discuss the situation. I assured him I would be politically neutral and said that all I could ask was that he judged me on my performance. He was firm but likeable and accepted the position, not that he had much option.

In the years since then I've become a bit of a William Hague fan. After he had given up the leadership of the Conservative Party I persuaded him to come and speak to my monthly management meeting, a group of about a hundred people from all parts of the BBC. He wowed them all. He was clever, funny, and profound about British and world politics. Timing is all: I suspect William Hague got the job as leader of the Conservative Party too early in his career and at the wrong time. I would not be at all surprised to see him leading the party again in the years ahead.

My journey into the BBC had actually started more than a year earlier, in July 1998, when I went for breakfast at the Ritz with Christopher Bland, my former chairman at LWT who had become Chairman of the BBC. At the time I was Chief Executive of Pearson Television, a company we had built by acquisition in a short time into one of the largest independent production companies in the world. I had recently failed in my efforts to expand it further by putting together a very large merger that would have combined the television assets of four large groups, United

News and Media, the Luxembourg group RTL, the German company Bertelsmann, and Pearson. If the merger had worked my idea was that I would have been Chief Executive of the new company.

The trouble was that getting four companies to agree on a merger at the same time was too difficult. There's simply too much plate-spinning involved. Just as three of the companies agree on the way forward the fourth plate begins to wobble. In the end the deal fell apart, although at a later stage three of the companies, RTL, Bertelsmann, and Pearson, did merge their TV businesses to create a large pan-European broadcasting and production company that in Britain owns 66 per cent of Channel Five and produces programmes like *The Bill*. It is now totally owned by Bertelsmann.

Christopher and I had stayed close after we left LWT in 1994. He'd been offered, and accepted, the job as Chairman of the National Freight Corporation and had asked me to join him as Chief Executive. I hadn't taken the job as I couldn't see myself getting excited about the trucking business. Over our breakfast at the Ritz, I told Christopher that now my major deal had fallen through I'd decided I wouldn't stay at Pearson for much longer, I'd certainly leave in the next year, and that I was trying to work out what to do next.

He said why didn't I consider coming to the BBC as Director-General to succeed John Birt, who was due to leave in 2000, having been in the job for seven years?

I'd never really seen myself as a BBC man. I had always made jokes about the sort of people who made it to the top of the BBC, suggesting that they were disproportionately made up of the public school, Oxbridge brigade. My own background was very different from that and I'd never seen the BBC as a likely home. In fact when I left LWT I was interviewed by Alan Titchmarsh on a BBC daytime chat show and asked whether I would like to run the BBC. I replied that I thought Saddam Hussein had a better chance of getting the job than I had. Of course when I was eventually appointed Director-General the clip was replayed endlessly on BBC news bulletins. When I did finally join the BBC I discovered that my views about BBC people were outdated and that the top of the organization was no longer dominated by public-school boys in the way it had been a decade or so earlier. By then the grammar-school pupils were largely in control.

Although I had never worked for the BBC I had flirted with the idea of joining the Corporation on a few occasions, although I only ever officially applied for two jobs with them. The first was as a reporter on BBC Radio Teesside when it was set up in 1970. I went to two interviews but did not get the job. At the second interview I was asked if I thought the people of Middlesbrough would understand my London accent. I pointed out that the taxi driver must have understood me as how else could I have got there from the station? I don't think the joke went down well. My second application for a job at the BBC, nearly thirty years later, was to be Director-General. In the intervening years I had been offered an executive role at the BBC by Michael Grade back in the mid Eighties when Michael was Controller of BBC One. He wanted me to join to sort out *Wogan*, BBC One's failing, five-nights-a-week chat show, by becoming its executive producer. It didn't excite me a lot, but to try to persuade me Michael offered a big carrot. He told me I would replace him as Controller of BBC One as soon as he succeeded the legendary Bill Cotton, who would soon retire as Managing Director of BBC Television.

Bill Cotton, or Sir William as he is now known, was an outstanding head of entertainment for the BBC for many years. He was also the son of the famous bandleader and looks remarkably like him. He tells a wonderful story of the day his dad became ill and couldn't lead the band on tour. The band's manager asked Bill to do it instead. Bill pointed out that he had limited musical ability and couldn't conduct. The manager looked at him, sighed, and told him that was totally irrelevant. All he had to do was get on the stage and wave his arms around, the band would do the rest. And that's what he did every night for a month.

It was Bill who had brought Michael Grade back from the USA to run BBC One. I had known Michael from my LWT days and loved his sense of fun, as well as admiring his flair and his knowledge about talent. Working with him again was a very attractive proposition. The problem was that, in typical BBC fashion, no one would put the offer to run BBC One on paper and, despite getting assurances from both Michael and Bill that they wanted me for the job, I refused to join without a letter. The BBC had a famous reputation at that time for offering the same job to a number of people. It was just as well I turned the job down because it wasn't long before Michael was poached to take over at Channel Four and wasn't in a position to deliver. But I did work with him there when

I became a director of the channel in 1988, having been appointed as an ITV representative on the Board by the Independent Television Commission.

In 1998, with the Chairman of the BBC saying that if I applied for the post of Director-General I would have a very good chance of getting the job, I began to think seriously about the prospect of running the BBC for the first time. The downside of the job was that I knew there was an enormous amount to be done. While John Birt had achieved a lot in modernizing the BBC since becoming Director-General in 1993 it was a deeply unhappy organization and Birt's BBC was also under attack from many on the outside.

In his 1992 McTaggart lecture in Edinburgh, the most important lecture in the UK television calendar, Michael Grade, by then the Chief Executive of Channel Four, had described Birt's BBC as 'a secret and forbidding place to work ... an airtight fortress from which no stray opinion is permitted to escape'. When he spoke of Birt's approach to running the organization he described it as a 'pseudo-Leninist style of management'. The following year, in 1993, the playwright Dennis Potter had gone even further in his McTaggart lecture when he said 'there are legions of troubled and embittered employees at the BBC who can scarcely understand any of the concepts of the new management culture'.

Even though the BBC had lost some of its cachet in the outside world, and was seen as a boring, process-driven organization, I was fascinated by the idea of trying to change it. This was a real leadership challenge that I knew I would find both difficult and stimulating. How easy was it to motivate and inspire an organization that had 27,000 full-time employees and countless other freelance workers?

After my first year at the BBC I was asked to record a long private interview with Ron Neill, who had retired from the BBC the year before I joined. The interview was for BBC archive purposes only. I recently re-read it and discovered that I had explained to him why I decided to go for the BBC job in the first place.

> It was a job I wanted but it was also a job I could have lived without. I like doing jobs where I'm not sure I can do them and you could see it was a job which was going to be difficult, and I found that attractive.

Ron then asked about the doubts I'd had concerning my ability to do the job.

> Firstly I'd never worked for the BBC which was a very large organization and secondly in recent years I'd been running profit and loss companies which meant the culture and ethos was going to be very different.

Ron also asked me what Sue's view had been.

> Sue didn't care a lot either way until the campaign against me started. Sue is like me in many ways and when you tell her she can't have something she'll resist. Once the campaign against me started, which I didn't expect, we just said well bugger them we'll fight this.

At a later breakfast in September 1998, again at the Ritz, I asked Christopher Bland if he thought my politics would be a problem given that I was an advocate of Tony Blair and New Labour and that I had given money to the Labour Party. Christopher, who knew me well and knew I had always separated my politics from my work, dismissed it as 'irrelevant', which I honestly believed it was. I had always been much more committed to the idea of independent broadcasting than I had been to Labour. When I had given the McTaggart lecture in August 1994 it had been on precisely that subject.

The donations I'd made to Labour totalled £55,000 over the previous five years, a significant sum but nothing compared to the £1 million I'd given to charity in the same period. That's not to say there haven't been times recently when I haven't been tempted to write to the Labour Party and ask for my money back.

Looking back now, I think Christopher and I convinced each other that my politics wouldn't be a major factor if I applied for the job. How wrong we were.

It was around this time that I shaved off the beard I'd had for thirty-three years. It is now part of Dyke mythology that I did it to make myself more presentable as a candidate for the post of Director-General, but the truth is less exciting. I grew it in the first place at the age of 19, when I was a young reporter on a local paper, to make myself look older. I shaved it off at the age of 52 to make myself look younger. Sadly, as I had grown older my beard had grown whiter and my kids, in the way that only one's own kids can, kept telling me that I looked like an old man. I think it was my daughter Alice who told me I hadn't got the nerve to shave it off. I told them I'd do it the night before we were due to go for a week's skiing, which is exactly what I did.

After a couple of days on holiday we had a family and friends vote on whether it should stay off or not. I voted to grow it again but I was outvoted 6–3, with only our eldest son Matthew and our daughter Christine supporting me. For some weeks I kept seeing this image in the mirror that bore no relation to the me I knew, but in the end I got used to my new look. My mum certainly liked it; she thought she'd got her boy back.

The possibility of my becoming Director-General was first raised publicly in a feature article in *The Guardian* in January 1999. A *Guardian* reporter, Kamal Ahmed, later political editor of *The Observer*, rang and said his editor, Alan Rusbridger, wanted him to do a profile of me. I always suspected that my old friend Melvyn Bragg had told Alan that he believed I was going to be the next Director-General and that he should keep an eye on me. The feature was very flattering with the headline 'Greg Dyke: TV's Man of the People'. In it, Kamal wrote that I was a strong candidate to become Director-General. I think it was the first time anyone inside the BBC realized that the job might go to an outsider.

In the same month Ladbrokes started taking bets on who would be the next Director-General and I was made the 3–1 joint favourite with Michael Jackson, who was by then running Channel Four, having replaced Michael Grade in June 1997. Michael later dropped out of the running and I stayed the bookies' favourite throughout the whole process.

The BBC formally advertised the job in the *Sunday Times* in March 1999. It so happened that it was a weekend when Sue, Joe, and I were in Northern Ireland staying, along with a number of other guests, at Hillsborough Castle. We had all been invited by Mo Mowlam, then Secretary of State for Northern Ireland, who liked inviting her friends over for the weekend to share the castle with her.

I remember being struck by the affection there was for Mo amongst ordinary people in Northern Ireland. We had Saturday lunch in the pub up the road from the castle and as we sat eating two elderly women came up to her and said, 'We just wanted you to know how much we love you, Mo.' It was very moving. Of course in the end Mo became too popular in the Labour Party for the Blairites. She always believed her downfall started when she got a standing ovation at the Labour Party conference during Tony Blair's speech.

On the Sunday morning someone in the party spotted the advert for Director-General in the *Sunday Times* and there was much discussion about whether or not I should apply. There were some BBC people amongst the guests that weekend, including Martha Kearney, the *Newsnight* and *Woman's Hour* presenter, and Jon Plowman, the BBC's Head of Comedy and the man who deserves enormous credit for spotting *The Office*, the best comedy, and probably the best programme, to come out of British television in the past decade. Months later, after starting at the BBC, I was at a meeting with staff at Television Centre when Jon walked up to me and gave me a rolled-up photograph that he knew would embarrass me: it was a picture he had taken in Hillsborough Castle of Sue and me sitting side by side on the thrones normally occupied by the Queen and Prince Philip.

Soon after the job of Director-General was advertised Matthew Horsman, the media analyst and former journalist, rang my office and said he wanted to join my campaign. I explained I didn't intend to run a campaign, that if I was asked to go for the job I would, but that was all I would do. Looking back now I realize how incredibly naive this position was. Given the campaigning that was to go on by those inside the BBC, by the candidates and other executives, I needed all the friends I could find if I was to succeed in getting the job, and Matthew would have been a valuable asset to any team.

To understand what happened in the coming months one has to understand John Birt. I had known him for many years and whilst we were not best friends we were mates. We originally got to know each other well at LWT playing football together every Friday lunchtime, when I was a reporter and he was my boss as Head of Current Affairs and Features. I played in the Friday game, on and off, for twenty years.

I owe John a lot. He played a big part in my getting a series of jobs, including succeeding him as Director of Programmes at LWT. In fact when he was due to become Director-General of the BBC he asked me to join as his deputy. I turned it down because by then I was Chief

Executive of LWT and had decided that, much as I liked him, I didn't want to work for him again. He was too much of a control freak. When I refused the job he lured Bob Phillis away from his job as Chief Executive at ITN to become Deputy Director-General. A few years later he effectively demoted him and tried to get him fired.

John Birt's autobiography, *The Harder Path*, might lead you to believe that he helped me become Director-General. When John's book was published in 2002 the press picked up on the story that he had 'rehearsed' me before my final interview with the Governors. They wrote that he had coached me. Journalists even found a few rent-a-gob politicians to denounce the appointment, saying that it had been a fix and unfair to the other candidates. The story simply wasn't true.

Whilst it was true I had spent an evening with John at the Governors' request I was certainly not coached by him, and in any case I knew by then the job was virtually mine. I only went for the dinner with John because I had been asked to go. I also knew by then how hard John had worked to stop me getting the job.

My memory of the evening was that John was much more concerned about how the press had discovered – and had published the previous weekend – the fact that he had been an active member of the Labour Party when he became Director-General. I now realize this had undermined one of the central arguments he had been using with the Governors to stop me being Director-General.

Nowhere in John's long and detailed book did he mention what he had done to stop me getting the job. All we were told was that he had helped me. We had to wait for the book (*The Fun Factory: A Life in the BBC*, published in 2003) written by Will Wyatt, Managing Director of BBC Broadcasting in John's time, to get the true story. It was typical of John to leave this out of his book. I can only presume it was because it was a battle lost, and according to John's account of his life he was always right and always won.

There is a story about the title of John's book that may or may not be true. Allegedly, his mother asked him what the title *The Harder Path* meant. John explained that you had a choice in life: you could take the easy route or the hard one. His mother looked at him and asked the obvious question, 'Why would anyone take the harder path if there was an easier one available?'

So why was John so hostile to my becoming Director-General when he had supported me in getting other jobs and, seven years earlier, had asked me to be his deputy when he took over the top job?

My own view is that John was desperate to go down in history as a great Director-General of the BBC. No story better illustrates this than the one about his portrait. As they retire, each Director-General has his portrait painted, which is then hung in the council chamber at Broadcasting House in central London. Before John, all the portraits were about the same size and depicted the subject from the waist up. And then came John's. He had a full facial portrait painted by Tai-Shan Schierenberg, which was done while he was still in the job, and thus ready to be unveiled as soon as he left, or soon after. It was a distinctive and brilliant portrait, but when it was hung it completely dominated the room, dwarfing everyone else's portrait. Wherever you sat, John's eyes followed you around the room. It was so typical of John. When the time came for John's picture to be hung Christopher made him dramatically prune the numbers he wanted to invite to the party for the official unveiling of his portrait.

I was never a great fan of the portraits. While I was a strong supporter of the BBC's heritage department I believed we should respect the past but not be dominated by it. With Broadcasting House currently being rebuilt, all the portraits are now in store or out on loan. I was asked what we should do with John's. Tongue in cheek, I suggested we should lend it to BBC Scotland, the part of the BBC where John was disliked the most. (I still have to have my portrait painted following my departure.)

When John left the BBC he went off to write his autobiography, which he wanted the BBC to make into a documentary. When Jane Root, the Controller of BBC Two, turned the idea down John wrote to her and complained, sending a copy of the letter to the Chairman, Christopher Bland. Typical John.

When I worked with him at LWT John Birt was great company, and widely respected. But the longer John was at the BBC, and he was there in all for thirteen years, the more he changed. He was constantly under attack and, as a result, became obsessed with himself and his image. He believed he had saved the BBC from Mrs Thatcher by making it more efficient, which is probably true. He also believed he had made a great financial sacrifice to join the BBC: again this was true. If he had stayed at LWT he could have made a fortune along with the rest of us. This was illustrated at one session at the annual Edinburgh Television Festival when he was on the platform and he turned to me in the audience and asked what would I have preferred, 'public vilification or £7 million'? That summed up John's views. He had saved the BBC, he had made financial sacrifices to do it, and yet he wasn't given public credit for having done so. The fact that he was widely disliked, both inside and outside the BBC, only strengthened his view that he had been unfairly treated.

My view of John was that he was always a man who worked upwards, someone who desperately wanted to be part of the power elite, part of the new establishment. Peter Mandelson, an average producer when we were all at LWT together, later became one of John's best friends when he became powerful. When he left the BBC, John not only received a peerage, he also got a job even closer to the centre of power, working on long-term strategy inside Number Ten.

In his last years as Director-General John Birt had the whole organization working on his twenty-year master plan for the BBC. In my experience the only thing you can be certain about when dealing with long-term strategic plans is that they will turn out to be wrong: there are too many variables for them ever to be right. For instance, when the BBC outlined its future for the next ten years in a document called *Extending Choice*, published in 1992, it made no mention at all of the Internet. Over the next five years the BBC's online services turned out to be its most exciting initiatives.

The failure of strategic plans is nobody's fault; it's just that the world changes faster, or in different directions, than predicted by the strategic planners. I always liked Christopher Bland's definition of strategy. He told me that any commercial decision made for 'strategic reasons' actually meant 'loss making'.

John Birt wanted as his successor someone who would not disrupt what he had done so far and would carry out the first part of his twenty-year plan. He wanted someone from inside the BBC who would carry the Birtist flame, who believed in the Birt way of doing things. He certainly didn't want someone like me coming in from outside who would probably never even read his plan.

Succession planning for the job of Director-General is close to impossible. Appointing and getting rid of the Director-General is the best sport the Governors have. BBC Governors don't actually have a lot to do and are removed from what is happening inside the BBC. But when it comes to hiring and firing the D-G they come into their own. In recent years the majority of D-Gs have left against their will. Hugh Carleton Greene was kicked upstairs to be a Governor in 1969, Alasdair Milne was fired in 1987, Michael Checkland was pushed out early against his wishes in 1992, and John only narrowly avoided an early departure in 1993 in a controversy over his tax arrangements. And then there was me.

After John Birt, the Chairman, Christopher Bland, and the majority of the Governors were of the view that they wanted to see a culture change at the BBC. They were tired of the staff loathing the management. So when it came to John's successor the Governors were not keen to appoint a Birtist from inside the organization, which meant they were interested in appointing an outsider.

Initially, John Birt encouraged all sorts of people inside the BBC to apply for the job. To his credit, he believed that everyone who wanted should be able to have the chance to go for it, even if they didn't have a realistic chance of getting the job. It was an egalitarian policy but in practice created real problems. People who had no chance of getting the job, people like the Head of Production Matthew Bannister, began to believe they might get it.

Contenders inside the organization began to work against anyone who might be a candidate, anyone who might stop them getting the job. They tried to kill off each other's chances. It was vicious, ruthless stuff, with BBC press officers being used full time to campaign for one candidate and against others inside the BBC.

The only candidate who seemed to steer well clear of the turmoil inside the organization was Mark Byford, who was Head of the World Service and had previously been the Director of Nations and Regions, responsible for the BBC's out of London activities. Mark was only forty at the time and, according to Will Wyatt in *The Fun Factory*, he was John Birt's chosen successor. When I first met Mark, having been appointed Director-General, I told him that I knew who had done what during the campaign and that by my reckoning he was completely clean. I thanked him for playing it straight.

A number of newspapers had taken against me, led by *The Times*, whose editor Peter Stothard had decided that, for political reasons, I shouldn't be the next Director-General. He launched a ferocious attack against me. In the spring of 1999 he published article after article and leader after leader criticizing me. The fight to stop me becoming Director-General became his campaign, supported by some senior managers inside the BBC.

When I look back now at the articles and leaders in The Times, they appear to me to be both pompous and ridiculous. In one leader the paper conceded that I was no 'full pedigree poodle' but pointed out that I had given money to Tony Blair's leadership campaign and that 'for anyone ambitious to climb the greasy poles of new Labour Britain, this was doubtless money well and sincerely spent'.

Four years later, of course, things were rather different when the BBC and the Blair Government were at war with each other over the events surrounding the reporting of the Iraq war. Like all Rupert Murdoch's papers, The Times had followed their master's voice and supported Britain's involvement in Iraq. As a result, The Times were squarely on Tony Blair's side in the battle with the BBC. Who was the Labour poodle now?

The strange thing about the Times campaign against me was that the paper's media editor Ray Snoddy, the doyen of media reporters for more than twenty years, first on the Financial Times and then on The Times itself, was of the opposite view. The more The Times rampaged against me, the more Snoddy, to his great credit, supported me in his column. He refused point blank to play Stothard's's game. When I eventually got the job it was Snoddy who gave Stothard the news.

My friends in television rallied round. Clive Jones organized a letter to The Times signed by all sorts of people who had worked with me in the past, people like John Stapleton, Peter McHugh, Mark Damazer, Adam Boulton, Trevor Phillips, and David Cox, who all knew I had no history of trying to distort the editorial process to match my own political views. Barry Cox, the former Head of Current Affairs at LWT, also defended my journalistic experience, which The Times had described as 'limited', and the actor Nigel Havers wrote to the paper to tell them that I was 'a fine man [whose] programme-making, from grass roots to the chairman's office, has been of a very high calibre indeed'.

And throughout it all, Melvyn Bragg advised and supported me, lobbying from the sidelines wherever he could. The help I got from him and his wife Cate Haste was invaluable. They helped to keep me enthusiastic despite the drivel that was being written in the papers, and they made sure I never got depressed.

The row went on in the columns of *The Times* for weeks but sitting in the Pearson building about half a mile away from Broadcasting House I wasn't that involved in it. I was still doing my day job at Pearson despite the furore going on around me.

Alan Yentob, the BBC's Director of Television at the time, then turned up in my office to say he wanted to join me and run as my deputy. I like Alan and think he is a talented man, and I could have done far worse than have him as my number two; but the last thing I was going to do was get involved in the inner politics of the BBC. Instead Alan announced his own candidacy, only to be publicly ridiculed as 'completely disorganized' by the other candidates and their press officers inside the BBC. It was nasty stuff.

Each candidate was asked to prepare a manifesto that was to be not more than three pages long. I had a lot to say, so the typeface I used got gradually smaller and smaller to ensure I could get it all on three pages. When I re-read my manifesto whilst writing this book I was pleasantly surprised by how much of it we had achieved in the four years I was at the BBC. In May 1999 I saw the BBC's single biggest problem as one of culture. I wrote then:

Most of all I believe I could bring to the BBC a style of leadership which enables creative talent to flourish at the same time as being financially and managerially accountable. Internally, I believe the BBC has a cultural problem. It has moved to a culture which is very top-down in style, internally competitive, too centralized, and one in which people are reluctant to question. It is very clear to me that many of the people who work for the BBC today don't like the new culture.

The interesting question this raises is: can the modernization process be continued and be successful with a different and more inclusive style of management? I believe it can. The most exciting organizations around the world are those with open and inclusive cultures. Interestingly, in terms of management style the BBC has moved in exactly the opposite direction to that chosen by the most successful companies of the 90's.

I believe the most important leadership challenge facing the next Director-General is to build an inclusive culture without losing the momentum for change.

I then listed what I believed needed changing in a number of areas. These included responding to devolution by expanding the BBC's production bases outside London, expanding the BBC's role as an international broadcaster, making the BBC's services more relevant to the young, and dramatically changing some of John Birt's internal organizational changes.

When I re-read it I also realized just how much of my manifesto was anti-Birtist. If he had read it, and I've little doubt one of the Governors would have shown it to him, I can understand why he didn't want me as his successor.

I had a series of interviews with different groups of Governors. The most bizarre was in a flat in Shepherd Market, Mayfair, which the BBC had hired for the day. It was later discovered it was normally used by prostitutes. I remember another where I told the Governors that I only had a certain amount of time as I was due to see Bruce Springsteen in concert at Earls Court. And I remember a final meeting with the whole Board, the day before I was appointed, at which Christopher had told me in advance that I was likely to get the job.

By the end there were four candidates left, two internal and two others who coincidentally both worked for the Pearson group. The internal candidates still in play were Mark Byford and the Head of News, Tony Hall. The two candidates from Pearson were Michael Lynton, an Americanized Briton who headed up Pearson-owned Penguin Books, and myself from Pearson Television. Michael didn't get offered the BBC job but was later offered the role of Chief Executive at Channel Four. He turned it down so it went to the BBC's Director of Television, Mark Thompson, instead. Michael went on to a major job in Hollywood as Chairman and Chief Executive of Sony Entertainment. Howard Davies, currently the Director of the London School of Economics, was also on the final list but he pulled out at the last moment.

To hear about both Pearson candidates Dennis Stevenson, the Chairman of Pearson, was invited along to see Christopher. To Dennis's surprise he found himself meeting the full Board of BBC Governors. I understand he was full of praise for me and that swung some doubting Governors my way.

Towards the end of a lengthy and very public process John Birt, Will Wyatt and friends decided that they should try harder to stop me getting the job and tried to directly influence the Governors against me. I know for certain that John told Heather Rabbatts, at that time Chief Executive of Lambeth Council and a relatively new Governor, that she mustn't vote for me as an outsider. Ron Neill, who by this time had left, was sent to see the Governor for Wales, Roger Jones, to try to turn him against me, but Roger, an entrepreneur in the pharmaceutical industry, was having none of it. Mark Byford was Ron Neill's protégé so naturally he wanted him to become Director-General.

There was also a good deal of leaking going on. In his book Will Wyatt owns up to placing a story in *The Times* about my giving money to both Chris Smith and Mo Mowlam to help fund their offices when they were shadow secretaries of state for culture. The story was true, but it was hardly a scoop, as the piece implied, as it came from a letter I had written to *The Independent* some years earlier. To be fair to Will Wyatt, he was the only person who later admitted straight out to me that he had opposed my appointment because he didn't think someone with such strong links to a political party should be Director-General. Later he wrote publicly that he had been wrong to oppose me and thought I had done the job well.

The only time I was seriously unnerved was late in the process when the remaining candidates were asked to write a confidential letter to the Governors outlining their political and business interests, including any political donations they had made. I outlined mine in full only to find the letter printed verbatim in *The Times* two days later. I suddenly realized that at least one Governor was leaking against me. Today I could make a good guess as to who it was.

But it was all to no avail, I had enough supporters with Christopher Bland and his Deputy Barbara Young (then Chairman of English Nature), Richard Eyre (the former Director of the National Theatre who had encouraged me to apply in the first place), Heather Rabbatts, Roger Jones, plus the support of at least two others.

I think it was on Wednesday 23 June, just before midnight, that Christopher rang me in the car. Sue and I had been to dinner with Jeremy and

Sue Beadle and it was memorable because Jeremy was on an odd diet and had walked into the restaurant with a bag of ingredients that he'd asked the chef to cook. When I picked up the phone Christopher said 'I'm afraid it's bad news. You got the job.' By then I was pretty sure it was mine, but I was still excited. It had been a long, tortuous, and unpleasant process, but I had made it. The boy from Hayes was going to run one of Britain's great institutions.

According to Will Wyatt, 'John was low. His plans and his strenuous efforts to influence events had failed.'

The following day I went to Broadcasting House to arrange the details of my contract. As my appointment had not yet been announced, and because the BBC wanted to keep it secret for as long as they could, I was taken into the building through a tunnel that ran from another BBC building on the other side of the road. It was a bizarre experience, as though I was going for a job in the secret service rather than the media. Inside I met Margaret Salmon, the rather cold Director of Human Resources, who outlined what I was being offered. I didn't question a single thing. I took what was on offer – including, I discovered later, a pension deal that was far inferior to the one enjoyed by other people in the BBC, including Margaret Salmon.

My view was simple. I had made a lot of money over the previous ten years, and this job wasn't about money. I had earned just under a million pounds in my last year with Pearson and was coming to the BBC to earn about a third of that. But I didn't care. I accepted the package they offered me, which included stipulations as to which shares I could keep, which ones I had to sell, and by when. Some months later that became important. The worst was that I had to give up being a director of Manchester United and give up my four seats in the directors' box at Old Trafford as both the BBC and Manchester United rightly saw it was a conflict of interest. You couldn't be on both sides of the negotiating table. My kids have never forgiven me for that.

I was joining as Deputy Director-General and Director-General Designate, which meant my initials inside the BBC now read as GD, DDG, DGD. With initials like that it was quite clear that I had joined the public sector. It was agreed I would join in November but would not become Director-General until 1 April 2000 to allow a five-month handover period – about four months longer than I reckoned was needed. In the end it was cut to three months because John Birt received his peerage and had to leave at the end of January 2000.

On Friday 25 June I turned up officially for the first time at Broadcasting House, where my appointment was to be announced, although it had been leaked and confirmed by the BBC the day before. I got there early and the only television crew outside was Sky News. The trouble was the cameraman had nipped off for a cup of tea and so missed my arrival. I felt sorry for him and restaged it.

We had a press conference with Christopher Bland, John Birt, and me on the podium. In discussions with James Hogan of the City public relations company Brunswick, who was advising me personally, I had decided that in the press conference or in any interviews I gave I would only talk about programmes because that was what I believed the BBC was all about. I also knew it was what the staff would want to hear and I had to start rebuilding morale immediately.

At the press conference virtually all the attention was on me, which was not surprising given that I was the new boy, but this immediately upset John Birt. I can only assume his ego was bruised. That weekend I took a call from Christopher saying that we had a problem with John, who was complaining that I hadn't been warm enough about him or praised his achievements enough at the press conference. In fact I don't think I'd mentioned John at all. I pointed out to Christopher that I was John's successor, not his mother; but as I certainly owed the job to Christopher's unswerving support, I did agree that from then on I would tell the staff at any meeting I attended what a great job John had done in modernizing the organization. But this would mean ignoring his biggest weakness: the fact that most of his staff hated him and everything he stood for.

I realized then what a long and miserable five months I faced before I finally took over and could truly speak my mind.

There were two further stories in the Murdoch newspapers that related directly to my joining the BBC. Both involved my private business dealings. When I'd first met up with Margaret Salmon, the BBC's Director of Human Resources, I'd offered to put all my business interests into a private trust, in the same way that politicians do when taking government office. She said that wouldn't be enough and that instead the BBC would want me to sell a whole range of shares by 6 April 2000, six days after I became Director-General.

The shares I was being asked to sell, which had all been outlined in the BBC's offer letter, included my shares in Granada, which I owned as a result of the Granada takeover of LWT, Pearson, and Manchester United. I agreed without question and started to sell all my shares in media companies.

On 16 January the *Sunday Times* published a story saying that I still owned £6 million worth of shares in Granada, the largest of the ITV companies. The story was true but irrelevant because I had been given until 6 April to sell them. The *Sunday Times* ran it as if it was a great exclusive and a scandal. It was a typically exaggerated Sunday newspaper story and quoted one BBC Governor as saying, 'Of course it's a conflict of interests, he must sell now', as if it was news to the Governor in question that I owned the shares. Richard Brooks, the journalist who wrote the article, even quoted Lord Rees-Mogg, a former Deputy Chairman of the BBC, saying, 'If he did not reveal to the BBC Governors that he had the shares when he was appointed, he should resign now', even though all my holdings had been revealed at the time of my appointment. I had told Brooks this myself.

It was the usual way in which certain journalists turn a small story into a large one. They phone people up who know nothing about the story and get them to say things on the basis that the story is true. There are always people, particularly opposition politicians of all parties, who are willing to do this simply to get their names in the papers. It is why, after four years at the BBC, I had little regard for those politicians who never let the facts stand in the way of publicity.

Where both the BBC and I had made a mistake was in not considering whether the date by which I had to sell the shares – 6 April – should have been brought forward when John Birt was appointed to the House of Lords and my starting date as Director-General was consequently brought forward to 1 February. Changing the sell-by date hadn't crossed my mind, or the Chairman's. In the end I decided that I could kill the story simply by selling all the shares, which I did the following week.

In late January *The Times* ran a story saying that I was involved in a property business in Devon at the same time as being Deputy Director-General – again implying that this was scandalous. They quoted John

Tusa, a former Head of the BBC World Service, as saying 'Call me old-fashioned but I think if you are running the BBC it ought to be a full-time job.' This time I heard that some of the Governors were concerned about this story, particularly Pauline Neville-Jones, the former Foreign Office official who had opposed my becoming Director-General. Soon after I joined the BBC John Birt told me that I should never assume the BBC Governors remembered what they'd decided at an earlier meeting: you always had to remind them. He was to be proved right on countless occasions.

When the Governors were discussing my property interests at their next meeting I took in the letter I had sent them during the application process outlining all my business dealings, the very letter that one of them had leaked to *The Times*. This included details of my political payments and my business interests, including property development. I also pointed out that I had offered to put these interests into a blind trust but that the BBC had decided this would not be necessary and that they had not asked me to sell the property interests.

That was the end of that particular story, but what both stories showed me was that my battle with certain sections of the press, particularly the Murdoch press, was only just beginning. During the appointment process *The Times* and its editor Peter Stothard had been humiliated. They were unlikely to leave it at that.

On 29 January 2000 I became the BBC's thirteenth Director-General, and the first who had not been either to a public school or to Oxbridge. I was also the first Director-General in peace time who had never previously worked for the organization.

CHAPTER EIGHT

The BBC Years (1)

At the end of my first week at the BBC I woke up very early thinking about what I had discovered. I was deeply depressed, so I got up and decided to write down what I was feeling. I thought it was important that I captured these feelings, if only for myself. I couldn't believe how bureaucratic and paper-driven the whole place was.

The worst point had been getting into my car on the Tuesday or Wednesday evening of that first week and finding an enormous pile of papers more than a foot high on the back seat. This was my reading for tomorrow. I pointed out to Emma Scott – who had been assigned to look after me as my business manager in the early weeks but who remained on my staff for the whole four years – that I hadn't read that much in my life and certainly wasn't going to start now.

What I learned in my first few weeks was that the main activity at the executive level of the BBC seemed to be writing and reading documents, reports, and policy papers. The aim seemed to be to produce the perfect policy paper; when it was completed and approved, that in itself would be enough. Of course that wasn't the case. I remember a senior figure at the BBC telling me in those early days that I needed to understand that if everyone at a BBC meeting appeared to agree on something you couldn't assume that they did agree, and you certainly couldn't assume that they would then do what had been 'agreed'.

After a while the message began to get around that I was refusing to read these ridiculously long reports. Instead of making them shorter some people started doing two – what they called the 'proper' one and a condensed version for me. In the end I managed to get all papers shorter, but the only way I could keep them that way was by complaining every few months when I spotted them getting longer again.

I'll always remember my first strategy conference. John Birt was still Director-General and he opened the session by saying that we weren't moving fast enough as an organization and that we had to get things done more quickly. He then proceeded to reject most of the detailed proposals on the agenda on the grounds that the papers that had been written for the conference weren't good enough. John was obsessed with getting everything dead right. Once a year he used to present his view of the BBC to the Governors' annual conference, usually held at a hotel somewhere in the South of England. His staff told me he would prepare as many as seventeen different versions of his presentation and rehearse it for days on end.

What I eventually worked out was that this was an organization that, at the top level, was risk averse. It commissioned more and more analysis and produced more and more papers to avoid taking risky decisions. The approach assumed, firstly, that the more analysis you undertook the more likely you were to take the right decision, not something that I have ever seen proven. Much more importantly, and the reason why the reports were so lengthy, was that if the policy went wrong you could point to an exhaustive paper trail to protect you. It was classic civil service mentality.

My own approach to organizations, business, and life is that you have to 'try things'. Some will work, others won't. If you try too many that don't work then you don't survive. It's as simple as that. On the other hand, if most of your initiatives work, then you end up being successful. What you can't do is analyse every good idea to death without taking a decision. If you do that everyone will lose enthusiasm for the project. At some time you have to decide to proceed, even if you are not 100 per cent certain, or else abandon the project – if only because everyone involved has had enough and is getting bored.

A good example of my approach came in my first year at the BBC when we decided to make a radical move, and make it quickly. The *Daily Telegraph* described it as follows:

This is a bad decision; for the BBC, for television in general, for the licence paying public, and for British political culture . . . In yielding to the forces of Philistinism at the corporation Mr Dyke is clearly signalling his priorities. They are evidently very different from those of the BBC's core viewers ... A philistine BBC is a supine BBC; a nation kept in ignorance is a nation easily led.

That was the *Daily Telegraph* leader on 15 August 2000. And the *Telegraph* wasn't alone. The media spokesmen for all three of the main political parties joined in the criticism of the BBC, as did some, though not all, of the other national newspapers.

According to the detractors, we were 'dumbing down' the BBC and the nation yet again. So what had we done? What momentous decision had we taken to bring such a tirade down on the heads of the BBC? The answer is that we had announced that we planned to move our nightly television news on BBC One from 9 p.m. to 10 p.m. Hardly the end of the civilized world as we knew it, but you wouldn't have known that from the reaction of politicians and the press.

ITV had occupied the ten o'clock slot with *News at Ten* for more than thirty-five years but had recently vacated it and were playing their news later. Their move had really upset the politicians and, under orders from Downing Street, Chris Smith, then Secretary of State for Culture, Media and Sport, had been trying desperately to 'persuade' ITV to move back. I had a lot of time for Chris and thought he was an excellent Secretary of State, and we were all surprised and disappointed when he was sacked after the 2001 election. But on this issue we disagreed.

Even before I joined the Corporation it was obvious to me that the BBC should move its news from nine o'clock into the 10 o'clock slot vacated by ITV. This would give the BBC two advantages. Firstly, it would increase the news ratings because the competition wasn't so strong at ten o'clock; secondly, it would allow the BBC to schedule more competitively at the crucial nine o'clock junction and enable us to start our drama, most of which couldn't be played before the nine o'clock watershed, at the same time as ITV rather than thirty minutes later.

We decided to make the move, got it unanimously approved by the BBC Governors, and agreed that I would announce it as part of the McTaggart lecture I was due to give at the Edinburgh Television Festival in August 2000, just six months after becoming Director-General. The story broke a day early, and I received an urgent phone-call from Chris

Smith asking me not to make the announcement. I told him I couldn't do that and phoned the BBC Chairman, Christopher Bland, to tell him what had happened. Christopher was indignant. His view was that the Governors had approved the change and that Chris Smith's view was therefore irrelevant. It was the Governors who were in control of the BBC, not the politicians.

So I went ahead and made the announcement and confirmed that we would be implementing the change some time during the following year, 2001. Then ITV announced on 21 September that they were going back to the ten o'clock slot that they had recently vacated. In a bizarre agreement between Charles Allen, the Chief Executive of Granada, and Patricia Hodgson, Chief Executive of the Independent Television Commission (who had clearly been heavily pressurized by the politicians), ITV had agreed to move their news back to ten o'clock but only on three days a week. Even more bizarrely, it wouldn't be the same three days every week. In return, the ITC was allowing ITV to run more advertisements in peak time. In scheduling terms the agreement was ridiculous. ITV's news eventually became known as *News at When* and its high reputation for news programming was seriously damaged.

When we heard about this our new Director of Television Mark Thompson and I decided we had two choices: scrap our plans or move quickly to implement them. We were helped by the weird proposal ITV had come up with. If their plan had been to move back into the slot five nights a week it would have made life difficult for us. As it was, Mark and I decided to press ahead quickly.

The Chairman, Christopher Bland, was all in favour and the Governors supported him. They all knew by then that the Government would take a dim view of it, but it was not, and must never be, the job of the BBC Governors to please the Government of the day – not that Governments and Secretaries of State ever fully understand that.

One journalist asked Christopher Bland if he would take the views of the Secretary of State into account when considering the matter of rescheduling the nine o'clock news. He famously replied: 'Yes, just like I would any other licence fee payer.' Downing Street was outraged; as I pointed out to Christopher, I thought he was there to stop me making injudicious remarks like that, not the other way round.

In my time at the BBC both Chris Smith and his successor, Tessa Jowell, couldn't resist lecturing us on what should and should not be shown on television. Politicians watch less television than any other group in the country but, sadly, this has never stopped them thinking they know more about it than the professionals. One of the problems we face in a representative democracy today is that politicians increasingly believe that they should be involved in all aspects of our lives and want us to accept that they know something about pretty much everything. And yet the people who go into politics are increasingly drawn from a narrow group who, having decided (probably at university) that they wanted to become politicians, have done little else with their lives. I know: I was nearly one of them. What most of them know about, and are obsessed with, is politics full stop.

Just two months after I had announced our plan to move the news to ten o'clock we did it, giving everyone in the BBC just two weeks' notice of the precise date of the change. Again we came under attack for making the change quickly, something publicly funded organizations are not supposed to do; doing it early, in response to ITV's announcement that it was moving its news; and doing it competitively, because we wanted to occupy the slot before they did.

The move excited the people inside BBC News because it meant doing something different and new. When the unions began to make noises about the move it was the staff who told them to back off. When we finally made the move we also doubled the length of the late-night regional news from three and a half minutes to seven and made it an integral part of the ten o'clock bulletin. This proved very popular across the BBC newsrooms in the Regions and Nations. I only heard of one person directly related to the BBC who was against the move: Michael Buerk's wife. Michael was one of two main presenters of the nine o'clock news and his wife realized it would mean that he'd get home an hour later. Quite understandably she didn't fancy that.

Moving the news was the single best thing we did in my first couple of years at the BBC. We stopped the decline in the ratings for the BBC's flagship news bulletin, they even went up a little, and the freeing-up of the schedule at nine o'clock was a major factor in BBC One overtaking ITV as Britain's most watched channel a year or so later.

But the biggest impact of moving the news at two weeks' notice was the message it sent to the whole of the BBC. It told everyone that we didn't have to be a large and unwieldy organization that analysed everything to death and couldn't take a decision quickly. We could move fast when we wanted to.

What the whole saga illustrated was the sort of intense public and political pressure an organization like the BBC comes under when it proposes even relatively minor changes. Opposition to change is not a new phenomenon at the BBC. As the Corporation's chief archivist said to me when I first joined: 'You do understand, don't you, the BBC has been accused of dumbing down from the day Reith invented it.'

In my McTaggart lecture I had foreseen the anguished cries we would get when I announced we were moving the news:

> Outrage from journalists, politicians, the great and the good and even some of the BBC's own staff at any change in BBC radio or television is a pattern you can find throughout the history of the BBC ... The point is that the real genius of the BBC is that it *has* adapted and changed over the years ... at crucial times in the BBC's history its leaders have recognized that change was essential and have taken the bold decision to introduce it despite loud protests from all around them.

I went on to say that change was essential at this particular time in the BBC's history:

> I believe the stark choice facing the BBC today is that we either change or we simply manage decline gracefully ... The changes happening in technology, in the wider society, and in our competitive environment make this one of those times in history when change at the BBC is essential.

We were only able to change the timing of the main evening news because the BBC was not controlled by the politicians, unlike most of the rest of the public sector. We, management and Governors, made our own decisions and took our own risks without reference to political masters.

In theory, taking risks ought to be easier in the public sector than in profit-and-loss companies: in the former, you don't go bust if the risk you take goes seriously wrong. But the reality is the opposite: publicly funded organizations are much more likely to avoid risk. The problem is that they are under much greater public scrutiny for the simple reason that they are spending public money. A single failure can be blown up by newspapers and politicians to such an extent that it does lasting damage to the organization, or to its leader.

As a result, there is a real danger that public-sector organizations err on the side of caution and do not take the calculated risks they ought to take if they want to improve the services they deliver to the public. For the downside of a risk going wrong in a publicly funded organization is public criticism, even public humiliation. Being wrong about the benefits of moving the news would have had serious consequences. On the other hand, the upside of taking the risk and being proved right was – what? I'm still waiting for the politicians and the newspaper editors who criticized our decision to concede it had, with hindsight, been the correct one.

The BBC I inherited would never have moved the news, and certainly not at the speed we did. There would have been at least a dozen policy papers on the issue, every possible ramification would have been considered at length – including the political opposition – and most likely nothing would have happened. Instead we just did it.

Moving the news was not the first major change I made at the BBC. Back in April 2000 a small group of us had produced a document entitled *One BBC*, which, amongst other things, proposed a new organizational structure for the Corporation. Soon after I'd arrived, John Birt and I had clashed over the appointment of a new Director of Broadcasting to replace Will Wyatt, who was due to retire in December 1999. John, who was still Director-General, wanted to make an immediate appointment. I didn't want to appoint a Director of Broadcasting at all. I couldn't see the point of the role and saw scrapping the Broadcasting Division in its totality as a good way of saving money.

The division had only been formed in 1995 as part of a McKinsey/Birt inspired reorganization known as the production/broadcasting split. In this everyone who produced programmes was put in one enormous division and had to sell their ideas to a much smaller but incredibly powerful Broadcasting Division. The important thing was that Broadcasting had all the money, and that gave it all the power. John had planned the production/broadcasting split in secret with McKinsey and hadn't even told his deputy Bob Phillis about it. He had 'just jumped it' on the organization, to use his words, because he believed that was the only way he could get it implemented.

In John's reorganized BBC, the Director of Broadcasting was responsible for virtually all the services – television, radio, and online. The role puzzled me: surely that was what the Director-General was meant to do? Why did the people in charge of television or radio have to report to the Director-General through another layer of management? In effect this meant the Controller of BBC One had to report to the Director of Television, who in turn had to report to the Director of Broadcasting, who then reported to the Director-General. It was nuts.

Having just been appointed to run the BBC, I knew that if I made a stand against the appointment of a new Director of Broadcasting the Governors would have little choice but to back me against John. Instead I suggested that the whole issue be referred to a small group I had set up to look at the changes I wanted to make inside the BBC, a committee that later became known as the 'One BBC' group, after the title of their report.

The Governors agreed with this suggestion but John was mightily upset because he knew what it meant: that this was only the beginning of the dismantling of some of what he had done. John was very wary of my small group and on at least one occasion he took one of the people on the 'One BBC' group away to a quiet room and 'suggested' to them, in a threatening way, that their role was to defend the status quo. It made no difference and only convinced me that, whatever happened, the group would not report until after John had left the BBC.

I don't know why he was so surprised that I wanted to restructure the organization. That's what all new chief executives do. There is no perfect organizational structure and constant rethinking is healthy for any organization. Mark Thompson, my successor as Director-General, has done precisely that.

I announced the 'One BBC' changes at a studio session on 1 April 2000, which was to have been my first day in charge had John not been elevated to the House of Lords in February. We also sent every member of staff a booklet entitled *Building One BBC*, which outlined the whole range of changes we planned to put into effect as quickly as possible.

In my introduction to the booklet I outlined the problems we needed to overcome:

> We have talked and listened to many people at all levels and in all parts of the BBC. We heard the same message again and again. People are proud to work for the BBC, but want to see changes . . . They think we have too many managerial layers and costly processes and that too much time is spent negotiating within the BBC. As a result, as an organization we simply move too slowly.

We disbanded the Broadcasting Division, saving about £5 million a year in the process, and in some areas like sport, children's programming, and radio we removed the artificial split between broadcasting and production altogether. Looking back now I wish we had been more radical and removed the split right across the BBC. I was too conservative and should have been bolder.

We divided the BBC's all-powerful Policy and Planning Department into two. I felt that the BBC's strategy was being too influenced by the policy people, who cared a great deal about what the politicians and Whitehall wanted and too little about the audience, the people who actually paid for the BBC. As a result of this decision Patricia Hodgson, who ran Policy and Planning, decided to leave the organization to become Chief Executive of the Independent Television Commission.

We centralized functions such as marketing so that there was only one Director of Marketing for the whole of the BBC rather than having a number of separate, competing marketing departments. This was an important change as marketing would clearly be taking on a bigger role in the BBC. In the multi-channel world more money has to be spent on marketing since there is no point spending millions on programmes if no one knows they are there or where to find them. We also set up a New Media department for the first time, bringing together all the online and interactive television departments across the BBC under a single director.

Probably the most controversial move came when we merged the old executive committee with the BBC's Board of Management; in future there would be only one management group running the BBC, the BBC Executive. In all there were to be seventeen in that group, all of whom would report directly to me. Some Governors asked, quite fairly, how could that many people all report directly to one boss? I believed it was possible and looked around for examples from around the world. I found what I thought was a good one – Enron, then one of the fastest growing, most successful companies in the world. When the Enron scandal broke a year later I prayed no one on the Board of Governors would remember that I'd held them up as an example.

The organizational structure was drawn up on paper as a series of colourful petals, with me at the centre. Christopher Bland always said I had only done it that way because I couldn't get all the people reporting directly to me on a normal organizational chart. Harsh, but probably true. The petal diagram was actually the work of our new Director of Strategy, Carolyn Fairbairn, who had a great artistic touch. The idea of the layout was to demonstrate a less hierarchical organization.

In my years at the BBC Carolyn was probably my closest confidante, along with the Finance Director John Smith. A former journalist on *The Economist* and a consultant with McKinsey's (I forgave her that), Carolyn had worked in John Major's policy unit in Downing Street and had the advantage of being a fairly recent recruit to the BBC. She is incredibly clever and good fun to work with. Most of all she shared my view of the world – let's just work it out and then get on with it, risks and all.

Over four years together, Carolyn and I dreamt up all sorts of initiatives for the BBC: just before I left we were writing the BBC's plans for a new charter together. In many ways she took on the role my old friend and colleague Tony Cohen used to play in my life: she'd do the detailed analysis and find an intellectual rationale for the things I instinctively believed were a good idea. But she would also tell me, in no uncertain terms, if she thought it *wasn't* a good idea, and at the beginning of my time at the BBC there weren't many people who felt able to do that.

The most important thing about the 'One BBC' reorganization was that it resulted in more programme people at the very top of the Corporation – after all, outstanding programmes were what the BBC was all about and why the public paid their licence fees. So of the seventeen jobs on the Executive, nine went to programme makers. But structure was only one part of 'One BBC'. It was also about money and my avowed aim to spend more of the BBC's income on programming and less on running the BBC.

I have always understood finance and on arrival was surprised to find how complex the finances of the BBC appeared; after all, it was only a spending organization. Everyone at the BBC used to say to me what a complicated organization it was. I used to reply that it didn't seem that way to me. We were given two and a half billion pounds a year and our job was to spend it. In the world I had come from, the hard bit was getting the two and a half billion.

The other thing I noticed at the senior levels of the BBC was that no one seemed to think anyone actually paid the licence fee. Even before I joined, I sat in a meeting discussing the likely licence fee settlement and was struck by how everyone just wanted as big an increase as possible. I suspect that most of the public sector is like this, but I kept thinking about the people 'out there', those for whom the licence fee is a lot of money. Shouldn't we have been talking about giving them value, not just seeing how big an increase we could get? This meeting simply assumed we gave them good value.

Within a couple of weeks of my becoming Director-General we got a comparatively generous licence fee settlement. Gavyn Davies, a distinguished economist who was later to become Chairman of the BBC, had written a brilliant paper on the funding of the BBC saying we needed more money and had recommended a two-tier licence fee in which people who had digital television and could receive the BBC's digital services would pay a larger fee. While it was a clever idea it was a non-starter. It met massive hostility from Rupert Murdoch's BSkyB, who believed it would be a deterrent to people going digital and as a result limit the potential of BSkyB's business. And, as I shall explain later, the New Labour Government was never likely to take on Rupert Murdoch.

However, the Prime Minister has always been a BBC supporter and he wanted a strong and vibrant BBC. In the end the licence fee agreement was an old-fashioned political carve-up. As so often happens in politics, Gavyn Davies's sophisticated analysis was largely irrelevant once the horse-trading started. There was initially a disagreement between Tony Blair and Chris Smith on one side and the Chancellor, Gordon Brown, on the other. Brown understandably didn't want to set a licence fee with an above-inflation increase for the next six years as he feared it would set a trend for the rest of the public sector.

But Blair and Smith were adamant. The BBC needed more money and some certainty about its funding, and in the end they got their deal – the BBC licence fee would increase by one and a half per cent a year above inflation every year until 2007. As it turned out, virtually all of the rest of the public sector got bigger average increases over the next four years.

While the discussions about the licence fee agreement were going on, Patricia Hodgson, who was then still at the BBC, organized a private meeting between Chris Smith and myself to discuss the future. My job was to convince Chris that any extra money would be well spent. It was private because John Birt was still Director-General and neither Chris nor I wanted to offend him and he was still running the licence fee negotiations for the BBC. John did a brilliant job in achieving such a good settlement.

At the meeting I told Chris I thought BBC One was underfunded, that we needed to spend more money outside London, that we had exciting plans in education, and that it was important that the BBC compete in the digital world. If we were to do all of this we would need some extra funding. When Chris Smith announced the licence fee settlement in February 2000 he fed my four priorities straight back to the BBC as part of the agreement and said that these were what he wanted us to spend the extra money on.

Chris also urged us to raise any further money we needed by making savings within the BBC – by selling assets and by expanding our commercial activities. Interestingly, four years earlier Virginia Bottomley, the last Conservative Secretary of State, had also urged the BBC to become more commercial. As a result, we did increase our commercial activities quite significantly over the next four years, as we'd been asked to do, and brought more money into the BBC as a result, only to find ourselves under attack from all sides for becoming 'too commercial'. In all, Chris Smith challenged us to raise an additional £1.1 billion over seven years. When I left the BBC we were on target to do better than that, though we had probably spent more than expected as well.

Led by the BBC's talented Director of Finance, John Smith, who had sat on my 'One BBC' group, we worked out a plan that would allow us to spend more money in my early years at the BBC, and claw it back in the later years. The logic was straightforward. The digital revolution was under way and we needed to play a big part in it immediately, not four years later when we would have the cash. By then it would be much harder to compete and make an impact.

At that time, the BBC had quite a large cash surplus and our plan was to spend it all, and more, and go into debt for the next three or four

My family in 1989. We had this picture taken to give to my mum and dad, who were celebrating their golden wedding. Sadly my dad died the following year. The children are (from left to right) Christine, Alice, Joe and Matthew.

TO ALL
LWT STAFF

As you may know I am Managing Director of LWT
as from today (Thursday, March 1).

I will be spending the day going round the building
in the hope of meeting as many people as I can personally.

My apologies if I miss anybody today. Over the next few months
I'll be meeting with all staff again, section by section,
to listen to what you think about our company
and to answer any questions.

If you've any questions about the company
that you'd like to ask today,
please drop them into my office by lunchtime.

Michael Aspel will put them to me on your behalf
at 3.45 this afternoon on the set of Aspel & Company.
You can watch us on Channel 6 on the internal monitors.

Lastly, if you are around at lunchtime,
do drop by the bar to say hallo.

Greg Dyke

Above: The message I sent to LWT staff on my first day as managing director. I wanted them all to know that my approach was different.

Left: Christopher Bland and I were a good team both at LWT and the BBC, and I learned a lot from him and liked him enormously.

Above: The great match at Wembley when I played in David Frost's team against Jimmy Tarbuck's side immediately before the 1987 Cup Final. I was scared to death playing in front of all those people. John Birt (fifth from left, back row) played in the same match and even scored a goal. I'm standing next to Daley Thompson.

Right: Steve Cram chopping me from behind in the same match, which ended in a 1–1 draw with Daley Thompson scoring a great goal for our side.

Left: A joke poster we drew up at LWT as we bid to retain the London weekend franchise. We managed to keep the size of our bid confidential to the very end.

CARELESS TALK
COSTS
FRANCHISES

Below: LWT's top management with our stars on the day we retained the franchise. We partied all night. Front row (left to right): Michael Aspel, Denis Norden, Michael Barrymore, Cilla Black, myself, Jeremy Beadle, Brian Walden. Back row (left to right): Brian Tesler, Brian Moore, Marcus Plantin, Matthew Kelly, Melvyn Bragg, Trevor Phillips, Christopher Bland.

years. The increase in spending would then flatten off. The idea was to end the charter period in 2007 with little or no debt and with our annual income exceeding expenditure. To achieve this we knew that some time during that period we would have to sell one of the BBC's large assets. In my last year at the BBC we began the process of selling BBC Technology, the proceeds of which would repay the overdraft and reduce our expenditure on technology going forward.

I explained this financial strategy to the audience at Edinburgh in my McTaggart lecture in August 2000. Of course no one took much notice. They were far more interested in the sexier announcements. But what I said was this:

> By 2007 this [the licence fee settlement] will produce a real increase of £250 million in that year compared with our income in 1999. But 2007 is too late. If we want to shine in the new competitive digital age, and we must, we need to spend more money now, which is why I've spent so much time in my first six months as Director-General looking for ways to save money right across the BBC.

By the year 2000, when I gave the McTaggart lecture, the BBC was already a very different place from what it had been a decade earlier.

At the start of the Nineties, most television companies in Britain, including the BBC, had absolutely no idea about the true cost of anything. Large standing armies of cameramen, sound men, editors, make-up people, and the rest were employed and apportioned out to programme teams. The teams didn't pay for them and had little choice whom they got. The cost was carried in a massive central overhead and the people who ran these facilities budgets were kings. They handed out the resources and in many ways they controlled television.

Programme makers in areas like sport always did pretty well because they controlled tickets to sporting events: whenever you went to any of these the managers of the facilities divisions were always there, being well looked after. It was a corrupt, inefficient, appallingly organized system and needed to be changed. We changed it at LWT when I became Managing Director in 1990 and the BBC followed suit in the early Nineties.

When John Birt began to introduce change at the BBC it was on a massive scale. It was called 'producer choice' and I remember when I was still at LWT being asked to go to meet two or three different groups who were being asked to come up with ways to modernize the BBC. On the first occasion I went to a breakfast meeting with one working party at Bush House, home of the World Service. I turned up to find we were all having a full silver-service breakfast with three people waiting on us.

As we started the discussion I asked who was paying for the waiters. I was the only non-BBC person there and everyone else looked at each other. One person finally said, 'Well, the BBC are paying,' to which I replied, 'Yes, but who? Whose budget is paying for them? Whose cash is it?' Silence again. So I said, 'Can I suggest that until you know who is paying for them the rest of this meeting is a waste of time.' Thankfully, John Birt's reforms meant that by the time I arrived at the BBC these sorts of excesses had disappeared. By then everyone knew what everything cost.

On another occasion I was taken by a group through their plans for 'producer choice'. What it meant was that every producer in the BBC would have the choice of either buying their resources, such as studios, film crews, and outside broadcast units, from inside the BBC or from outside providers. I applauded the idea of knowing what everything cost and having internal trading at proper market prices but I cautioned against going full scale down that route. I pointed out that if you had the people and resources you needed sitting idle while producers were spending real cash outside the building you were in danger of paying for everything twice. I was told, by a group of people who had only ever worked in the public sector, that I was not being ambitious enough, that this sort of change would only work at the BBC if it went all the way. No half-way solutions would work there. It was like meeting a group of zealots.

This was madness and the system was still in operation when I got to the BBC. One of the first things I did was to stop the Children's Department from moving *Blue Peter* to Granada's studios in Manchester. It was explained to me that this would be cheaper for the programme as Granada were offering a good deal, even though it meant laying out real cash both for the cost of the studios and travel and hotel accommodation every week to get the team to Manchester. I pointed out that while it might be cheaper for a particular programme, it would cost the BBC overall a lot more because it was already paying for the studio in London that *Blue Peter* was vacating.

No commercial organization would or did operate like this, and in my first year I had to persuade all sorts of people that we needed a more pragmatic approach: producer choice was a good idea in principle, but not if you took it to extremes.

One of the first questions I asked when I joined the BBC was, what proportion of our expenditure was being spent on running the institution of the BBC itself? I was shocked to find that the figure was 24 per cent. It meant that almost a quarter of everyone's licence fee was being spent on the organization's overheads – going on things that had little to do with programmes or services. All organizations have overheads, but 24 per cent was a ridiculous figure and I set a target to reduce that to 15 per cent by 2004. In fact we did better than that: the figure for the financial year ending April 2004 was down to 12 per cent.

We achieved this partly by making some easy moves, such as not spending £20 million a year on outside consultants, most of which was going to McKinsey, and massively reducing the amount of internal charging between departments, which meant we could cut the spending on bureaucracy. We reduced the number of business units that could send invoices to each other from three hundred down to sixty. With the processing cost of each invoice at around £100 a transaction, this alone saved serious money.

We also made big savings in areas like personnel, where the BBC had one personnel employee for every forty members of staff whilst the average across British companies was closer to one for eighty. Too many managers at the BBC simply handed over people management to the Human Resources Department.

One particular cost-saving move got a good deal of publicity by accident. One day, early on, I said to my PA that I didn't want croissants at any of my meetings because I was putting on weight. I'm one of those people who will eat a croissant if it is there, even if I'm not hungry. She sent out an e-mail saying that I didn't want croissants at my meetings in future. Within days it was all over the newspapers that I had banned croissants from the BBC.

I didn't object to the publicity as I wanted everyone in the BBC to know that I intended to cut back on anything that diverted money away from programmes; but the story wasn't true. What I did ban was people taking cabs between the BBC's various sites in London. Instead I laid on a free bus service between the centres and saved hundreds of thousands

GREG DYKE: INSIDE STORY

of pounds in the process. In his autobiography, *Chance Governs All* (2001), the former Chairman of the BBC, Duke Hussey, relates the tale of a taxi driver moaning bitterly to him about me for undermining the livelihood of London cabbies. The three C's – croissants, cabs, and consultants – thus became part of the legend of the spending cuts I was making all around the BBC.

But the biggest savings of all came as a result of changes in the finance area where we went through the agony of changing all our software systems across the organization to enable us to know far more about what we were spending and where. This meant we could have a more effective central purchasing system so that we could negotiate much better pan-BBC deals. We reduced the number of companies supplying services to the BBC from 150,000 to 9,000.

In doing all this we also found out some amazing things. For instance we discovered we were paying 120 different stationery suppliers, despite the fact that the BBC was supposed to use only one. We also discovered that 90 per cent of the bills we were paying did not have a proper purchase order. All this changed and we saved a fortune. We had far fewer bills to pay and overall we needed far fewer people working in finance. John Smith halved the size of the finance department from 1,000 staff to 500 over four years while also making the systems much more efficient.

As part of 'One BBC' every division inside the BBC was asked to produce its own plan to cut the overhead. By this initiative alone we cut 1,100 jobs. The total savings from 'One BBC' came to £166 million a year, significantly more than we received from the increase in the licence fee in my time at the BBC.

I explained all this in my McTaggart lecture in August 2000. Having announced to everyone that we were moving the news I went on to talk about money. I told the audience of broadcasters and programme makers that we were increasing the spend on programmes and services by £100 million that year, by £250 million the next year, and by a further £130 million the year after. I said:

That means in the year 2002/3 we will be spending £480 million a year more on our programmes and services than we spent last year, a 30 per cent real increase in programme spend over just three years. This amounts to the biggest increase in programme expenditure in

BBC history ... More than half of that money will have been saved inside the BBC and this will not be achieved without real pain and a lot of people will have lost their jobs through no fault of their own ... however, the obligation must be on us to spend as much as possible on programmes.

The next section of the lecture was the bit that really interested the audience. If we were increasing our spend by £480 million a year, where were we going to spend it? Most of the audience were interested because they wanted to know if they were going to get any of it. I explained briefly that some of the extra money had already been allocated to BBC One, which had been doing particularly badly in the ratings. It had been short of cash for some years, and was being widely criticized for being old-fashioned and out of touch. There were politicians who were saying we couldn't justify the licence fee if the figures for BBC One didn't improve. Four years later some of the same people were complaining it was too successful. This is the great dilemma all Director-Generals of the BBC face. When you do well in the ratings you are accused of 'dumbing down' and not taking minority programming seriously enough. When you are doing badly you are accused of failing the popular audience. As I've said many times, it is the only job in the world where you get crap for losing and crap for winning.

To try to revive the failing BBC One I had decided to increase the annual spending on it by £115 million a year, a 15 per cent increase. The Director of Television, Mark Thompson, and his new Controller of BBC One, Lorraine Heggessey, spent most of the additional money on drama. Some went on increasing *EastEnders* to four slots a week, *Holby City* to 52 weeks a year, and increasing the run of *Casualty*. But the vast bulk of the money went on drama series for the new 9 p.m. drama slot: *Waking the Dead*, *Judge John Deed*, *Merseybeat*, and *Red Cap* were all products of this new money. When Mark Thompson left the BBC for Channel Four his replacement, Jana Bennett, carried on very much the same strategy of investing heavily in drama.

What none of us knew at that time, in 2000, was that advertising revenue worldwide was about to drop dramatically. ITV's revenue was at an all-time high, but over the next two years it fell by 15 per cent, and in real terms it is unlikely to get back up to the 2000 figure until the latter part of this decade. So at the very moment I had boosted spending on BBC One, ITV had to cut spending as its advertising fell. Within two years BBC One had overtaken ITV as Britain's most popular channel for the first time, not because BBC One's ratings share was growing dramatically but because ITV's was falling fast.

We also allocated a great deal of the extra money to developing a series of new digital channels. Anyone who had followed broadcasting developments in the United States over the previous twenty years understood what had happened to the big three broadcasters, CBS, NBC, and ABC. In his book *Three Blind Mice* Ken Auletta, the distinguished media columnist for the *New Yorker* magazine, had described how the three network companies had gone into decline because they failed to expand as the multi-channel world hit the USA. As a result, all three were bought by enormous conglomerates and have become small, if important, parts of the wider broadcasting landscape.

With the coming of BSkyB and cable television to Britain there was a danger of the same thing happening here. The advent of the digital revolution meant that there was more broadcasting capacity and many more channels would be made available. The BBC and ITV, who had both seen significant falls in their share of viewing since BSkyB was launched, were in danger of being marginalized over the coming years.

My predecessor, John Birt, had recognized this and had opened up new channels with BBC Choice, BBC Knowledge, and News 24 – but only News 24 had been properly funded. That day in Edinburgh, just six months after taking over at the BBC, I announced the biggest expansion in television services in the BBC's history. I said:

> We believe that in the age of digital television it will not be sufficient for the BBC to offer only two mixed genre channels which are somehow supposed to meet the needs of everyone. This is not how audiences will want to receive television in the future. We need a more coherent portfolio of channels.

I announced that we planned to scrap BBC Choice and BBC Knowledge and launch two children's channels (CBeebies and CBBC), a new network for younger people (BBC Three), and a cultural network (BBC Four) to add to BBC News 24 and BBC Parliament. I explained that this would be our channel portfolio for the digital world and that there were a number of guiding principles involved.

One was that all the channels would eventually be available free to everyone whether on cable, satellite, or digital terrestrial. When the whole of Britain was digital, everyone would have access to all our channels. I explained that as the number of channels on digital terrestrial was limited, we therefore had to limit our expansion. I also explained that these initiatives represented the most we could afford.

By far the most important principle I outlined was that these would be overwhelmingly *British* channels, commissioning and broadcasting original *British* programmes. The greatest danger of multi-channel television is that it will lead to television around the world being dominated by American programming. As the richest market in the world, the USA can afford to make more programmes than any other country. The result could well see the world becoming dominated by US culture.

So far in Britain we have avoided that, largely because of the BBC and the way it is funded. We spend more money per head on original television programmes than any country in the world, including the USA, because of the way we fund the BBC. To compete with the BBC, both ITV and Channel Four have to spend a lot of money on original UK production. Take away the BBC and ITV would certainly spend less. In announcing a new tranche of channels for the BBC our aim was both to keep pace in the expanding multi-channel world and also to ensure that some of the new digital channels were overwhelmingly British, reflecting our society and our culture.

Having announced the channels we wanted to broadcast we still had to persuade the Secretary of State to give them the go-ahead. There was a lot of opposition to the children's channels from the large US media companies such as Disney, Viacom, and Rupert Murdoch's Fox, which had already started children's channels on satellite television in Britain. This was an easy battle to win.

These channels were overwhelmingly cartoon-based, broadcasting American programming on services littered with adverts. Our case was that British parents had the right to choose whether or not their children watched American channels or two BBC children's channels that were wholly British, reflected our culture, and carried educational material, all without ads. I met all sorts of US executives at that time bleating that it wasn't fair that the BBC was using public money to compete with them. My reply was that it wasn't fair that they were building new businesses in Britain by 'dumping' US programming in the British market. I love winding up American media executives because so many of them suffer from the disease of not understanding that American hegemony might not be in the best interests of the world.

We secured permission for the children's channels and they were launched in February 2002. CBeebies was an instant hit amongst the under-fives but CBBC took longer to connect with the older audience at which it was aimed. Both are now very successful. There was little opposition to BBC Four, which was launched the following month in March 2002. The big battle was over BBC Three and it was a battle with Channel Four.

It was about this time that Mark Thompson left the BBC to take over as Chief Executive of Channel Four. I encouraged him to go, even though I didn't want to lose him. He had only ever worked at the BBC and needed wider experience if he was to succeed me as Director-General. At that time there were only two potential candidates as my successor inside the BBC – the two Marks, Thompson and Byford. While both had real talents, Mark Thompson was always the more likely to get the job.

Mark Thompson had moved around the BBC a lot: as he openly jokes, he never stayed anywhere long enough to be found out (an experience I fully understand). One of his great claims to fame was when, as editor of *Panorama*, he broadcast the programme revealing that Robert Maxwell was fiddling the 'Spot the Ball' competition in the *Daily Mirror*, which of course he owned. When I gave Mark's farewell speech at the BBC in 2002 I mentioned this, but also pointed out that the programme hadn't spotted that Maxwell had also stolen the whole of the Mirror Group's pension fund.

Mark had been an outstanding Controller of BBC Two and was a natural for the Channel Four job when Michael Jackson gave it up to go to the States. I always remember Mark's words to me when he told me he had got the job: he said that whatever happened at Channel Four, he would continue to support our application to launch BBC Three. Someone from Channel Four must have heard this because within days, before Mark had actually joined them, Channel Four came out against BBC Three on the grounds that it could damage their advertising revenue. Given that Channel Four's income had grown by 13 per cent per annum for the past decade this was pathetic. The problem was that 2001 was the beginning of the slump in advertising revenue in the UK and people at Channel Four were panicking. For the first time their total revenue was falling.

In the middle of this process we had the 2001 General Election and Chris Smith was replaced by Tessa Jowell as Secretary of State at the Department of Culture, Media and Sport. Tessa had a terrible first couple of years and was regarded as a lightweight in the media industry. We all thought she was there because she was a Blairite who would do what Downing Street told her to do. That was certainly the case during the passing of the 2003 Communications Act: measures her department didn't agree with were put into the bill, and thus became law, at the initiative of Downing Street. There is no doubt that the change in the rules that allowed US media companies to own ITV, even though European companies are prevented from owning networks in the USA, was a Downing Street initiative and had nothing to do with Tessa Jowell and DCMS. In time, after the departure of Alastair Campbell (to whom Tessa was very close) and after Blair had been weakened by public reaction to the Iraq war, the general view across the industry has been that she became far more effective as a Minister. It was left to Tessa Jowell to make the decisions about our new channels, particularly BBC Three. In the end it got the go-ahead, and I have to admit that the channel was better for the process Tessa put it through. BBC Three was finally launched in February 2003.

The coming of the digital age did not only affect television. We recognized that we had to expand across the whole digital world, which meant moving into digital radio as well as digital television, developing interactive television, and expanding our online activities. Digital radio eventually took off in 2003 when the radio manufacturers finally decided to produce digital radio sets and, surprise, surprise, found there was a great demand for them. The consumer response was immediate; people were keen to get more radio stations and the better quality signal that came with digital radio.

Up until then the history of digital radio was a classic chicken and egg situation. The manufacturers wouldn't produce digital radios until there were more digital services available, and the BBC and commercial radio stations wouldn't fund new digital services until the manufacturers produced and sold enough radios. It was Jenny Abramsky, the BBC's Director of Radio, who broke that deadlock. When the history of radio in this period is written, Jenny should get most of the credit for turning British radio digital.

Jenny is an infuriating person. Some days she is charming and reasonable; on others her paranoia that radio is a second-class citizen to television within the BBC makes her difficult to deal with. She believes passionately that inside the BBC radio is unloved and as a result is underfunded. Her argument is simply wrong: BBC radio stations are probably the best funded in the world, and are certainly significantly better funded than any competitors in Britain. The same, however, is not true of BBC One or BBC Two: ITV and Channel Four are at least as well funded. For instance, there is not a radio station anywhere in the world that receives the £70 million a year it costs to run Radio Four. As a lifelong Radio Four listener I am a true supporter of the channel; but sometimes it has to be acknowledged that it is well funded – just as it has to be recognized that Radio Four is a service that disproportionately appeals to, and serves, the South of England.

In the end it was the BBC who broke the stalemate with the radio manufacturers, and this was completely down to Jenny Abramsky. Without her commitment to, and promotion of, digital radio it simply wouldn't have happened. She persuaded, cajoled, and threatened everyone inside the BBC to support the plan to develop a series of new BBC digital radio services. And it was the arrival of those services that finally persuaded the radio manufacturers to start producing digital radios.

The BBC took the decision to spend £18 million a year on a range of new digital radio services at the same time as we committed to expanding our television portfolio. It was the right decision, even though it also meant our spending many more million actually paying for the transmission system that would enable 85 per cent of the population to receive digital radio. The truth is that none of us would have dared to suggest that we shouldn't set aside the money to fund our new digital radio stations when we were expanding in television. We would have all been too scared of incurring Jenny's wrath.

There was no problem persuading the Secretary of State to approve the new radio stations because the commercial radio companies were actually in favour of the BBC expansion. They wanted digital radio to work and knew that only the BBC was big enough to drive it. So over the next eighteen months the BBC launched four new radio stations: Five Live Sports Extra, 1Xtra, 6 Music, and BBC 7. We also turned the Asian Network into a national network.

BBC Radio's share of the total market went up almost every year during my time at the BBC, driven mainly by the incredible success of Radio Two nationally but also by the performance of Radio Four in the London area, where it is the most listened-to radio station, ahead of all the commercial stations. When I joined the BBC, I hadn't listened to Radio Two for years. I still thought it was the service for my Auntie Muriel and thought of it as *Sing Something Simple* and *Friday Night is Music Night*. It was only when I started listening that I, like millions of others of my age, found it was now playing 'our' music. All my favourite artists – Bob Dylan, Bruce Springsteen, Crosby Stills & Nash, and others – were now all to be found on Radio Two.

But I suppose it was discovering Jonathan Ross's show on a Saturday morning that finally changed my attitude to Radio Two. In some ways I was responsible for the Ross family being on television and radio in the first place – I had given Paul, Jonathan's elder brother, his first job in television when I was running *The Six O'Clock Show* at LWT, and Jonathan followed Paul into the business. I was really touched when Jonathan gave £500 towards the fund to buy the advert in the *Telegraph* the weekend after I left the BBC. Jonathan's radio show is essential listening for me. I listen not for the music but to hear his banter, wit, and personal anecdotes. He has the same skill Victoria Wood possesses: that amazing ability to talk about the everyday things of life and make you laugh about them.

The third major growth area in my time at the BBC was online services. The BBC's online activity had started, like so many good ideas in many organizations, without anyone on top knowing much about it, but it was eventually championed by John Birt. The BBC spent a considerable amount of time, both before my arrival and after, deciding how much of the BBC's online services should be commercial and how much should be public service, funded by the licence fee. This was an occasion where moving comparatively slowly saved us from disaster.

When I arrived it was at the height of the dot-com boom, and with the BBC owning the most visited websites in Europe there was a potential fortune there for the taking. But by the time we had worked out where the boundary between public service and commercial activity should lie, it didn't matter any more. The dot-com bubble had burst and it was clear that, other than in exceptional circumstances, people were not going to pay for information on the web. It became obvious that brilliant online services like BBC News, BBC Sport, and many of our educational sites could only exist if they were publicly funded.

Ashley Highfield joined us to run the newly created New Media division. Ashley is one of the most inventive people I know and our one-to-one monthly meetings were amongst the most creative and stimulating I had in my time as Director-General. He always had a new or different idea that he wanted to bounce around. With my limited knowledge of new media I enjoyed testing his ideas and acting as his technically illiterate sounding-board.

Ashley didn't have an easy task bringing all the BBC's online activity under one division, but he did it with great success. By early 2004, when I left, the BBC's website, bbc.co.uk, was reaching ten million adults every month, making it the BBC's fourth biggest service after BBC One, BBC Two, and Radio Two. More than 50 per cent of the people of Britain are now online, and nearly 50 per cent of them regularly use the BBC's sites.

The BBC is criticized by other British content providers on the web, particularly the national newspapers, for spending too much public money on its services and squeezing its competitors out of the available space. This is largely irrelevant. What is certain is that the BBC's websites are outstanding and that UK-originated sites of this quality would simply not have happened without the BBC and without public funding. Again the choice was straightforward: either the BBC developed and competed in this area or the Americans would have free rein to dominate the web in the UK. I'd challenge anyone to go onto, say, the CBeebies website and fail to recognize its value to the young children of Britain today.

The facts simply don't support the argument that if the BBC had not moved into providing online broadcasting services other British companies would have done so instead. It was *because* the BBC was publicly funded that it could be original, take risks, and develop sites in great depth. The commercial sector would never have done this: as the dot-com collapse demonstrated, there was no revenue base for these sorts of sites. Increasingly, in the broadband era, the web will be used for delivering moving pictures as well as text, and then newspapers will be left far behind. What the BBC has achieved on the web is remarkable.

Ashley Highfield was also put in charge of developing interactive television on the BBC. Here he was starting with a clean sheet. His first big venture turned into an amazing success when BSkyB viewers were able to receive interactive Wimbledon coverage for the first time in 2001, enabling them to choose any one of four matches being played at the same time. In all, 63 per cent of the audience watching on the BSkyB platform pushed the red interactive button and watched the service at some time during the championships. BBCi, as the interactive service is called, now offers viewers the chance to vote, watch additional footage, and find out more information about a whole range of programmes from *Test the Nation* to *Restoration*, and from *Question Time* to coverage of the Chelsea Flower Show.

Looking back now I find it remarkable how fast we moved in that first year at the BBC. We reorganized the whole place, found ways of saving enormous amounts of money, and outlined what we planned to do over the next two years. We then simply did it.

CHAPTER NINE

The BBC Years (2)

For many years I have objected to, and feared, the stranglehold Rupert Murdoch has been securing on the British media. I could never understand why so few people seemed to understand or care about it. When it was recently suggested that Murdoch might move his papers in Britain en masse away from supporting Labour, virtually no one seemed alarmed that we had ended up in this country with such a significant concentration of power in the hands of one person. One person who is not even British: an Australian who is now a US citizen and who lives in New York. Similarly, when it was reported that Tony Blair had decided to hold a referendum on the issue of a European constitution as a way of trying to keep the Murdoch papers on side, it was remarkable how little reaction it caused.

It could be that Britain has grown to accept the power that Rupert Murdoch wields, but I still find it deeply offensive and worrying.

It is extraordinary that, after having had cross-media laws in this country since 1963, we have ended up in exactly the position those laws were intended to prevent. The legislation was aimed at stopping anyone getting too much power over the media, and as a result having too much power over the politicians. Yet in Rupert Murdoch that is precisely what we now have. Controlling 35 per cent of the national daily circulation of newspapers in this country, and 41 per cent of the Sunday market, makes him very powerful indeed. By chairing and effectively controlling BSkyB he also runs Britain's most financially successful broadcasting operation, which, if unchecked, could in the years to come dominate broadcasting in the way Murdoch's News International dominates the print media.

British broadcasting is in danger of sleepwalking into Murdoch's control.

Of course the editors of Murdoch's newspapers all pretend they don't jump to his tune, but no one doubts that on the really big issues he calls the shots. Murdoch was an avid supporter of the war against Iraq and all his 175 newspapers around the world supported the policy. The story that there was one exception, a small paper in Papua New Guinea, turns out not to be true. It simply gave prominence to a reader's letter that was against the war. All 175 newspapers just happened, by chance, to follow the Murdoch line.

So far Sky News, Murdoch's excellent television news operation in Britain, has followed the British broadcasting tradition of aspiring to political impartiality, but there is no guarantee that this will continue into the future. Fox News, Murdoch's 24-hour news channel in the USA, has been incredibly successful by adopting a blatantly right-wing agenda. During the Iraq war its ratings went up by 300 per cent and it overtook the market leader, CNN. Andrew Heywood, President of CBS News, was deeply concerned about the success of Fox News. He said that the long tradition of objective and fair journalism in the USA was threatened by the Fox effect. A University of Maryland study found that Fox News viewers in the USA were the most likely to believe three major misperceptions of 'facts' about the war: that US troops had found evidence of close pre-war links between the Saddam regime and al-Qaeda; that the US had found weapons of mass destruction in Iraq; and that world opinion was in favour of the US going to war.

When the Hutton report was published in January 2004, Fox News said on air that 'the BBC was forced to pay up for its . . . frothing at the mouth anti-Americanism that was obsessive, irrational and dishonest . . . it felt entitled to not only pillory Americans and George W. Bush but it felt entitled to lie'. There are some who believe that Murdoch wants Sky News to follow the same commercially successful route as Fox News. He reputedly calls Sky News 'BBC Light'.

The British Labour and Liberal parties should be very nervous of this happening: it would mark the beginning of the end of impartial broadcast news as we know it today in Britain. On both radio and television people in the UK have access to a range of political views in a way they don't in the newspapers they read. One of the reasons you buy the *Daily Mail* or *The Guardian* is that it tends to reflect your own political views. So far that hasn't been true of broadcasting. One thing we can now be certain of in the UK is that the politicians are not strong enough successfully to resist Murdoch.

Back in the early Nineties, when I was Chief Executive of LWT, I persuaded Barry Cox, then Director of Corporate Affairs at LWT, to have a chat with his friend and former neighbour Tony Blair, at that time a rising star in the Labour Party. I wanted Barry to warn Blair about the scale of the operation Murdoch was building up with his expansion into television in Britain. Barry told me at the time that the warning had completely backfired. Tony Blair had recognized the danger but his reaction to the warning was not the one either of us expected. Blair had said, in effect, that he believed Labour might have to do a deal with this man.

Although unable to stand up to the Murdoch empire – for Blair and Alastair Campbell, having *The Sun* supporting Labour was much more important – when he became Prime Minister Tony Blair recognized that a strong BBC was essential as a counterweight to Murdoch, which is why he supported an increase in the licence fee. The great tragedy is that New Labour would have won the 1997 General Election with or without the support of Murdoch's newspapers and so could have campaigned on a policy to reduce the size and power of his empire. Sadly, after eighteen years out of power, they didn't have enough confidence to do it. Instead, New Labour has allowed Murdoch's power to grow and has done very little, if anything, in seven years that is likely to offend him.

In fact this Government would have allowed Murdoch's empire in Britain to grow even larger. Had the original Government bill outlining the 2003 Communications Act gone through, BSkyB would have been allowed to buy one of the traditional terrestrial broadcasters, Channel Five. Thankfully, the parliamentary joint committee chaired by Labour peer Lord Puttnam insisted that the Act should include a media plurality test, which makes it extremely unlikely that Murdoch will now be allowed to own a terrestrial television station. According to David Puttnam, he was not thanked by Downing Street for his efforts.

All of this might suggest I'm not a fan of Rupert Murdoch, which is not true. I admire the way he has built up his enormous media empire; I admire the loyalty he gets from his staff, and the speed at which he moves; and I admire his drive and imagination. He is without doubt the most successful media operator of the last twenty years. Whenever I've met him I, like many others, have fallen under the Murdoch spell. But I find the way he uses politicians, as well as his attitude to democracy, worrying. He has found a way of subverting the democratic process to extend his own power and his own business interests. For electoral reasons politicians around the world, including both main political parties in Britain, have gone along with it.

Murdoch has never been a fan of the BBC. I suspect the idea that a publicly funded broadcaster should be so successful offends his very view of the world. It certainly limits his business potential in Britain. So whenever the opportunity arises, Murdoch or his people will always criticize the BBC, as they did on several occasions during my period as Director-General.

Now I'm no longer at the BBC I will happily admit that many of the moves I made in my years there, particularly in my last two years, were designed to ensure that the organization was big enough and strong enough to stand up to Murdoch. It was my view that Murdoch and his people would do all they could to damage the BBC, not because they believed it was in the public interest to do so, but because it was in their commercial interests to have a smaller and less influential BBC. To counter this, I believed anything I could do to limit the power and influence of BSkyB would, in turn, be very much in the public interest. In my last two years as Director-General we made two moves that I believed were to the long-term advantage of the BBC and broadcasting generally in Britain, moves which would prevent BSkyB from dominating broadcasting in this country. The first was perhaps the most important decision I took in my four years at the BBC: the launch of Freeview.

The story of Freeview goes back to 1998 when two ITV companies, Carlton and Granada, joined up with BSkyB to bid for the new digital terrestrial television (DTT) licences. At that time DTT was seen as an exciting new way of delivering digital television to the home through traditional television aerials. The On Digital consortium, as the three bidders called their new venture, were awarded the licences but existing broadcasters such as the BBC and Channel Four were also given additional spectrum on the new system.

Michael Green, Chairman of Carlton, was a DTT enthusiast from the beginning and his company did all the research and analysis for the bid. He believed it was an important strategic move for his company. Sadly, it went seriously wrong for him. The Granada involvement was very different. Up to a couple of weeks before the consortium won the licences Granada had had no intention of bidding: they'd undertaken no research, and were only involved because they didn't want to be left out when they discovered that Carlton and BSkyB had joined together to bid. Granada bid blind.

The consortium's original business plan estimated that their maximum investment would be £350 million. After they'd lost £1.2 billion of their shareholders' money, Granada and Carlton finally pulled the plug and ITV Digital went bust in early 2002. Oddly, the company changed its name from On Digital to ITV Digital when it was in dire economic trouble, perhaps one of the worst branding decisions of all time.

Things began to go wrong for the company even before the services were launched. From the moment the European Commission ruled that it was anti-competitive for BSkyB to be part of the consortium, as they already dominated the satellite pay-television sector in the UK, the business was in trouble. That was the moment when Granada and Carlton made their crucial mistake. Instead of pulling out they decided to compete head to head with BSkyB in the pay-television market. They were murdered. BSkyB simply had too much money and muscle for the fledgling On Digital to compete.

When BSkyB started giving away digital boxes, On Digital had no option but to do the same, even though they couldn't afford to. And in June 2000, when football rights were being sold for enormous figures, On Digital was in there paying a fortune for the rights to broadcast Football League matches. They paid three times what they were worth.

But what really killed On Digital was that the technology didn't work. Only about 50 per cent of the population could get any sort of DTT picture, and less than a third of homes in the UK could get a clean, clear signal. In some homes the picture was interrupted by simple things like opening the fridge door or by a passing bus. As a result, the number of people giving up ITV Digital each month because of the quality of the picture meant the company was struggling to stand still.

In the autumn of 2001 it became clear that ITV Digital was in serious trouble. When we discovered this, Carolyn Fairbairn and I got talking and we dreamt up an idea. We went to Carlton and Granada and offered to help turn ITV Digital into a platform for free-to-air broadcasters like the BBC, ITV, Channel Four, and Channel Five on which they could all develop new channels. We and others would help by marketing our digital channels, as Freeview was later marketed, to attract people who didn't want pay television. But every set-top box would also be capable of being used for pay television, allowing ITV Digital to try and persuade people to switch to pay once they had a box. That way Carlton and Granada could continue to bring in some income for the pay channels.

ITV Digital liked the idea but negotiating with Granada and Carlton was difficult because of a lack of mutual trust. Then one day, just before Christmas 2001, the Managing Director of Carlton, Gerry Murphy, whom I did trust, came to see me and told me to be careful. He honourably advised me to stop talking about this possible solution to their problems in public: even if we all reached a deal, he doubted whether there was enough money to keep ITV Digital going. From that moment on we began to develop version two. We called it Freeview.

Our research had shown that there were a lot of people who wanted a wider choice of television channels but didn't want to pay for it. They were the pay television rejecters, who tended to be older and more middle class; in effect, they were traditional BBC viewers and listeners. They wanted to have twenty or thirty channels but didn't want pay television. On the basis of this research we came up with Freeview. We first had to win the DTT licences that ITV Digital had handed back to the Independent Television Commission when the company went bust. I told my team, led by Carolyn Fairbairn, the BBC's Director of Marketing Andy Duncan (whom I had persuaded to join us from Unilever and who is now Chief Executive of Channel Four), and Emma Scott, that we had to win. So far I had won every bid for a licence I had been involved in – LWT, GMTV, and Channel Five. I didn't want to lose this 100 per cent record.

At a day's notice, I decided to turn up at a seminar being held at Number 11 Downing Street and outline the idea for Freeview. It was probably the concept's turning point.

The pitch was pretty simple. Part of the reason ITV Digital had failed was the failure of the technology: we knew how to fix that. They had also failed because they'd gone head to head with BSkyB: we had no intention of doing that because this would not be a pay service. Finally, ITV Digital became involved in buying expensive rights: we'd avoid this because we were only proposing a distribution system in which the risk belonged to the channel providers. The great trick of Freeview would be to persuade consumers to buy the box and to see it in the way they saw their television set. If it didn't work it was their problem, not ours.

We got a break when Tony Ball of BSkyB phoned me to ask if we'd consider letting them in. It so happened that we needed someone to take up some of the spare channel capacity we would have if we won the bid as both Mark Thompson at Channel Four and ITV had turned us down, a decision history will show was a bad one for both of them, particularly for ITV. At the BBC we didn't want, and certainly couldn't afford, to take all the extra channels, so I welcomed Tony's approach. I was also keen on BSkyB's joining us because it meant they would be inside the proverbial tent rather than criticizing us from the outside. I've never really worked out quite why BSkyB wanted to help us build Freeview. To me, it was always obvious that if it worked it would undermine their own basic-tier pay business. This is now happening, and again, I think history will show that it was a business mistake for BSkyB to help us grow Freeview.

In a two-man consortium with Crown Castle, who owned the whole distribution system, including the masts, and with BSkyB as a partner in supplying channels, we bid for the licences and won. My 100 per cent track record was safe.

In less than two years Freeview has become a massive success. This doesn't surprise me. It was Andy Duncan's marketing department who came up with the basic selling idea – more 'normal' television but no contract. We started with Freeview boxes on the market for £99, although the price has now dropped dramatically. It is an easy sell. For a relatively small one-off payment you can get thirty television channels, including all the new BBC television and radio channels, and make no further payments. In twenty months four million homes had boxes able to receive Freeview, making it the fastest take-up ever for a new consumer electronic product in the UK. The four million are all in the 75 per cent of the country that can currently receive Freeview.

So what had all this to do with the BBC? Why should we have been interested in the first place? I can partially answer that with one simple statistic.

In traditional five-channel analogue homes, the BBC's share of viewing in 2003 was 49 per cent, nearly half of all viewing. In Freeview homes the figure was just over 45 per cent, while in BSkyB homes it was 26 per cent. Given that the Government plans to turn off the analogue signal in the early part of the next decade, it is obviously very much in the BBC's interest for people to go digital via Freeview rather than through BSkyB. In Freeview homes, they watch 8 per cent less BBC programming than in traditional five-channel homes; but in Sky homes the loss is a massive 50 per cent.

There were two other reasons for the BBC's involvement. It was, and still is, important for the BBC that the UK goes fully digital because that is the only way to ensure that all the BBC services – on radio and television – are available to everyone. Given that everyone pays the licence fee, it is only right that, within a reasonable time, all its services are universally available. If we hadn't developed Freeeview the chances of the UK being able to turn off the analogue signal were virtually nil. In those circumstances it would have been hard to defend continuing with our range of digital services.

Freeview was also important to the BBC defensively. Opponents of the licence fee always argue that once everyone can get pay television the licence fee as a means of funding the BBC will be unnecessary. If people want the BBC they will choose to pay for it; and if they don't want it, then why should they pay for it? This is a superficially attractive argument that eventually some political party will fall for and adopt. But there is a good argument against and it is this: it is imperative that everyone can receive the BBC, even if they don't pay their licence fee. It is part of the glue that binds the UK together and must be available to everyone.

Freeview makes it very hard for any Government to try to make the BBC a pay-television service. The more Freeview boxes out there, the harder it will be to switch the BBC to a subscription service since most of the boxes can't be adapted for pay TV. I suspect Freeview will ensure the future of the licence fee for another decade at least, and probably longer.

The second move we made against BSkyB was a more obvious victory. When the BBC first put its television services onto BSkyB's digital platform it took the rather odd decision to pay BSkyB £5 million for the privilege of doing so. It was a decision taken back in 1998 and it was odd because BSkyB were desperate to get the BBC on board and would happily have paid them to get them. In Italy the state broadcaster RAI later looked at what had happened in the UK and made sure that Sky paid them a lot of money to carry their services. The BBC were total mugs.

ITV stayed off the BSkyB platform for several years and only went on, reluctantly, in 2001. By then the platform was a roaring success and ITV needed to get on it, so they agreed to pay BSkyB's price of £17 million a year for the privilege – a decision that ITV appealed against to Oftel, the appropriate regulator. When Oftel decided it was a perfectly fair price, we at the BBC knew we were in trouble when our current contract with BSkyB ended in late 2003.

By then, however, two further things had happened. First, a new satellite had been launched with a smaller footprint that only covered the UK and part of Northern Europe. This meant that if we switched all our services to the new satellite we could beam our channels largely at our own home market. Second, I had discovered from my colleagues in the German equivalent of the BBC that they happily put their signals out unencrypted, even if it meant they were accessible all across Europe – this was allowed under European legislation on overspill.

With BSkyB telling us that eventually they would expect us to pay at least the price ITV was paying them we saw this as our opportunity to strike. If we decided to beam all the BBC services from the new satellite we could broadcast them unencrypted: we no longer had to pay BSkyB to scramble the signal and then unscramble it again.

This would bring real advantages for the BBC. In one move we'd be free of the BSkyB satellite monopoly; we would save a lot of money; and, finally, all our regional services would be available throughout the country. This would mean, for instance, that a Scot living in London would be able to watch BBC Scotland. I have to admit we also saw it as one in the eye for BSkyB, an organization that only respected you if you played it tough.

We did know, however, that BSkyB would hate it and would play tough themselves: if we got away with it the other terrestrial broadcasters were bound to follow suit over time, and this would cost BSkyB millions of pounds in lost revenue. We worked through all the things they could do to us and decided the risk was worth taking. For instance, we knew that the first thing they would do would be to try to demote the BBC from the good positions we had on the BSkyB electronic programme guide, but we also guessed that the Independent Television Commission wouldn't allow them to do this.

When Carolyn Fairbairn and I first came up with the idea of going unencrypted, everyone else in the BBC told us why it couldn't be done. No one was on our side. Jana Bennett's Television division said we wouldn't be able to buy films or US series because the Hollywood studios wouldn't sell to an unencrypted service. Peter Salmon's people in Sport said roughly the same thing, that it would prevent us acquiring sports rights; and the people in Pat Loughrey's Nations and Regions division objected because it could mean that the only way you could find their services on the electronic programme guide was down amongst the porn channels. My joke that it might increase the audiences was not well received.

I thought they were all behaving like wimps, but then I sometimes forget that not everyone else sees life like me. They don't relish battles the way I do. My reckoning was that we represented half the free television market: who in their right mind was going to try to sell sports rights or movies without half the market? Only we could do this, because only the BBC was big enough to take on BSkyB, the sports organizations, and the Hollywood studios in one go. I knew the Hollywood studios of old. The chances of their deciding together on a policy and sticking to it were nil. They would certainly get together and swear allegiance to each other in the battle with the BBC, but then one of them would break ranks if they could get a decent deal.

So despite everyone's fears we went ahead. We didn't give BSkyB any warning of the announcement and we planned our PR strategy very carefully. When we announced the move we blamed it on BSkyB for trying to charge us too much money. We argued that this was public money and that there were better things to do with it than hand it over to Rupert Murdoch. It worked brilliantly. It was a complicated move that journalists found difficult to explain; but they recognized that it was game, set, and match to us as there was little BSkyB could do about it.

At the BSkyB headquarters at Osterley there was a deafening silence. No one there had believed we would do it – after all this was the BBC. But the BBC had changed.

Predictably, the US studios all got together to protest, but Disney came round the back and did a deal, so that was the end of that. Once one studio had broken ranks, the rest of them folded one by one. As I told John Dolgen, the boss of Paramount, when he took Jana Bennett and me out to lunch to tell us we were following the wrong strategy, I wasn't pleading with him to take the BBC's money and we were happy to spend it elsewhere.

In the sports area we were in the middle of negotiating a £280 million-plus deal with the Football Association. When they said that it was only a deal if our signal was encrypted our negotiators simply got up, said that there was no point continuing the discussion, and left. They were all soon back at the table. We got the deal and our signal remained unencrypted.

Then there was BSkyB's electronic programme guide. As we'd predicted, BSkyB immediately said that they could no longer keep BBC One at 101 and BBC Two at 102, the two best slots on the guide. In turn we appealed to the Independent Television Commission, arguing that BSkyB didn't have the right to do this. The ITC set up an investigation and the weeks passed. Then one day I got a call from a mutual friend who said that Tony Ball at BSkyB, whom I hadn't spoken to since we announced we were going unencrypted, would like a chat.

Although we were on opposite sides on this issue, I liked Tony and had always found him friendly and straight to deal with. I rang him and we had an affable conversation about sports rights and the coming FA contract. Over the next couple of weeks our conversations got friendlier still and we began to talk about a deal involving the FA contract, the electronic programme guide, and the possibility of what we called a regionalization service. We wanted to make sure that the right signals for BBC One and BBC Two went to the right regions in satellite homes and we were prepared to pay for that. We had to ensure that if you were in Wales and went to 101, not only would you get BBC One but you also got the service that included all the Welsh regional programmes.

I became suspicious: we were getting too good a deal. BSkyB even agreed to move BBC Three to slot 115 and BBC Four to 116 on their programme guide, slots we'd been trying to get for two years. And then it dawned upon me. BSkyB were keen to get an agreement with us *before* the ITC adjudication on our dispute was published and were prepared to be very generous to stop it being published. For a negotiator it was a wonderful position to be in; but in these circumstances it is important not to screw the opposition into the ground. I had discovered over the years that what goes around comes around.

Then I got the call from the ITC Chief Executive, Patricia Hodgson, who asked me, seemingly in all innocence, if we and BSkyB were likely to reach agreement before their publication date in a week's time. I said it looked like it and, as a result, we would withdraw our complaint, which meant the ITC's ruling would never be published. She laughed and said something like 'You appear to have got all you wanted.' It was very clear that the ITC had discovered something that would have been deeply embarrassing to BSkyB if it became public. That was why we had achieved such a good deal. Patricia has always refused to discuss it with me so, to this day, I don't know what the ITC found. But I do know they found something.

During my time at the BBC I had a high public profile – not always of my own choosing. According to sections of the press, I took every decision at the BBC and was personally responsible for making every programme on television and radio. The reality was exactly the opposite. I only ever commissioned one television programme the whole time I was at the BBC, a two-part biography of Nelson Mandela that played on BBC One in 2003.

I happened to be having breakfast with the South African High Commissioner, Lindiwe Mabuza, and told her that someone should make the definitive Mandela documentary and that we would love to do it. I heard no more until I was on holiday in Australia in the summer of 2002 and got an urgent message from my PA, Fiona Hillary, saying an outline of the project was needed within three days. There was no way I could do that; instead I wrote a couple of pages about why such a documentary needed to be made.

I quoted my daughter Alice, who was 17 at the time. I explained that, like most 17-year-olds, she had no interest in politics, no understanding of international affairs, and was obsessed by popular culture. (This was the same daughter who, when I told her I was going to run the BBC, told me I shouldn't do it because I'd only screw up Radio One.) And yet when I'd asked her whom she would like to meet most in the world it wasn't someone from film or pop music: it was Nelson Mandela. In my note I said that this was the reason we should make the documentary. Mandela had transcended politics and was an icon to young and old. It worked and we made two one-hour films.

The press also believed I was obsessed by ratings, which again wasn't true. When I first arrived at the BBC we certainly had to do something about the declining numbers on BBC One, and we did that by increasing our spend on the channel, largely in the areas of drama and sport. But if you look carefully at the numbers in my time at the BBC, BBC Television still lost share overall. The problem was that ITV was in free fall for a couple of years. We didn't overtake ITV by increasing our ratings; theirs simply fell faster than ours did. In fact, looking at a graph of what has happened to ITV's figures over thirty years, you find a pretty dismal picture, although there are some signs now that, under their new Director of Programmes, Nigel Pickard, ITV's decline has slowed down.

My real concern was that the whole television industry had now adopted the Channel Four model of commissioning, whereby a relatively small number of people decide which programmes should be made. They have all the money and, as a result, they take virtually every decision, even though they don't actually produce any programmes themselves. The danger of this system is that a channel only reflects the personalities and tastes of a very small number of people. The BBC adopted this system when John Birt introduced the producer/broadcaster split in June 1996, and although I changed some of it with my 'One BBC' changes when I first arrived, I didn't change it enough.

It meant that the production community in the BBC cared too much about what the channel Controllers wanted. I used to try to tell current affairs or documentary producers I came across that we wanted their ideas, not those of the channel Controllers; but at the end of the day the producers knew who had the money. I should have been more radical and done more to change this.

There were two other areas where I believe, over four years, we made a big difference to the BBC. The first was in the area of equal opportunities.

If anyone had walked round the BBC in the late Eighties they would have found it was still very white and very male. When I arrived a decade later it was no longer very male: women had broken through as a result of a series of positive initiatives introduced by John Birt, who felt passionately about the issue. This made it possible in my time for us to promote a lot of women, on merit, to the most senior positions in the BBC. By the time I left the Directors of Television, Radio, Strategy, and Policy and Legal were all women. Equally importantly so were the Controllers of BBC One, BBC Two, Radio Two, Radio Four, BBC Northern Ireland, and BBC Wales.

Women were in charge of numerous parts of the organization, particularly in the regions, which until recent years had been very much a male preserve. Mark Byford tells the story of when, as Director of Nations and Regions in the mid Nineties, he organized a meeting of all his senior staff from around Britain to meet John Birt. They were virtually all men. John took Mark aside and told him this simply wasn't acceptable and *had* to change. Today it has changed and the glass ceiling for women, which existed for decades at the BBC, has been well and truly broken. However, in 1999, when I arrived, the same was not true for ethnic minorities.

As Director-General I was invited to speak at the annual Campaign for Racial Equality in the Media awards presentation in April 2000; in my speech I made it very clear that improving the ethnic mix of the staff at the BBC would be one of my priorities. I announced that we were to have targets so that, by the end of 2003, people from ethnic minorities would make up 10 per cent of the staff, as opposed to the 8 per cent figure in 1999, and that in management the figure would increase from the pathetically small 2 per cent to at least 4 per cent. I also said we wanted radically to change on-screen representation of ethnic minorities.

Soon afterward I was interviewed by Anvar Khan, the presenter of a Radio Scotland programme called *The Mix*. She asked me about ethnic representation in the media and didn't I think it was hideously white? I replied that I certainly thought the BBC was hideously white and thought no more about it until the comment appeared as the front-page lead story in the following week's *Mail on Sunday*, predictably followed by papers like the *Daily Telegraph*. The letters column of the *Telegraph* had to be seen to be believed. It seemed like every retired colonel in the Home Counties had written in to complain about me. Their argument was that the BBC was white because this was a white country.

Everyone assumed I would be embarrassed and realize I'd made a mistake in the interview. On the contrary, I was rather pleased with the publicity because it told people inside and outside the BBC that I was serious about change in this area. It also told the members of BBC staff from ethnic minorities that I was serious. This wasn't about being politically correct; it was about making sure the BBC properly reflected a significant change that was happening in our society.

After four years we hit our employment targets, just. It had been very hard work to get there and we only achieved them by introducing a 'name and shame' policy. Every three months the Executive would receive a report outlining which divisions were doing well and which were doing badly in our efforts to change. For instance, when the Asian Network was switched out of Nations and Regions and into the Radio Division it was suddenly apparent that we had a major problem in cities like Leeds, Manchester, and Birmingham where a high proportion of the population were from ethnic minorities. Andy Griffee, who was in charge of the English regions, told us that in two years he would change that and that if he didn't we should fire him. True to his word, he introduced a whole range of equal opportunity initiatives and delivered what he had promised. In January 2004, only a couple of weeks before I left the BBC, I announced another four-year target: by 2008, 12.5 per cent of staff were to be from ethnic minorities, whilst the figure for management would be increased to 7 per cent.

As for on-screen representation, there has been a big change in the number of Afro-Caribbeans appearing on the BBC, but we didn't do as well increasing the number of people of Asian descent, particularly Muslims. A great deal was achieved in drama, largely thanks to Mal Young, a Liverpudlian who was in charge of drama serials at the BBC. He changed the racial mix of programmes like *Holby City* and *Casualty* by making the producers go into hospitals and see what they were actually like. He pointed out that the existing racial mix in BBC hospitals was very different from the average UK hospital.

I was once on a train on my way back from watching a football match in Manchester when I found myself sitting opposite a black guy who had been in Manchester to see a play he had written. I didn't recognize him as Kwame Kwei-Armah, an actor from *Casualty*, and he didn't recognize me as the Director-General of the BBC. When we both found out who we were he told me the story of the day he saw another black actor being auditioned for *Casualty*. He'd said to himself, 'That's it, then. I'm out' – on the assumption that they only ever had one black actor in *Casualty*. Thanks to Mal Young those days are long past in BBC drama.

I think in this area I did make a difference. I suspect my determination over four years to change the mix of people working at the BBC means the process is now unstoppable, and I know that Mark Thompson regards the issue as being as important as I did. I regularly got accused of promoting positive discrimination in favour of ethnic minorities, which wasn't true. What I wanted was a workforce that more properly represented twenty-first-century Britain. I believe multi-cultural Britain is an exciting place and I wanted more of that excitement to rub off on the BBC.

The other area in which I tried to make real change was in making the BBC less focused on London and the South of England. Historically, ITV had been the regional television system in Britain and the BBC more a national service. But as the ITV companies merged, and with greater commercial competition undermining their profitability, it was clear to me that ITV would have no option but to reduce its commitment to the regions. I thought this meant that, over time, our respective roles might be reversed and that the BBC would have to make more programming away from the South. Personally I saw it as an opportunity, not an obligation.

From the moment I joined the BBC I realized just how much a problem the bias towards the South of England was. In my early months, when I spent a lot of time out of London, I discovered a disillusioned workforce, people who believed that London stopped them doing this or that, who felt that London was biased against them and that you could only get on by working in London.

By making Mark Thompson the new Director of Television soon after I arrived at the BBC I created a vacancy for Director of Nations and Regions. In recent years the post had been given to high fliers on the way up – Byford followed by Thompson – but by promoting Pat Loughrey to the job we were promoting someone who had spent his whole career in Northern Ireland and had never worked in London. It was intended to give a signal to staff outside the capital.

Oddly, a lot of extra money had already been spent in Scotland, Wales, and Northern Ireland as a result of devolution, but it hadn't changed the relationship with 'head office'. In Scotland, in particular, the hostility towards London was very evident. For some reason the Scots and John Birt hadn't got on at all well.

My view was that devolution was very important and that it wasn't just about politics. It was about devolving real decision-making out of London. So we set aside an extra £50 million a year to be spent in all three countries, money without strings attached. I told the Controllers that my advice would be not to spend it just covering politics but to use it to try to build the production industry in the three countries. But in the end I told them it was their decision. That was what devolution was about.

Over the four years I was Director-General we increased production in the nations for local consumption quite markedly, but we also succeeded in building up production for the network, particularly in Scotland, where network output doubled over four years. Interestingly, it transformed the relationship between London and Scotland. Suddenly BBC Scotland became a serious and well-respected player within the BBC.

Then it became very obvious that we had a problem in England, particularly in the North of England. The BBC regularly asks people what they think of the Corporation. What we found was that the further north you went in England the lower the BBC's approval figures were. It wasn't hard to see why. The vast majority of our programmes were made in the south. So early on we set aside some money and created the Northern initiative. As a result we got new northern dramas like *Cutting It* and *Merseybeat*; we developed an important writers' initiative across the North of England; Radio Four became active in Manchester again; and we introduced a completely new regional service for East Yorkshire based in Hull. We also decided to do a major research project on the impact of broadband in the city of Hull itself, and set up a new journalists' video training centre in Newcastle upon Tyne. The decision was taken that this should be out of London and the first suggestion was Oxford. I exploded and pointed out that Oxford was London in the country and could we please go further north. So it went to Newcastle.

We increased our spending on regional news with great effect. In terms of the numbers viewing, we overtook ITV's regional news in virtually every region in England; by the time I left we were only losing in the north-east, and BBC Scotland's news had even overtaken Scottish Television north of the border. That the BBC's regional news should become so successful had been unthinkable only five years earlier.

By spending a lot of time myself in the north, and encouraging other members of the BBC Executive to do the same, we improved morale in places like Manchester, Leeds, and Newcastle, but I still thought more needed to be done. Everyone in the UK pays a licence fee and it was wrong that so much of that money was being spent in the south. The BBC needed to reflect the whole of life in the UK, not just one part of it.

I therefore planned a major change. I wanted to move some of our services out of London to an expanded BBC operation in Manchester. My plan was to move Radio Five Live, both our children's channels, half our new media operation, and BBC Three to Manchester in the second half of this decade.

At the same time I planned to move other parts of the BBC out of London for more practical reasons. Our outside broadcast headquarters needed to be on a motorway somewhere, not in Acton in West London, whilst our back office operations did not have to be in Central London. We weren't big payers and many of our back office staff increasingly couldn't afford to live in London. I also planned that at least two members of the Executive would in future be based in Manchester.

When I told my Executive colleagues what I was proposing most, though not all, were against the idea. Jenny Abramsky threatened to resign if Radio Five Live were moved, although she never actually said so to me. Jana Bennett felt that BBC Three had to stay in London, while the Children's department were adamant they weren't going anywhere. They all said this had been tried before when 'Youth' and 'Religion' had been moved north a decade earlier and it hadn't been deemed a success. My point was that this plan moved the money to Manchester, not just a production department. The real reason most people objected was that it would disrupt their lives. My answer to that was, 'Bad luck'.

Sadly, this was unfinished business when I left the BBC. I took my plan to the Governors at the end of 2003 and they agreed with the proposal to move services to Manchester. The idea was that it would be announced as part of our commitment for the next charter period. And then I left. The plan still exists and the BBC say they are going to implement some of it, but I have no doubt that the forces against it are regrouping even as I write.

The opposition I hit was exactly the same as the opposition Gavyn Davies met when he made his speech suggesting that too much of the BBC's money was being spent on the southern middle class. He was savaged for daring to say such a thing. But then of course that is how a comparatively small South of England elite has managed to keep such a strong grip on the BBC and on this country for so long.

CHAPTER TEN

Why Did They Cry?
(Culture Change at the BBC)

In my manifesto for the post of Director-General of the BBC, written in the summer of 1999, I had said that the biggest challenge facing a new Director-General was to build an 'inclusive culture'. This was not based on any detailed analysis; it was simply something I sensed was a problem at the BBC from what I had heard. But I was shocked by what I found when I got there. It was worse than anything I had expected. Much worse.

When I joined the BBC I faced the prospect of spending five months shadowing John Birt and learning by his example, which is what I suspect he had in mind for his successor when he planned the ridiculous concept of a five-month handover. Five weeks would have been more than adequate. Instead I decided to find out about the BBC for myself, and so I took to the road. I spent a great deal of time outside London and talked to thousands of people who worked for the BBC in different parts of the UK.

The first thing I had to do was to put a stop to the whole pomp and paraphernalia that had traditionally surrounded visits from the Director-General over many years. This meant getting rid of the inevitable entourage and dissuading people from seeing me as a visiting dignitary. I didn't want the red carpet treatment that most Director-Generals had received in the past. On most of my visits I went alone or with one other person, Emma Scott, my business manager.

If this approach was to work it meant persuading the managers of the places I was visiting that I wanted to see business as usual, not a spruced-up version; more importantly, that I wanted to talk directly to the people who worked for the BBC, not just the local bosses. I therefore insisted on eating in the canteen with the staff instead of attending formal lunches or dinners, and I wanted to have time to talk to people on a one-to-one basis.

The message began to get around. Early on I went to visit BBC Radio Lancashire in Blackburn to find I was being served tea in a cup and saucer, not the sort of thing you normally found in local radio. The boss, a great bloke called Steve Taylor, told me that he'd sent someone down to Blackburn Market to buy it especially but that I needn't worry about the expense as he was taking it back after my visit.

I went to BBC offices that no Director-General had visited in decades. I found that some of our staff were working in buildings that should have been condemned years earlier. I remember visiting our building in Leicester, the home of BBC Radio Leicester and the Asian Network, and saying to people afterwards how awful it was. I was told that if I thought it was bad I should wait until I went to Stoke. When I finally visited Stoke I was pleasantly surprised; it wasn't *that* terrible. But over the next four years BBC Radio Stoke moved to a better building. We also moved to a new building in Sheffield and started work on replacement premises in Birmingham, Leeds, Hull, Liverpool, Glasgow, and finally Leicester. We also renovated buildings right across the country.

On my visits I found staff doing what had been required of me in local newspapers thirty-five years earlier, when I had to buy my own typewriter. Some were buying their own recording equipment because the gear the BBC was supplying was so out of date. In particular the younger staff coming straight from media courses found they had to use equipment that was significantly inferior to what they'd been used to at college. Over the next four years we digitalized every local radio station in the BBC. I also found that many of the staff I met felt unloved, unwanted, and unnoticed.

Everywhere I asked the same two questions of the management and the staff. What do we need to change in order to improve our service? And what can I do to make your life better? Some of the suggestions were ridiculous, such as wanting their total budget doubled; but most of them were small and practical and would cost peanuts to implement. In most cases we did this in my first few months in charge. A few of the suggestions were more difficult because, in some areas, the Birt–McKinsey-inspired reorganizations of the BBC had resulted in institutional madness.

A classic example was the library service, a fundamental resource in any broadcasting organization. Access to books, cuttings, and CDs had been priced at such a high level in the internal pricing system that many programme makers couldn't afford to use them, given the size of their budgets. In the case of CDs, for example, it was cheaper to go to the local High Street and buy them than borrow them from the BBC library. This was simply crazy and we put a stop to it as part of the 'One BBC' changes.

Worst of all was the climate of fear I found everywhere inside the BBC. I knew John Birt and his senior team weren't popular, but once I was on the inside I discovered that they were disliked, even loathed, by large numbers of people working for the BBC. Around the organization people didn't talk of the Director-General as 'John' or even 'Mr Birt': he was described only as 'Birt' in a disparaging tone. There was little affection for him or the wider leadership anywhere, and the further down I went into the organization the greater the feelings of hostility and distrust I found.

For instance, in local radio every station had to cut 2 per cent from its budget every year, year after year, because that was the saving that head office theoretically believed was achievable. Yet anyone who actually visited a local radio station could see they were being run on a shoestring and that more and more cuts would only damage the service. It may not have been fair but the staff in local radio blamed John Birt personally for this, and virtually every other problem they had.

I realized I would have to try to change the relationship between the Director-General and the staff at every level of the organization. It never occurred to me, for example, not to be friendly to the people on security or at the reception desk and I always chatted to the staff doing these jobs wherever I went. At Broadcasting House in Central London, where I was based, people on reception told me later that they had found my style very different from that of my predecessor, who had tended not to acknowledge them. He certainly never stopped and chatted. In contrast to this approach, I always wanted to get to know as many members of staff as possible.

I suspect John was intrinsically shy and found it difficult to be informal and friendly with people he didn't know. I don't do this naturally either, but over the years I've worked on it and learnt how to do it. Gareth Jones, whom I brought in to be Director of Human Resources, saw this in me and said one day, 'You're not really an extrovert at all, are you?'

He was right. Sadly, Gareth didn't like the BBC much and in particular he didn't take to the BBC Governors. He left after a year.

I also found that there was little trust between members of top management. Obviously there were friendships between people, but I detected no feeling of common purpose. They had learnt how to operate as competing individuals within a climate of fear, but I didn't feel they were a united team. When Jana Bennett returned to the BBC in 2002 to become Director of Television, after spending two years in the United States, she told the story of turning up late for her first Executive meeting. As she reached the room she heard laughter so she assumed she was in the wrong place. According to her, no one laughed at Executive meetings when she had last been at the BBC.

A year later, when things had begun to improve, I remember discussing what it had been like with a board-level colleague who had been a senior member of the previous regime. He told me that at the time he had genuinely believed in what they were doing and the way they were doing it and that their critics were totally wrong. He said he had since discovered a different world and what he had discovered in the process was that behaviour he had believed to be acceptable had actually been completely inappropriate and ineffective. Lorraine Heggessey, now the Controller of BBC One but then Joint Director of Factual Programming, demanded at an early meeting of the Executive, which she had just joined, that all those who had supported the Birt regime should explain and account for their actions. An uncomfortable silence followed, broken by a long-serving member saying, 'I vas only following orders.'

The reason I was so shocked by what I found at the BBC was that I couldn't conceive that anyone could have believed that this was the way to run a creative organization. What I knew for certain was that the traditional leadership model based on exaggerated status, self-importance, and ordering people around was over. It was obsolete. Expecting people to deliver because you, as their boss, told them to do so didn't work any more, and was certainly not the way to get the best out of staff.

I had discovered this for myself many years earlier when I first ran programme teams, but my views of management and leadership had developed over the years and had been reinforced by the period I had spent at the Harvard Business School back in 1989. The twelve weeks I spent there showed me that my gut feelings on how to run organizations and motivate people had an intellectual rationale. That gave me the confidence to continue putting my ideas into practice as I found myself running larger and larger organizations.

In many ways my approach to leading groups of people is rooted in what my father taught my brothers and me all those years ago when he used regularly to talk to the local road sweeper. When he died, all three of us were asked to write a piece about him to be read out at his funeral. I wrote that, more than anything else, he had hated pompous people who thought that they were somehow better than those around them. He believed *everyone* was worthy of respect. It was always obvious to me that people would do a better job if their boss respected them and what they were doing. Once you grasp this simple human truth there are a set of ideas that logically follow, which I've used as a basis for running organizations over the years.

As a leader you need to be yourself. It is lethal to try to ape the behaviour of the stereotypical manager just because you've got a job in management. You were appointed because of who you are and you need to keep faith with that: if you are naturally rather eccentric, as I am, then *be* eccentric. Your staff will like you for it. On the other hand, if you try to be something you are not, you'll pay a high price, waste a lot of personal energy, and your staff will see straight through you. It takes courage to simply be yourself; it means you have to be confident, understand your strengths and weaknesses, and be willing to admit the latter. But the results are worth it.

As a leader, communication *really* matters. People working in the organization are more likely to support you and what you are trying to achieve if they feel they are involved in a two-way conversation with you. We used a variety of means at the BBC to try to do this. I sent regular e-mails always signed Greg, did frequent internal broadcasts, used our in-house magazine, and made a series of videos – all with the aim of creating a one-to-one relationship with nearly thirty thousand people. It is important to be direct and to the point; most important of all, never lapse into the language of management, the gobbledegook of consultants and business schools. Avoiding jargon is essential if you want to be a good leader.

For instance, when I publicly apologized for the *Question Time* programme that was broadcast the week of the September 11 disasters I immediately sent an e-mail to all the staff saying very clearly why I thought it had been a mistake, that the programme hadn't matched the mood of the moment. I went on to say that we all made mistakes and that was the end of it. There would be no recriminations. This up-front approach worked. Many of the thousands of people who took to the streets, or who wrote to me following my departure from the BBC, had never met me, but they told me they felt we had a relationship.

As a leader you also have to be honest with your staff. It shouldn't be a problem to say, 'I'm sorry. I got that wrong.' The problem is pretending you are right when you know you are wrong. At the BBC we once tried to reform the expenses policy right across the organization. It was a good idea but I soon discovered by talking to the staff that we were being too mean and that some of the new allowances were too low. I listened, changed the policy, and personally took the blame, admitting the error on the front page of *Ariel*, the BBC's in-house magazine. Making the apology actually won me new friends.

As a leader you set the example. Don't tell your staff to do one thing and then do another yourself. They'll spot it immediately and your credibility will be undermined. It's about practising what you preach. If, for instance, you urge your managers to be less hierarchical and mix more with the staff then you, as the leader, need to be seen to be doing it yourself. Every day I got my sandwiches or salad from the canteen and talked to the people I met in the queue. It would have been easier and quicker to have sent someone from my office to get my lunch, but my going to the canteen sent an important and symbolic message to everyone: I was both accessible and one of them; that's what I wanted my managers to be.

As a leader you have to recognize that leadership is often about the stories told about you – either positive or negative – by others in the organization. You'll be judged more by those stories than by anything you say or write. As an example, in October 2002 there was a serious fire at my house that kept me up all night. The next day I was exhausted and up to my eyes dealing with the aftermath of the fire, but I had a long-standing commitment to speak to 350 BBC staff from the Nations and Regions at an event in East London. The organizers assumed I would cancel and made contingency plans. But I turned up, if only to tell those 350 people that they mattered. The downside of this approach is that, as a leader, you are always under the spotlight. That's why big leadership jobs are so exhausting, if you do them properly.

As a leader in an organization you have to be able to convince those working for you that they are capable of achieving great things, more than they ever imagined. In turn, this means giving people responsibility and letting them get on with the job. I'm always amazed by how many so-called leaders manage to achieve the opposite. People perform better when they are trusted and encouraged rather than when they operate in a climate of fear or intimidation in which everything they do is double checked. When I arrived at the BBC such checking was institutionalized: in some areas nothing of real importance happened without being scrutinized by McKinsey, the management consultants. As a result, many senior managers in the BBC felt powerless and deeply frustrated.

As a leader you have to understand the finances. Numbers are far too important to be left to the accountants, who, in my experience, will only succeed in confusing you. You have to insist that the accountants give you the numbers in a form you can understand, not in a way that only they understand. This is a constant battle, for often finance people will not do this willingly. Managers who don't understand the finances are vulnerable: they are not really in charge. I found this all the time at the BBC, and I suspect this is a particular problem in the public sector. However, the problem doesn't only apply to finance. There's always a danger that other support services such as human resources, strategy, and facilities management end up running the operation. The leader's job is to understand enough to be able to remind them every so often that they are only the support machine.

Finally, if you are the leader of an organization you must care about the people who work for you, all of them, and show them you care. Only then can you succeed.

By the year 2000, when I took over at the BBC, this kind of thinking wasn't exactly rocket science. Business schools had been teaching the importance of leadership, as opposed to management, for more than a decade. But many organizations in Britain had continued to pursue the management philosophies of the 1970s and 1980s – years after most reputable academics had stopped teaching them. This was, and is, particularly true of the public sector.

Two years before I joined the BBC I had first-hand experience of this problem when I spent nearly a year looking around the National Health Service. In the summer of 1997, soon after Labour had been elected, I bumped into Margaret Jay, then Minister of State for Health, at David Frost's garden party, where the great and the good converge in large numbers every summer. It was at that same event six years later, when the Gilligan affair had just broken, that all the press photographers tried to get a picture of Alastair Campbell and me together. Instead we studiously avoided each other.

I told Margaret that as a committed Labour supporter and a believer in what the NHS stood for I would be happy to help if I could and that if there was anything I could do she should give me a ring. A few weeks later Margaret and the then Secretary of State for Health, Frank Dobson, asked me to come up with some new ideas for the Patients' Charter. With the help of Alison Nield, a former nurse and now a manager within the NHS, I spent nearly a year simply wandering around the organization. I quickly found the idea of the charter uninteresting but became fascinated by how you run and motivate an organization that employs a million people, the biggest employer in Europe.

What we found was an NHS whose frontline staff, particularly in the hospitals, overwhelmingly believed that what they achieved, they achieved *despite* their management, not thanks to it. I found small oases where the frontline staff and the leadership worked together in pursuit of common goals, but they were the exception. In my report I tried to tell the politicians that they didn't have a hope in hell of changing the NHS fundamentally unless they first addressed this problem, which was a problem of leadership.

In terms of culture I'm not sure much has changed since then, although the coming of foundation hospitals – in which the local management have real power – could make a big difference. I recently heard of an NHS Trust where one hospital had lost all its stars. The frontline staff had celebrated this because it was one in the eye for 'the management', who would now lose their bonuses. Until this ugly divide between 'us' and 'them' is tackled I do not think the NHS can move forward properly.

Changing the culture of the NHS will require real commitment over a number of years, but it also requires spending real money on change programmes. This is a difficult sell in the NHS. People both inside and outside the service seem to believe that any NHS money not spent directly on health care is somehow wasted. And the likes of the *Daily Mail* would have great fun dismissing expenditure on culture change as wasted money when it could go on hip replacements. Yet every commercial organization in the world knows that you *have* to spend money on these things if you are to succeed.

In the introduction to my NHS report I wrote:

> My approach to this task reflects my own approach to management. I believe that most people are capable of achieving outstanding performance – well beyond what many have been led to believe they can achieve – but that can only be brought out by an inclusive management style. I do not believe people are best motivated by fear but by being involved in the decision-making process, by taking part in the setting of goals for an organization and by being able to celebrate achieving them.

What the report recommended was that the top-down approach of running the NHS, which the Government was pursuing at the time, was largely doomed. I argued that, while the NHS needed a few central principles, power needed to be shifted quite radically from the centre towards the coalface. This was hardly revolutionary stuff, but it proved far too radical for the politicians and the Department of Health back then. By the time the report was published, in November 1998, Margaret Jay had moved on to become the Labour Leader in the House of Lords, and no one else was really interested in it or was in a position to deliver on its recommendations.

In my experience, politicians understand very little about how to manage and motivate a workforce. Few of them have held senior jobs in large organizations and they still tend to believe that the critical component in making change is deciding on the policy. It's not. The hardest thing is getting the support of the staff who have the job of implementing policy: they are the people who will determine whether it succeeds or fails. Most civil servants have the same problem: too much of their energy is focused on managing upwards.

As far as the NHS is concerned, I believe that it is only when the politicians stand well back and let the senior managers really become the leaders that there is any chance of positive change. And the majority of those managers should come from the medical professions themselves rather than being 'professional' managers. This happens in almost every other organization, yet giving a doctor a management role in the NHS is somehow seen as a misuse of his or her training and talents. Only when this happens will the leadership have a chance of getting the staff on their side.

In one sense I wasted a year of my life on the NHS report, but in another it was invaluable experience, because when I joined the BBC I found myself facing many of the same challenges.

On my first day as Director-General I was determined to do something similar to what I had done a decade earlier on my first day as Managing Director of LWT. I wanted everyone to know that things were going to be different. But doing it in a relatively small organization where everybody worked in the same building was easy; it was going to be much harder getting that message across to the nearly thirty thousand BBC people working in more than six hundred offices in the UK and around the world. I could hardly buy them all a drink.

I decided to make a speech and hold a question and answer session in a studio at Television Centre in London that would be broadcast live across the BBC on the internal ring main. I insisted that we have a cross-section of staff in the studio audience, not just senior managers as had happened in the past. Compared with the kind of events we were running a couple of years later it was a rather conservative affair; but I did manage to make some jokes and to send some signals about the vision I had for the organization.

I said that my aim for the future was simple:

I joined the BBC because I wanted it to make wonderful programmes . . . So how do we do that? I think we need two things. We should spend more of our money on programme making and we must ensure we have a culture within the BBC where we believe everything and anything is possible.

In answer to one of the subsequent questions, I suggested that if people were so unhappy with the BBC that they felt the need to moan all the time, then they should consider leaving. There were thousands of people outside who would be grateful for their jobs. To my amazement this drew a sustained round of applause.

Sue Lawley, who was MC of the event, asked me whether my management style was closer to Michael Grade's or John Birt's. I explained that I hoped to bring the flair of Grade and the analytical ability of Birt. I added that if I got it the other way round the organization could find itself in real trouble. When Michael Grade was appointed BBC Chairman in April 2004 he was asked a similar question about me and John Birt. He told Jon Snow on Channel Four News that he was a 'Dykeist' rather than a 'Birtist'.

So I made it clear to the staff that changing the culture of the BBC was on my agenda from day one. But it was two more years before I had the confidence really to do something about it, two years before I felt I'd earned sufficient credibility and support within the organization to launch a fully fledged culture-change initiative.

By then we'd restructured the organization, taken out several layers of management, put more programme people onto the BBC Executive, cultivated more collaboration, and encouraged the organization to move faster. We were also ahead of target in reducing the amount of money the BBC spent on overhead departments, which meant much more money was going into programmes.

I can't say I enjoyed my first year at the BBC and eighteen months after I joined the organization I was beginning to wonder whether I would ever be able to make real progress in the area that I knew mattered most: doing something about the entrenched BBC culture that had developed over decades. Like all big organizations the BBC was inbred, which made changing its culture even more difficult. BBC people tended to live their lives with other BBC people. They were their friends, their lovers, their husbands and wives. Even when they got divorced it was often to go off with or marry someone else from the BBC.

Parts of the BBC culture were very positive: a commitment to strong editorial values, a willingness to go the extra mile to achieve excellence, and a strong team spirit within certain units. But other aspects were negative. Many staff felt badly treated by their bosses and many more felt they weren't valued by the organization. Internal rivalry was rampant, and many people saw the competition as being someone else inside the BBC. There was little trust or collaboration; middle management tended to be risk averse; and there was still contempt for many in senior management.

Our staff also told us that, despite producing some great programmes, it was a difficult place in which to be creative or innovative. The annual staff survey in 2001 showed that some things had improved since I arrived – staff believed the senior team had a much clearer vision of the future and they also felt communications were getting better; but, overall, the results of the survey painted a bleak picture of our internal culture. I hadn't made much of an impact.

The condition I'd identified in the NHS in 1998 was prevalent when I joined the BBC, and was still there. People still believed that what they achieved, they achieved *despite* the management.

In the end, a number of factors encouraged me to make the move to try and tackle the cultural problems in late 2001. The most significant was the arrival of three new people onto the BBC Executive team: Stephen Dando, who joined as Director of Human Resources; Andy Duncan as Director of Marketing and Communications; and Roger Flynn as Managing Director of BBC Ventures. They changed the balance on the Executive.

All three came from the private sector and all three had the same initial impressions of the BBC that I had had eighteen months earlier. They reminded me of my feelings that change to the ingrained culture was essential. Urged on by the three of them, I decided that this was a good time to make the move. In performance terms the BBC was in good health. Our revenue was secured, our output was strong, and our main commercial competitors were in trouble due to an advertising recession. I also believed, having channelled millions of pounds of extra money into programmes, that the production community was more on my side. Without the support of the programme makers there was little hope of effecting any real change in the culture since more than nineteen thousand of the staff worked directly in programme making or content creation.

My overall calculation was that the staff would now give me the benefit of the doubt if we went for wholesale culture change. In the end we finally decided to do it after three BBC executives – Andy Duncan, Alan Yentob, and BBC Two Controller Jane Root – went on a fact-finding trip around a number of successful companies and organizations in the USA. They came back like converts, preaching the gospel of culture change, corporate values, and the importance of nurturing your staff. I was particularly taken by the slogans they brought back. My favourite was 'We employ people for attitude and train for skills', which came from Southwest Airlines in Dallas; but I also liked the Stanford Research Institute's advice to 'Kill the cynics'. I later went with another group of BBC executives on a similar trip and we saw what could be achieved for ourselves.

Having decided to back a culture change programme, the question was how to go about it. Over the years the BBC had been littered with the corpses of failed change programmes, which meant that BBC staff were likely to be cynical and resistant to yet another initiative. So the Director of Television, Mark Thompson, and his Radio counterpart, Jenny Abramsky, both veterans of previous ventures, offered to look back and see what lessons could be learnt.

They found that too often the programmes had been run by external consultants, had been owned only by management and imposed on the organization from the top, and that they'd been shot through with man-agement jargon. As a result they'd tended to be short lived and had been resisted very effectively by an intelligent, articulate, and sceptical workforce. So we now knew what not to do. In particular, we knew that if we were to launch a change programme we had to see it through over a number of years. There's a lot of evidence to suggest that at about the time a change programme is having an impact on the staff the senior management have got bored and moved on to the next initiative.

On 7 February 2002, almost two years to the day since I'd become Director-General, we launched our culture change programme, which we called 'Making it Happen'. When I look back now, I'm not sure we knew what we were doing; we simply knew we had to do something. Luckily Susan Spindler, an experienced programme maker who, as a senior man-ager, had worked in a whole range of areas across the BBC, agreed to be director of the project for six months. In the end she did twenty. She was then replaced by another senior manager, Katharine Everett, who carried on the good work Susan and her team had started.

Susan took the job against the strong advice of her family and most of her senior BBC colleagues. They told her she was mad and that by getting involved in something that sounded like pure 'management bol-locks' she was certain to blight her career. Having agreed to do the job, her biggest asset was her determination that this change programme would not degenerate into meaningless management jargon like so many others before it.

The day before the launch of 'Making it Happen', we explained what we were planning to my 100-strong Director-General's briefing group. I had set up the group early on and used it as a way of communicating to the most senior managers in the BBC. Like most big organizations, the BBC tends to be too introverted, so I always invited a guest speaker to our monthly meetings to broaden everyone's horizons. These ranged from politicians to academics, from business leaders to senior clerics. In fact at one meeting Jonathan Sacks, the Chief Rabbi, made one of the most persuasive arguments in favour of public service broadcasting that I've ever heard – far more persuasive than most of the arguments the BBC has ever come up with.

I can't say that the briefing group was initially wild about 'Making it Happen'. I suspect they thought I had bounced the idea on them and that we were all being dangerously evangelical. But they gave me the benefit of the doubt and over the next two years fully supported the idea.

Next came the whole staff. In an ambitious studio session that was transmitted across the BBC I announced a new vision for the Corporation. I told them that John Birt's vision 'to be the best managed public sector organization in the world' was laudable and worthy but not designed to get creative people out of bed in the mornings. We were replacing it with an aim 'to become the most creative organization in the world'. I believed this best summed up what the BBC should be about.

In my off-the-cuff speech I urged everyone in the BBC to 'imagine, just imagine what a great place the BBC could be if we all worked together to change it'. But what the press picked up on, and which was by far the most publicized aspect of the event, was a yellow card emblazoned with the words 'CUT THE CRAP'. It was like a football referee's yellow card and I promised the staff that everyone who asked for one could have one, to use in meetings when they couldn't get something to happen. It was a good gimmick, if a little corny, and we sent out thousands of cards to staff right across the BBC. We even had it translated into Chinese and Arabic.

But the key message we were trying to get across was that the BBC did not have a 'God-given right to exist' and that we needed to pay more attention to our audiences. After all, they were our paymasters. In order to do this we needed to address aspects of our own culture in the BBC.

At the same event we screened a video showing some of the good things already happening at the BBC that we wanted to see more of. One of them was the story of the atrium at our White City building. It demonstrated very clearly a lot of the things that were wrong at the BBC.

The White City building in West London was only built in the late 1980s, but it was a disgrace. It was a terrible off-the-shelf design and looked like it had been built by an old Eastern European communist state. Around the place it was called Ceausescu Towers, after the former communist leader of Romania. When I arrived at the BBC I noticed that the only nice part of the building, the open atrium in the middle, was actually closed to the staff. It had been closed since the building was first opened and to go into the atrium you had to wear a hard hat.

I asked why the staff weren't allowed to use it and was told the magic words: 'Health and Safety'. But because I was the Director-General I could push a bit more. I asked for an explanation of the Health and Safety problems. Some months later I was told staff couldn't use the atrium because there was no wheelchair ramp and it needed another exit to meet fire safety regulations. No one could explain why people had been wearing hard hats for the last decade!

I raised the matter at the BBC Executive. I asked everyone around the table if they'd known about all this and why they hadn't done something about it. I remember Mark Thompson, then Director of Television, saying 'We tried but it was too difficult, so we just gave up.' We all sympathized with this. We all knew changing things was hard.

So John Smith, who by now was in charge of property as well as finance, and I arranged for the fire exit and wheelchair ramp to be installed and opened up the atrium. On the opening day I wrote a piece in *Ariel* in which I asked, 'How many equivalents are there around the BBC, things which we can't do because someone, at some time, has told us it can't be done?'

I also held a party in the atrium that night for all the staff who worked in the building. As I wandered around many of them were excited and asked 'Does this mean we can go on the balconies now?' or 'Does it mean my office doesn't have to be painted grey?' I found the man from property and told him about this. His answer was a classic: 'Look what you've started now.'

The opening-up of the White City atrium became an incredibly important story around the BBC. It symbolized what 'Making it Happen' was trying to do and helped convince people that things could be changed. It showed the staff that the Director-General was on their side in attacking the mind-numbing negativity of much of the BBC bureaucracy. It also told the jobsworth bureaucrats that we were after them.

As part of 'Making it Happen' we set up seven working groups, each with a high-profile and powerful leader at the helm. Importantly, none of these came from the BBC Executive. They covered the areas we thought needed addressing: creativity, audiences, valuing people, improving leadership, transforming our work spaces, and attacking bureaucracy. The seventh group was asked to develop a set of written values for the BBC. These groups were charged with coming up with a five-year change plan to transform the BBC; at the same time we asked every division to form its own 'Making it Happen' team to suggest and implement more immediate change at a local level.

The launch event seemed to go down well and there were positive reactions reported in the BBC's in-house magazine, *Ariel*. One person said:

It was the clearest sign yet that we've changed course and it's all hands on deck. It reminded me how much had been squashed out of the organization by the old regime. At last we've moved on to discussing the BBC's soul instead of being distracted by crazy charges for borrowing a CD.

Another commented:

Some fantastic, inspirational stuff. This is something that everyone should own. Greg is backing us to question things and change them if we need to.

Perhaps less positively:

Shame that after leaving the session I shared a lift with two 'BBC types' who said how funny it was hearing a cockney DG. Maybe we've got further to go than even Greg realizes.

'Making it Happen' was now up and running, with a decent budget, a good team, and an inspirational leader in Susan Spindler. What Susan and her team always believed was that it was very important that they reported directly to me as Director-General and weren't sidelined as a Human Resources initiative. They needed it to be seen that they were supported from the very top. The basic idea of 'Making it Happen' was that by getting rid of the crap, by freeing people to make their own decisions and to take their own risks, our programmes and services would improve.

Over the next two years we took communication within the BBC to a higher level. The BBC was full of great programme makers and writers and we started using them properly for the first time to tell stories about BBC people to people *inside* the organization. One example. We made a film to tell the story of two BBC engineers who were the real heroes on the day John Simpson 'liberated' Kabul. These two engineers had transported a satellite dish and other equipment through Russia and into Afghanistan. When their Russian lorry driver refused to go any further into the mountains they refused to give up. They hired thirty mules, divided up the equipment, and strapped it on the mules. They then walked for days with the mules through snow-covered passes and down into Kabul to be ready and waiting when John arrived. They were the true heroes of Kabul.

This sort of thing happened all the time at the BBC, but no one ever got to hear about it. We decided to change that and over the next two years made many similar films and showed them all around the organization. Many revealed for the first time the great work that was being done by staff outside London, which helped to offset the BBC's ingrained pro-London bias. One film featured the work of BBC Radio Leeds in a city-centre primary school in one of the most deprived areas of Britain. It showed how a comparatively small project had transformed the lives of the children, their families, and their community. It was impossible to watch it without getting a lump in your throat, tears in your eyes, or both. When I was next in Leeds I visited the school and the headmistress told me that, as a result of the project, the children's confidence had soared and their results had improved.

These films, and dozens of others like them, opened the eyes of BBC people to the scale and range of the organization and made them proud of what was being achieved and of those involved. The real point about 'Making it Happen' was that it engaged people's emotions, not just their brains. Culture change is above all an emotional experience, not an intellectual one.

On launch day I'd promised staff that *everyone* would have a chance to be involved if they wanted. At the time I had no idea how we would do it, but Susan Spindler and her team found a way. They created something we called 'Just Imagine', borrowing the title from my launch speech. In the first six months more than ten thousand staff voluntarily took part at more than two hundred meetings all over the UK and across the world.

It is difficult now to remember how risky it felt to embark on something quite as radical as 'Just Imagine'. It was very non-BBC, an organization in which people tended to leave their emotions behind them when they came into work. In sessions ranging in size from fifty to four hundred, people paired up and took turns to interview each other about their positive experiences at the BBC. Instead of moaning, people talked about their proudest and most successful moments. They then discussed these in groups of ten, and finally the most powerful stories were shared with the whole group. Everyone was asked: If those great experiences were to become the norm, how would the organization have to change?

For thousands of people it was the first time anyone had ever listened to what they thought and felt about the BBC. These were often very moving occasions, and it wasn't unusual for people to shed a tear as their feelings of pride, loyalty, and deep affection for the BBC were reawakened. Often those feelings had been buried years earlier, to be replaced by disappointment and cynicism.

Many sceptics came to the meetings thinking this was 'happy-clappy management' but left excited after an incredibly rewarding experience. I was surprised by the success of these sessions and certainly found them an emotional experience myself, largely because some people I had secretly written off as 'change refuseniks' were transformed.

The data that came from the sessions – in all there were 25,000 separate ideas and suggestions – was analysed and then fed back to the divisional and pan-BBC change teams. Often good ideas that were popular at the sessions and easy to do were implemented almost immediately: simple things like putting a cash machine in the reception at BBC Cardiff or allowing staff to busk in the foyer of Bush House in London at lunchtime.

As a result of one suggestion at a 'Just Imagine' session we introduced job shadowing so everyone could learn about other parts of the BBC; and as a result of another we introduced news hotlines so that if a member of staff came across a story they knew who to ring. When this happened we told the world so that people could see change was happening and that their ideas were not being ignored.

Another vital aspect of 'Making it Happen' was the creation of a large group of senior leaders known as the 'Leading the Way' team. They came together for the first time in May 2002 at a two-day event in London's Docklands. This was the first time the top four hundred at the BBC had ever come together at one time. Some didn't want to come and protested vehemently that they didn't have time for this sort of nonsense. In my speech on the first day I said that in many ways the BBC was an immature organization, that I didn't know of any other company or institution of comparative size that did not bring its senior leaders together at least once a year to discuss strategy and performance and to build relationships.

I invited my old mentor from the Harvard Business School, John Kotter, to talk about leadership, and people were spellbound. The event was extremely effective in building a bigger group – a 400-strong team. People wanted us to hold more events of a similar nature.

Dave Gordon, a thirty-year veteran of BBC Sport, talked about the first meeting in a film made for his own area. He said:

I've been in the BBC for thirty years and I've seen initiatives come and go. I went along to the event in Docklands thinking 'Oh my God, another one of those sessions', but within minutes I found the whole climate was so positive. I met people I'd never met before and we exchanged ideas. I came out feeling the BBC really did have a future.

All the 'Making it Happen' divisional groups produced action plans and new ideas and initiatives sprang up everywhere. Within a year staff opinion started to change. All those earlier responses from the staff survey that had convinced us we had to do something about the prevailing culture began to shift.

The amount of raw data that came from staff who had participated in the 'Just Imagine' sessions was worth its weight in gold. Most of all, it gave me a powerful mandate for change. I no longer had to say, 'This is what I believe should happen' or 'This is what the Executive believes should happen'. I could look staff in the eyes and say, 'This is what you told us you wanted.'

A year after we launched 'Making it Happen' the cross-BBC groups came up with their proposals in the form of a single five-year change plan. Central to the plan was a new set of values that would guide everything that happened in the organization from now on. This was the first attempt in the BBC's eighty-year history to articulate the things the organization stood for. They were drawn up by a group from within the BBC that looked both at the way other successful organizations expressed their values and, crucially, boiled down the four thousand suggestions about values that had come in from the 'Just Imagine' sessions. These values hadn't originated with me or the Executive; they'd come from the staff, which made them easier to sell across the organization.

The six values were as follows:

- Trust is the foundation of the BBC: we are independent, impartial and honest.
- Audiences are at the heart of everything we do.
- We take pride in delivering quality and value for money.
- Creativity is the lifeblood of our organization.
- We respect each other and celebrate our diversity so that everyone can give their best.
- We are one BBC: great things happen when we work together.

These values were not necessarily what characterized the BBC at that time, but they were what the people at the BBC aspired to achieve.

Every value carried with it examples of what we, as individuals, needed to do if we were to achieve it. For instance: 'I support the best idea, not just my own' (creativity); 'We have internal debates and external unity: we are ambassadors for the BBC' ('One BBC'); 'We resist pressures on the output from political parties and lobby groups' (trust).

The largest and most expensive single element in the change plan was that the BBC would start one of the biggest ever leadership training programmes in the UK. With the help of Ashridge Business School we planned to give six thousand BBC leaders proper training over the next five years. It was one of those initiatives that, historically, the staff would have said was a waste of money. Instead I told them all that the 'Just Imagine' data had overwhelmingly shown that the staff wanted better leaders; it had emerged as their highest priority. And for managers who didn't want to go on the programme I was able to tell them that their staff wanted them to go and that it wasn't voluntary. If you wanted to be a leader at the BBC you had to have leadership training. I spoke about my views of leadership on every course.

We also started an induction programme that was one of our quick wins. Everyone joining the BBC now had to spend three days getting to know the organization, learning some basic programme-making skills – even if they were working in accounts – and meeting other new recruits from other divisions. The idea was simple: we wanted to make them feel they were part of 'One BBC' from the outset. And we wanted to excite them about the organization.

The overall change plan consisted of more than forty separate initiatives, many of them involving quite radical changes to the status quo. We introduced coaching and mentoring for managers to give them support, and a new recruitment programme based on the BBC's newly stated values; we gave programme makers more and better information about audiences, and we gave people more control over the areas they worked in. In the area of creativity, there was a recognition that single acts of creative genius were the exception rather than the norm and that BBC people needed to learn how to work together, in creative teams, to come up with and improve on good ideas. Many in the independent production sector were already doing this.

The next challenge was how to launch the change plan so that as many people as possible would be aware of it and have a chance of being part of implementing it. We came up with the idea for something we called 'The Big Conversation' – a title that was later used by Downing Street. Our 'Big Conversation' involved seventeen thousand members of staff in a huge live discussion. We agreed to spend £250,000 permanently to extend the BBC ring main so that an additional eight thousand staff could watch and take part in this event. We tried to create a party atmosphere with four hundred large events. We had events in Delhi, Moscow, Cairo, and Nairobi, as well as right across the UK. At Television Centre in White City we followed the event with Cerys Matthews singing live in the courtyard outside the studio. There was food and drink available to everyone and we all felt something special was happening.

The event began with a half-hour film in which I was the presenter. I explained the headlines of the change plan and linked all the initiatives back to what the staff had told us. This was not top down, it was bottom up. Everyone – all seventeen thousand of them – then discussed what they had seen in their separate meetings before joining together in a BBC-wide debate. For the first time, people could see the size, scale, and sheer variety of the organization. I believe this was the biggest and most ambitious staff communication event ever to take place in the UK.

It lasted two and a half hours and at the end of it I felt exhilarated. I thought we had achieved the impossible. Everyone seemed excited and there was an incredible sense that we all belonged to this huge, amazing, and wonderful organization. If we could only harness this spirit, everything would be achievable. As I left Television Centre that day I was accosted by a man who said to me, 'Greg, you've got to understand I'm about as cynical as you can get about the BBC, and even I thought that was pretty good.' Praise indeed.

Once the plans were announced we began to act on them very quickly. People began to see the difference and this was reflected in the results of the annual staff survey at the end of 2003. In 2001 the survey had revealed that just 28 per cent of people at the BBC felt valued by the organization. It was one of the main reasons we launched 'Making it Happen'. Two years later the figure stood at 58 per cent.

'Making it Happen' – and in particular the 'Just Imagine' sessions – changed the BBC profoundly. They helped the organization to grow up and to reduce the 'them and us' divide. People discovered that they didn't need permission to do things; they could do them for themselves. They also discovered management couldn't wave a wand and solve all their problems. They told us that, at last, they felt they were being treated as human beings, not just cogs in a machine.

It was a cathartic experience for many at the BBC, but not for all. Most of the BBC Governors were simply not part of it, which, given that their role only requires spending a day or two a month in the building, is not surprising. The main exception was the Chairman, Gavyn Davies, who understood about culture change programmes, having been through one at Goldman Sachs. Gavyn made the effort to attend the 'Just Imagine' sessions himself. He had warned us at the beginning that we shouldn't start the process if we weren't intending to see it through. Richard Eyre, who had himself changed the culture of the National Theatre when he ran it, also understood what we were trying to achieve.

Sadly, when the BBC Governors decided my future that evening in January 2004 they didn't take into account what we had achieved with our staff – an achievement that is now a Harvard Business School case study and widely recognized as a highly effective change programme. The reason was most of the Governors didn't even begin to understand what had been achieved.

When I am asked, as I am all the time, why thousands of staff took to the streets in support of me, why they bought the ad in the *Telegraph*, and why my going was so emotional for so many of them, when I was forced to leave the BBC, my answer is: 'Making it Happen'.

In two short years we convinced most of our staff that we really wanted change, that we wanted to empower them, that we wanted to be better leaders ourselves, and that we wanted everyone working for the BBC to have more rewarding and more fulfilling working lives. They knew we weren't doing this just to be nice. It was the means of achieving the ambition we all shared for the BBC: to become 'the most creative organization in the world' and as a result make the best programmes and provide the best possible services to our audiences. But, most of all, I hope we persuaded them that we cared.

The street protests weren't really about me. In the eyes of the staff, I represented the changes that 'Making it Happen' had already brought about in the organization and their hopes for the future. They understood instinctively that the whole initiative itself would now be vulnerable. They had lived through the Prague Spring and feared they could hear the distant rumble of the tanks.

CHAPTER ELEVEN

Television and Sport

Sport has always played a big, even a dominant, part in my life. I was brought up in a household where winning at football was always more important than exam results, which was just as well given that the Dyke boys weren't exactly from the top drawer academically.

My eldest brother Ian was an outstanding sportsman and a particularly good footballer. He was a left winger, back in the days when there were still left wingers, and one of my earliest recollections as a child is that of Bill Dodgin senior, the manager of Brentford, turning up at our house to try to sign him up. These were the days of the £20 a week maximum wage for footballers and my dad made it very clear that Ian was not going to be a professional footballer but instead was going to get a 'proper' job. He ended up spending his life in the insurance industry just like my father. Both hated it.

Ian did join Brentford as a junior and we've all had an affection for the club ever since, although they were never first choice for any of us. My father had been a big Arsenal fan since he was a boy, and he talked endlessly about their great side of the 1930s. He was a particular fan of their winger Cliff (Boy) Bastin and their centre forward David Jack. According to him, there were no players in modern-day football who could match Bastin and Jack.

A couple of years before he died I took both my dad and my mum to the 1988 FA Cup Final and we watched one of the biggest upsets in modern footballing history when Wimbledon beat Liverpool. It was only the second Cup Final he'd ever been to – the first was when Arsenal beat Huddersfield in 1930 and he reckoned he'd watched the match from the roof of the stand at Wembley. We worked out that there were fifty-eight years between his first final and his second.

When we were young my grandmother had a pub called the Seven Sisters in Markfield Road off Broad Lane in Tottenham, within walking distance of the Spurs ground. All the customers were Tottenham fans through and through so both my brothers followed suit, much to my father's dismay. If you are an Arsenal fan, there is nothing worse than your sons supporting Tottenham.

To be different from my brothers I perversely decided to support Manchester United, largely because John Rixon, a neighbour in our street in Hayes, was a United supporter. He was a friend of my eldest brother and was nearly ten years older than me, so I was always a bit in awe of him. Forty years later, in May 1999, I searched John out and took him with me in the private plane I had hired to fly to Barcelona to watch Manchester United in that amazing European Champions League Final. By then I was a Director of Manchester United and felt I owed John; if it hadn't been for him I might have had to support Tottenham for all those years, or – even worse – Arsenal.

As a sports freak it was natural that when I became Director of Programmes at LWT I also became Chairman of ITV Sport and took over responsibility for sport across the network. The full-time head of ITV Sport at that time was John Bromley, or Brommers as he was known, a legendary figure and one of the most loved men I have ever met. He never remembered anyone's name but overcame the problem by calling all women 'darling' and all men 'captain'.

Soon after I became Chairman we ran into problems concerning our contract with the American heavyweight boxer Mike Tyson. ITV had the exclusive rights for five Tyson world championship fights. As it turned out, the fifth was the big one: the fight between Tyson and the British boxer Frank Bruno. Suddenly Tyson's people, led by his manager Bill Cayton and Don King, the legendary US promoter, got a much bigger offer for the fight from the fledgling Sky and decided ITV didn't have a contract after all – even though we'd broadcast, and paid for, the first four fights.

We went to court to argue that we had the right to show the fight, although this was not without some risk. As always in such circumstances, our barrister told us we might win or we might not (I've often wondered why we all pay barristers so much money to tell us the obvious). The problem was that the only written contract we had was an agreement signed in the Rififi Club, a private members' club and restaurant just off Berkeley Square in London's West End, and written on a Rififi club napkin. When John Bromley went into the witness box the barrister for Sky decided to try to embarrass him about this. 'Do you normally write contracts on napkins in clubs?' Brommers was asked. 'Absolutely,' he replied, and everyone in court fell about laughing. Bromley's wit didn't make any difference, however. We lost the case, very unfairly we all believed, and Sky showed the fight.

Brommers was a decade older than me and came from a different period in ITV's history, a time before ITV was in any sense a proper business. Bromley's expenses were legendary and as Chairman of ITV Sport I had to sign them off. I left them on the kitchen table once and Sue picked them up. She couldn't believe that anyone could possibly claim for so much food and drink, and it was certainly true that Brommers had great difficulty meeting anyone without both of them having a drink in their hand. Oddly, he didn't eat a lot himself; he merely paid for everyone else to eat.

My favourite Bromley story was when LWT's Managing Director had to try to defend Bromley's expenses before the Board of LWT. The Finance Director was in full flow about how much Bromley had charged the company while in Seoul covering the Olympics in 1988. 'And then we come to the boat,' he said. 'Ah,' replied the MD, 'I can explain that. The guys out in Seoul were working so hard that John decided to take them for a party on the boat. What's wrong with that?' The Finance Director looked up. This was the moment all finance directors dream of. 'That would be fine except this boat wasn't in Seoul, it was on the Thames,' he said. Like all good stories it's probably been exaggerated over the years, but it tells you all you need to know about ITV sport in those days.

When Brommers was dying of cancer a couple of years ago I went to visit him at the Cromwell Hospital in London. When I told the desk whom I was visiting the receptionist looked dismayed and said, 'Oh no, not another one.' I think the rules said that there were only supposed to be three visitors at a time around his bed but Brommers had never taken any notice of the rules at any stage in his life, and he certainly wasn't going to start in his dying days. In his room there were at least thirty people. He'd had a bar set up in the corner and every night there was a party, while he lay in bed welcoming visitors.

I had been warned what to expect so I'd taken along a bottle of gin as a present. Brommers' voice was the same as it had always been, but the man in the hospital bed was a shrunken version of the wonderful character we'd all known. When he died there was standing room only at his memorial service held in St Martin-in-the-Fields in Trafalgar Square. It was a true celebration of the way he'd lived: LWT even picked up the bill for the celebrations afterwards. If you have to die, that's the way to go.

In those days boxing was big on ITV and one of my early sports decisions was that we should try to secure the rights for the fight between Frank Bruno and Joe Bugner for ITV. Bugner was coming out of retirement in Australia especially for the fight, and although it always had the look of a mismatch about it I believed it would be great box office. It was Barry Hearn's first ever fixture as a boxing promoter; up until then he was Mr Snooker in the UK, and this was the first time I'd ever met him.

Barry always tells the story that he asked me for a certain figure for the television rights to the fight; rather than arguing, I'd replied that if he could deliver the fight I'd pay him more. I don't remember this, but it didn't matter: the fight turned out to be a win for both of us. It was staged at White Hart Lane, the home of Tottenham Hotspur, and I even persuaded Sue to come and watch it. She hated the boxing but as a trained sociologist was fascinated by the mix of people who got all dressed up to watch it.

We got sixteen million viewers for the fight, the highest-rated sports programme on television in 1987, and it lasted eight rounds. Now how long a fight lasted was very important to ITV as you had to include as many advertisements as possible between rounds. A first- or second-round knockout might have been great for the crowds, but it was a disaster for a commercial broadcaster.

Barry is another of those big characters you find in sport. He walks around with a wad of notes in his wallet and has a new idea every day that he is prepared to back with his own money. Barry is the man who turned fishing into a spectator sport by building grandstands around a lake near Coventry where every year he stages *Fishomania* live on Sky

Sports. People sit all day, either in the grandstand or by the television set, watching motionless fishermen waiting to catch fish. It is a bit like watching paint dry, but Barry still manages to make money out of it. Amazingly, it has become an annual event.

My favourite Barry Hearn story was when Chris Eubank fought Dan Schummer of the USA in South Africa for the World Boxing Organization super middleweight world championship in October 1994. Eubank lost virtually every round. When it came to the end of the fight he sat down and asked Barry, who was his manager, 'What do you think?' At that very moment the WBO judge looked across at Barry and gave him a big wink, implying Eubank had retained his title. 'What do I think, Chris?' he said. 'What do I think? I think this is another country we can't come back to.' The crowd and the press went mad.

Barry once even asked me to be part of the English fishing team in the World Marlin Championships in the West Indies. I told him I'd never fished for big game and had certainly never caught a marlin. 'Don't be ridiculous. Neither has anyone else in the team,' he replied. He later sent me a tape: it was hilarious. I think there was only one marlin caught all week.

I also used to do business with another boxing promoter, Frank Warren, who was shot and wounded one night in Barking in London's East End. One of his boxers, Terry Marsh, was charged with the shooting but found not guilty. Soon afterwards Frank came for a lunch at LWT and I asked him if his business was going well. He replied that he was having a rough time and the banks weren't supporting him. Why not? I asked. 'Because banks don't like you if you get shot,' he explained.

During my years at ITV Sport I tried to refocus the network away from traditional magazine programming onto big sporting events. Early on I scrapped television wrestling and was threatened with Big Daddy and Giant Haystacks coming round to my house to sort me out. I believed the money spent on wrestling would be much better spent on boxing. But my five years as Chairman of ITV Sport were dominated by one sport above any other: football. It is difficult to believe today but until the mid Eighties there was virtually no live football on British television. Apart from the odd English international, the only live game was the FA Cup Final, and virtually everyone stayed indoors to watch it. In those days, towns were empty on FA Cup Final day.

But by the late Eighties pay television was emerging on the scene and out of the blue the fledgling British Satellite Broadcasting (BSB), the competitor to Sky before the two companies merged, bid for and was on the verge of winning the rights to broadcast live First Division matches on their pay channel, due to be launched in April 1990. It was around the same time that I came onto the sports scene and I decided my job was to try to derail the process and pinch these live football rights from BSB.

For advice on how I could go about this I turned to Trevor East, Deputy Head of Sport at Thames Television and a football specialist. I asked him whom we could talk to 'off the record' and he suggested we should meet David Dein, the Deputy Chairman of Arsenal and a member of the Football League management committee. The three of us met at

YES FOLKS, GREG DYKE IS BEING ASKED TO RECONSIDER HIS DECISION!

One of my first decisions when I was in charge of ITV Sport was to scrap Saturday afternoon wrestling. Many people hated me for taking that decision, including Big Daddy and Giant Haystacks. I did it because I wanted to change the image of ITV.

Suntory, a Japanese restaurant in London's West End, and David and I struck up a close friendship that lasts to this day.

We realized at once that we both had something to gain from each other. I wanted to pinch the football rights from BSB's grasp and he might be able to deliver them. He in turn wanted more money for his club and the other big clubs and I could afford to pay it. His view was very clear. The viewing public wanted to watch the big clubs on television so those clubs should get the bulk of the television money, which at that time was still spread around ninety-two clubs. In a series of meetings over a couple of weeks David, Trevor, and I worked out a plan. We would go direct to the big five clubs of the day – Arsenal, Liverpool, Manchester United, Tottenham, and Everton – and offer them a minimum of a million pounds a year each for the exclusive right to broadcast their home matches. This was massively more than any of them had received in the past. The Football League could sell the rest of the old First Division matches to whomever they wanted, but of course without the big clubs' home games they were worth much less.

I met the men who controlled the big five clubs in a bar one evening. Phil Carter of Everton, who was Chairman of the Football League at the time, came along with Martin Edwards from Manchester United, Irving Scholar, the Chairman of Tottenham, John Smith, Chairman of Liverpool, and of course David Dein from Arsenal. I took John Bromley with me for that first meeting but he was uneasy about doing a side deal with the big clubs so I didn't take him to the next one. That's a tactic I discovered was widely used at the BBC when I joined them a decade or so later. If someone doesn't agree, hold the next meeting without them.

In his book about his life in football – *Behind Closed Doors*, published in 1992 – Irving Scholar describes the turning point at this first meeting as the moment I admitted that I thought there had been a cartel between ITV and BBC to keep the price paid for televised football artificially low. The club chairmen had always believed it and I semi-confirmed it. From that moment on all five were on my side.

At our second meeting, held on a Sunday night, the five chairmen asked which club I supported. I told them I supported Manchester United, at which Martin Edwards beamed. A few years later this statement was to have real significance. At that second meeting we decided to extend the initial group of five to include five more clubs who would receive a lesser figure: West Ham, Newcastle, Aston Villa, Nottingham Forest, and Sheffield Wednesday.

The problem for me during this period was that every time I went to lunch with David Dein the price tab for the contract went up. I even recollect having to pay for the lunches as well. But the strategy we had devised worked. Threatened with a rebellion by the top ten clubs in the First Division, the Football League folded and opened negotiations with ITV. We eventually reached agreement with the League to pay £11 million a year for twenty-one live matches, to be played mostly on Sunday afternoons. We also bought the recorded rights for ITV but chose not to use them. For the next four years there would be no *Match of the Day* on Saturday evenings on BBC One.

Early in the negotiations I'd invited Paul Fox, then Managing Director of BBC Television, to join us in trying to defeat the fledgling BSB but he told me that he didn't think it would help make the BBC popular with the Government at a time when the Corporation's charter was up for renewal. It's interesting that they didn't take the same view a few years earlier when they very nearly killed off TV-am by launching a competitive breakfast television service.

Within ITV, and particularly within LWT, there were those who believed I had overpaid by paying £11 million a year. Only two years earlier the Football League had received only £1.6 million in total from the BBC and ITV. Because virtually all the games would be played at the weekend, LWT would pay more than a quarter of the total £11 million bill, so I understood the concern within my own company. But I believed the doubters were wrong. Anyway the deal was done and there was little that could be done about it. Eight years later the same rights were sold for the unbelievable figure of £167 million a year, so perhaps it wasn't such a bad deal.

The ramifications of the way we had done the deal were enormous within the Football League. The old Second Division clubs were angry that they had been outmanoeuvred by the big clubs and took action that later would cost them dear. Phil Carter, the League's Chairman, was fired and David Dein was made to step down from the management committee as the Second Division clubs took total control of the Football League. In taking their revenge against the representatives of the big clubs they sowed the seeds of what was to come four years later.

ITV honoured the deal we'd made with the bigger clubs. They were all guaranteed a certain number of games a season on television, which we delivered, and all received the heady sums we'd promised them. But this strategy also made ITV vulnerable four years later. Where the old Second Division clubs had upset the big five, we'd upset the smaller clubs in the First Division, who became resentful about the deal we'd done with their stronger brethren. They, too, would have the opportunity to take their revenge.

Although, like so many sports contracts in those days, the deal was never actually signed by either party, it turned out to be a good one for both. ITV, in particular, got a real bonus at the end of the first season. The First Division title went right to the wire with Liverpool and Arsenal very close in first and second places respectively. Amazingly, the last game of the season was between the same two clubs and was to be played on a Friday night, live on ITV. Liverpool had won the FA Cup the previous Saturday and were three points clear of Arsenal, so the famous double was there for the taking. They only had to draw to become champions, while for Arsenal to take the title they had to win the match at Anfield by two clear goals. It was probably the most exciting end to a season ever.

Arsenal scored their second goal in the last minute to win 2–0 and to take the title. I had flown up to the game with members of the Arsenal Board and ended up celebrating with David Dein and the Arsenal team in the winners' dressing room. I found it revealing that only two of the Liverpool team, Bruce Grobbelaar and Peter Beardsley, came in to congratulate the Arsenal players that night. But the Liverpool fans were magnificent; they were obviously desperately disappointed but applauded the Arsenal team off the pitch. ITV got an audience of nearly eleven million, making the £11 million a season look cheap.

By the autumn of 1991 it was time to talk about the next football deal. Trevor East, David Dein, and I decided another dinner between ITV and the big five clubs was called for. We fixed the dinner and I offered to host it in London, in the hospitality suite on the eighteenth floor of the LWT building on the South Bank. Many have claimed they were the architects of the Premier League; but when the official history of the Premier League is written, this dinner meeting will surely be seen as the time and the place at which it became a reality.

229

By and large the same people turned up from the clubs as four years earlier, although by this time John Smith had retired as Chairman of Liverpool and had been replaced by Noel White. Just as we had four years ago, David Dein and I discussed tactics in advance. We agreed I would open up by saying I thought it unlikely we could do another deal with the Football League negotiators that would be as favourable to the big clubs as the last one, which was certainly true. So the big clubs had a choice: either take less money, as the total was likely to be spread around more clubs, or take radical action.

They were unanimous. They all resented the way Carter and Dein had been treated by the Football League and they opted for the radical approach. They very quickly decided that they wanted the First Division clubs to break away from the Football League and set up the Premier League, which would be run by the twenty member clubs in the interests of those clubs. They would sell their own television rights and the proceeds would go to them.

No one had predicted things would move so fast, but everyone remembered a few years back when a similar move had failed. This time they all agreed that if they were to succeed they needed to get the Football Association onside. Everyone knew that there had never been much love lost between the FA and the Football League. I once met Alan Hardaker's daughter at a football match and asked her why her father, the legendary Secretary of the Football League, had moved the organization's headquarters to Lytham St Annes. Her reply was that he wanted to get it as far away from the FA as he could.

In 1992 the relationship between the two bodies was particularly bad and this made it more likely that the FA would support the clubs if they decided to break away; but it had to be handled properly, so another significant decision made that night was the choice of who would lead the delegation to meet Bert Millichip, the ageing Chairman of the FA. These were the days when Liverpool had dominated English football for at least a decade and they had to be seen to be onside; so the five clubs decided that the Chairman of Liverpool, Noel White, who was then and still is a member of the FA's international committee, would lead the delegation, supported by David Dein.

The rest is history. Within months the top clubs had resigned from the Football League and by the start of the following season the FA Premier

League was up and running. The only problem was that ITV didn't get the television rights. By then BSB had merged with Sky to form BSkyB and Rupert Murdoch was in control and very keen to win the rights.

It was probably my fault that we lost them. I'd been too complacent, believing that with the big five clubs supporting us we were bound to win. Trevor East tried to warn me that we ought to be spending more time with the smaller Premier League clubs, but I didn't take any notice. I've always hated making polite small talk in a bid to get people onside, a character trait that was later to cost me dear with the BBC Governors.

My view back in 1992 was that my strategy of working with the big clubs had been successful last time, so why wouldn't it be the same this time? Trevor himself had actually shaken hands on a deal with Rick Parry, the newly appointed Chief Executive of the Premier League, at a boxing match in Manchester, so we thought we were in pole position.

In fact I did have lunch with the Chief Executive of BSkyB, Sam Chisholm, during the bidding process. Chisholm was an overweight, mouthy Australian who had been brought up as one of Kerry Packer's henchmen and styled himself on Packer. He had been brought in by Murdoch to save the company. Over lunch he was pretty blunt. He told me that Rupert Murdoch had approved what he was about to say. 'Mr Dyke,' he said, 'why don't we get together to fuck these football clubs?' My view was that if he wanted a deal with us it meant we were in prime position and didn't need him. How wrong I was.

I also misjudged the situation because in the time between the Premier League actually being set up and the television contract being settled Irving Scholar had sold Spurs to Alan Sugar. Sugar owned the electronics company Amstrad, which at the time was the main supplier of satellite dishes to BSkyB, and he was very close to the Murdoch operation. As a result, Spurs switched sides and supported BSkyB.

In fact when it came to the crucial vote, Sugar played an important part. We had received intelligence from within the Premier League during the weekend before the meeting on Monday 18 May that we were in danger of losing. We worked all through Sunday night and on the day of the meeting we hit the clubs with a new offer, which Trevor East delivered personally to each club representative. He had also delivered the new bid to Rick Parry earlier that morning. It was high enough to be the winning bid.

A few minutes after the meeting at the Royal Lancaster Hotel started Trevor was standing outside the meeting room when Sugar came rushing out of the meeting and got on the phone. Trevor heard him say, 'You've got to blow them out of the water.' He was clearly talking to someone at BSkyB and – lo and behold – a new BSkyB bid arrived.

I also misjudged how much the Premier League contract mattered to BSkyB. Rupert Murdoch himself flew over to Britain to get involved and did his usual job of flattering the people who would be influential in the decision. In fact when ITV put in its final bid Alan Sugar wasn't the only person to ring BSkyB: Rick Parry had already done so. Between shaking hands with Trevor East on the deal and the meeting of the clubs actually taking place, Parry had been heavily courted by both Chisholm and Murdoch. They'd even flown him to Scotland in their private jet to show him the BSkyB call centre. Rick Parry told me later that 'Mr Murdoch was the most impressive man I ever met'.

In spite of all this, Trevor and I believed we had enough votes to win. When it came to the vote, six of the twenty Premier League clubs supported the ITV bid – four of the big five plus Leeds and Aston Villa. Two other clubs abstained. We lost by a single vote as seven clubs would have been enough to stop BSkyB. We discovered later that Nottingham Forest, whose Chairman had promised to vote for us, had actually sent along an office secretary because no one else was available. That vote in favour of BSkyB turned out to be crucial.

Actually, we would still have won had it not been for the personal intervention of the Chairman of the BBC, Duke Hussey. Again Rupert Murdoch was involved. When Murdoch took over the Times Group he kept Hussey, who had been a pretty disastrous Chairman of Times Newspapers, as a board member. They became friends, and there are even suggestions that it was Murdoch who suggested to Margaret Thatcher that she should appoint Hussey as Chairman of the BBC, a remarkable decision in itself given that Hussey didn't actually own a television set at the time. Personally I've always liked Hussey: he's loud, eccentric and a wonderful character, exactly the sort of person whose company I enjoy, although I'm not at all sure I would have enjoyed working for him. When he and John Birt were Chairman and Director-General respectively of the BBC they didn't talk to each other for months on end, though that was not necessarily all Hussey's fault.

In the run-up to the Premier League bid, as Hussey later admitted, he had discussed the issue with Rupert Murdoch. As a result, the BBC put in a bid of around £20 million a year for the *Match of the Day* rights but only on the condition that ITV didn't get the live rights. What it meant was that we at ITV had to bid £20 million more than BSkyB to win. As it turned out, that £20 million would have been enough to have swung the contract our way.

Knowing the BBC so much better now than I did then, I find Hussey's actions even more extraordinary today than I did at the time. What on earth was the Chairman of the BBC doing getting himself involved in football negotiations in the first place? That is not his role. The BBC had effectively used public money to favour the Murdoch bid following a conversation between Rupert Murdoch and the Chairman of the BBC. What was Hussey doing using money raised by the licence fee to favour Murdoch? It was, to say the least, questionable. But Rupert Murdoch's activities in Britain – first in the Thatcher/Major years and, since 1997, during the Blair era – have consistently escaped real political scrutiny. In other countries politicians intervened when it looked like their major football league was likely to end up on pay television; in Britain they didn't. Winning elections is too important to British politicians and the Murdoch press can influence who wins and who loses. As a result, most of them don't have the nerve to take on Murdoch.

So my days involved in sport at ITV ended on a disappointing note. By this time I had become Chief Executive of LWT and had moved away from any close involvement in programming. Once the Premier League negotiations were over I gave up being Chairman of ITV Sport and for a while wasn't involved in sport at all. It was only after LWT had been taken over by Granada and I was sitting at home unemployed that I got the chance to become involved again.

I received a call in the autumn of 1994 from Robert Charles, Head of Sport at Yorkshire Television, who told me that Channel Four wanted a new current affairs programme about sport and that Yorkshire were planning to bid for it. He wanted to know if they could use my name as the prospective presenter in their bid document. I agreed and we got the commission for a series of programmes called *Fair Game*. Now television broadcasters traditionally avoid making controversial programmes about sport for obvious reasons. If you expose wrongdoing or inefficiency in a sporting organization they are unlikely to sell you their rights again; but this would not have been a problem for Channel Four because the channel wasn't reliant on sport.

By the time of *Fair Game* I had been around the boardroom of television companies for close on a decade, so going back on the road making programmes was a novel experience. If you run television companies you believe television production is an efficient, well-organised, well-oiled process. When you go back on the road you discover it is just as chaotic as it ever was. You spend hours hanging around, you shoot masses of material you never use, and there are always people who simply don't show up. One day we spent hours in a field waiting to meet a bent jockey. He never came. Why? Because he was a bent jockey and wasn't reliable.

We did programmes about a range of sports but the one that really hit the headlines was on rugby union and it led to Will Carling's being fired as captain of the England rugby team for something like thirty-six hours after he had described the Rugby Football Union's management committee as 'fifty-seven old farts'.

The aim of this particular programme was to demonstrate that the people running English rugby were from a different age. These were the days before the game went professional and the RFU's management committee really did believe the game was for them and that the players were largely irrelevant. When we interviewed Dudley Wood, the Secretary of the Rugby Football Union, for the programme we kept asking him about the players and in the end he got a bit agitated. 'You keep asking me about the players but I want to tell you what a wonderful job the committee does.' One has to wonder what planet he was living on.

Never in any sport have I met a bunch of players who so hated the people who ran the game as I found in rugby. It was a straight divide between a bunch of old blokes who loved the 'amateur' nature of rugby and players who trained and played like professional athletes but didn't get paid. It was a divide both of generations and of class.

When the producer of this particular programme first arranged to meet Carling and Rob Andrew in a pub, Andrew was late turning up; so the producer explained to Carling what the programme was likely to be about. When Andrew finally arrived Carling turned to him and said 'They're out to get the RFU. Are you up for that?' Both of them agreed they were 'up' for it.

I interviewed Carling at the Richmond Hill Hotel, the traditional meeting place for England players before an international. He said a lot of controversial things, including describing the committee as 'old farts'. Later there was some dispute about this particular statement with Carling saying it was said off the record when the camera wasn't running. The programme team denied it, although it was true they only had it on the audio tape not the video. My own recollection at the time was that Carling knew what he was saying and had been waiting a long time to say it. Although Carling initially complained to Channel Four, his agent later withdrew the complaint.

The programme, called 'State of the Union', was broadcast on Thursday 4 May 1995 at 8 p.m. On the following Saturday morning I got a phone call from John Bromley, by then a sports consultant, who had in turn taken a call from Carling's agent, Jon Holmes. 'They're going to fire Carling this morning,' Bromley told me, 'for disrespect to the committee. Jon Holmes is desperate to talk to you.' It was true, and Carling was fired.

Unfortunately for Dudley Wood and Dennis Easby, that year's President of the RFU, there was a game at Twickenham that afternoon with Wasps playing Bath in the final of the 1995 Pilkington Cup. The ground was full to capacity with 73,000 spectators. Word got around that the committee had fired the England captain for disrespect and as Dennis Easby walked onto the pitch the whole crowd started booing, and carried on booing. In one afternoon the RFU Committee had to face up to something they had spent years trying to avoid: they finally had to admit that the spectators, the people who paid to watch rugby and who indirectly paid for the committee's expenses and their grand dinners, regarded the players as infinitely more important than committee members.

The following day Jon Holmes persuaded me to go on a live radio discussion programme with Dennis Easby of the RFU. It was on Talksport and the presenter was another ITV man, Gary Newbon. Somehow, live on air, we managed to patch things up and Carling was reinstated.

In many ways the 'old farts' saga marked the death of one era of rugby in England and the birth of another. Not long afterwards the game went professional. The RFU was reformed, a more professional management team came in, and nine years later a professional England side won the Rugby World Cup. For my birthday that year my friend Jeff Wright gave me a car number plate as a present: GD 57 RFU 0.

What I'd discovered in making *Fair Game* was that the people who were organizing and running sport in the UK were largely hard-working, well-meaning, enthusiastic amateurs. Sadly, in many sports they still are. I remember Graham Taylor telling me that when he became manager of the England football team he expected to be quite an important figure at the Football Association. According to him, he quickly discovered he was less important than the FA council member for Norfolk.

Stories of committee members flying 'club class' while the competitors are back in goat class are still to be found in British sport. On one of the *Fair Game* programmes David Mellor captured all that was suspect in British sports administration when he said: 'Sport in Britain will only improve when a lot of old men in blazers fall on their swords.' Unfortunately, what we have discovered since is that there are always a lot of young men in blazers prepared to replace them. Without structural change in sport not much will improve.

I made two series of *Fair Game* whilst I was also holding down my new day job of running and building Pearson Television. In fact I was negotiating the deal to buy Grundy, the Australian production company, for $386 million while I was standing, freezing cold, on the Yorkshire moors filming a programme on horse racing. At the end of the second series I decided I couldn't be both a presenter and an executive so I wanted out of *Fair Game*. Channel Four and Yorkshire Television agreed there weren't that many more sports stories to cover so we all happily called it a day and my involvement in sport ended again, but only for a while.

The following year I took a call from Mike Southgate, who at that time was, amongst other things, responsible for sport at the ITV network. Mike is a great guy to have working for you. He works hard, is a good leader, but most of all he's a problem solver. Talk to Mike about a difficult issue and he'll be back the next day with a solution, and then he'll go away and actually get on with it. Any successful Chief Executive needs the Mike Southgates of this world. Mike is always complaining that I take him with me to new jobs and then leave him behind when I go, which is unfortunately true. When I first left LWT he stayed behind. I then lured him to TVS, back to LWT, to Pearson Television, and then to the BBC.

Mike had phoned to tell me that Martin Edwards of Manchester United had been asking him where he could find me. So I rang Martin and fixed up to meet him for a drink at the Lancaster Hotel. When I turned up he was there with Sir Roland Smith, Chairman of Manchester United plc. They sat me down and told me they wanted someone with television experience to join the Board of Manchester United and that, after a long discussion, they had decided I was the person they wanted.

Of all the things that have happened to me in my life, this was the most humbling. I was a kid from Hayes who had supported United since the early Fifties. I'd cried myself to sleep on the night of the Munich air crash in February 1958; I'd celebrated the night we beat Benfica to win the European Cup in 1968; I'd despaired as Liverpool came to dominate English football and United didn't win the title for sixteen years. Suddenly I was to be elevated to the Board of Manchester United. Martin told me that with the place on the Board came four seats in the directors' box. I played it very cool and told Martin and Roland I would think about it and discuss it with Sue.

I rushed home and found Joe, my youngest son and a fellow United supporter. He was nine at the time. I told him that I was going to be a director of Manchester United. 'What does that mean, Dad?' he asked. I replied: 'It means tickets, Joe, tickets.'

Telling my partner Sue was a different proposition. She has always hated football with a passion and believes to this day that her greatest failure as a parent was in not preventing me from indoctrinating three of our four children with my love of football. Now I was going to tell her I'd be away at football matches most Saturdays, as well as midweek evenings, following United. It was not without some trepidation that I raised it. Amazingly, she was relaxed. 'I've been thinking you ought to be doing something just for you,' she said. I couldn't believe it. Was this the woman that I knew and loved? I thought about it and then said, 'Could you write that down and sign it, please?' Now all I had to do was to get the agreement of my employers, Pearson plc. I went to see the Chairman, Dennis, now Lord, Stevenson. I explained what I'd been offered and then said that if it came to a choice between United and Pearson, I'd opt for the former. He laughed and agreed.

The Chairman of Manchester United plc, Professor Sir Roland Smith, was another great character. He was a fount of fascinating and funny stories. He had been in and around big business for many years and at one time he held more directorships in companies listed on the Stock Exchange than anyone else in Britain. He was Chancellor of UMIST, the second university in Manchester, had been on the Board of the Bank of England, and had also been Chairman of British Aerospace. As Chairman of House of Fraser he was the man who had sold Harrods to Mohamed Al Fayed and was threatened by Tiny Rowland in the process. In the battle for Harrods Roland had famously told Tiny Rowland to get his tanks off his lawn. In turn, Rowland said that after shaking hands with Roland Smith you had to count your fingers. It was Roland who had first suggested floating Manchester United on the stock market in 1991. I remember buying some shares back then out of loyalty. Richard Webb, my best friend, business partner and accountant, told me he didn't think they were a good buy but that I shouldn't worry about losing money because we needed some capital gains tax losses to offset against the profits we were making elsewhere. In fact it was a brilliant investment. I bought at 28p a share and sold at 214p.

The United Board had clearly been under pressure to recruit some proper independent non-executive directors. There was inevitably tension between the main plc Board, on which I sat, and the football club Board, which was supposed to run the actual footballing side of the business. As Mike Eddelson, still a member of the football club Board, once said to me: 'I don't care about the money or making profits. I want us to buy the best players so we can win.' Mike summed up the challenge facing any football club when you try to run it as a business. Virtually no one – not the manager, the players, the staff of the club, and certainly not the fans – cares whether you make any money. They'd rather you spent more money on players, and in football most of the income does go to the players. It is not unlike the movie business where most of the money goes to the on-screen talent. That old joke 'How do you make a small fortune in movies? Start with a large one' applies equally to football. The exception in Britain has been Manchester United and it was the duty of the main Board to make sure we made profits, paid dividends to the shareholders, and grew the overall value of the business. The two different concepts inevitably led to clashes.

When Manchester United bought Dwight Yorke for £12.6 million from Aston Villa in 1998 it was on the strict understanding that Ole Gunnar Solskjaer was to be sold to Tottenham for £5 million. I have my doubts whether Alex Ferguson and the football club Board ever had any intention of selling him, and once Yorke had arrived, at a bigger price than we'd been told, suddenly Solskjaer didn't want to go. As it turned out, he won the European Champions League for United so the football club Board were probably right.

Martin Edwards was the Chief Executive of Manchester United and Chairman of the football club Board so he was on both boards. He was very interested in the share price because at that time he was the club's biggest shareholder. Of course running a football club is a thankless task because in the end the fans always turn on you, but this usually only happens when you are losing. With Martin it was different. In the time Martin was running United they won the Premier League seven times in nine years and yet every time he walked onto the pitch the fans booed him. They didn't believe he really loved the club in the same way as they did because, on at least three separate occasions, he'd tried to sell it and cash out. I was on the Board for the last of these, when Rupert Murdoch and BSkyB tried to buy the club. I ended up being the only director opposed to the sale for quite a long time, but being on my own in such circumstances has never worried me, and it didn't on this occasion. I think it was Enoch Powell who said, 'I've never felt being in a minority of one was in any way an indication that I might be in error.' On that I agree with him.

The first I knew that BSkyB wanted to buy Manchester United was at the beginning of July 1998 when I turned up at the monthly United board meeting to find that both Roland Smith and Martin Edwards wanted us to scrap the normal agenda to discuss something else – selling the business. It was to be another two months before the *Sunday Telegraph* broke the story, two months in which I did my best to kill the deal.

I should have known something was up at the earlier June board meeting. It was intended that we would discuss long-term strategy, not something the Board of Manchester United was used to doing. When we got there, however, Roland Smith announced that he had urgent business in London and was planning a truncated meeting. We were out of the room in a couple of hours. At the next meeting we were given the news of the BSkyB bid.

The plan to sell had been Martin's. We were told he'd had a series of meetings with Mark Booth, the Chief Executive of BSkyB, and that they had agreed a deal. BSkyB would buy the whole of Manchester United at 212p a share, valuing the business at nearly £600 million. This compared with a share price at the time of 159p. Martin explained that Mark Booth had run the numbers and that 212p a share was the most BSkyB could afford to pay. I laughed and said, 'He would say that, wouldn't he?'

As the club's biggest shareholder, Martin was not only willing to sell; he was also willing to pledge his shares to support the bid, even at this early stage. He clearly wanted the cash. He had also got Roland on his side for more altruistic reasons. Roland truly believed United would benefit from being part of a large, high quality business with a strong balance sheet. I disagreed with Roland and for a whole range of reasons was against the deal.

I thought the price was too low. I didn't see any advantage to the club in being part of a large media empire; in particular I thought United had a strong enough balance sheet to survive on its own as, unlike many other football clubs, it had no debt. I also argued against the idea that BSkyB would put money into Manchester United. When companies pay a premium over the share price to buy another company they reckon on saving money, not putting more money into the new business.

I also said I had real doubts whether the deal would get through the competition authorities, since here was a single television company effectively buying Manchester United's television rights for ever. I had one final reason for being against the deal, though I didn't tell the Board. I didn't want my beloved Manchester United to be controlled by Rupert Murdoch, but I could hardly put that forward as a business reason for opposing the deal.

At that July meeting we decided, as a board, that we needed to do more work, to bring in our merchant bankers and make our own assessment as to whether or not it was a good deal. That work went on during July and August. I brought in Janice Hughes from Spectrum, a media consultancy, to give us a long-term view as to what television rights would be worth. She was pretty optimistic and I thought I might persuade the Board to drop the deal.

When Martin Edwards told Mark Booth that he was meeting opposition on the United Board, Booth increased BSkyB's offer to 220p a share. So much for 212p being the most he could afford to pay. Our bankers were HSBC, led by the remarkably named Rupert Faure-Walker.

At 220p a share they told us we had a fiduciary duty to put the offer to our shareholders to let them decide, as they thought it a good deal. I disagreed and pointed out to them that I didn't think this was an entirely unbiased view given that HSBC would make millions if the deal went through and a few hundred thousand if it didn't.

One by one the members of the Board began siding with Martin and Roland. By the end of August the only people against the deal were myself and the Finance Director David Gill, now the Chief Executive of Manchester United. Then the story broke. I was at my house in Hampshire on the afternoon of Saturday 5 September when I got a call from the Pearson press office saying that Neil Collins of the *Sunday Telegraph* had a story about BSkyB buying Manchester United. They'd laughed at the story but Collins had assured them it was true and said that he wanted to speak to me as I was known to be the director most opposed to the deal.

I didn't return the call but managed to get hold of David Gill and asked him to alert the rest of the Board. I also rang BSkyB and managed to speak to Mark Booth, whom I knew quite well, though we'd never discussed the takeover. I told him about the *Sunday Telegraph* story and we got on to talking about the deal. He asked me why I was against it. I gave him my reasons and also explained why I believed the deal would be thrown out by the Monopolies and Mergers Commission. We ended up making a £50 bet on whether it would go through or not. He duly paid up when it didn't.

It had been a good old-fashioned Sunday paper scoop and Neil Collins rightly won a number of awards for it. Everyone believed I had given him the story, but it wasn't in my interests for it to become public. I had more chance of stopping it if it remained confidential. To this day I have no idea who Collins' source was, but it was a good piece of journalism.

What happened next was politically interesting. On the Sunday morning the Sports Minister Tony Banks appeared on *Frost on Sunday* making it pretty clear that he was against the deal. He said that he was sure the Department of Trade and Industry would want to take a very close look at it. He and every other Government minister then disappeared and never said another word about the proposed takeover from beginning to end. The Labour Party had spent a long time wooing Murdoch and were not going to blow it over this. Banks had clearly been told to keep quiet.

The Manchester United Board met virtually non-stop for two days on the Monday and Tuesday following the *Sunday Telegraph* article. It got pretty unpleasant at times. Late on the Monday night Martin Edwards threatened to sue me personally if my opposition stopped the deal, to which I pointed out that I was the only truly independent director on the Board and said I wouldn't be threatened by him. He later said it had been a joke, but it hadn't felt like it at the time.

Our stockbrokers, Merrill Lynch, supported me – they, too, thought the offer was too low – though they came under enormous pressure for doing so. Their top man in London told me that he'd been ordered by his bosses in New York to stop supporting me otherwise they wouldn't get their share of the impending US flotation of Fox – owned, of course, by Rupert Murdoch's News International. To their credit, Merrill Lynch remained steadfast. The pressure got worse. Early on the Tuesday morning Rupert Murdoch himself rang Roland Smith and warned him against me. He told him I shouldn't be allowed to vote as I was a known enemy of BSkyB.

I took my own legal advice from Stephen Cooke, at the City firm of Slaughter and May. Stephen had represented LWT in the takeover bid by Granada and I'd been impressed with his work. We had also become friends. His advice on this was clear: I had to recommend acceptance of an offer if I thought it was a good financial deal for the shareholders. According to him, the law was unambiguous: only the shareholders mattered. The fans, the players, the staff were all secondary to the shareholders in law.

By this time the bid was up to 230p and even David Gill had decided it was time to accept. I was now completely on my own. I came up with a proposal on the Tuesday morning that I would accept a price of 240p but I would simultaneously announce that any profit I made on the shares I owned as a result of the deal would be given to an appropriate charity in Manchester. I certainly didn't want to profit personally from this deal. I said that if the deal stayed at 230p I wouldn't oppose it but nor would I recommend it; I'd also put out a statement giving my view that there was no reason for Manchester United not to remain an independent company. Roland Smith, wise old bird that he was, knew that he had to have all his board onside and he instructed Martin Edwards to tell Mark Booth that the price was 240p or no deal. Booth went mad, saying that there was no way he would pay 240p and that the offer would come off the table at 5 p.m. that afternoon.

The BSkyB Board were meeting all afternoon in Isleworth, with Rupert Murdoch in attendance; we were at the HSBC offices in Lower Thames Street. It was now a game of chicken. Coincidentally, my chairman at Pearson, Dennis Stevenson, was also on the BSkyB Board at the time and he later told me that a number of profanities were used as adjectives in front of my name every time it was mentioned at the BSkyB meeting. Dennis stood up for me and said I was only doing what any non-executive board member should be doing – trying to maximize the return for the shareholders. I don't think he mentioned that I was also having great fun screwing Rupert Murdoch.

The question was, who would crack first? I was praying that the Board of BSkyB would stay firm because that way Manchester United would remain independent; but it wasn't to be. At about 4 p.m. they folded and agreed to pay 240p per share. I had won, but I had also lost.

The following day there was a press conference at Old Trafford at which a reporter from the *Daily Mirror* asked Mark Booth one of the great questions of sports journalism. 'Who plays left back for Manchester United?' Booth, an American who knew nothing about soccer, was completely lost and couldn't answer the question. In some ways I think the credibility of the deal collapsed with that question. At the same time, I made my announcement about giving the profit from my shares to a local charity. Our bankers had tried to persuade me, in the strongest fashion, not to make the announcement. I ignored them.

The takeover deal was duly referred to the Monopolies and Mergers Commission and hundreds of individuals and organizations submitted evidence arguing against the deal. Virtually no one outside of BSkyB and Manchester United plc argued in favour. In the end, the Commission took the view that a takeover of Manchester United by BSkyB would be anti-competitive. Their report was so conclusive that even a Government that had tried so hard not to offend Rupert Murdoch had to accept it. The BSkyB takeover of Manchester United was dead.

Being on the Manchester United Board meant that all sorts of people would ring you up to try to get that most precious of commodities – tickets. However, the oddest request I received during my time on the Board came from Downing Street, and it was not for tickets. Cherie Blair, whom I knew quite well, rang one Christmas to ask if I could get a discount on a Manchester United shirt. I said I could and asked what name and number she wanted on the back. The reply came: Blair, number 7. Her son, Euan, wanted David Beckham's number. I offered to give her the shirt for free, but she insisted on paying. For a while I was tempted to keep the cheque Cherie sent me for the shirt and frame it; in the end I decided the money was more important than the memento, so I cashed it.

My last year on the United Board coincided with one of the most successful seasons in the club's history, by the end of which we'd won the treble. I took most of my family and a few friends, including John Rixon from Hayes, out to Barcelona to watch the third leg of the treble, the match with Bayern Munich. I very nearly didn't get in. I had enough tickets for my party but my personal ticket was being held by the United staff. I was due to meet them at the hotel in Barcelona to collect it but unfortunately the private plane I'd hired was late and the mini-bus driver who collected us from the airport didn't come from Barcelona and couldn't find the hotel. By the time I did get to the hotel everyone had left and I still didn't have a ticket. The only way to see the match was to bluff my way in. We got through the first police cordon by pretending we had more tickets than we had; after that at every barrier I insisted I was a director of Manchester United and asked to be escorted in. In the end I got onto the pitch itself before finding Ken Merrick, the secretary of Manchester United, who had my ticket and accreditation. It's amazing how far bullshit can get you.

In my time on the United Board two matches stand out above all others. I was at Villa Park in April 1999 on the night we knocked Arsenal out of the FA Cup with one of the greatest goals I've ever seen. Peter Schmeichel had already saved a penalty in the last minute of normal time and Roy Keane had been sent off when Ryan Giggs ran from the halfway line to score, having only touched the ball three or four times during a wonderful run. We went on to win the FA Cup, the second leg of the treble. The second game was that match in Barcelona just a couple of months later, where for eighty-eight minutes we were terrible and then scored twice to win the match. The following day I threw a party for all my staff at Pearson Television to celebrate.

My time on the United Board came to a natural end when I was appointed Director-General designate at the BBC. Everyone agreed that you couldn't be both the buyer and the seller of the same sports rights, and so I resigned. I also had to sell all my Manchester United shares. But it had been an interesting experience.

When I joined the BBC, sport was one of the biggest problems I faced. Until the late Eighties and the arrival of BSkyB, the BBC had been pre-eminent in sport and had most of the big sports contracts. But by 2000 many of these had been lost. The FA Cup and Formula One motor-racing had gone to ITV, cricket had gone to Channel Four, as had racing at Cheltenham and the Derby, we had no contract for the next football World Cup, and BSkyB had most of the domestic football.

The BBC had taken the decision not to compete for many of these sports. John Birt's view was quite logical: that the BBC had limited funds that could be better used in areas like drama and news where the BBC added more value. It was a perfectly rational strategy but, like so many of John's strategies, it ignored one factor: what the audience wanted. Our research showed the British public liked sport on the BBC, without advertisements, and were very resentful that it was no longer available. For many of them, that was why they paid their licence fee.

The second problem with BBC sport was easily fixed. For ideological reasons – driven by the consulting firm McKinsey – sport at the BBC had been split into two. There was Sports Broadcasting, the people who bought rights and were responsible for exploiting those rights on television and radio, and Sports Production, who produced the programmes that owning the rights entitled you to make. It was madness, and everyone involved knew it was madness – except of course for McKinsey and the people around John Birt. When I produced my first reorganization plan for the BBC, 'One BBC', I scrapped the system and recreated a BBC sports department that handled everything.

I then persuaded Peter Salmon, who at that time was Controller of BBC One, to take over BBC Sport. He was not only a natural leader prepared to take bold decisions but also a naturally caring person who, unlike some others at the BBC, saw it as his job both to inspire and look after the people who worked for him. When I started my culture change programme at the BBC he was an important part of it.

Sadly, before Peter took over the job in the autumn of 2000, things got worse: the BBC lost the rights to *Match of the Day* once again. In June 2000 the television rights to the FA Cup, the Premiership, and the

Football League were all sold in a single week – a week of madness when ridiculous prices were paid that I doubt will ever be paid for football rights again. At the BBC we wanted to retain *Match of the Day* and regain the FA Cup and the English internationals. ITV was not interested in recorded highlights but was desperate to retain the FA Cup.

The then Chief Executive of the FA, Adam Crozier, clearly wanted the FA Cup back on the BBC so he encouraged us and BSkyB to get together to bid. We ended up with a great deal for the BBC that rankled with Sky Chief Executive Tony Ball for some years. We paid only a third of the money and got all England's competitive home internationals live, as well as two matches from every round of the FA Cup, including the pick of the best game.

We were delighted when we were told unofficially that we'd got the deal. The trouble was that Adam Crozier also told ITV that they'd lost the FA Cup – something he denied later but which I know to be true. He didn't do it to be malicious; he was simply trying to be fair. Of course what happened was that the following morning, when all the final bids for Premier League rights had to be submitted, our £40 million bid for the *Match of the Day* rights, which was very expensive in any case, was dwarfed by ITV's bid of £60 million plus. If Crozier hadn't rung ITV we would have won both. Either way, it was the economics of the madhouse and was to cost ITV dear: they estimate they lost between £20 and £30 million a season on the contract. In fact things were worse than that for ITV because that was the same day that ITV Digital, the struggling digital service, bid £315 million to acquire the television rights to the Football League for the following three years. It was the size of this bid that eventually brought down the whole company and left the Football League short of £80 million a year.

The BBC and I were both savaged in the press for losing *Match of the Day*. No one was interested in our rather good FA deal, and the fact that ITV had massively overbid was ignored: most journalists know little about money but sports journalists know the least. This all happened while the European Nations Cup was happening in Belgium and Holland and the ITV sports boys out there gave our people a hard time.

In fact that 'mad' week, during which record prices were paid for the FA Cup, England internationals, Premier League and Football League rights, was the beginning of the end of the period of massive inflation in sports rights. It had been fuelled by two things: the arrival of competing pay television platforms in the shape of BSkyB, ITV Digital, and the cable companies, and a massive boom in advertising revenue. In two years both these factors had disappeared, as I explained in a speech at the Manchester Evening News Business Awards in November 2001. By then ITV Digital and the cable companies were heading for bankruptcy and administration respectively, and ITV's advertising revenue was 15 per cent down year on year. The bubble had burst. 'So what does all this mean?' I asked in my speech. 'Well, if I was still on the Board of Manchester United I would be warning my fellow directors to be very careful. The boom in television revenues has funded an amazing escalation in players' wages in recent years but that boom is now coming to an end.' I was right, but I'd reckoned without Roman Abramovich and his Russian millions.

Despite losing the rights to *Match of the Day*, BBC Sport, under the leadership of Peter Salmon, gradually recovered. We had a great 2000 Olympics in Sydney, where the BBC was named by the International Olympics Committee as the number one broadcaster, and we wiped the floor with ITV when it came to the 2002 World Cup. First we had the exclusive rights to that wonderful night in Munich when England beat Germany 5–1, thus virtually qualifying for the finals. I was there that night and bumped into John Motson the following morning at the airport. He said it was such a great victory, wouldn't it be a good idea to repeat the match again that night? I grabbed Mark Thompson, the Director of Television, who was also at the airport and we both decided we should show it, if only so we could both see it again ourselves. We phoned Lorraine Heggessey, the controller of BBC One, from the airport and bullied her into changing that night's schedules.

When it came to the World Cup finals we completely outmanoeuvred ITV by playing hardball on the allocation of matches for the finals themselves. When negotiating the deal for the World Cup – which we got at a decent price because Kirsch, the organization selling the rights, was going bust – we told ITV that we wanted to change the way we split the matches. Once we'd both signed the contract we told them we were planning to show all the England matches live and didn't mind if they showed them live as well. The ITV people went berserk because they knew we'd attract twice or three times as many viewers as they would if we both broadcast the same match. In the end we took two England matches and ITV took one. When we went head to head on the final we beat ITV by nearly four to one in ratings – 12.4 million viewers against their 3.6 million.

We retained the rights to both the Premier League and cricket for Radio Five Live; we won back the Derby and the whole of Five Nations rugby for BBC One, and we won athletics for BBC Two. But the comeback of BBC Sport was sealed in 2003 with the next round of football negotiations for the 2004/5 season. Not only did we agree a good deal with the FA by which we acquired all England's home internationals and three matches from each round of the FA Cup, we also won back the *Match of the Day* rights with a bid of £35 million – nearly half the figure ITV had been paying. In fact by the time I left the BBC we had more live and recorded football planned for the 2004/5 season than the BBC had ever had before.

The great advantage of being Director-General if you are a sports fan is you get access to tickets for virtually anything you want to watch. Every year I tried to arrange a couple of visits to Wimbledon as both Sue and I enjoyed watching tennis. At least one of them was usually in the Royal Box as a guest of the All England Lawn Tennis Club itself. One year we were in the front row of the box watching a match when someone announced that tea was served. The box emptied and Sue and I were on our own in the front row when the game finally ended. The players came up, looked up and bowed to us. It was hysterical. A couple of years later the Club ended the tradition of players bowing to the Royal Box.

Sport in Britain has changed beyond all recognition in the fifteen years I've been involved with sports broadcasting. The coming of pay television has brought billions of pounds into certain sports – the ones the public want to watch on television week in and week out – to the disadvantage of others. It has also changed when and where live sports events are played: the traditional Saturday afternoon football match, to take one example, is now close to disappearing as broadcasters want matches spread right across the weekend.

The traditionalists, including many sports journalists on newspapers, who hate the control broadcasters now have, constantly tell us what a terrible thing this is. But in today's sports world money is all. The broadcasters supply the cash, so they call the tune.

All sports organizations today face a dilemma: how much of their sport to put on pay television and how much on traditional terrestrial television.

The former pays more, the latter gets much bigger audiences and helps build the sport. The best example is rugby union. When England versus Wales at Twickenham was broadcast on Sky in 2002 it got an audience of only a few hundred thousand; Wales versus England at Cardiff the following season, on the other hand, was broadcast on BBC One and attracted seven million.

When I look back now, losing the rights to the Premier League back in 1992 was a blow for ITV but was probably inevitable. If it hadn't happened then it would have happened next time around. The value of Premier League football to a pay television operator is so much greater than it is for a traditional commercial broadcaster funded by advertising. Millions of people in Britain pay BSkyB £40 a month just to get their football; the advertising revenue involved is worth nothing like that.

Sport is a world in which money talks. All sorts of people and sports bodies promise you undying loyalty as a broadcaster because you cover their sport so well, only to sell the rights to someone else because they're prepared to pay more. But it goes both ways. Broadcasters often offer sports organizations the world to get their rights only to treat them in a cavalier fashion once they've won them.

In many ways sports organizations and broadcasters deserve each other.

CHAPTER TWELVE

Gilligan, Kelly, and Hutton

One of the standing jokes amongst my team at the BBC was that I always seemed to be away when the really big stories about the BBC hit the papers.

I had been on a beach in Barbados when the Secretary of State announced what the BBC's funding would be for the next six years. I had been sailing in Turkey when Rod Liddle had been forced to resign from the editorship of the *Today* programme after he wrote an article attacking the Conservatives and the Countryside Alliance. I had been in Australia when a potential bust-up about what a BBC website had said in a fictitious story about the death of the Queen Mother had surfaced. I remember it well because the then Chairman, Christopher Bland, had insisted on ringing me at 4 a.m. to 'discuss' it. And I was away skiing in France when the Queen Mother actually died and the colour of Peter Sissons' tie became a big issue.

Now, true to form, I was on holiday in the west of Ireland on the day – 29 May 2003 – when Andrew Gilligan's story on weapons of mass destruction in Iraq was broadcast on the *Today* programme on Radio Four. Once again my holiday was interrupted. But it wasn't the Gilligan story that was the controversial issue that particular week. That was to come later.

What dominated that week in Ireland was whether or not we should include pictures of dead British soldiers in Iraq in a documentary made for BBC Two's *Correspondent* series the following Sunday. Jana Bennett, the Director of Television, was in charge while I was away and her view, supported by Mark Damazer, the Deputy Head of News, was that we should.

I tended to agree, but it wasn't an easy call. The BBC had not done it before, *The Sun* had gone to town on the story, the relatives of the soldiers were understandably upset, and the Chairman of the BBC, Gavyn Davies, was worried. The argument in favour of showing the pictures was that we were planning to show pictures of dead US and Iraqi soldiers, so why not play a two-second shot of the unidentifiable British soldiers? Surely this was the reality of war?

In the end I backed Jana and Mark but made sure I got to see a tape when I arrived home on the Friday evening before *Correspondent* was broadcast on the Sunday, just in case I wanted to change my mind. I watched it and I didn't. When the BBC Governors' complaints committee considered the issue a couple of months later they took the view that we'd made the wrong decision and should not have broadcast the pictures. However, they recognized it had been a close call.

What this all meant was that another holiday had been disrupted. I'd sat out at sea in an open boat discussing the issue for hours on end with all sorts of people. At one time, distracted, with mobile phone in hand, I'd even untied the wrong boat on the quayside and was left with the task of stopping someone else's boat drifting out of the harbour.

In these circumstances none of us had taken much notice of the Gilligan story on the *Today* programme on 29 May. Although you can get a perfectly good Radio Four signal in that part of Ireland, I was on holiday and wasn't up in time to listen to the broadcast at seven minutes past six. Eight months later that broadcast would lead to my exit from the BBC.

My private view of the Iraq war, like that of the BBC's Chairman Gavyn Davies, was that I was marginally in favour of trying to get rid of Saddam Hussein. I regarded him as a nasty bastard whom the world could well do without. Mistakenly, as it has turned out, I had also been convinced that Tony Blair and the Government knew more about Iraq's weapons of mass destruction than they were able to tell us and that there was a real and serious threat. My support for the war made me very unpopular with some of my friends, one of whom described me publicly in her speech at her fiftieth birthday party as a neo-conservative.

In terms of my role as Director-General of the BBC my own feelings about the war were irrelevant. Our job was to report the events leading up to the war, and the war itself, as fairly as we could. It was certainly not the job of the BBC to be the Government's propaganda machine, but nor was it our job disproportionately to represent the views of those protesting against the war. Our job was to be impartial, to tell the story as fairly as we could. At times we would get it wrong – journalism is not an exact science; but the duty we owed to the public was to do our best to tell the story as our journalists saw it. As our value statement made clear, 'Trust is the foundation of the BBC' and we should do nothing to endanger that trust, which was why we needed to avoid being seen as either side's mouthpiece.

It was Huw Wheldon, the former Managing Director of BBC Television, who had said that when Britain as a nation is divided the BBC is on the rack. It was clear from well before the war started that we were going to be on the rack this time: not since Suez had Britain been so divided over taking military action. History shows very clearly that it is at times of war that the relationship between the BBC and the government of the day is at its most tense. During Suez the Prime Minister, Anthony Eden, even considered taking over the BBC when it agreed to give the Leader of the Opposition, Hugh Gaitskell, airtime to explain why Labour was against the war, following Eden's broadcast explaining why he had gone to war.

Today such an even-handed approach is seen as the norm, but back then it brought accusations from Eden that the BBC was betraying the nation at a time of crisis. He wrote privately to Winston Churchill saying, 'The BBC is exasperating me by leaning over backwards to be what they call neutral and to present both sides of the case.' He asked William Clark, his press secretary, 'Are they enemies or just socialists?' Clark noted in his diary that Eden had a growing 'passion and determination to teach the BBC a lesson'. It is remarkable how history repeats itself. The same hostility from the Government was seen at the time of the Falklands war in 1982. When Dick Francis, a senior BBC executive, expressed the view that the grief of a widow in Buenos Aires was no less than that of a British widow, he was roundly condemned by a Government that told the nation it should 'rejoice' at military victories.

John Simpson, the BBC's brilliant World Affairs Editor, summed up the position in an article published just weeks before the Iraq war:

At the times of Suez, Biafra, Vietnam, the Falklands, the American bombing of Libya and the NATO attacks on Kosovo and Serbia, the BBC reported the opposition to these wars fully. On every occasion the Government – Labour or Conservative – tried to bully the BBC into supporting the official line. On every occasion the BBC resisted; sometimes energetically, sometimes not as energetically as it ought to have done ... Governments have as much right as anyone to put pressure on the BBC; it's only a problem if the BBC caves in.

For Alastair Campbell and his team in the Downing Street press office our refusal to report what they wanted us to, in the way they wanted us to, made us a target even before the war itself began. It was easy to see why he was so anxious. With a million people on the streets of London protesting about the war, and a Labour rebellion on an unprecedented scale happening in the House of Commons, Tony Blair's whole future as Prime Minister was in the balance. In one letter Campbell even complained that we hadn't properly reported the views of the Labour MPs who had supported the Government – this on the day after 139 Labour MPs voted against their own leadership, the biggest backbench rebellion ever against a sitting Government.

The criticisms from Downing Street of the BBC's reporting in the run-up to the war were largely confined to complaints to Richard Sambrook and his people in BBC News. I heard nothing directly from Downing Street until the week the war started, when both Gavyn Davies and I received private letters from the Prime Minister. The Prime Minister's letter to me, sent on 19 March 2003, said that while he accepted that in a democracy it was right that 'voices of dissent' were heard, the BBC had gone too far and that he had been shocked by some of the editorializing of our inter-viewers and reporters. He said:

It seems to me there has been a real breakdown of the separation of news and comment ... I know too that Alastair has been pressing you to ensure more reference is made to reports from inside Iraq about the restrictions under which the media operate ...

Tony Blair went on to complain that our reports were full of complaints from 'ordinary' Iraqis but that there was no such thing in modern-day Baghdad, as anyone who criticized the regime risked execution or torture.

He ended by saying that he had never written to me or my predecessor in this way before and added:

> I believe, and I am not alone in believing, that you have not got the balance right between support and dissent; between news and comment; between the voices of the Iraqi regime and the voices of Iraqi dissidents; or between the diplomatic support we have, and diplomatic opposition.

Gavyn was later told by an official at Number Ten that the Prime Minister hadn't wanted to send the letters in the first place. He'd been persuaded to send them by Alastair Campbell, and later regretted it. Gavyn and I discussed how we should respond. We agreed that he should send a conciliatory reply whilst mine should be more robust, since I deeply resented this obvious attempt by Campbell to try to bully us. The first three paragraphs of my letter to Tony Blair, sent on 21 March, said:

> Firstly, and I do not mean to be rude, but having faced the biggest ever public demonstration in this country and the biggest ever back-bench rebellion against a sitting government by its own supporters, would you not agree that your communications advisors are not best placed to advise whether or not the BBC has got the balance right between support and dissent? Given these circumstances they are hardly in a position to make a reasoned judgement about the BBC's impartiality.
>
> You have been engaged in a difficult battle fighting for your particular view of the world to be accepted and, quite understandably, you want that to be reported. We however have a different role in society. Our role in these circumstances is to try to give a balanced picture.
>
> It is perfectly legitimate for you or your advisors to complain about particular stories – journalism is an imperfect profession – and if we make mistakes, as we inevitably do, under my leadership we will always say we were wrong and apologise. However for you to question the whole of the BBC's journalistic output across a wide range of radio, television and online services because you are

concerned about particular stories which don't favour your view is unfair.

My view was straightforward: if the Government was going to try to bully the BBC then I was going to fight back. Looking back now there is an argument that I should have been more circumspect, but I don't agree. I believed passionately in the argument I made in my reply to Blair: that the media and the Government had crucially different roles in a democracy and that one of the central roles of the broadcast media was to question the government of the day and to stand up to any bullying from them. That the BBC's charter was soon up for renewal was irrelevant to me.

I had first outlined my views on the relationship between broadcasters and government in my first McTaggart lecture back in 1994 and my opinions hadn't changed since then. Back then I had quoted Grace Wyndham Goldie, the former BBC News executive who had dealt with Eden during the Suez crisis in 1956. In her book, *Facing the Nation: Television and Politics, 1936–1976*, published in 1977, she expressed what I believed:

> Nowhere more than in broadcasting is the price of freedom eternal vigilance; resistance to political pressures has to be constant and continuous. But it must be realised that such pressures are inevitable, for the aims of political parties and those of broadcasting organizations are not the same.

The war in Iraq was not a moment of national unity. There were more than a million people marching through the streets of London opposed to it, and it was important that their voice, and what they represented, was properly and fairly reported. Writing this book more than a year after the war ended, it is quite clear now that Blair's Iraq policy has been disastrous for Blair, for the Labour Party, and for Britain's reputation virtually everywhere in the world other than in the United States. It would have been outrageous if the BBC hadn't tried properly to report the opposition to the war, which is in effect what Campbell wanted.

I think that from the moment my reply reached Number Ten all the gloves were off; that Campbell saw it as a personal rebuff, that I had humiliated him. I am told by people who know him well that he now regarded it as personal. In a later letter, sent to me the day after he went ballistic in front of the Foreign Affairs Committee, he complained that my reply to the Prime Minister had been 'dismissive'.

Everything that happened later in the year has to be put into the context of the person with whom we were dealing. Alastair Campbell, while a brilliant operator, has a classic obsessive personality and he had decided that the BBC was the enemy. From then on, if not before, I suspect he was looking for revenge.

As the Director-General I believed I had already gone to great lengths to make sure we would report the run-up to the war, and the war itself, fairly and properly. I had set up and chaired an ad hoc group that met every morning to discuss our coverage of the Iraq issue. All the most senior editorial figures at the BBC were on that group. In particular I'd made strenuous efforts to ensure that the Government position was fairly reported.

It was this group that had decided to prevent any senior BBC editorial figures from going on the anti-war march if they wanted to be involved in the coverage of Iraq. It was this group that had decided there was a danger of our phone-in programmes being dominated by the anti-war lobby and had ordered more phone lines to be opened to ensure we got a proper balance. And it was this group that insisted we find a balanced audience for *Question Time* when it was hard to find many supporters of the war willing to come on the programme, even though the polls showed that the country was evenly split.

That same group had also discussed, on several occasions, the point the Prime Minister had made in his letter about whether or not our correspondents inside Baghdad were restricted in what they could and couldn't say. Our view was that this hadn't been the case and that, although all our reporters had Iraqi minders, they were not unduly hampered in their reporting. In fact, during the war itself, Rageh Omaar's minder even asked if he could have a day off because it was his child's birthday. Of course the American broadcasters pulled all their people out of Baghdad as soon as the war started, but then the US broadcasters were hardly a model of good and fair reporting during the war. In fact they were the opposite and most of them simply became cheerleaders for Bush, which is why viewing and listening figures for the BBC's services in the USA increased so markedly during the conflict.

I pointed out what we had done in terms of ensuring fairness to the Prime Minister in my reply to his letter. I said:

> My point is that we have discussed these sorts of issues at length and made the best judgements we could. That our conclusions didn't always please Alastair is unfortunate but not our primary concern.

I received no more complaints from Tony Blair during or after the war. But the complaints from Campbell never stopped. They arrived on Richard Sambrook's desk with regular monotony and Richard and I discussed them on several occasions. We both came to the conclusion that Campbell had become obsessed by the BBC. Peter Stothard, the former editor of *The Times* who spent thirty days following Blair during the war, said on the *Today* programme, when interviewed during the Hutton crisis, that he believed antagonism towards the BBC was 'hard wired into Downing Street'.

Andrew Gilligan was reporting from Iraq for the whole of the war and his reports were not always popular with Campbell. On one occasion we actually agreed with Campbell when Gilligan talked about a particular claim he said 'could be true rather than more rubbish from Central Command'. Campbell complained and we wrote back saying that we agreed the use of the word 'rubbish' was a mistake. On another occasion we received identical letters complaining about Andrew Gilligan from Campbell and the Chairman of the Culture, Media and Sport select committee, Gerald Kaufman. It was clear that Campbell's department had written this letter for him.

But the biggest argument came on the Monday after the war ended when Gilligan, who had been in Iraq for the whole of the war, filed a report for the *Today* programme in which he said that for many people in Baghdad conditions were more dangerous that morning than they had been before the war. He said:

> Baghdad may in theory be free but its people are passing their first days of liberty in a greater fear than they've ever known. The old fear of the regime was habitual, low level. This fear is sharp and immediate – the fear that your house will be invaded, your property will be taken away and your daughters will be raped.

Campbell and his team in Downing Street complained again. We discussed the complaint at some length but decided that what Gilligan had said was also being said by other journalists. We felt that his comments were reasonable: for some in Iraq, life was clearly now more dangerous. Of course within weeks many military people were saying very similar things, and no one could doubt that is the position in Iraq today. When Gilligan returned to the UK Richard Sambrook thanked him for staying on in Baghdad and putting his life at risk. He told him that some of his reporting had been very good, but he also told him that he needed to be more careful and that too often he went 10 per cent too far.

The war was over and we had a period of relative quiet in terms of our relationship with Downing Street. Then came Gilligan's broadcast of 29 May when I was away in Ireland.

One of the major criticisms of the BBC made by Lord Hutton when he published his report in January 2004 was that the BBC's editorial system that day was 'defective', implying that if the proper procedures had been followed Gilligan's broadcasts would never have got to air. This wasn't true. The BBC's own internal inquiry has recently reported that in fact the proper procedures *were* followed. Quite how Hutton reached this conclusion is beyond me: he never asked for evidence from the one person most responsible for implementing the editorial procedures on the *Today* programme, its editor, Kevin Marsh.

The BBC didn't put Marsh forward as a witness because our legal advice was that you didn't nominate witnesses; you waited for the inquiry team to call them. This was based on our QC's firm belief that all your bad days would come when your witnesses were in the witness box and all your best days would come when it was the turn of the Government witnesses. He was absolutely right; that is exactly what happened. But it did mean that Kevin Marsh was never given the opportunity to explain the editorial process the *Today* programme applied to the Gilligan report. As a result, Hutton has been allowed to create the myth that Gilligan's report went to air without any proper editorial control being exercised beforehand. It was one of the many myths Hutton has been allowed to foster. I shall discuss the others in the next chapter.

Gilligan's story began when he met Dr David Kelly – a former senior UN weapons inspector, a government adviser, and an international expert in biological warfare – on 22 May 2003 over Appletize and Coca Cola at the Charing Cross Hotel in London.

Gilligan didn't expect to get a story at all; he was meeting Dr Kelly for a chat. When he realized that what Dr Kelly was telling him was indeed an important story he discovered he had no notebook with him. He therefore asked Dr Kelly if it was OK for him to take notes on his personal organizer. The story Gilligan was told is now well known. In essence, Dr Kelly told him of deep concern within intelligence that the Government's September 2002 dossier had been made 'sexier' by Alastair Campbell and others in Downing Street.

With a good, exclusive story on his hands, Gilligan began the process of checking and cross checking. He ran the story by a couple of senior government contacts. They were unable to confirm it, although one did encourage him to keep digging. He discovered that similar stories were circulating in the USA.

He also did extensive analysis of the 2002 dossier that suggested to him that the language had been hardened up in some areas. The dossier was supposed to be an assessment from the Joint Intelligence Committee (JIC). But Gilligan had seen earlier JIC assessments and the September dossier did not feel to him like the usual JIC product. The language was much more assertive than a conventional intelligence assessment, as the House of Commons Foreign Affairs Committee later pointed out.

Gilligan did a search of the cuttings, which threw up the remarkable fact that, although the claim that Iraq could deploy nuclear and biological weapons within 45 minutes had been made so much of when the dossier had been launched in September 2002, it had almost completely dropped out of government speeches over the following six months. This suggested that the Government did not place all that much faith in the claim.

Then there was the context. Firstly there was the second dossier, which the Government had published in February 2003 – just a few months before Gilligan spoke to Dr Kelly. This had been shown to have been based on a student thesis on Iraq, which had then been embellished in Downing Street to exaggerate the threat. The Government had form in this area.

Gilligan's suspicions were increased when he looked at the claim in the September dossier that Iraq had been trying to import uranium from Africa – one of the things Dr Kelly had raised questions about when they met. The International Atomic Energy Authority had been very critical of this claim and said it was based on forged documents. Once again the claim had been dropped from ministerial speeches on the Iraqi threat.

There were other factors too. Gilligan's cuttings search revealed a number of press stories published shortly before the September dossier appeared saying that there was little new in the dossier, which was then circulating in draft form in Whitehall. This seemed to support Dr Kelly's claim that it had been 'transformed in the week before publication'. Later stories reported rows between Alastair Campbell and the intelligence services over the dossier, again supporting one of Dr Kelly's claims.

Then there was Robin Cook, who, in his speech given in the House of Commons after resigning from the Government in March 2003, said that he did not believe Iraq possessed weapons of mass destruction in the commonly understood sense of the term. And of course no weapons of mass destruction of any size had yet been found by the allies in Iraq.

None of this directly corroborated what Dr Kelly had said, but it did suggest he was not a lone voice with an axe to grind. He seemed to be well informed about the dossier. His claims were consistent with other information – and the extensive checks Gilligan had made had turned up nothing to suggest they were wrong. Gilligan also knew that Dr Kelly was a highly credible and authoritative source who had given him information before that had proved reliable. Finally, Gilligan knew that Dr Kelly was not a novice when it came to dealing with the media: he was perfectly aware of what journalists were likely to do with the information he gave them.

Gilligan spent six days checking out the story before he was sufficiently confident to take it to his editors on the *Today* programme. On Wednesday 28 May 2003 he rang the day editor, Miranda Holt, an experienced senior assistant editor. She was interested in the story but she thought she should run it by her editor, Kevin Marsh.

Marsh was still new to the job of editing *Today*, although he was not new to BBC radio news. Now approaching fifty, he'd joined the Corporation straight from Oxford in 1978 and, apart from a brief stint at ITN, he was a BBC lifer. In 1989 he became editor of Radio Four's *PM* programme, and four years later editor of *The World at One*. By 1998 he was editor of a group of Radio Four programmes that included both *PM* and *The World at One*, along with the newly launched Sunday morning show *Broadcasting House*. In January 2003 he became the editor of *Today*.

Marsh is one of the BBC's most experienced editors and was long used to dealing with politicians upset by what he had broadcast. He also had extremely good contacts throughout Whitehall but was disliked by Campbell and New Labour because in his time editing *The World at One* he was a constant thorn in their side. When the BBC broadcast a drama called *The Project*, a film based on the early years of New Labour, the character of the BBC editor in the programme was widely thought to have been based on Marsh.

Marsh was interested in Gilligan's story. But, as any sceptical editor should, he raised a series of questions about it. In particular he wanted to know if the source was as senior as was being claimed; whether or not he was really in a position to make an informed judgement about the preparation of the dossier; whether or not he was credible and reliable and had a decent track record; what exactly the source had said to Gilligan; and how accurately Gilligan had recorded what he said. Marsh also wanted to know if the claims fitted into a broader picture.

Marsh was told that the anonymous source was a former Porton Down scientist; that he had been a lead United Nations weapons inspector in the 1990s; that Gilligan had known him for two years; that he was planning to return to Iraq as a senior member of the Iraq survey group; and that he would have seen much of the intelligence on chemical and biological weapons referred to in the September dossier. Miranda Holt also showed Marsh a note Gilligan had written for her. Among other things it recorded the source as saying there was a 30 per cent chance that Iraq had had a chemical weapons programme six months before the war started. Marsh took comfort from this because it indicated that the source did believe Iraq constituted some sort of threat – this was no pro-Iraqi peacenik trying to spin facts for a particular cause.

Marsh was now reassured on many of his concerns, but still not completely convinced. He decided to consider a number of other factors.

There had been a general feeling, since the revelation of the 'dodgy dossier' in February 2003, that government dossiers on Iraq were not to be wholly trusted – a feeling heightened by the doubts cast on the uranium claims in the earlier dossier.

There were the recent comments from Hans Blix, the UN Chief

Weapons Inspector, that intelligence offered to his inspectors by the UK and USA had turned out to be unhelpful, faulty, or misleading.

There was also the fact that stories in the press from reputable journalists alleging unhappiness in the intelligence services over information being 'spiced up' in the dossier had not been denied by the Government.

And there was more.

Marsh himself had two separate sources of unimpeachable authority who had given him information that lent credence to the source's claim about the inclusion of unreliable intelligence in the dossier. One was Clare Short, the former Cabinet Minister, who was still in her job at the time the dossier was produced. Marsh happened to have had lunch with her that very day. Short had insisted that she had seen no intelligence that conclusively demonstrated that Iraq was an imminent threat. She believed, she told Marsh, that policy had driven the interpretation and presentation of intelligence rather than – as is supposed to happen – intelligence driving policy. She had also told Marsh that she was convinced that Alastair Campbell had played a central role in the way intelligence had been presented to the wider public.

Marsh's second source was a very senior serving member of the intelligence services. Marsh and John Humphrys had recently had lunch with him, and Marsh had left the meeting with the clear impression that the intelligence available did not suggest that Iraq was the most immediate threat to the region and that Iran and Syria were a greater threat to British interests. Given this, it was difficult to justify attacking Iraq at that time.

On reflection, it seemed to Marsh that the story passed all the tests he had set. The source was senior, credible and reliable; was in a position to know what he was talking about; and it was obvious why he couldn't go on the record. Much of what the source was saying was validated by what he, Marsh, knew from other sources and he believed Gilligan's notes were full enough to justify the story. Finally, Marsh believed there was obvious public interest in broadcasting the story.

He decided to go ahead, but he made two further stipulations. One was that Gilligan should script his main report and that Marsh should see it before it was broadcast. The second was that, in the interests of balance, the bid that *Today* had already made for a Ministry of Defence minister (to respond to a different report about the coalition's use of

Another celebration:
Claire Rayner and I
celebrating Labour's
great victory in 1997.

Sue and I on election night in May
1997. We had waited a very long
time for Labour to win again. I
enjoyed the night, but Sue thought
it was too triumphalist. She turned
out to be right.

Outside Old Trafford
soon after I became a
director of Manchester
United in 1997.

Left: With Alex Ferguson and other directors of Manchester United in 1999, the year we won the treble, which is probably the greatest achievement in the history of football in this country.

Below: Directors and officials of Manchester United before the match on that magic night in Barcelona when we scored twice in the last minute to win the European Champions League. I managed to blag my way onto the pitch without a ticket.

Left: The day I became Dr Dyke! In 1999 York University gave me an honorary doctorate. I received it twenty-five years to the day after I got my first degree. In 2004 I became Chancellor of the University.

Right: On the same day that I appeared before the Hutton Inquiry, I gave a reading at Thora Hird's memorial service. Victoria Wood and Alan Bennett paid moving tributes to a wonderful actress and a great character.

Below: The BBC's Board of Governors led by the chairman Gavyn Davies, in July 2003. The current system of governance is antiquated and needs to be changed. Back row, left to right: Lord Ryder, vice-chairman; Baroness Hogg; Professor Fabian Monds; Dermot Gleeson; Angela Sarkis; Sir Robert Smith; bottom row, left to right: Dame Ruth Deech; Ranjit Sondhi; Gavyn Davies, chairman; Professor Merfyn Jones; and Dame Pauline Neville-Jones. Seven of these voted to get rid of me.

Above: Outside Television Centre on the day I left the BBC. Thousands of staff in all parts of Britain took to the streets to protest about my departure. Many were in tears. I am forever grateful to them for their support.

Left: Taking out tea to the television crews outside my house the day after I left the BBC. The pictures were shown on the national news. I am not at all sure anyone drank the tea!

cluster bombs in Iraq) should be widened to include a response to Gilligan's story.

Marsh was now satisfied. He did not – nor was there any reason for him to do so – formally refer the story up to his own boss. However, I suspect that if Marsh had known the story would turn into the most celebrated BBC report of the century he would at least have discussed it with those above him. But then, at that point, who was to know?

There was one other decision to be made by the *Today* team – where the story should go in the running order. The cluster bomb story had more immediate appeal, so that was planned as the lead item, which now seems an odd decision. Gilligan's story would run some time later. It was decided that the minister who was due on the programme would first take questions on cluster bombs, and then on Gilligan's story.

The decision was taken to run Gilligan's scripted story some time between 7 and 8 a.m. but that, in accordance with usual practice, there would also be an unscripted 'two-way' between the presenter and reporter between 6 and 7 a.m.

Within the programme the early two-ways were seen as curtain-raisers, trails for the main event later in the programme. They were never scripted – although since they were based on the scripted item to be broadcast later in the programme, it was assumed that they would faithfully reflect the scripted content.

During that evening before the broadcast there were a number of phone calls to the Ministry of Defence both from the *Today* office and from Gilligan (who had been away from the office for the whole of the day). There is a dispute about what was said during these calls. Gilligan is sure that he outlined his story – that the dossier had been exaggerated at Downing Street's behest – to an MoD press officer, Kate Wilson. She is equally sure he did not and that they spoke mainly about cluster bombs. Since neither took notes the dispute is impossible to settle. Various members of the *Today* production team also put in calls to the MoD – and here too there is a dispute over what calls were made when, and who said what to whom. Neither side kept a good enough log of these calls.

Wherever the truth lies in these disputes, the Armed Forces Minister, Adam Ingram, did appear on *Today* the next morning, 29 May, and was sufficiently well briefed on the background to confirm one key piece of information immediately: that the 45-minute intelligence came from a single source. And Mr Ingram, who has a reputation as a robust and direct minister who makes his complaints to *Today* personally, made no complaint about his treatment or suggested he had been 'ambushed'.

When Marsh arrived at the *Today* office early on that Thursday morning, he read Gilligan's proposed script for the planned 7.30 a.m. broadcast and passed it for transmission. The stage was now set. As it turned out, it was the early unscripted two-way conversation between Humphrys and Gilligan that was to cause all the trouble. I shall examine this in detail in the next chapter.

So Gilligan's story did not just fall onto the air. There was an extensive and well-tried editorial process in place which was followed, although it was not faultless. The record keeping of interview bids by the *Today* team was not what it should have been; it was unwise to break a story such as this in an unscripted two-way; and Downing Street should have been asked to comment on the story as well as the Ministry of Defence. But the process was fully in place, Kevin Marsh followed it, and the BBC's subsequent internal inquiry confirmed this.

Lord Hutton got this wrong. But then Lord Hutton got a lot wrong.

I returned from Ireland on the Friday night, 30 May, the day after Andrew Gilligan's reports on the *Today* programme, and went into the office on the Monday.

There was a bit of noise around about the *Today* programme story from the previous week but nothing particularly unusual. I later discovered that there had been a complaint on the day of the broadcast from Anne Shevas, a Downing Street press officer, that the Government's denial of the Gilligan allegations had not been properly reported. Reading the statement today is instructive as it included a paragraph saying: 'Any suggestion that there was any pressure or intervention from Downing Street is entirely false.' The evidence given to the Hutton inquiry some months later shows that statement to be wrong. There *was* pressure and it is obvious to me that John Scarlett, Head of the Joint Intelligence Committee in Downing Street, changed the dossier as a result of that pressure. But I am running ahead of events.

It so happened that I had one of my regular meetings with Stephen Whittle, the BBC's Head of Editorial Policy, on the following Wednesday

THIS IS NOT USED

and we discussed the story. By then I had read an article by Andrew Gilligan that had appeared in the *Mail on Sunday* in which he had outlined the same story but, crucially, added that his source had told him the September dossier had been 'sexed up' by Alastair Campbell himself. Campbell was never named in any BBC programme.

That morning, Wednesday 4 June, the Chairman of the Labour Party, John Reid, had appeared on the *Today* programme and had attacked the story; in particular he'd attacked 'rogue elements in the security services' whom he believed had given the story to Andrew Gilligan.

I asked Stephen Whittle to take a look at Gilligan's original story and make sure we were happy with it and the process by which it went to air. He sent me back a two-page e-mail outlining the process and finished it with one line: 'As you can see, a strong and well sourced story.' When I was later criticized for not having involved myself early enough in the process I pointed to this action I had taken even before we had received our first complaint from Campbell. My mind was put at rest by Stephen's reply, although over the next week or so I did discuss the issue with Richard Sambrook. When we received Campbell's letters of complaint they were addressed to Richard so he dealt with them, which was the normal BBC process.

It was two days later that Alastair Campbell sent his first complaint. Campbell's complaint letters were often very long. He clearly suffered from verbal diarrhoea, which I always thought strange given his background as a tabloid journalist. In some of his letters it was also quite difficult to work out what he was actually complaining about.

In a four-page letter, dated 6 June, Campbell complained that Gilligan had failed to understand the role of the Joint Intelligence Committee and that we had broken our own BBC guidelines by the use of a single unattributable source. He ended the letter by saying he wondered why we had guidelines at all, given that they were so persistently breached. Richard Sambrook replied on 11 June and told Campbell quite clearly that there had been no breach of the guidelines and that the BBC had several sources who were expressing concern about the way intelligence was used and presented in the September dossier.

A day later came another letter from Campbell, again sent to Richard, again complaining that Gilligan had misunderstood the role of the Joint Intelligence Committee; and again he was complaining that Gilligan's

THIS IS NOT USED

265

story had broken the BBC's reporting guidelines. Richard replied in detail on 16 June. This time he quoted the BBC guidelines, which made it clear they had not been broken. I had received copies of both Campbell's previous letters and at my suggestion Richard offered Campbell the opportunity to take his complaint through the BBC's official complaints process. If he had taken this route it could have eventually gone to the relevant Governors' committee for a final ruling. Campbell never replied to that invitation.

Campbell's letter of 12 June is very interesting and tells us a lot about him. In the final paragraph he complained that BBC news bulletins on Sunday 8 June had reported a *Sunday Telegraph* story saying that Campbell had written a letter of apology to Sir Richard Dearlove, Head of the Secret Intelligence Service (MI6), over the failings in the second, February, dossier. Campbell said this was untrue and he was demanding an apology. We later discovered that the story was essentially true: he had apologized to Sir Richard Dearlove. The only thing wrong in the article was that Campbell hadn't apologized by letter, but verbally.

This was a typical Campbell tactic. He would try to discredit an entire story by denying a tiny detail. Everyone was aware of this and it undermined the credibility of his complaints.

After this spurt of letters over ten days, complete silence. No more complaints from Campbell and we all assumed that the complaints and the story had gone the way of so many others. Richard Sambrook and I were later criticized for not taking the complaints seriously enough, which was unfair. Richard received letters like these from Campbell on such a regular basis that when he received the second letter he described it to me as 'just another Alastair rant'.

Around this time the House of Commons Foreign Affairs Select Committee was holding a series of hearings on the decision to go to war in Iraq and wanted Alastair Campbell to appear before it. In particular, they wanted to know about the 'dodgy' dossier, which Campbell's staff had taken from the Internet, changed to improve the case for going to war, and then published in February 2003 as their own work.

To get the full picture you have to go back a few weeks. The Foreign Affairs Select Committee announced their inquiry on 3 June 2003. One of their first actions was to ask Campbell to appear. He refused point blank.

But then things started to go wrong. Campbell began to attract a lot of criticism – particularly over the February dossier. Downing Street was forced to confirm that, in the wake of the 'dodgy' dossier, it had written to the heads of the intelligence agencies promising greater care would be taken in future.

On the same day Iain Duncan Smith, then leader of the Conservative Party, made his first intervention in the affair, calling for an independent inquiry into the way intelligence was used to make the case for war and pointing the finger at Campbell: 'My concern is the way that this was twisted and fiddled and spun by people like Alastair Campbell.'

Meanwhile, the flow of stories continued in the press, raising questions about misuse of intelligence. *The Observer* ran a story on 8 June saying that 'two vehicles that he [Blair] had repeatedly claimed to be Iraqi mobile biological warfare production units are nothing of the sort'. The *Mail on Sunday* ran a second piece by Gilligan. It didn't have much new to say but it kept the story on the boil – and Campbell's paranoia about the BBC at full pitch.

Then, on 9 June, Clare Short, who had resigned from the Cabinet over the war in May, before the broadcast, went on the attack. In the *New Statesman* she wrote: 'My conclusion is that our Prime Minister deceived us . . . He exaggerated the imminent threat from WMDs.'

The next day the Intelligence and Security Select Committee (ISC) published its annual report in which it criticized the way intelligence had been used in the 'dodgy dossier'. The report also contained a few lines of qualified support for the September dossier, but press comment, not surprisingly, focused on the 'dodgy' document. This upset Campbell. He later told Hutton: 'The BBC and other parts of the media chose to focus not on that part of their [the ISC's] report [concerning the September dossier] but on the part which criticised the Government over the February briefing paper.'

A week later, more bad news. Clare Short and Robin Cook gave evidence to the Foreign Affairs Select Committee in which they said that they had received intelligence briefings before the war that did not justify the claim of an imminent WMD threat from Iraq.

The next day it was the turn of Pauline Neville-Jones, a former JIC Chairman (and, incidentally, a serving BBC Governor), who, as usual, did not mince her words. The February dossier, she said, was 'a serious mistake . . . it discredits the earlier material [the September dossier], it is a mistake. I think you should not do cut and paste jobs.'

By now the pressure was mounting for Campbell to appear before the Foreign Affairs Committee. But Downing Street was still holding firm. At Prime Minister's Questions on 18 June, Tony Blair, pressed on the issue, refused to give ground, citing an apparently unshakeable constitutional precedent: 'It has never been the case that officials have given evidence to Select Committees.'

The day after that another Foreign Affairs Committee witness, Ibrahim al-Marishi, whose doctoral thesis was the unacknowledged source for the 'dodgy dossier', said that the 'reckless' use of his work had endangered the lives of his family in Iraq.

The Foreign Affairs Committee now wrote to Campbell again asking him to appear. Campbell took a few days to reply.

It was now clear that the sheer weight of evidence against Campbell was likely to result in a report that was severely critical of him. The Sunday papers on 22 June were full of stories on this theme. The *Mail on Sunday* claimed that Campbell was 'on the brink of resignation' and that 'the powerful FAC has stepped up the fight to force him to answer for his actions'. The *Independent on Sunday* even managed to get a Labour member of the Committee, Eric Illsley, to go on the record: 'Given the evidence so far that Campbell's staff put this document [the 'dodgy dossier'] together, made a complete botch of it, and then put it out as serious research, I think the report is going to point the finger at him.' Campbell was later to tell Hutton: 'I sensed over that weekend, through reading some of the comments of the Labour MPs in the Sunday press, that the FAC was moving in a very, very bad direction for the Government.' What he meant, of course, was a very, very bad direction for Alastair Campbell.

By now Campbell's position was weakened. Even the usually loyal Foreign Secretary, Jack Straw, had told the Committee on 23 June that the February dossier was 'a complete Horlicks'.

Campbell decided the time had come to act. He consulted Tony Blair, who said the constitutional precedent was not so unshakeable after all and that Campbell could go before the FAC. On 25 June Campbell gave evidence.

*   *   *

The proceedings opened with the chairman making a feeble joke about 'Campbell in the soup' – an indication of the weakness of Campbell's position. But Campbell was not fazed for a moment. Instead he used his appearance to launch a full frontal verbal assault on the BBC. He accused it of lying and of running an anti-war agenda. It was an unprecedented attack on the BBC's journalism from the man in charge of all the Government's information services, a civil servant with unprecedented powers.

So why did Campbell do it? Why make such a public attack on the BBC, an attack that was eventually to lead to Campbell losing his job and which did lasting damage to the Labour Government he was supposed to be representing?

An article in *The Scotsman* the following morning captured what happened:

Mr Campbell did exactly what he wanted to do. He blunted the attack immediately by putting his hands up for the dodgy dossier and then used the remaining three hours to perform the oldest trick in the spin doctor's manual: distract attention from the government's shortcomings by feeding the media with an alternative story.

And the media – in particular the Murdoch press – lapped it up. *The Sun*'s headline the next morning was 'Campbell: BBC Liars'. *The Times* took the same tack: 'Campbell accuses BBC of lying'. No wonder Campbell was pleased. As he later told Hutton: 'I felt a lot better ... I had opened a flank on the BBC.'

It is clear that the whole attack on the BBC from Campbell was a means of diverting attention away from the 'dodgy dossier' and the disgraceful way he and his team had produced it. He decided that attack was the best means of defence. It was as cynical as that. And for Campbell, in the short term, it worked. Every time he was asked a difficult question by the Foreign Affairs Select Committee he attacked the BBC.

I suspect that Campbell had been wanting to 'get' the BBC for a long time as a way of exacting revenge for our refusal to follow his agenda during the Iraq war. In particular he had wanted to 'get' Gilligan and the *Today* programme. Campbell had told me personally how much he disliked the programme and we knew, in particular, he disliked its main presenter, John Humphrys. We had also received complaints about Gilligan, who, in his time on the programme, had embarrassed both the Ministry of Defence and the Government with good stories. It was Gilligan who had shown up the tactical ineffectiveness of the bombing in Kosovo and the lack of any link between Saddam Hussein and al-Qaeda. He had also revealed that British troops had not been properly equipped on a number of occasions; and of course Campbell had hated Gilligan's reports from Baghdad during the war. But his dislike of Gilligan went back to 2000 when Gilligan had warned that a proposed European Union 'Code of Law' could be an EU Constitution that would form the basis of an EU super state. After that, Campbell called him 'gullible Gilligan'.

At the Select Committee Campbell personalized his attack by saying we had accused the Prime Minister of lying, which was completely untrue. Again this was a typical Campbell ploy. No one had ever mentioned the Prime Minister, but it suited Campbell to claim that criticism of Number Ten or the Government meant directly accusing the Prime Minister of lying. By the same logic the Prime Minister would have had to have taken personal responsibility for the 'dodgy dossier', even though no one had suggested that Blair himself knew it was nonsense. Campbell turned what Dr Kelly had told Gilligan into a personal attack by the BBC on the Prime Minister. To his discredit, Tony Blair later went along with this.

The ferocity and wide-ranging nature of the attack meant that the BBC had little choice but to go into battle. Campbell had attacked much of the BBC's output and in particular its coverage of the war. A comprehensive Cardiff University study later showed that, if anything, the BBC had slightly favoured the official Government position rather than an anti-war one.

On the day of Campbell's attack on the BBC at the Select Committee, 25 June, the BBC Executive was away at one of the strategy conferences we held three times a year. This time we were at Witley Park in Surrey, where we went every June. As usual we had some bonding activity, in which members of the Executive did silly things to make them feel more of a team. On paper these sorts of events seem ridiculous but they are very effective at bringing a team of people together as a group of friends.

At the 2003 BBC Executive conference we had an 'It's a Knockout' competition. We were halfway through when Richard Sambrook took a call on his mobile phone. He walked over and told me that Alastair Campbell had gone ballistic at the Foreign Affairs Committee attacking the BBC; but as we only had the headlines we decided to carry on with the game, probably because my team was winning. We were still ahead until the last round when we all had to do country dancing. At that moment Alan Yentob came into his own and his team won on 'artistic merit'. What a joke!

An hour or so later we had the full report of what Campbell had said to the Committee and I agreed that we had to respond. Richard set off back to London to prepare himself for being interviewed on the *Today* programme about the attack the following morning; the rest of us stayed at the conference. We all agreed the next morning that Richard had done a pretty good job defending the BBC and making the point that it was not the BBC who had made the allegations against the Government but a high-level source who had been involved in preparing the September dossier.

I got home from the conference to find a fax Alastair Campbell had sent to the office. It was clearly an attempt to be friendly saying that he had always admired both my career and my commitment and that he was 'sorry' he had had to attack the BBC in the way he had. I didn't believe a word of it. Campbell had refused to take advantage of any of the official complaints channels open to him – going through our complaints process or taking his complaint to the Broadcasting Standards Commission, or even coming unofficially to Gavyn or myself. If he had wanted to be friendly he could have phoned to say that Number Ten regarded the Gilligan report extremely seriously and asked us to take a look at it.

It was very clear to me that Campbell's attack was a mixture of diversionary tactic and revenge against the BBC. He was not interested in a proper investigation: he wanted a public bust-up for political reasons. His letter to me was part of his game and I didn't want to play along with it. I decided not to respond.

Richard Sambrook, too, had received another three-page letter from Campbell in which, in typical Campbell style, he had demanded the answers to a series of questions, and wanted a reply that same day. He had also released his letter to the press.

On the Friday I was supposed to be one of a panel judging a competition to decide on the architect for the new BBC music centre planned for

White City. Ever since joining the BBC I'd taken a keen interest in the architecture of any new BBC buildings. At one time the BBC had wonderful buildings everyone could be proud of, but in recent years we had built inappropriate extensions and some really ugly new structures. I was determined that this wouldn't happen in my time as Director-General. John Smith, who was in charge of property, agreed with this approach, and Alan Yentob, a trained architect, played a major part in implementation.

After talking to Gavyn Davies first thing on the Friday morning I decided to pull out of the panel and spend the day with Richard Sambrook and Mark Damazer helping to draft the BBC's official reply to Campbell.

Replying quickly was a mistake, my mistake. We allowed ourselves to be driven by Campbell's timetable and, as I later explained to Lord Hutton, what I should have done that day was to stop the process, refer the whole complaint to the BBC's Programme Complaint Unit, and ask for a speedy judgement. We should then have told Downing Street what we had done and that they would have to wait for their reply.

Instead we sent a detailed response to Campbell that only upset him even more. He received it while he was watching the tennis at Wimbledon, got into his car, and drove to the studios of ITN. He demanded to be interviewed live on Channel Four News and laid into the BBC once more in a quite extraordinary fashion. He told Tony Blair what he was doing and Blair reluctantly agreed. Even Campbell later accepted that his behaviour had been over the top; Blair clearly had little control over him. We all thought that by then Campbell was completely out of control. Evidence is now emerging that suggests we were right.

According to *Alastair Campbell* by Peter Oborne (political editor of *The Spectator*) and Simon Walters (political editor of the *Mail on Sunday*), published in June 2004, Campbell rang Jon Smith, the Press Association's political editor, a few days later and started to shout at him when he wouldn't file a story about an issue that Campbell wanted reported. Smith told him to stop shouting and Campbell reportedly replied, 'I can't, I can't, they're after me, everybody's after me.' Smith told Campbell that he was 'going round the twist again'.

Campbell's diaries – parts of which were published on the Hutton Inquiry's website – show that his intention had been to 'fuck Gilligan'. According to Oborne and Walters, at a later event held by the Blairs to say goodbye to Sir David Manning, who was leaving Number Ten to become Britain's Ambassador to Washington, Campbell is reported to have embarrassed people by saying openly that he wanted to wreak vengeance on 'that fucking little shit Gilligan'.

In one of a number of conversations Gavyn Davies had with Tony Blair over this period, all initiated by Blair, Gavyn said that he thought Campbell's behaviour was over the top. Blair replied, 'Don't we all'. Incidentally, Gavyn is convinced to this day that Blair had surmised what would be in the Hutton Report a couple of months before it was published because, suddenly, the calls from Blair dried up.

It was around this time that Mark Damazer remembered that *Newsnight* had run a story on weapons of mass destruction at about the same time as the *Today* programme report. When he pulled out the tape he found incredible similarities between the story on *Newsnight* by their science editor Susan Watts and Gilligan's reports on the *Today* programme. This was important because either Watts had a different source, in which case there were now two anonymous sources for the same story, or it was the same source and supported Gilligan. Either way, it was good news for the BBC because it corroborated the story.

Richard Sambrook saw Susan Watts and asked her who her source was. She refused to tell him. She also failed to tell him that she had recorded the conversation with her source, a fact that was not to come out for several weeks. She later complained to Lord Hutton that Richard had bullied her. She must be very sensitive, since Richard is about the least bullying person I know. Of course what we all found out later, when we heard the tapes, was that David Kelly was her source, that he'd given her the whole story before giving it to Gilligan, and that she'd missed it.

Watts herself seems to have realized this. The tape of her interview with Dr Kelly records her telling him: 'I've looked back at my notes [of her interview with him on 7 May] and you were actually quite specific at that time – I may have missed a trick on that one.' Later the editor of *Newsnight*, George Entwistle, asked Mark Damazer if he thought *Newsnight* had missed a great story.

Gilligan had given evidence to the Foreign Affairs Committee before Campbell's attack on the BBC. His appearance was barely reported – real evidence that the story was dying until it was reignited by Campbell. We now thought the Committee should see the item on *Newsnight*, which was broadcast in two parts on 2 June and 4 June, before they published their report. We therefore sent them the tapes as a matter of urgency and pointed out their importance.

The *Newsnight* report only convinced us further that Campbell was running a vendetta against Gilligan and the *Today* programme. Why hadn't he complained about *Newsnight* since it had reported virtually the same story as the *Today* programme?

It is true that Susan Watts did not say the Government probably knew the 45-minute claim was wrong and had ordered it to be put into the dossier. But she did report her source saying that the 45-minute figure 'was seized on and it's unfortunate that it was. That's why there is the argument between the intelligence services and Cabinet Office/Number Ten, because they picked up on it and once they'd picked up on it you can't pull it back from them.'

Watts had also said that she had been told by 'a senior official involved with the process of pulling together the dossier' that 'in the run-up to publishing the dossier the Government was obsessed with finding intelligence on immediate Iraqi threats. The Government's insistence the Iraqi threat was imminent was a Downing Street interpretation of an intelligence conclusion.' She quoted her unnamed source (Dr Kelly) at length. For example, on the imminence of the Iraqi threat, Kelly had made it clear that while there might be a future threat, the current threat was less serious. 'But that unfortunately was not expressed strongly in the dossier because that takes away the case for war.' In other words, her reports made clear that the intelligence services were unhappy because Downing Street had exaggerated the scale of the threat from Iraq. In essence, this is exactly the claim made in Gilligan's report. The Prime Minister later said he would have had to resign if the Gilligan story was true, but he has never mentioned the Watts story. Surely if this had been true the same would have applied? And yet no one from Downing Street has ever denied the Watts story.

We had already told the Foreign Affairs Committee that if they unanimously told us that our report was wrong on the basis of concrete evidence that they had seen, then we would accept that the Gilligan report was wrong and that we would withdraw it and apologize. There was not much chance of that happening because Number Ten was, not surprisingly, refusing to let the Committee see the various drafts of the September dossier.

We now know that if the Committee had seen the drafts its conclusions would have been embarrassing for Number Ten. When they were all revealed to the Hutton Inquiry, the drafts showed that not only had people in Number Ten suggested significant changes to the relevant parts of the dossier but that Campbell himself had deliberately misled the Foreign Affairs Committee. Campbell had told the Committee of the changes to the dossier that he himself had suggested but, crucially, he omitted any reference to the point he made about the 45-minute claim – the very detail they were interested in. He didn't tell the Committee that he had had an exchange with John Scarlett, the Chairman of the Joint Intelligence Committee, on this very point. If he had told the full story it would have supported what Kelly had alleged.

That neither Hutton nor the Committee has ever taken Campbell to task for misleading them is, at the very least, a failure of our democratic system. Hutton left it to the Committee and the Committee has since ducked it. It seems that if you are the Government's head of information you can mislead Parliament with impunity.

The story was not going away and during that week Gavyn was anxious that the Governors be given the opportunity to discuss the matter. He, personally, had investigated the whole thing in great detail since Campbell's public outburst and discussed it privately with a number of Governors who were concerned at the ferocity of the attack on the BBC's independence. With the Foreign Affairs Committee report due to be published the following week, he wanted to call an emergency Governors' meeting, but I cautioned against. I thought it wasn't necessary to bring the full force of the Governors into the battle at this stage and could see that it might leave the Governors in a difficult position if Gilligan's story was eventually shown to be wrong.

On the Friday, 4 July, I was in Northern Ireland for one of my regular out of London visits. In particular I was there to open the BBC's new roof gardens where the staff could relax at lunchtimes or in the evenings. It was a classic 'Making it Happen' initiative.

While in Belfast I got a phone call from Simon Milner, the BBC Secretary, to tell me that Gavyn had called a meeting of the Governors for that Sunday evening and that we would all be receiving a pack of information over the weekend. I told Simon that I thought it was a mistake but that obviously I would be there.

The following morning *The Guardian* ran the story as their front-page lead story with the headline 'Dyke Summoned to BBC Crisis Meeting'. Later, when the Governors were accused of being management patsies, I regularly pointed to that headline to show that this wasn't how it was seen at the time.

On the Sunday Sue and I were due to go to Wimbledon for the men's tennis finals. As luck would have it, Cherie Blair was sitting in front of us, so the photographers had a field day. I've known Cherie for twenty years but that day she said hello to Sue and then looked straight through me as if I didn't exist. I remember thinking then how sad it was that she didn't recognize that old friendships are far more important than temporary battles. But then perhaps that can't apply to people who spend their lives in politics. As Enoch Powell once said, 'There are no friendships in politics, only alliances.'

I went straight from Wimbledon to the Governors' meeting, still in my cream suit. I remember being asked on the way into Broadcasting House one of those banal questions that journalists shout at you when it's clear you won't be interviewed. The question was, 'Is this the end of the BBC?' I replied with one word: 'Hardly'.

I agreed with Gavyn that I wouldn't go to the first part of the meeting. When I did go into the meeting, along with other members of the management team, Richard Sambrook and I were closely questioned about the story and the processes we'd followed. We'd been through all this with Gavyn over recent weeks and he understood all the detail. He hoped the Governors would support the position we had all taken. Interestingly, perhaps the most supportive Governor that day was Sarah Hogg, who was not physically at the meeting but was on the line from her home in Lincolnshire. She was adamant that we shouldn't show any weakness. The only waverer that day was the Deputy Chairman, Richard Ryder.

Of course at that time none of the Governors knew who Gilligan's source had been. At that meeting only Richard Sambrook knew Kelly's name, although I knew his position. At the meeting Richard described Andrew Gilligan as a reporter who tended to 'paint in primary colours', meaning that subtlety was not his strong point and that, as a result, he occasionally went too strongly on a story.

In the end the Board put out a statement that said that it 'emphatically rejects Mr Campbell's claim that large parts of the BBC had an agenda against the war' and it called on Campbell to withdraw the allegations. They also said that the *Today* programme had properly followed the BBC's producers' guidelines in broadcasting the Gilligan story and that it had been in the public interest to do so.

However, the Board did say that the *Today* programme could have put the allegation in the story to Number Ten as well as to the Ministry of Defence before it was broadcast – something we all agreed with – and that it intended to look again at rules under which BBC reporters and presenters were permitted to write for newspapers. I think the Governors felt that if Gilligan had not named Campbell in his newspaper article Campbell would not have reacted the way he did.

Finally, the Governors said the following:

> The Board wishes to place on record that the BBC has never accused the Prime Minister of lying, or of seeking to take Britain to war under misleading or false pretences. The BBC did not have an agenda in its war coverage, nor does it have any agenda which questions the integrity of the Prime Minister.

Later, Michael Grade (soon to be the next Chairman of the BBC) happened to be on *Question Time* and discussed the Governors' actions that night. His comments are very instructive. He said:

> I applaud the governors of the BBC. I wish I'd had them when I was at the BBC when we were going through *Real Lives* and everything else, because the first time there was ever a sabre rattled by Downing Street in our direction the governors shopped the management straight away . . . I applaud Gavyn Davies and the governors for standing up to Downing Street and making sure that everyone understood that the independence of the BBC was not going to be compromised.

The day after the Governors' meeting, 7 July, the Foreign Affairs Committee report was published. It was a bit of a damp squib with both sides claiming victory. Jack Straw, the Foreign Secretary, came out and said that the Committee had cleared Campbell and that the BBC should with-draw its allegations. He didn't point out that the report had divided on party lines and that it had cleared Campbell by one vote only.

We in turn pointed out that the Committee had said unanimously that the 45-minute claim did not warrant the prominence given to it in the September dossier and that the Committee had asked the Government to explain why it had done so. The Foreign Affairs Committee report also criticized the September dossier for using language that was too assertive in relation to the underlying intelligence – or, as some might say, 'sexed up'. The Committee also said the Government should set out whether or not it believed that what it had said in the dossier was still true.

Around that time there were two attempts to broker a peace between Downing Street and the BBC. First Peter Mandelson rang Caroline Thomson, the BBC's Director of Policy and an old friend of both of us. He suggested a way out; it required the BBC's accepting that Gilligan's story wasn't true whilst maintaining that we were right to broadcast it when we did. Caroline, Richard Sambrook, and I discussed this suggestion and agreed that we needed to try and find a compromise but that this wasn't it. We couldn't say the story wasn't true. When we discussed it with Gavyn he was against dealing with Mandelson at all because, he said, we couldn't be sure that our discussions would stay private and, more importantly, he didn't think there should be a backstairs deal on a matter of such public interest.

When Caroline took the message back to Mandelson, a former Labour spin doctor himself, he told her that the BBC would now have the full force of the Government's PR machine thrown at it. Nice people.

The second approach came on the morning of 7 July, the same day the Select Committee published its report, when the Prime Minister rang Gavyn Davies in what Blair said was an attempt to calm the whole thing down. He offered the same deal as Mandelson, but Gavyn told him that he couldn't agree to it because we were not prepared to withdraw the story. Blair also said he had told Campbell to back off and needed us to make a similar gesture. As a result, in a speech I was making at the Radio Academy Festival in Birmingham the following day, I added a phrase thanking Alastair Campbell for withdrawing his more outrageous remarks about the BBC. I suggested that we should all agree to disagree and that we should all move on. Some hope.

Whether Blair genuinely wanted to calm everything down is highly questionable. On the very day he spoke to Gavyn we now know he spent the rest of the morning in a series of meetings in Downing Street, none of them minuted, with political staff and civil servants deciding what should be done to exploit the fact that an official called David Kelly had now come forward to say he could have been Gilligan's source. Kelly had told the Ministry of Defence that, while he had talked to Gilligan, he hadn't said what Gilligan claimed he'd said. The strategy of how the Government should put Kelly's name into the public agenda was devised that day at a meeting attended by the Prime Minister.

For some reason Campbell, the Defence Secretary Geoff Hoon, and others had convinced themselves that once it was known that Gilligan's source was not an intelligence officer – which, to be fair, was how Gilligan had once mistakenly described him – the whole story would fall apart. Campbell's diary entry for that day notes that he and Hoon had agreed that it would 'fuck Gilligan' if Kelly turned out to be his source. Of course that didn't happen as the BBC refused to name its source even after Kelly had been named.

Over the next couple of days the Ministry of Defence and the Downing Street press office jumped through all sorts of hoops to make sure Kelly's name became known, including the farcical stunt of allowing journalists to suggest name after name until finally they hit on the right one, which the Ministry of Defence then confirmed.

On Monday 7 July Gavyn got a call from a Labour MP telling him that he'd had dinner the night before with a senior member of SIS (MI6) who happened to be an old friend. He had told the MP that Gilligan's story was absolutely right and that the original intelligence on the 45-minute claim had come through a reliable Iraqi contact who had been given the information by a brigadier in the Iraqi army. SIS had forwarded the information with provisos, only for these to be taken out, and what was left was then used as definite intelligence. Interestingly, when the Butler Inquiry, which reviewed the use of intelligence on weapons of mass destruction, reported in July 2004 it told virtually the identical story.

I got in touch with the MP and asked him if he could fix up a meeting between me and his friend. That was in the process of being arranged when David Kelly committed suicide. Gavyn also got a call from a Liberal Democrat peer who told him that a friend had been told by the Attorney

General himself that his original opinion on the legality of the war had been judged not sufficiently strong and needed to be strengthened. These were just two of many calls we were getting at that time from people in high places telling us to keep chasing and that the story was right. Some of them were from people close to the security services themselves. I myself was told by a very senior military official over dinner that it was very unlikely that they would find any weapons of mass destruction in the conventional sense and he personally doubted if there had ever been any.

At this time there were few moments of light relief but one came when I was phoned and offered a special number plate. I was asked if I'd like to buy it for £250. The number was MI6 WMD. I bought it with the intention of giving it to Richard Sambrook as a Christmas present when the whole story had died away. I hid it away in a cupboard for nearly a year but it is now the number plate on my Lexus.

Once Dr Kelly had been named, the Foreign Affairs Select Committee wanted to interview him. I have no doubt that the Ministry of Defence and Number Ten believed Kelly would go before the Committee, say he was Gilligan's source, and then dump all over Gilligan. Instead when he appeared before the Committee on 15 July he convinced them that he was not Gilligan's source at all. He also told at least one deliberate lie when talking about dealing with Susan Watts. When the Conservative MP Richard Ottaway read from the transcript of the *Newsnight* programme Dr Kelly looked particularly uneasy.

I watched his appearance and was surprised that Kelly didn't play the game Campbell and others expected. By then I knew he was Gilligan's source and suspected he was also Susan Watts'; and yet the inept performance of members of the Committee in interviewing him had left them and the public totally confused. I felt terribly sorry for Dr Kelly: he looked like a man whom the politicians wanted to hang out to dry and who had been abandoned by everyone he'd worked with. He looked uncomfortable and his evidence was vague.

Two days later Andrew Gilligan gave evidence to the Committee for a second time, this time in private. It was a very hostile affair and some of the Labour members of the Committee had files in front of them that we suspected had been prepared for them by the Downing Street Information Department. So much for the independence of the legislature.

The Labour chairman of the Committee, the deeply unimpressive Donald Anderson, whom the Government had tried to dump from the chair after the last election, said after the session he thought Gilligan an 'unsatisfactory witness'.

Much later I had a long discussion with a senior member of the FAC who has asked for his name to be withheld. He told me that he now recognized that the Committee had made a great error. He said that they had disliked Gilligan and hadn't believed him, but that they had liked and respected Kelly and had believed what he'd told them. Now, he said, they recognized they had got it the wrong way round: Gilligan was telling the truth and Kelly wasn't.

We now know that at exactly the same time as Gilligan was being attacked by the Committee and Tony Blair was being given a standing ovation in Congress on his trip to Washington, having said that history would prove him and President Bush right with regard to their Iraq policy, Dr Kelly was lying dead in a field in Oxfordshire.

Until that happened I believed the story was running out of steam. Neither the BBC nor the Government were going to back down, nor were we going to say whether or not Dr Kelly was our source. All stories die in the end because the journalists covering them – and, more to the point, their editors and news desks – get bored with them. I thought that was happening to this story when the following morning, Friday 18 July, I took a call in the car on my way to work from Richard Sambrook, who told me the dramatic news that Dr Kelly was missing from home. He had left the day before to go for a walk and hadn't returned. We later heard that a body had been found. The story was back on all the front pages.

For the BBC this changed the world. We no longer had a source to protect. When she heard the news, Susan Watts told Richard Sambrook that Dr Kelly *had* been her source and that she had tape recorded her last conversation with him. Richard, Mark Damazer, and I all agreed that, with no source to protect, we should now tell the world that Dr Kelly had been our source, but that we couldn't do this until the body had been identified and we had informed Dr Kelly's family.

On the Saturday afternoon, after Dr Kelly's body had been identified, we told the family that we were going to make a statement and discussed with them what it would say. They asked us to hold off until the Sunday, which we willingly did. The last thing we wanted to do in these terrible circumstances was to cause the family even more distress.

On the Sunday Sue and I were at the eighteenth birthday party of Michael Pallett, the son of my friend from university, Marianne Geary, and her husband Keith. To be truthful Sue was at the lunch party being held in the garden, I was in the house talking to all and sundry at the BBC. Midway through the afternoon I got a call from Mark Damazer asking me to ring Andrew Gilligan.

There were real worries inside the BBC about Gilligan's state of mind, and even fears that he might commit suicide. He was a relatively young man who lived on his own and was not known as someone with lots of friends. He was also under enormous pressure. Campbell had thrown the whole PR operation of the state against him, just as Peter Mandelson had promised, and he was being attacked by anyone and everyone. He was being blamed for Dr Kelly's death by politicians and journalists alike. I couldn't understand why he was being blamed as he'd done everything he could to keep the identity of his source confidential.

I rang him, left a message, and a few minutes later he rang back. We talked at some length and it was clear he was very agitated that he wasn't being allowed by the BBC to make a press statement. I judged that a controlled statement would do no harm and would certainly calm Andrew down, so I agreed. It did the trick and by the evening he seemed much more relaxed.

We got back home to find a *Sun* journalist outside the door of our house, so I parked the car further up the road and went in through one of the numerous other ways into the house. Later, when I thought the journalist had gone, I walked up the road to get the car only to find the journalist shouting at me, saying things like, 'Mr Dyke, haven't you got blood on your hands?' Who would willingly do a job like that?

In the week after Dr Kelly died we all gathered in the BBC lawyers' office – Gavyn, Richard, Mark Damazer, the lawyers, and me – to listen to Susan Watts' tape of her interview with Dr Kelly for the first time. The outside world still didn't know a tape existed but it proved to be remarkable in that it supported much of what Andrew Gilligan had reported back in May.

Here was Dr Kelly naming Alastair Campbell, talking about Number

Ten being 'desperate for information' to put into the dossier and about the 45-minute claim being a statement 'that just got out of all proportion' and about which he was 'uneasy'; he also said that it was difficult to get certain views into the dossier 'because people at the top of the ladder didn't want to hear some of the things'. Talking of Iraq, Kelly said that the concern wasn't the weapons that Saddam had but what he might have in the future, 'but that wasn't expressed strongly enough in the dossier because that takes away the case for war to a certain extent'.

It was remarkable stuff and showed very clearly that Dr Kelly hadn't told the truth either to the Ministry of Defence or to the Select Committee. Everyone in the room that day thought it massively strengthened the BBC's position, and Gilligan's. And yet Lord Hutton never seemed to take the Watts tape on board. It should have been dynamite at the inquiry but wasn't. It showed that Gilligan's story had been overwhelmingly true. Those who still believe that Gilligan exaggerated what Dr Kelly had told him should re-read the transcript of the tape. When Hutton replayed the tape in court it had been remastered and much of the really incriminating evidence was inaudible, so it didn't have the public impact it deserved. As William Rees-Mogg said later: 'I found Lord Hutton's report a defective document . . . he gave too little weight to crucial parts of the evidence, including David Kelly's interview with Susan Watts and the colourful extracts from Alastair Campbell's diary.'

There were two more events of note in the weeks that followed. First, I had another exchange of letters with the Prime Minister with me writing to complain that one Cabinet Minister had briefed journalists in the days after Dr Kelly died saying that 'the problem with the BBC was that it had too much money and Greg Dyke' and that after Hutton the Government would 'sort these things out'. The Minister had used the word 'revenge' on several occasions. The journalist who had been briefed said it sounded like the Minister had been reading from a script prepared by someone else.

In my letter to Tony Blair I said that both Gavyn Davies and I regarded this as 'a blatant threat to the funding and editorial independence of the BBC from a member of your Cabinet' and that while I was sure that the Prime Minister hadn't sanctioned the briefing I was also sure he would recognize 'the political and constitutional implications' of what was said. He sent back a letter in which he said he totally supported the independence of the BBC and that there was no question of the licence fee decision being affected by any of this. He also said that he was fed up with stories driven by 'anonymous sources'. But mine wasn't an anonymous source – I knew for a fact which Cabinet Minister had done the briefing.

The second event was of course the resignation of Alastair Campbell. The BBC's Political Editor, Andy Marr, had got a very strong hint some weeks earlier that Campbell was going to go, but it wasn't until 29 August that he finally announced his departure. He spun himself out brilliantly, making it look like it was his decision, but it wasn't. Blair later told Gavyn Davies in one of their conversations that Campbell had to go.

From the moment Dr Kelly killed himself it was obvious that Campbell's decision to go to war with the BBC had backfired spectacularly on the Government, on Blair, and on Campbell himself. An eminent and loyal public servant had died. Campbell had wanted Kelly named. Now Kelly was dead and Blair was insisting that Campbell was out of Downing Street. Amongst other things, there was a real fear that his diaries would prove embarrassing and that the untruths he had told to the Foreign Affairs Committee about his involvement in the September dossier would rebound on the whole of Number Ten. By Campbell leaving, the Prime Minister would be able to say that Downing Street had cleaned up its act.

In many ways the death of Dr Kelly was the end of the whole saga for a while and things calmed down. The Government announced that Lord Hutton would conduct an inquiry and everything went quiet while we waited for the process to start. I'd persuaded my family that we should spend our summer holiday walking the Inca trail, cycling and white water rafting in Peru. Sadly, they all had to go without me. As they left, Sue said: 'I was only doing this because you wanted to go. Do you really think this is how I wanted to spend my summer holiday?' I did manage to get out for the second week, though I missed the difficult bit of walking the trail.

I arrived back from Peru for the first day of the Hutton Inquiry on 1 August. We were all impressed by the way the inquiry was run. I was particularly impressed by the barrister for the inquiry, James Dingemans, who seemed to be seriously interested in getting at the truth. The only time when I thought he and Hutton let themselves down was when they were too reverential to Tony Blair when he gave evidence. He should have been recalled for cross-examination as there were questions that should have been put to him. In particular, he should have been asked about his role in the 'outing' of Dr Kelly as he clearly played a part. Hutton has since said he didn't recall Blair for cross-examination because he didn't want the Prime Minister to receive a public mauling. Surely Hutton's job was to get at the truth and not to be over-concerned about the sensitivities of the Prime Minister? This is an illustration of Hutton's whole attitude when it came to writing his report.

We judged that there were three particularly bad moments for the BBC during the inquiry. The first was when an e-mail from Kevin Marsh to his boss was revealed saying that Gilligan's report was 'marred by loose language'. I had never seen this before, or heard the sentiment expressed.

The second was when Gilligan was answering questions and said that when he reported Dr Kelly as saying that the Government 'probably knew it was wrong' it was not a direct quote but his interpretation of what Dr Kelly had told him. Again this was not what we believed he had told us.

The third was the e-mail that Gilligan had sent to the Liberal Democrat member of the Select Committee David Chidgey saying that Dr Kelly had been Susan Watts' source. At that time none of us – including Gilligan – knew this for a fact, and it was a totally unacceptable thing for Gilligan to have done.

Although these were all serious concerns, the Government and the Ministry of Defence faced even more embarrassing moments during the inquiry, particularly over the way in which they had conspired to 'out' Dr Kelly.

The day before I was due to appear before Hutton I rang my mother to warn her that there would be some more publicity. To cheer her up I told her that on the same morning I was doing a reading at Thora Hird's memorial service at Westminster Abbey. My mum thought for a moment and came back with two lines only an 88-year-old could come up with. On Hutton she just said, 'Yes, dear. I read in the paper you were going to a meeting'; and on Thora Hird she went quiet, thought for a moment, and then said: 'She's dead, you know.'

My own appearance before Hutton was rather a non-event. I wasn't called in the first round of witnesses, was called almost as an afterthought, and was not recalled for cross-examination. I was rather nervous and stuck very much to the witness statement I'd submitted in advance, as advised by our QC. When I wandered off it to try to point out something I thought was really important, Mr Dingemans rapidly chopped me to pieces. I realized then that this was the barristers' pitch and the barristers' game and that I had to play by their rules.

The inquiry closed on 25 September and Lord Hutton said he hoped to report before Christmas. In the end it was 28 January before he published his report. And when he did, it took virtually everyone by surprise.

CHAPTER THIRTEEN

Why Hutton Was Wrong

In the months after Gavyn Davies and I left the BBC, which in my case was the same day that Lord Ryder made his abject apology, the BBC stopped trying to defend the position it had taken throughout the Hutton Inquiry that it had been right to broadcast Andrew Gilligan reporting Dr Kelly's concerns.

What this has meant is that in the months since Lord Hutton's report was published a myth has been fostered. The myth is that Gilligan and the BBC made a series of very serious mistakes. This is simply not the case. Gilligan did make errors, a couple of which were serious; but it was Lord Hutton, not the BBC, who got it fundamentally wrong.

Over the months, the BBC could have countered this myth. Instead, led by the acting Chairman, the BBC ran for cover. From the moment Lord Ryder made his apology, with a worried acting Director-General by his side, no one from within the BBC has been allowed to argue the opposite case. This has done great damage to the BBC's integrity and to the reputation of its journalism both in Britain and, more importantly, around the world.

The Governors of the BBC have allowed the myth to become accepted wisdom for fear of reopening the whole issue and reigniting the battle with the Government, while some in management, who know the real story, were so badly bruised during the Hutton process that they have chosen to say very little in public. As a result, the fallacy that was at the heart of the Hutton Report has been left to fester undisturbed. It is time that was corrected.

We now know for certain that Andrew Gilligan's story was nothing like the 'mountain of untruth' that Tony Blair described it as in the House of Commons on 4 February 2004. Nor was it '100 per cent wrong', as Alastair Campbell claimed in a letter to me of 26 June 2003. We know this because Lord Butler's Review of the intelligence on weapons of mass destruction told us so. It also meant that when Campbell said that the BBC – from Chairman and Director-General down – had lied, it was an inaccurate and disingenuous statement from a man who had himself deliberately misled the House of Commons Foreign Affairs Select Committee when giving evidence on the Kelly affair and who is not unknown for being economical with the truth.

There was a clear public interest in the BBC broadcasting what Dr Kelly had told Andrew Gilligan because of what it told us about the Government's case for going to war in Iraq, about how some in the security services disagreed with the way intelligence was used to justify that decision, and about the Blair Government's obsession with public relations and spin.

Lord Hutton got it wrong on many points, as I shall demonstrate later, but in particular he made a mistake on one crucial issue: his ruling that it was not part of his remit to consider what sort of weapons of mass destruction the Government's dossier on Iraq actually referred to. It is not going too far to say that the entire structure of Lord Hutton's report, and its recommendations, were deeply flawed because of that ruling.

This is not to say that Gilligan didn't make mistakes; he did, and he should not have made them. But his mistakes did not mean the story he was reporting wasn't valid, and not all the mistakes were of his making. Sometimes he reported accurately and in good faith something Dr Kelly had told him that later turned out to be an exaggeration by Dr Kelly himself.

The best way to understand what Hutton got wrong is to analyse what Gilligan actually said in that early-morning broadcast at seven minutes past six on 29 May 2003 and ask how it stacks up against what we know today. It was this early, unscripted, broadcast that caused all the problems.

First, there was an introduction from *Today*'s main presenter John Humphrys:

[JH]: The Government is facing more questions this morning over its claims about weapons of mass destruction in Iraq. Our defence correspondent is Andrew Gilligan. This in particular, Andy, is Tony Blair saying they'd be ready within 45 minutes.

[AG]: That's right, that was the central claim in his dossier which he published in September, the main case if you like against Iraq and the main statement of the British Government's belief of what it thought Iraq was up to. And what we've been told by one of the senior officials in charge of drawing up that dossier was that actually the Government probably knew that that 45-minute figure was wrong even before it decided to put it in. What this person says is that a week before the publication date of the dossier it was actually rather a bland production. It didn't, the draft prepared for Mr Blair by the intelligence agencies, actually didn't say very much more than was public knowledge already and Downing Street, our source says, ordered it to be sexed up, to be made more exciting and ordered more facts to be discovered.

[JH]: When you say 'more facts to be discovered' does that suggest that they may not have been facts?

[AG]: Well, our source says that the dossier as it was finally published made the intelligence services unhappy because, to quote the source, he said there was basically – that there was, there was – unhappiness because it didn't reflect the considered view they were putting forward: that's a quote from our source. And essentially the 45-minute point was probably the most important thing that was added and the reason it hadn't been in the original draft was that it was – it was only, it came from – one source and most of the other claims were from two, and the intelligence agencies say they don't really believe it was necessarily true because they thought the person making the claim had actually made a mistake, it got – had got – mixed up.

[JH]: Does any of this matter now, all this – all these – months later? The war's been fought and won.

[AG]: Well, the 45 minutes isn't just a detail. It did go to the heart of the Government's case that Saddam was an imminent threat and it was repeated four times in the dossier including by the Prime Minister himself in the foreword. So I think it probably does matter. Clearly, you know, if – if it was, if it was wrong in good faith, things do – things are – got wrong in good faith. But if they knew if it was wrong before they actually made the claim, that's perhaps a bit more serious.

In the course of his report Gilligan covered about a dozen points but serious questions were only ever raised about five of them. By far the most important, and the one that caused most of the fuss, was when Gilligan said he had been told by his source that 'the Government probably knew that the 45-minute figure was wrong even before it decided to put it in'. I shall return to that later but first I shall analyse the other four points.

First was Gilligan's description of Dr Kelly as 'one of the senior officials in charge of drawing up that dossier'. The mistake here was Dr Kelly's, not Gilligan's. Dr Kelly appears to have overstated his own role in the dossier. Gilligan told the Hutton Inquiry what had happened:

At the end of our May 22nd meeting I asked him how he wanted to be described in the reporting and offered him two alternatives, a senior official involved with the dossier or one of the senior officials in charge of drawing up the dossier. He was happy with both alternatives, he said: fine.

There is no reason to disbelieve Gilligan's account of what Dr Kelly told him, but from what we now know the first of these two descriptions ('a senior official involved with the dossier') is clearly the more accurate. Dr Kelly did draw up one part of the dossier, and he was consulted about the accuracy of the whole document. But he was not in charge of drawing up the dossier. Dr Kelly seems to have been quite keen to underline his role in the dossier. In the interview with him that Susan Watts of *Newsnight* taped he is heard saying: 'I reviewed the whole thing, I was involved with the whole process.'

In these circumstances Gilligan would have been covered by the law of qualified privilege, as defined under the Reynolds defence ruling of October 1999. (Reynolds provides a complete defence to media organizations, even where false allegations of fact have been reported, so long as publication was the result of 'responsible reporting' on a matter of 'legitimate public interest'.) Lord Hutton got the law wrong on this point when he said 'the right to communicate such information is subject to the qualification . . . that false accusations of fact impugning the integrity of others, including politicians, should not be made by the media'.

What this exposes is that Lord Hutton, who trained as a criminal lawyer, knew little about media law and yet this is what the whole inquiry was about. If Hutton's findings in this area had been a legal judgment they would, arguably, have completely rewritten the rules of journalism in the UK. Had the BBC been able to appeal, we could have shown that Hutton had misunderstood the law and that the whole inquiry was not a 'fair' legal process: the Government chose the judge and then he failed to permit full examination of the witnesses.

In any case, whether Gilligan properly described Dr Kelly is a relatively trivial matter as no one now questions the fact that Kelly had played an important role in drawing up the dossier. As the story unfolded the Government's public relations people did try to underplay Kelly's role. They initially dismissed him as 'a middle ranking official' and Tom Kelly, one of Campbell's lieutenants, famously called him a 'Walter Mitty character'. (Tom Kelly has since been promoted inside Downing Street.) But at the Hutton Inquiry there was no questioning of Dr Kelly's credibility as someone in a position to know about the dossier and weapons of mass destruction in Iraq.

The second point in Gilligan's broadcast that has been questioned was the use of the word 'ordered' in 'ordered more facts to be discovered'.

Gilligan accepted during the inquiry that he had no record of Dr Kelly's using this precise word. Again, on the face of it, this was a serious journalistic error. But in the light of the evidence revealed during the inquiry we can see that although 'ordered' was the wrong word to use, it was not all that far from the right one.

Gilligan's own notes record Dr Kelly as saying 'transformed week before publication to make it sexier'. Later there is a reference to 'Campbell', and then, two lines later, 'not in original draft – dull, he asked if anything else could go in'.

In his evidence to Hutton, Gilligan partially justified his use of the word 'ordered' by explaining that:

He [Kelly] clearly stated that the transformation of the dossier was
the responsibility of Campbell, who had asked if anything else could
be put in. So again, it was a reasonable conclusion to draw from
what he had said.

Gilligan's logic here is not perfect. But we do know that Dr Kelly also
told *Newsnight*'s Susan Watts: 'They were desperate for information. They
were pushing hard for information that could be released.' What is clear
is that the Government was not pushing for evidence that didn't support
the case for war. Quite the opposite. It is also clear that pressure for that
evidence was coming from the very top. On 3 September 2002 Tony Blair
had said at a press conference held in his constituency of Sedgefield:

There is a real and existing threat we have to deal with . . . What
is that threat? The threat is an Iraq that carries on building up
chemical, biological, nuclear weapons capacity.

And yet on 3 September there was virtually no hard evidence to support
that position. By 24 September, when the dossier was published, it had
miraculously appeared.

What Dr Kelly told both Gilligan and Watts was strongly supported
by the revelation during the Hutton Inquiry of a memo headed 'Questions
from No 10'. This was written by someone in the Cabinet Office drafting
team only a few days before the dossier went to the printers. It was
addressed to the intelligence agencies and set out a number of areas where
Downing Street was pressing hard for more information. It ends with the
faintly despairing plea:

I appreciate everyone, including us, has been around at least some
of these buoys before . . . But No 10 through the Chairman [of the
JIC] want the document to be as strong as possible . . . This is
therefore a last (!) call for any items of intelligence that agencies
think can and should be included.

This doesn't amount to an 'order' in the strict technical sense of the word,
but it's not far off it. Imagine yourself as a member of one of the intelligence agencies when this appeared in your e-mail box with all the majesty

of the Number Ten address at the top. Would it not feel like an order? Would you not respond as if it were an order? What would be the consequences of not reacting to such a high level 'request'?

There was another consequence of this relentless pressure to find new intelligence from the very top. As the Butler Report says, it resulted in dubious information being passed up the chain to satisfy the demands of the politicians:

> Because of the scarcity of sources and the urgent requirement for intelligence, more credence was given to untried agents than would normally be the case.

This was to have serious consequences as we shall see later.

The third point is Gilligan's claim that Dr Kelly had told him the dossier was 'sexed up'. Hutton decided that this allegation was 'unfounded' and dismissed it out of hand. Yet the evidence on this point is unarguable.

Kelly certainly made the claim, although the actual word 'sexier' was not the sort of word he normally used. Gilligan probably introduced it into the conversation and Dr Kelly picked it up, as so often happens in interviews. Without doubt Gilligan's notes record Kelly as saying that the dossier 'was transformed in the week before it was published, to make it sexier', so Kelly clearly said it.

Another BBC reporter, Gavin Hewitt, having spoken to Kelly, said that it was Kelly's judgement that 'some Number Ten spin did come into play'. And Susan Watts of *Newsnight* taped Kelly saying, 'The word-smithing is actually quite important, and the intelligence community are a pretty cautious lot on the whole, but once you get people presenting it for public consumption then of course they use different words.'

It is clear that Kelly's allegation was of spin, that the dossier had been exaggerated to increase its impact. It was certainly the charge made by one of Kelly's colleagues, 'Mr A', a chemical weapons expert consulted in the preparation of the dossier. He e-mailed Kelly when the dossier was published and described it as 'another example supporting our view that you and I should have been more involved in this than the spin merchants of this administration'. When asked to explain this by the Hutton Inquiry, Mr A said: 'The perception was that the dossier had been round the houses several times in order to try to find a form of words which would strengthen certain political objectives.'

The phrase to 'sex something up' has now gone into the language – as witnessed by the latest edition of the *Concise Oxford Dictionary* where it is defined as to 'present something in a more interesting or lively way'. But Hutton chose to interpret 'sexing up' in a totally different way, which just happened to support the Government's position. In his report he spells out the meaning he chose to put on it: '[that] the dossier had been embellished with intelligence known or believed to be false or unreliable'. This is a much more serious charge than Gilligan believed Kelly was making when using the term 'sexier'.

Yet even on Hutton's interpretation, the evidence that the wording of the dossier was tampered with in a way that fundamentally altered its meaning is overwhelming. Key passages were hardened up. Caveats were removed or softened, and conditional language was replaced with absolute language.

For example, the draft of 16 September says, in the section called Main Conclusions: 'The Iraqi military **may be able** to deploy these within forty-five minutes.' Three days later, in the draft of 19 September, the same section reads: 'The Iraqi military **are able** to deploy these within forty-five minutes.' A possibility had become a certainty.

Similarly, the first draft of the Executive Summary, written by Alastair Campbell and Tony Blair, says that: 'Intelligence **indicates** that Iraq **could deploy** [chemical and biological weapons] within 45 minutes.' But by the final draft the sentence has been hardened up to: 'We **judge** that Iraq has military plans for the use of chemical and biological weapons, some of which **are deployable** within 45 minutes.'

Now these two significant changes might have been justifiable if new intelligence had become available. But we know that there was no new evidence on the 45-minutes claim after 9 September; yet these redrafts took place after that date.

Throughout the dossier caveats were removed or softened, and conditional language was replaced with absolute language. When the Butler committee, which reviewed all the intelligence, reported in July 2004 it made this point in spades. It said:

The language in the dossier may have left readers the impression that there was fuller and firmer intelligence behind the judgements than was the case; our view . . . is that judgements in the dossier went to (although not beyond) the outer limits of intelligence available.

A simpler way of putting it would have been to say that the dossier had been 'sexed up'. What Lord Butler conspicuously failed to tell us was who took out the caveats, who replaced the conditional language; in other words, who 'sexed up' the dossier.

These changes were what so upset Dr Brian Jones, Britain's most experienced intelligence official working on weapons of mass destruction, who had seen the original intelligence and knew that it did not reflect what was being said in the final draft of the dossier. For him, this change of language was not just a matter of spin, of putting the best gloss on available facts, of pushing intelligence to its outer limits. For Dr Jones, changing the language of an assessment was tantamount to changing the facts on which it was based.

When Dr Jones described to the inquiry the serious concerns his team had expressed on seeing the final draft of the dossier, Hutton interjected to ask if these concerns were just 'matters of language'. Dr Jones, a man of some dignity, gave a memorably withering reply: 'My Lord, they were about language, but language is the means by which we communicate an assessment so they were also about the assessment.'

This was not the view of those at the top, such as the Defence Secretary Geoff Hoon, who gave the impression that he simply couldn't understand what all the fuss was about over a few words here and there. 'I was aware,' Hoon told Hutton dismissively, 'that two officials had expressed some concern about certain language used in the dossier . . . I emphasize that this was of a *linguistic* kind.'

Hutton, as ever, came down against the views of the lower ranks in favour of those in higher places. But the evidence that the dossier was definitely 'sexed up' is there on the website for everyone to read. Hutton's verdict cannot change the truth revealed by the unexplained alterations to the drafts of the September dossier. And remember these were the very drafts that Downing Street refused to allow the Foreign Affairs Select Committee to see. We now know why.

The fourth point at issue is the assertion that the 45-minutes claim was not included in the early drafts of the dossier because it was single, not double, sourced. This was a straightforward mistake by Andrew Gilligan.

The reason the intelligence was included late in the drafting process was because it arrived late. Whether it should have been included because it was single sourced is itself a serious matter, particularly given the unreliability of the primary source, but it was not the reason for the lateness of its inclusion.

Gilligan's mistake was to link two of Kelly's concerns – that the information came late and that it was single sourced. He was wrong to have made such a connection, but was right to highlight both points.

It was the fifth point in the original broadcast that caused the most fuss, when Gilligan used the phrase: 'the Government probably knew that that 45-minute figure was wrong even before it decided to put it in'. This statement did more damage to the BBC case than any other during the inquiry when Gilligan told Lord Hutton that he now accepted that Dr Kelly did not use these precise words and that instead the phrase was his interpretation of what Dr Kelly had told him.

On the face of it, this was a serious mistake. But deeper analysis shows what Gilligan actually said is by no means indefensible. Gilligan himself defended his reporting by telling Lord Hutton:

> He [Dr Kelly] did say that the statement that WMD were ready for use in 45 minutes was unreliable, that it was wrong and that it was included 'against our wishes'; and it was a logical conclusion to draw from this that those wishes had been made known.

Whether or not what Gilligan said is justifiable is entirely dependent on who knew what about the 45-minute claim and what they thought it meant.

To understand what happened here you have to retrace some steps. It was in January 2002 that President George W. Bush made his 'Axis of Evil' speech, naming Iraq, Iran, and North Korea as sponsors of terrorism. Of these, Iraq was quickly singled out as the next target. Bush was quite open about his objective: 'We support regime change.'

In London, Tony Blair rapidly adopted the new Washington line. John Scarlett, Chairman of the Joint Intelligence Committee (JIC), was instructed to start trawling the intelligence data so that the British Government could publish a dossier showing the dangers posed by the 'Axis of Evil' states, particularly Iraq. Other officials were instructed to start examining the legal basis for military action against Iraq.

The work rapidly ran into problems. There was *no* new intelligence to suggest Iraq was doing anything it hadn't been doing for years.

The Butler Report sets this out with remarkable clarity in a passage discussing Blair's change of policy in early 2002:

> There was a clear view [by the Government] that, to be successful, any new action to enforce Iraqi compliance ... would need to be backed with the credible threat of force. But there was no recent intelligence that itself would have given rise to a conclusion that Iraq was of more immediate concern than the activities of some other countries.

And this was not the only problem. The officials charged with assessing the legal basis for action were being sticky too. President Bush might be gung-ho for regime change, but, as Lord Butler puts it:

> [British] officials noted that regime change of itself had no basis in international law.

The only way military action could be legally justified, said the officials, was if it could be proved that Iraq was in breach of its obligations under UN resolutions – but even then the proof would have to be 'incontrovertible and of large-scale activity'. Butler notes drily:

> The intelligence then available was insufficiently robust to meet that criterion.

But by now the die was cast. While this work was going on in the early part of 2002, Bush invited Blair to his ranch at Crawford in Texas. They met in early April and the two men had long discussions on Iraq, often with no officials present and no notes taken. Immediately afterwards Blair made a speech to an American audience and gave public endorsement to the Bush policy of removing Saddam by force. Blair said:

> We must be prepared to act ... If necessary the action should be military and again, if necessary and justified, it should involve regime change.

It seems that Blair had committed himself to removing Saddam from power. But his officials were advising that this was illegal under international law unless 'incontrovertible' evidence of 'large-scale activity' by Iraq could be found. And Blair was being advised at this time that this evidence did not exist. Blair obviously wanted and expected to get United Nations support for his position, but was prepared to take military action alongside the USA if it wasn't forthcoming.

As it happened, military action was postponed and the dossier to demonstrate Iraqi guilt was put on ice. But in the summer, as war came closer, the dossier idea was revived. Only now there was a new element in the mix: Alastair Campbell.

Campbell had had nothing to do with the first draft of the dossier in early 2002. But now he was given an important role in the preparation of the document. He was to be in charge of presentation. At the end of August, on a flight back from a visit to Mozambique, Campbell and Blair agreed that a new dossier should be published. On 3 September Blair made a public announcement that the dossier was on its way. Campbell wrote in his diary: 'Why . . . now? Why Iraq? Why only Iraq . . .'. And he identified the 'toughest question' the dossier had to answer: 'What new evidence was there?'

The awkward truth was that at this stage there *was* no new evidence of the sort Blair needed, as Campbell discovered when he took his first look at the latest version of the March dossier. He immediately ordered a substantial rewrite. 'It had to be revelatory,' he wrote in his diary. But at this stage there was nothing new to reveal. And it was less than three weeks before the dossier was to be published.

But then Blair and Campbell had a remarkable stroke of luck. SIS helpfully came up with two brand new pieces of intelligence. The first had arrived on 29 August and was already wending its way through the JIC assessment process. It seemed to suggest that the Iraqis had chemical and biological weapons that could be ready for use within 45 minutes. Blair and Campbell had the revelation they needed.

Or did they?

According to Butler, this new evidence was based on an intelligence report that was 'vague and ambiguous'. A proper assessment of its significance, says Butler, would be something like:

A source has claimed some weapons may be deployed within 45 minutes of an order to use them, but the exact nature of the weapons, the agents involved and the context of their use is unclear.

According to Butler, that is the phrase that should have gone into the dossier, but it didn't because it wouldn't have convinced anyone that it was the basis for going to war. So a much stronger version was included. What the dossier said was: 'The Iraqi military are able to deploy these within 45 minutes.' And what Blair said in his introduction to the dossier was: 'We judge that Iraq has military plans for the use of chemical and biological weapons, some of which are deployable within 45 minutes.'

There was one thing all the officials handling the 45-minute intelligence agreed on: that the weapons were short-range battlefield munitions, not rocket warheads that could threaten other states. Again this was not how it appeared in the dossier. There the clear impression was given that these were weapons that could inflict mass destruction on British subjects.

How could this have happened?

We know from evidence revealed during the Hutton Inquiry and since that there were a significant number of people in Whitehall who had real concerns about the way the 45-minute claim was presented in the September dossier and that these included intelligence analysts in the Defence Intelligence Staff. One of these, Dr Brian Jones, took the almost unprecedented step of formally minuting his concerns to his boss. He told the *Independent* newspaper in February 2004:

My belief is that right up to publication of the dossier there was a unified view not only amongst my own staff but all the DIS experts that on the basis of the intelligence available to them the assessment that Iraq possessed a CW or BW capability should be carefully caveated.

On the 45-minute claim he said:

There was no indication the original or primary source had established a track record of reliability. Furthermore, the information reported by the source was vague in all aspects except, possibly, for the range of times quoted.

The Butler Report backs Dr Jones, concluding that the 45-minute claim should not have been included in the dossier

> without stating what it was believed to refer to. The fact that the reference . . . was repeated in the dossier later led to suspicions that it had been included because of its eye-catching character.

This was not the only time that intelligence on this issue would be massaged to make it more 'eye-catching'.

SIS, having produced the 45-minute evidence, then came up with their second revelation. The second piece of intelligence arrived on 10 September and caused great excitement. A brand-new source was reporting that 'the production of biological and chemical agents had been accelerated by the Iraqi Government, including through the building of further facilities throughout Iraq'.

At last, here was incontrovertible proof of large-scale activity by the Iraqis in breach of UN resolutions. Here was the evidence Blair needed. Except that it was not incontrovertible. It came from an entirely new and untested source with no track record. According to Butler, when the head of SIS, Sir Richard Dearlove, personally briefed Tony Blair on the news, he said that the case was 'developmental and that the source remained unproven'. What the Butler Report didn't tell us was that Alastair Campbell was also at that briefing meeting.

SIS were adamant that, to protect the source, this material should not be used in the dossier, although they agreed it could be used 'through assertion'. That was enough for Campbell and Blair. Four days later, Campbell, who had been at the SIS briefing with Blair, produced a draft of what Blair wanted to say in his foreword. It said that Blair had been briefed in detail about the intelligence concerning Iraq and that he now believed it established 'beyond doubt' that Iraq had continued to produce chemical and biological weapons. Yet both Blair and Campbell must have known this wasn't established 'beyond doubt' as Britain's top spy, the head of the SIS Sir Richard Dearlove, had told them personally that the case was 'developmental' and the source 'unproven'. Dearlove later made a specific point of explaining to Lord Butler that he had told them this.

Both Blair and Campbell chose to ignore these caveats; they were not included in Campbell's first draft of the foreword or in the later versions which were approved by John Scarlett. It is clear to me that the Prime Minister's conviction was stronger than the evidence justified. In his foreword to the dossier Blair also hinted that he had information too secret to reveal, a claim which we now know was also partly based on evidence from this 'unproven' source. It, too, was used to convince us all of the threat from Iraq. Maybe there was a bit of 'sexing up' going on here.

We later discovered from the Butler report that this new source provided by SIS, a source so secret that his information didn't go through the proper assessment process, turned out to be unreliable. The evidence he supplied was withdrawn by SIS in July 2003, the month before the Hutton Inquiry started. Neither Sir Richard Dearlove nor John Scarlett, two eminent public servants, told Lord Hutton that the evidence was no longer regarded as reliable when they appeared before his inquiry.

This second new piece of intelligence was also used to support the first – the 45-minute claim. When Dr Jones complained about the over-strong use of language in the dossier on chemical and biological weapons, he was told that there was new intelligence, so secret that he was not allowed even to see it, that justified the language of the dossier.

And so the 45-minute claim, shorn of the caveats about its reliability, and presented in such a way as to make the implied threat much more serious, made its way into the dossier.

Jonathan Powell, the Chief of Staff inside Number Ten, drew attention to a serious problem in the dossier. Just before it went to the printers he sent an e-mail to Campbell and Scarlett. In it he pointed out that the paragraph in the latest draft of the dossier saying that

Saddam is prepared to use chemical and biological weapons if he believes his regime is under threat

was actually an argument against going to war with Iraq, not one in favour of it. He described that phrase as

a bit of a problem ... it backs up the argument that there is no chemical and biological weapons threat and we will only create one if we attack him.

301

Powell suggested that the relevant paragraph be redrafted. What John Scarlett then did is another example of how the dossier was 'sexed up' – changed not because there was new intelligence, but simply to make a better case for going to war. He took out the crucial qualification 'if he believes his regime is under threat' and in so doing changed the meaning of the dossier.

What is important here is not only *what* was changed but the timing of the changes. Powell's e-mail was sent, and Scarlett's redraft written, after the final deadline for changes to the dossier had passed. The redraft was never discussed by the rest of the Joint Intelligence Committee and yet any substantial changes to the dossier were supposed to go back to the full JIC for approval. Clearly Scarlett decided that the changes he was making were not substantial.

So it was Scarlett who took out the crucial line saying Saddam would only use his weapons if he was under threat. In doing so he changed a key emphasis of the dossier as a result of an e-mail from the Prime Minister's Chief of Staff, a political appointee. Scarlett's unilateral redraft meant that nowhere did the dossier say that attacking Saddam brought its own dangers. Nor did it say that the weapons of mass destruction it referred to were short-range munitions. As a result, the world was given the wrong impression.

In the same e-mail Powell also asked Alastair Campbell what the head-line in the *Evening Standard* would be when the dossier was published, demonstrating that headlines about the dossier mattered to Downing Street. The answer was that the newspapers reporting the publication of the dossier put terrifying headlines on their stories such as:

45 MINS FROM ATTACK
(*Evening Standard*)

BRITS 45 MINS FROM DOOM
(*The Sun*)

Both papers talked of the threat to British troops in Cyprus and *The Sun* even suggested that tourists in Cyprus could be 'annihilated by germ warfare missiles launched by Iraq'. Other regional papers picked up on the same line.

Many in Whitehall – politicians, spooks, and civil servants alike – knew these newspaper stories were wrong and yet they made no attempt to correct this scaremongering. One can only assume they failed to do this because they got the headlines that Downing Street wanted. In fact Tony Blair built his case for war on the supposed imminence of the Iraqi threat to Britain and British interests. He did it in the dossier:

> I am in no doubt that the threat is serious and current, that he has made progress on WMD, and that he has to be stopped ... the document discloses that his military planning allows for some of the WMD to be ready within 45 minutes of an order to use them.

He did it again in the Commons on 24 September 2002:

> His [Saddam's] weapons of mass destruction programme is active, detailed and growing. The policy of containment is not working. The weapons of mass destruction programme is not shut down; it is up and running now ... he has existing and active military plans for the use of chemical and biological weapons, which could be activated within 45 minutes.

And just before the war began, in reference to the threat of weapons of mass destruction, he again raised the spectre of

> a real and present danger to Britain and its national security

when addressing the House of Commons in March 2003. We now know that the basis of all three of Blair's statements was wrong.

It is interesting to compare the Prime Minister's statements with an earlier e-mail of 17 September 2002 from Jonathan Powell. Writing to John Scarlett, with a copy to Campbell, he said, having read the latest draft of the dossier, that

> We will need to make it clear in launching the document that we do not claim we have evidence that he [Saddam] is an imminent threat.

And yet Tony Blair claimed exactly that.

What is certain is that the Head of the Secret Intelligence Service, Sir Richard Dearlove, knew that the intelligence concerning the threat of WMDs that could be fired in 45 minutes did not constitute a threat to Britain or British interests. During the Hutton Inquiry Sir Richard was asked by the inquiry counsel if he accepted that the 45-minutes claim had been given 'undue prominence'. His answer was astonishingly frank:

> Well, I think given the misinterpretation that was placed on the 45-minutes intelligence, with the benefit of hindsight you can say that is a valid criticism.

At this point Lord Hutton himself interjected to ask what Sir Richard meant by 'misinterpretation'. There was a significant pause before Sir Richard replied:

> Well, I think the original report referred to chemical and biological munitions and that was taken to refer to battlefield weapons. I think what subsequently happened in the reporting was that it was taken that the 45 minutes applied, let us say, to weapons of a longer range.

Sir Richard was not alone in knowing the truth. The then Leader of the House of Commons, Robin Cook, also knew it before the war was started. In his published diaries, entitled *Point of Departure* (2003), he records an intelligence briefing from John Scarlett, Chairman of the Joint Intelligence Committee, in February 2003 – just a month before the war began:

> My conclusion at the end of an hour is that Saddam probably does not have weapons of mass destruction in the sense of weapons that could be used against a large-scale civilian target.

According to Cook, he shared these concerns with Tony Blair shortly before the war began. His diary records what happened at the meeting:

> The most revealing exchange came when we talked about Saddam's arsenal. I told him, 'It's clear from the private briefing I have had that Saddam has no weapons of mass destruction in a sense of weapons that could strike at strategic cities. But he probably does

have several thousand battlefield chemical munitions. Do you never worry that he might use them against British troops?' [Blair replied:] 'Yes, but all the effort he has had to put into concealment makes it difficult for him to assemble them quickly for use.'

Cook says he was 'deeply troubled' by his conversation with the Prime Minister:

Tony did not try to argue me out of the view that Saddam did not have real weapons of mass destruction that were designed for strategic use against city populations and capable of being delivered with reliability over long distances. I had now expressed that view to both the chairman of the JIC and to the prime minister and both had assented in it. At the time I did believe it likely that Saddam had retained a quantity of chemical munitions for tactical use on the battlefield. These did not pose 'a real and present danger to Britain' as they were not designed for use against city populations and by definition could threaten British personnel only if we were to deploy them on the battlefield within range of Iraqi artillery.

If Robin Cook's diary is an accurate record of his conversation with the Prime Minister it is inconsistent with Tony Blair's account of events in two important areas.

Firstly, it would mean that the Prime Minister knew that, even if these weapons of mass destruction did exist, they couldn't be used in 45 minutes because they had to be assembled first. Yet in his foreword to the September dossier the Prime Minister had talked about the 45-minute threat as if it was real and immediate and had done the same in his statement to Parliament the day the dossier was published. He has made no attempt to put the record straight on this.

Secondly, and more significantly, Blair's answer to Cook also suggests that by then he must have known that these were short-range weapons and that they couldn't threaten British interests, yet he has denied that he knew the truth about this until after the war was over. This means that either Cook's recollection of the conversation is suspect, or that Blair's subsequent denial of this knowledge has to be questioned. They cannot both be right.

Recent evidence published in Bob Woodward's book *Plan of Attack*, which was based on interviews with all the main US players, including President Bush, shows quite clearly that the CIA didn't believe the 45-minute claim. George Tenet, the Director of the CIA at the time, referred to the claim as 'they-can-attack-in-45-minutes shit'. Even more importantly, Woodward says that Tenet and the CIA had warned the British not to make the allegation, presumably before the dossier was published, as they believed the source was questionable and that the claim only referred to battlefield weapons.

The charge against Blair is damning. He was either incompetent and took Britain to war on a misunderstanding or he lied when he told the House of Commons that he didn't know what the 45-minute claim meant. Either way it can be argued that the Prime Minister should have known what sort of weapons he was talking about: after all, it was his foreword, his dossier, and subsequently his war. And in his foreword he did say: 'I and other ministers have been briefed in detail on the intelligence.'

The Defence Secretary, Geoff Hoon, accepts that he knew the truth although, he says, not until 'shortly after' the dossier was published, which was still six months before the war began. He told the Defence Select Committee on 5 February 2004:

> I asked within the Ministry of Defence what kinds of weapons were in effect being referred to as part of the so-called 45 minutes claim, and the answer was . . . that they were of a battlefield kind.

It is interesting that Hoon didn't ask the question until *after* the dossier was published. As the member of the Government responsible for defence one would have thought he might have asked *before* it became a public document. What we learnt during the Hutton Inquiry was that Hoon was only a bit-part player, like many in Tony Blair's Cabinet, and was often excluded from the crucial discussions about Iraq. We do know that Hoon made no attempt to correct the public record when he discovered that the dossier was not clear on this point and that the public had been given totally the wrong impression.

John Scarlett certainly knew the truth before the dossier was published since he had seen all the original intelligence. At the BBC we also knew he was 'uncomfortable' with the public case being made for the war because that is what he had told one journalist on a bench in the grounds of Ditchley Park, the exclusive Oxfordshire house used as a centre for high-level discussions on international affairs. Scarlett told the journalist he was particularly worried about the way the dossier had been interpreted in the press. He may have been worried, but Scarlett – like Hoon – didn't do anything about it.

I also find it difficult to believe that the group responsible for producing the dossier, which included Alastair Campbell and three other press officers from Number Ten, didn't know all the facts about the 45-minute claim before publication. Surely Campbell, a man who prides himself about knowing the detail on such matters, would have asked what actual weapons the dossier was referring to?

And yet the full picture on these points never made its way into the dossier. Why? One can only assume it was because it would have weakened the case for going to war.

Lord Hutton should have realized that Dr Kelly and his friends in the Defence Intelligence Services knew a whole range of things about this issue:

- They had serious doubts about the validity of the 45-minute claim and where it came from.
- They believed that the dossier presented the 45-minute claim to the press and public in a way that was misleading about Iraq's WMD capabilities.
- They knew that the 45-minute claim didn't refer to long-range weapons of mass destruction that could threaten Britain and British interests.
- They had been excluded from seeing the new evidence that SIS had presented directly to the Prime Minister, evidence that was formally withdrawn in July 2003.
- They knew that the September dossier had been changed at the very last moment. They suspected it had been done at the suggestion of people in 10 Downing Street.
- They knew that the very clear statement that Saddam would only be able to use his weapons of mass destruction against British interests if Britain attacked Saddam had been taken out of the dossier. Again, they suspected that this had been done at Number Ten's suggestion.

When Dr Kelly told Andrew Gilligan that the dossier had been sexed up by Downing Street we can see why he said it. From his perspective something very serious and unusual had happened. A deeply flawed dossier had been produced and he had grounds to believe, from what he knew, that this was as a direct result of interference from Downing Street. It is hardly surprising, then, that he told Andrew Gilligan, in so many words, that Downing Street probably knew it was wrong. That's what he clearly believed. Gilligan and the BBC only reported what Dr Kelly had told them, as they were perfectly entitled to do under the Reynolds legal ruling.

If Lord Hutton's remit was to find out the truth concerning the circumstances surrounding the death of Dr Kelly, then it was essential for him to understand and take on board what the 45-minute point meant. That was one of the key points of Dr Kelly's conversation with Gilligan. That Hutton failed to do this is a remarkable omission. Lord Butler understood this only too well. In his report he said the 45-minute report should not have been included without stating what sort of weapons it referred to.

One therefore has to ask, on what basis did Lord Hutton make the crucial decision that it was not relevant to his inquiry what sort of weapons of mass destruction the dossier referred to? How could he possibly have decided this?

It has been suggested that the Government constrained Lord Hutton's inquiry by the narrowness of the terms of reference. This is unfair to the Government and untrue. It was Lord Hutton himself who defined his terms of reference on this crucial point. It was Lord Hutton who chose not to consider the difference between a 45-minute claim based on battlefield deployment and one based on long-range use. In fact Lord Hutton included sixteen references to the '45-minute claim' in his report without once saying which of the two radically different meanings he was referring to.

His stated reason for making this decision was that the distinction between the two sorts of weapons was not made in the reports that Gilligan broadcast so it wasn't relevant. Lord Hutton said:

A consideration of this issue does not fall within my terms of reference relating to the circumstances surrounding the death of Dr Kelly.

When he appeared before the Public Administration Select Committee in May 2004 Hutton was asked why he hadn't gone into the nature of the intelligence or the 45-minute claim in his report. He replied that he didn't think he would have been able to resolve the issue and that it would require a different kind of inquiry. The question Lord Hutton didn't and doesn't answer is, why not? Surely his job was to find out what Dr Kelly was talking about?

The BBC's QC, Andrew Caldecott, made this one of his main points in the BBC's final submission to Lord Hutton:

> It seems to have been common knowledge within Government that the intelligence referred to battlefield munitions only, though this was never made clear in the dossier . . . the Government's failure to correct is wholly indefensible. The best governing minds of the country closely considered the outing of Dr Kelly, but on this funda-mental misrepresentation to the public . . . there was nothing.

So it was pointed out to Lord Hutton how crucial the 45-minute point was. He chose to ignore it. Was there another reason for Lord Hutton's deciding that this issue was not relevant? Was it a genuine mistake or a deliberate decision not to probe into an area in which his findings would inevitably have been very embarrassing for Number Ten, for others in Government, and for some in the intelligence services? Did Lord Hutton just get it wrong, or was there a more sinister reason?

Lord Hutton's failure to take on board what sort of weapons Kelly was talking about when he met Gilligan was not his only mistake in this area of the inquiry. There were many others, as there were throughout the report.

Lord Hutton made no real attempt to explain why he accepted John Scarlett's evidence that he alone had made the change to the dossier that turned the threat from Saddam Hussein from a defensive threat to an offensive one. Lord Hutton seems totally to have disregarded Powell's e-mail and believed that Scarlett was acting unprompted. This was despite the fact that the rest of the JIC had signed off on the earlier interpretation.

Lord Hutton also refused to take on board the clear evidence that

Campbell had deliberately misled the Foreign Affairs Committee when he told them that the drafts of the dossier concerning the 45-minute issue had not changed, and had failed to tell them that he had suggested changes himself to this part of the dossier. Campbell also misled them about the number of changes he had suggested.

Lord Hutton gives no explanation for why Scarlett changed the title of the dossier from *Iraq's Programme for Weapons of Mass Destruction* to *Iraq's Weapons of Mass Destruction*. He did so late on without discussing it with the rest of the Joint Intelligence Committee, and of course in doing so radically changed the meaning of the title. Yet another example of 'sexing up'.

In his report Lord Hutton also refused to see any mitigation for the BBC's actions in view of the public nature of the attack from Campbell; he also made no reference to Campbell's failure to use the official complaints process and his decision instead to go public with his wide-ranging attack on much of the BBC's journalism. Lord Hutton also failed to allow Blair to be cross-examined while allowing Hoon to be cross-examined before Campbell's diary was made public, thus saving him from having to answer some very embarrassing questions. The mistakes are numerous.

There are countless stories in circulation about why Lord Hutton behaved in the way he did, virtually all of them unprintable because of Britain's libel laws. Personally I have never been a conspiracy theorist and have difficulty believing that there was some sort of sinister motive.

Lord Hutton clearly knew little about journalism, had spent many years living closely with the security services, and was naive about the way Blair's Downing Street operated – all of which could explain why he made the mistakes he did. He certainly had no experience of running a major public inquiry – the nearest he'd come to it before was an inquiry in Northern Ireland in relation to drainage works in a river. But does this explain why he did what he did?

What I do know is that Philip Gould, one of the architects of New Labour and very much part of Tony Blair's inner circle, was asked by one Labour member of the House of Lords before Hutton was published if he thought the Government faced a problem over the Kelly affair. Gould replied: 'Don't worry, we appointed the right judge.' So in appointing Lord Hutton the Government was pretty confident this was not a man to rock the boat. He was appointed because the Government believed he would deliver for

Blair, the security services, and the Establishment. He did precisely that.

Lord Hutton didn't intend to be biased, but those who selected him knew the man and his views on the world. His mistake was that he over-delivered; as a result the public, quite rightly, didn't believe him or accept his judgment.

Many people, including myself, have suffered as a result of Lord Hutton's report. But so has Lord Hutton's reputation, particularly since the publication of Lord Butler's report, which made him look foolish in a number of areas. There are some in the legal world who believe he has done lawyers in general, and judges in particular, a great disservice by producing such a lightweight, one-sided document.

What an analysis of the five controversial points tells us is that Gilligan's original story, although flawed in places, was nowhere near Tony Blair's 'mountain of untruth' or Campbell's '100 per cent wrong'. The 45-minute intelligence *was* misused. There *was* unhappiness in the intelligence community as a result. The government *did* want the dossier sexed up. They *did* demand that the intelligence agencies discover more facts to strengthen their case for going to war. And people inside Downing Street *did* know the impression given by the dossier, as reported in the press, was the wrong one.

In his role as Chairman of the Joint Intelligence Committee John Scarlett has a lot to answer for. It is very clear that the dossier was written in a way that included any information that supported the case for war and excluded any arguments against. If Scarlett's job was to insist that the document presented a fair and balanced picture based on the information available to the intelligence services at the time, he failed. Instead, Scarlett allowed what was supposed to be an intelligence dossier to be turned into a public relations document.

It was very clear to most people who listened to the evidence given to the Hutton Inquiry that while working in Downing Street John Scarlett crossed the line and became part of Blair's team. He went native. But then the story of a courtier trying to please the king is as old as time. Interestingly, the only time I ever met John Scarlett he sat next to my partner Sue at a dinner. I asked her what he was like. She thought him both interesting and charming but said, 'He likes Tony Blair a lot.' Even Lord Hutton suggested that Scarlett might have been influenced by his closeness to Number Ten when, in one of the very few criticisms of anyone from the Government side, he said:

> I consider that the possibility cannot be completely ruled out that the desire of the Prime Minister to have a dossier which . . . was as strong as possible . . . may have subconsciously influenced Mr Scarlett . . . to make the wording of the dossier stronger than it would have been.

Logically, this statement from Lord Hutton must have meant that he believed the document was strengthened – even 'sexed up' – because of political pressure, whether it was done subconsciously or not. But Lord Hutton does not go on to say that. It's another fundamental contradiction in the Hutton Report.

Lord Butler is rather blunter; he believed that the pressure from above for a strong dossier that supported Tony Blair's position 'will have put a strain on them [SIS] in seeking to maintain their normal standards of neutral and objective assessment'.

It is little wonder that some in the intelligence services were upset by the dossier. They are reported to have told the Butler Inquiry that they were 'embarrassed' by what happened and that they never want to see their intelligence used in this way again. Given that much of their intelligence was misused this is hardly surprising.

In fact John Scarlett and the leaders of the intelligence services should be more than embarrassed by their role in the production of the September dossier. They should be ashamed. Virtually all the new intelligence they supplied was inadequate; much of it has turned out to be totally discredited. The intelligence from the 'unproven' source that Blair and Campbell used as the basis for hardening up the introduction to the dossier has now been withdrawn by SIS. It has also cast real doubts on the reliability of the 45-minutes report. The CIA tells us that Saddam's agents didn't try to buy 'significant amounts' of uranium from Niger as the dossier claimed; no mobile biological agent production facilities have been found in Iraq, which according to the dossier 'recent intelligence' said were there; the 'specialised aluminium tubes' that the dossier said were needed for Iraq's nuclear weapons programme we now know were actually for conventional weapons only; above all, the dossier was called *Iraq's Weapons of Mass Destruction*, and we now know there weren't any.

Scarlett and the intelligence services should also be ashamed that they allowed themselves to be manipulated by the Downing Street machine to produce a political document, not an intelligence dossier, a piece of advocacy, not a dispassionate assessment. That John Scarlett should later be appointed to run SIS, having been responsible for the publication of such a document, does not bode well for the future of the intelligence services in this country.

Putting out documents of selective information to improve the Government's case was food and drink to Campbell and his team in Number Ten; it's what they had been doing for seven years. They simply did to weapons of mass destruction in Iraq what they had done to so many other issues in the years since New Labour came to power. Take the evidence, sift out the stuff that doesn't support your position and publish the rest, exaggerating it a bit if needs be. That was their trade.

Whether you should be doing that as a Government information organization is debatable; whether you should be doing it when the stakes are as high as people being killed in a war is not. The people of this country were entitled to know the full picture about Iraq and they were not given it by Campbell and Co.

Nothing illustrates the way the Downing Street information machine worked more clearly than the second dossier, which has become known as the 'dodgy dossier' and which was published in February 2003. It was Campbell's idea to produce it because he didn't think the September dossier was powerful enough. His department then simply found a twelve-year-old thesis on the Internet written by a PhD student, plagiarized it, and, most of important of all, changed it – or in Kelly and Gilligan's terms 'sexed it up' – to improve the case for going to war with Iraq. They then published it as if it was an original piece of work. The US Secretary of State Colin Powell described the document as 'a fine paper that the UK distributed'. In fact it was a travesty of the truth.

The best example of what Campbell's team did in the 'dodgy' dossier was when they changed the phrase 'aiding opposition groups in hostile regimes' to 'supporting terrorist organizations in hostile regimes', which has a completely different meaning. They changed and hardened the language throughout the paper, and if a Cambridge academic hadn't spotted striking similarities between the dossier and a paper he had read on the Internet the 'dodgy' dossier would still have stood today, and no doubt Campbell would still be saying it was all true.

In a parliamentary statement on 3 February Tony Blair described the dossier as an 'intelligence report', and yet it was nothing of the sort. When Blair discovered the truth about how the dossier had been produced he should have been outraged and fired Campbell. That he didn't tells us a lot about Blair.

Doing this sort of thing was what Campbell's Number Ten information department saw as their job and they saw nothing wrong with it, until they were found out. But if anyone tried to point out what they were doing, as Dr Kelly did when he met Andrew Gilligan, they in turn became the enemy and had the whole apparatus of the state's PR machine turned on them.

To understand how this all came about one has to understand the whole psyche of Blair's Number Ten and the enormous power wielded by Alastair Campbell. In many ways Campbell is a political genius and there is enormous respect amongst the Conservative opposition for the way he operates. But over seven years he turned Downing Street into a place similar to Nixon's White House. You were either for them or against them. And if you opposed them on anything you became the enemy. As a Watergate groupie I was quite shocked when writing this book by these similarities between the Nixon White House and Blair's Downing Street.

Now all governments, of whatever political colour, get upset with the media. They all claim that what they are doing is what they promised when elected and that their policy is the right one. If the public disagree, governments always blame the media, saying that the public doesn't understand this or that because the media isn't reporting it properly. As a result, they all try to manipulate the media. It was just that Campbell took this to new extremes. Quite how such an obsessive man had become so powerful is interesting. This was a man whom a judge had described in a court action in May 1996 as 'less than completely open and frank'. The judge further said that 'I did not find Mr Campbell by any means a wholly satisfactory or convincing witness'. And yet, until he resigned in 2003, he was in charge of all the government's information services, and many regarded him as the most powerful man in the Government after Tony Blair and Gordon Brown.

When Labour was elected the law was changed to allow Campbell to become a civil servant and to control all the Government's information services whilst being a political appointee. As a result, he had unprecedented power and was able to order Cabinet Ministers around to do his bidding. Quite why they put up with it is, in itself, a sign of how our democratic system has been undermined.

As Director-General I always remember the hostility from Blair's Government to the BBC over the *Panorama* programme called 'Spin Doctors' back in 2000, one of the first programmes to show that Labour were announcing the same spend on things time and time again – classic spin. The same happened in May 2001 when *Panorama* produced a not dissimilar programme called 'The Labour Years' the week before the general election. The team producing it were treated as enemies by the Labour Party press office led by Campbell.

There are legions of stories of Campbell helping friendly journalists, people like Tom Baldwin on *The Times*, while attacking journalists he saw as his enemies because they wouldn't run stories the way he wanted them run. I asked the editor of *The Times* if he wasn't embarrassed by Baldwin's closeness to Campbell. The reply was that 'he got very good stories'. The question is, at what cost?

When the BBC gave a confidential briefing to a team at *The Times* it was Baldwin who reported it word for word to Campbell. And guess which journalist first revealed that a Ministry of Defence employee had come forward and said he might be Gilligan's source? Baldwin again. But it was worse than that. Campbell's department regularly misled journalists in an attempt to try to kill stories they didn't want published. We had experience of this at the BBC.

In recent years Campbell's department had issued denials and then later changed their position when new 'facts' emerged on a whole range of stories, including the Martin Sixsmith 'resignation', the advice given by Peter Foster to Cherie Blair, the Britishness or otherwise of LNM (the steel company owned by billionaire Lakshmi Mittal, who was a big Labour Party donor), and the nature of a phone call between the then Italian Prime Minister (Romano Prodi) and Tony Blair involving discussions about Rupert Murdoch's business interests. The problem was that the tactics Campbell employed in everyday life – spin, manipulation, and at times threats – were bound to catch up with the Government in the end, and they have with a vengeance over Iraq.

The Hutton Report was quickly dismissed by the British public. A poll in the *Daily Telegraph* two days after the report was published found that 56 per cent of the people interviewed agreed with the statement that 'Lord Hutton, as a member of the establishment, was too ready to sympathise with the Government and in the end produced something like a whitewash'. Another poll in *The Guardian*, published the same day, said that three times as many people trusted the BBC to tell the truth as trusted the Government.

Government ministers were genuinely shocked when the people of Britain treated Hutton with such contempt. As one minister said the weekend after, 'It cleared us and no one believed it, what are we supposed to do?'

So why did the public dismiss Hutton as a 'whitewash'? The answer to the question is that in many ways Lord Hutton was hoist by his own petard. He had held a ground-breaking inquiry. It was open to the public; all the evidence was available on the Internet, and Hutton ran it in a fair and open manner in an unprecedented way. The problem was that Lord Hutton's findings didn't line up with the evidence that the British public had seen and heard for themselves.

But the hostile reaction was based on more than that. By the time Hutton reported, the public increasingly didn't trust the Prime Minister. Blair's trust ratings, in fact, had collapsed. In 1997, according to the research organization Gallup, Tony Blair's trust rating was plus 37; by February 2004 a YouGov survey put the figure at minus 39. And the public certainly didn't trust a Downing Street information machine that had spun just once too often. Campbell's pompous and vitriolic performance on the steps of the Foreign Press Association certainly didn't help Blair's cause.

What all this tells us is that it was Government and the people in Number Ten who misled the British people, not Dr Kelly, Andrew Gilligan, or the BBC. The September dossier was only a public relations exercise designed to persuade sceptical Labour MPs and a sceptical public to support a policy of going to war in Iraq.

In fact most of the story broadcast on the *Today* programme on that May morning was right, and while Gilligan made mistakes they were nowhere near as serious as those made by Downing Street when producing their two dossiers warning about the threats from Iraq: the BBC was not sending British soldiers to war. In producing and promoting the September dossier Tony Blair and those involved, including John Scarlett, Alastair Campbell, and Geoff Hoon, sold the British people a false bill of goods.

Only Campbell has, so far, paid a price for this by being forced out of Downing Street, although he was planning to go at some stage anyway. But Blair and Hoon struggle on damaged, while Scarlett has got the job he always wanted as Head of SIS. Tony Blair could have stopped that appointment but didn't.

The king repaid the courtier.

CHAPTER FOURTEEN

Some Final Thoughts

This book has had three themes: broadcasting, politics, and me. I'll end by saying something about all three, beginning with broadcasting.

As I finish this book I am, oddly, more optimistic about the future of the BBC than I was before the whole Gilligan saga started. I'm of the view that the pressures the BBC will face in the renewal of its charter in 2007 will be significantly less as a result of the torrid events of 2003 and 2004.

The BBC has a good man as its new Chairman in Michael Grade, so long as someone can stop him trying to be the Director-General at the same time, which is bound to be a risk when you have a hands-on man like Michael in the Chairman's role. Michael was a good and brave Chief Executive of Channel Four, willing to stand up for his programme makers and willing to stand up against the bullying from politicians that all broadcasting organizations face – not that Channel Four ever faced the intensity of political pressure the BBC faced. I suspect that if Gilligan's report had been on Channel Four News it would have gone unnoticed.

To do his job well Grade needs better and more knowledgeable Governors than he currently has to support him. I hope that the six current Governors who voted to get rid of me – Dermot Gleeson, Merfyn Jones, Fabian Monds, Pauline Neville-Jones, Robert Smith, and Ranjit Sondhi – will realize, having read the Butler Report and my chapter on Hutton, that what they did on that January night was bow to pressure from a political thug called Alastair Campbell. What happened to me is irrelevant – Director-Generals come and go; but there is no greater betrayal of the principles on which the BBC is based than to fold under political pressure, particularly when it comes from the Government of the day. These Governors got it seriously wrong and they should accept that. They should now resign. The BBC deserves better.

The BBC has a second good man in Mark Thompson, the new Director-General. He is both clever and potentially an outstanding leader. He sorted out the finances at Channel Four but wasn't there long enough to have an enormous impact on its programmes. He was a good Controller of BBC Two and made a big impact in his short period as Director of Television at the BBC. Both Michael and Mark are people who will not fear making changes and taking calculated risks, even when their decisions are unlikely to be popular with politicians, the press, or the BBC's commercial opponents. But the reason why I'm now optimistic about the BBC going forward is not because of its leadership but because Michael and Mark find themselves in a unique position with a unique opportunity.

Rather than being damaged by the Hutton affair the BBC has been strengthened by it. The battle over Hutton was so fierce that the public had to choose between the politicians and the BBC. The polls make it very clear that, overwhelmingly, they chose the BBC. What that means, I suspect, is that it will be a very long time before any Government tries to bully the BBC in the hysterical way that Campbell did and Tony Blair allowed him to do. And it will be a very long time before any Government will want to have another row on that scale with the BBC. There were no winners but the polls show quite clearly that public trust in the BBC wasn't damaged. The main casualty was the public's trust in Tony Blair and the Government.

In fact I don't believe Michael Grade would have become Chairman of the BBC had it not been for the Gilligan affair: he certainly believes that. When the staff took to the streets to support me, Downing Street was deeply unnerved. They had seriously misjudged the position. The advertisement in the *Daily Telegraph* and the demonstration organized by the trade unions protesting against Government interference in the BBC the week after my departure shocked them further. They thought they'd got the right result from Hutton. They hadn't. As a consequence Tessa Jowell, who had always favoured Grade becoming Chairman, was able to get her way despite the machinations of some inside Downing Street, particularly John Birt.

Birt and Grade, friends when they were both at LWT in the Seventies, had hated each other for nearly two decades. They fell out when John joined the BBC as Deputy Director-General and started trying to tell

Michael how to run the television service. Rather than be bossed around by John, Michael left the BBC and joined Channel Four. He later used the McTaggart lecture to launch a massive attack on Birt's BBC.

Inside Downing Street, Birt fought against Grade's appointment as Chairman of the BBC, tried to influence Tessa Jowell, and, when he lost, sent a letter to Tony Blair telling him that Grade's was the worst public appointment he had made since becoming Prime Minister.

But the whole affair had another beneficial impact on the BBC. It has led to a significant improvement in the relationship between the BBC and the Conservative Party: a party that was in danger of writing off the BBC as a bunch of pinkos and liberals has had to rethink. And of course they too must have recognized the strength of public opinion on the BBC's side.

Some things are bound to change with the BBC's next charter. In fact some things should change. The current system of governance should certainly be scrapped. You cannot carry on running one of the biggest media organizations in the world with a governance system more suited to a small charity: a system in which the great and the good are appointed for no obvious reason other than they are Welsh, Scottish, black, Asian, a businessman, a card-carrying former politician, a mate of the Minister's, or a trade unionist. This is particularly so when most of them bring with them little knowledge or understanding of broadcasting or the media.

And the logic of the current system whereby the Governors are both regulators and also responsible for management no longer holds water either. While it may have worked over the years it no longer stands up to intellectual analysis in a world more and more obsessed by accountability.

There needs to be a separation of powers with a BBC Board, made up of executives and knowledgeable non-executives, responsible for the running of the BBC, and an outside regulator with the job of checking on it. By the time I left the BBC most of the BBC Executive had come round to this way of thinking. We believed the BBC had spent too much time trying to defend the current system of governance: we had used up too much political capital trying to defend the indefensible. This wasn't true of the Board of Governors, who still hadn't changed their views and when I left were still fighting desperately to retain their current status. Michael Grade certainly knows and believes change is necessary.

This is not to argue that regulating the BBC should be the responsibility of the new communications super regulator Ofcom. It should not. It would be too dangerous to have only one content regulator across the whole of British broadcasting. As a society we need a plurality of regulators, just as we need a plurality of broadcasters. There is too great a threat of a single regulator being 'captured' by the government of the day, in much the same way as John Scarlett was 'captured' when he was Chairman of the Joint Intelligence Committee.

But that isn't the only reason. Once the commercial sector and the BBC are regulated by the same body I fear that economic interests will predominate and the public interest will be left very much in second place. That will prevent the BBC from continuing to innovate and expand in the public interest as technology changes. My solution would be for the Government to establish a small and separate regulator for the BBC and the BBC alone, but place it outside the BBC and not make it responsible for the running of the organization. When I first joined the BBC Carolyn Fairbairn and the former BBC Secretary Michael Stevenson made a cogent argument on the BBC Executive for such a system. At the time it was rejected. They were right and the rest of us were wrong.

In a changing media world in which BSkyB will grow ever stronger it is essential there is a strong BBC to counterbalance the Murdoch interests; a BBC that is not overly constrained by the commercial sector; a BBC that is driven by the public interest in delivering the best possible services to as wide a group of the UK population as possible. The BBC is not and should not be there principally to please an intellectual, South of England elite.

A strong and well-funded BBC is particularly important given what has happened to ITV. In many ways it is sad that Granada bought LWT. It should have been the other way round since our management was far superior to theirs: we were committed broadcasters, they were cost-cutting caterers who knew little about television. They had no vision for ITV other than consolidation. That simply wasn't enough in a fast-changing media world. They screwed up over ITV Digital and made a serious mistake when not backing Freeview. As an ex-ITV man I feel terribly sad about the decline of ITV as a serious force in British broadcasting, and I am not confident it can recover without radical change.

I also worry that what we have seen in the USA is happening here to ITV. During the Iraq war the US broadcasters abandoned their role as impartial observers to become cheerleaders for American involvement in the war. They did it for many reasons. The fear of the religious right, the after-effects of 11 September, and the fear of being accused of being anti-patriotic were just three of them. But I suspect there was a business agenda too. The big American media companies wanted a change in the ownership rules on US television to allow them to own more stations. If they had upset the Bush administration during the war this would not have happened.

This was exactly what I warned could happen in Britain in my first McTaggart lecture delivered in 1994. Now there are real signs that what has happened in the USA is beginning to happen to ITV in this country. In the last couple of years there have been at least three occasions when there has been attempted interference in programming from 'on top' because what was planned didn't suit the ITV companies' commercial interests. The first was with the drama *The Deal*, written by Peter Morgan and directed by Stephen Frears, which won the best single drama at the BAFTA awards in 2004. It told the story of the Brown/Blair pact. When it was broadcast, the piece was very sympathetic to Gordon Brown but far less so to Tony Blair. Nick Elliot, ITV's head of drama, commissioned the project for ITV and planned to play it on ITV. The powers that be inside Granada found out about it. With the company trying to persuade the Government to agree to the merger of Carlton and Granada they put enormous pressure on the ITV Network Centre for it not to go out on ITV. The drama eventually ended up on Channel Four.

The second came with a three-part factual series about Rupert Murdoch that the ITV Network Centre had actually commissioned. All was agreed and the programmes were about to be made when a senior executive stepped in and said that even if the series was made he would not broadcast the programmes, which were likely to be critical of Murdoch.

Thirdly, on the day the story came out that Michael Green was receiving a £15 million payout for leaving ITV, ITV's news provider ITN was asked by a senior executive of ITV not to run the story. To their credit the news people told him it was none of his business and ran the story anyway.

Successful commercial broadcasters only succeed if they care about more than just business. You can't have portion control television, nor can you only be obsessed about finance and management. Television is most of all a creative business and success comes if you recognize that.

If broadcasters end up as *just* commercial entities, as ITV is in danger of becoming, they will fail, both as broadcasters and as businesses. As I ended my McTaggart lecture back in 2000, 'It's the programmes, stupid.'

This book has also been about politics.

I first met him when he was sitting next but one to me at a dinner at Barry Cox's place. It was around 1980 and at the time I was a producer at London Weekend Television. I remember the evening well, and in particular I remember this fresh-faced young man with a very upmarket accent, which was unusual in the circles I moved in. In those days in the media, even people brought up with plums in their mouths spent most of the time pretending they didn't have them. This guy had no such inhibitions.

As part of polite conversation I asked him what he did. He told me he was a barrister but what he really wanted to do was to 'serve' his country. I remember thinking, what does he mean, 'serve'? I genuinely thought he meant that he wanted to join the priesthood. He later explained that by 'serve' he had meant that he wanted to serve his country by becoming a Labour MP.

I didn't say much but as the evening went on I returned to the subject. In those days I regarded myself as being from the Labour left and I thought one of the great problems of the Labour Party was that it was full of lawyers, barristers, journalists, and academics – people who had never actually run anything. Twenty-five years later my politics have moderated, but I still have the same view about many of the people who go into politics.

As the wine flowed I began to explain to my next but one neighbour that I didn't think his idea of becoming a Labour MP was a particularly good one and that I wasn't sure that the Labour Party needed another posh-sounding barrister as an MP. I think my exact words were, 'I think the Labour Party needs another barrister like it needs a hole in the head.'

Roll forward to May 1997. It had been a beautiful day and was a beautiful night. Sue and I were at the Festival Hall with the great and the good of the Labour Party to celebrate Labour's election victory. The man who had led the party to victory that night arrived amid huge jubilation in the early hours of the morning. I was one of many who had turned out to greet him.

It was the same man who had been my table companion at that house in North London nearly twenty years earlier. I had told Tony Blair that the Labour Party needed him like a hole in the head.

My feelings the night New Labour won were mixed. It really hit me that I had been young when Labour had lost in 1979 – just thirty-two. I was about to be fifty and Labour had only just got back into power. But I enjoyed the night. Sue, on the other hand, hated all the triumphalism and she rightly had forebodings about the future.

We got home from the celebrations at the Festival Hall at about 5 a.m. The sun was just coming up. I remember the excitement of the following day as if it were yesterday. I had a couple of hours' sleep and then had to go to a meeting of the Pearson plc Board – not the natural home of the Labour Party. It was beautiful weather and on my way there everyone on the streets seemed to be smiling and waving. We all felt it was a new beginning, that New Labour would not only be in control but would bring new politics to Britain.

When I look back now maybe we were all ridiculously optimistic. I even remember one friend saying to me that Tony Blair was the first prime minister who looked like he might have been round Tesco's. I checked that out with Cherie at a later stage and she laughed at the idea. Seven years later all that optimism has gone. All that initial hope has gone. Tony Blair has turned out to be just another politician and in some ways worse than those before him. They never promised us a new sort of politics. He did.

For me, the disillusionment came late. In my time at the BBC I took no part in any political activity and studiously kept my feelings about politics to myself. And then came Iraq, Gilligan, and Hutton and suddenly it struck me how naive I had been.

It is now obvious; the decision to go to war was made first and the intelligence to support that move was discovered afterwards. The trouble was, the evidence wasn't right.

There was no current threat to British interests or to anyone else from Iraq's weapons of mass destruction. There were no weapons of mass destruction. There was no uranium being imported from Niger. Iraq played no part in the 11 September attacks. There were no international terrorists then operating out of Iraq, although there are today. In particular, Iraq was not supporting al-Qaeda. We now know that George W. Bush was obsessed with attacking Iraq *before* 11 September. Even the moral arguments for getting rid of Saddam were damaged when we saw the way the Americans troops were then encouraged to behave in Iraq by people at the top.

One by one the reasons the Prime Minister gave us for going to war have been proved to be wrong. But it's even worse than that. He took us to war on the basis of intelligence about weapons of mass destruction and the 45-minute threat which, at the very least, he didn't understand and didn't question.

It was Mr Blair who said that Gilligan's reports were 'a mountain of untruth'. That wasn't the case. But there *were* 'mountains of untruth' – they were the dossiers he and his colleagues in Downing Street produced to justify going to war in Iraq. And yet the Prime Minister has never stood up and said to the British people, 'I am sorry.' There was a moment when he could have done so, and we might have forgiven him. That moment is past.

So why did we go to war? In researching this book I have become convinced that there is a relatively simple explanation. In April 2002 Tony Blair told George W. Bush that he would support him in a war against Iraq. He did so because he believed, as have all prime ministers since the Suez fiasco nearly fifty years ago, that Britain has to stay close to the USA, and in particular support their foreign policy. But unlike Harold Wilson, who supported the US involvement in Vietnam without committing British troops, Blair decided we should go to war alongside the USA; in April 2002 Blair committed us to support George W. Bush if he launched offensive action.

This left Blair with some problems. He had to persuade his Cabinet, Parliament, the Parliamentary Labour Party, the general public, and the Government's law officers to support him and follow his lead. He couldn't tell them his real reason for going to war. There was no legal basis for it, and he was clearly concerned that, across Britain and much of the world, if he did he would be seen as Bush's poodle. Instead he told us that Iraq had weapons of mass destruction; that work on them was increasing; and that they were a current threat to British interests. I've no doubt he believed this. He recruited the intelligence services to try to help him prove it and, to their eternal shame, they went along with it. As a result, intelligence turned into advocacy and public relations. In a series of speeches, press conferences, and two separate dossiers he outlined the case for war. Unfortunately for Blair none of it turned out to be true. No matter. We are told by Mr Blair that a tyrant has gone, that history will show he was right, and that we should all rejoice.

It's not a complicated story, but what it means is that we were all duped. History will not be on Mr Blair's side. It will not absolve him but will show that the whole saga is a great political scandal. What is really frightening is that Tony Blair still doesn't believe or understand that what he did was fundamentally wrong.

If you look deeper you see our democracy is in trouble as a result of Blair's style of leadership. In the thirty years since I studied political theory Britain has moved, first with Thatcher and even more so with Blair, from cabinet government to a prime ministerial, even a presidential, system of government. But we have no separation of powers, and none of the checks and balances that such a system needs. As a result, the Prime Minister is now all powerful.

Parliament is supposed to hold the executive in check and yet with a Labour majority of 161 it has little chance of doing so, particularly when the Labour benches are disproportionately made up of people who, understandably, want to further their careers. In a system dominated by patronage they can only do that by currying favour with the very executive they are supposed to be holding in check.

As both the Hutton Inquiry and the Butler Report showed so clearly, most of the major decisions in Government are now made in Downing Street, with few elected politicians other than the Prime Minister being involved. The evidence presented to Hutton didn't give the impression that Geoff Hoon was in charge of Defence.

But, as we saw with the Foreign Affairs Select Committee during the Gilligan affair, we have too many MPs who are willing to do what the whips or the Prime Minister tell them to do; or, even worse, did what his unelected Director of Communications told them to do.

I don't subscribe to the theory that all politicians are liars and only out for themselves. I believe there are some very good people in all parties who are trying hard to do their best for their constituents, their country, and what they believe in. It is not the individuals who are flawed but our system of democracy in which the executive arm of government has been allowed to become all powerful.

A decade ago, in a very small way, I helped Tony Blair to become leader of the Labour Party by giving £5,000 towards a fund to help him run his leadership campaign. Of course he would have become the leader of the Labour Party without my money, but today I regret giving it. Not because he's not a decent man but because I don't like what he has allowed to happen to our political system. I don't like Number Ten's obsession with spin, and I believe he misled the nation on Iraq.

Tony Blair is, in electoral terms, the most successful Labour leader ever and New Labour can claim some real achievements. And yet I suspect Blair's legacy will be summed up in two words: 'Iraq' and 'spin'. The Gilligan affair was about both.

And then we come to me.

I have a cartoon on the wall of my study of me sitting in my office with a bullet hitting my back and a caption saying, 'Who shot Greg Dyke?' It was published when I left TV-am in May 1984, which was around the same time that the big story on *Dallas* was 'Who shot JR?' The irony is that that same cartoon could have been used again in 1994, when I left LWT, or in 2004, when I left the BBC.

Writing this book I have discovered the uncanny pattern that I was unemployed in the summer of 1974 when I left university and again in parts of 1984, 1994, and now 2004. I hope that by 2014 I'll be too old to be fired. At one point I was jokingly advised by my accountant and best friend Richard Webb that I had received so many tax-free payments as compensation for loss of office that there was a danger that the Inland Revenue might take a different view this time. He felt that the Revenue might say, 'No, Mr Dyke. This is not an exceptional tax-free compensatory payment for loss of office. This is how you earn your living.'

Soon after I'd left the BBC Sue, always one to get straight to the point, asked me a profound question. 'Why,' she said, 'don't you ever leave an organization like anyone else? Why is it always a drama?' I tried to point out that this wasn't entirely accurate, but when I looked back at my time in television I could only genuinely claim my departure from TVS as being without incident.

In the last few months, as I've been writing this book and thinking about my life, I've got to thinking more about what she said. Were the events of the last year somehow my fault? Was I simply too combative?

Do I look for confrontation when others don't? As I look back now on the whole Gilligan affair, as I call it, could I, or should I, have played it differently?

Having again reviewed all the evidence in the process of writing this book I am still of the view that the September dossier was sexed up and that there were people in Downing Street who knew that.

I believe that in Alastair Campbell the Government had a time bomb waiting to go off. He just happened to go off in the direction of the BBC.

Of course I could have backed down. Of course we could have done a deal. Of course I could have abandoned our people and settled. But to what purpose? If the BBC means anything it has to stand by what it believes to be fair and right.

For me to have been cowed by an out of control bully in the shape of Alastair Campbell, whom the Prime Minister himself was clearly unable to control, would have betrayed everything I believed in. So the answer is, no; I wouldn't have acted differently. I just wish the BBC had had a Board of Governors who understood that what they were doing in getting rid of me was giving in to political bullying. But it didn't.

So what of those three days in January 2004 now?

I have always believed that there are days of your life, some good, some bad, some truly exciting, but all of them days that stand out from the ordinary when you look back.

Some such days are intensely personal and mean much to you as an individual. For me, the days my children were born were like that, days that can never be replaced. Then there are days when everything goes right, like the day at LWT when we won two ITV franchises on the same day and ended up having the most amazing party. And days that are just memorable for you, like the one on which I played football at Wembley in front of 80,000 fans, or when I finally got to meet Bob Dylan, or the night I watched Manchester United win the European Champions League in Barcelona, or sat watching the Queen's Jubilee concert at Buckingham Palace.

But not all such days are happy. For me the day I knew my marriage was over and the day my father died are memorable for the wrong reasons. Luckily, in my life the good days have far outweighed the bad.

And then there are the days when memorable events happen to all of us, like the first man walking on the moon, or when England won the football World Cup, or more recently when the English rugby team won the rugby World Cup. Again these days are not all good news days. For anyone of my age the assassination of John F. Kennedy was traumatic, and of course no one alive on 11 September 2001 will ever forget the events of that day.

So where does Thursday 29 January 2004 sit for me in those memories of special days? It was certainly special. It was a day when the swings in my emotions were enormous, ranging from the shock of being sacked from a job I loved through to the elation of finding just how many of the staff had been touched by what I had been trying to achieve over the previous four years.

It was both a good and a bad day, but I suspect over the years the reaction of the staff will play a bigger part in my memories. I suspect for some people working at the BBC that day will matter to them too; it will be one of those days that matters in their lives, a day when logic and rational behaviour were rejected and instead were overruled by emotion.

I found it exciting that thousands of people from different parts of the BBC and different parts of the UK believed enough in what we were trying to achieve together to go out onto the streets to express their emotions and their support for me. The fact that more than 20 per cent of the staff e-mailed me and thousands paid for the ad in the *Daily Telegraph* will always live in my memory. Jobs have come and gone in my life but the reaction of those people on that day will be with me forever. I thank them from the bottom of my heart for turning a terrible day into an uplifting one.

For me it was also special because of the reaction to the events of that day from people outside the media, ordinary people who saw what had happened and sensed that an injustice had been done to someone they didn't know but who was clearly liked and respected by the people who worked for him.

But everything needs to be put into context. Three weeks to the day after I had been fired I visited Robben Island off Cape Town, the prison where Nelson Mandela spent many of his twenty-seven years in captivity. Today it is a museum.

I found the visit an incredibly emotional experience. The man who showed us round was a former prisoner and I felt humbled just to be in his company and to listen to the stories of people who had shown such dignity in such adversity; people who had been imprisoned for so many years by a barbarous regime that treated them appallingly. And yet these prisoners understood humility and forgiveness.

When I went to Robben Island, everything about me was still raw. I was still angry and upset about being fired from the BBC. As I wandered around the prison on that day my tears flowed quietly: tears for what had happened on this horrible island, but also tears for what had happened to me in those three days in January. But as I walked around, it put much into perspective. I began to ask myself, how dare I feel angry? Nobody had taken away my freedom, my possessions, my family, my friends. What I saw on Robben Island was real injustice, and what had happened to me was insignificant in comparison.

As I finish this book, what I still feel today is sadness. I am still sad that something so exciting was taken away from me and that my relationship with so many people at the BBC is no more. But perhaps if the events of 29 January 2004 had not happened I would never have known what I know now. I would have retired from the BBC, probably within a couple of years, and there would have been the boring statutory speeches at the statutory retirement parties and I would never have known what all those people felt about me. And I wouldn't have known what I felt about them.

From the day I left the BBC I've been determined that I wouldn't become obsessed by what happened. While writing this book has been cathartic, it hasn't helped me to put the whole business behind me. That time is now; it is time for me to move on, to do something else with my life.

Gavyn Davies and I left the BBC because we were criticized by Lord Hutton, we think wrongly and unfairly, for failing to ensure the BBC's editorial controls were sound on a particular story broadcast on one BBC radio station at seven minutes past six one May morning. Tony Blair took Britain into a war in which thousands were killed, including many British troops, on the basis of shoddy intelligence. Some of that intelligence he knew was unproven; and some of it he should have questioned and didn't. He is still the Prime Minister.

Index

A, Mr (chemical weapons expert), 293
Abbott, Paul, 32
Abramovich, Roman, 247
Abramsky, Jenny, 11, 176, 197, 210
ACI (distribution company), 129
Ahmed, Kamal, 141
Ainsworth, Peter, 135
Airey, Dawn, 132
Aitken, Jonathan: invites GD to join TV-am, 68, 72–4; takes over TV-am, 71–2; prosecuted and convicted, 72; Sue mistrusts, 75; steps down as Chief Executive of TV-am, 76; and TV-am's problems, 85; relations with Arabs, 86
Aitken, Lolicia, 74–5
Aitken, Timothy, 72, 76–7, 82–3, 86–9
Al Fayed, Mohamed, 238
al-Marishi, Ibrahim, 268
All American (US production company), 130
Allen, Charles, 123, 158
Anderson, Donald, 281
Andrew, Rob, 234
Anglia Television, 123
Ariel (BBC house magazine), 23, 203, 213
Ashbridge Business School, 217
Aspel, Michael, 64
Auletta, Ken: *Three Blind Mice*, 172

BAFTA awards, 32
Baker, Danny, 64, 75
Baker, George, 95
Baldwin, Tom, 315
Ball, Tony, 186, 190, 246
Ballard, Robert, 95
Banks, Tony, 241
Bannister, Matthew, 146
Barlow, Frank, 105, 128–9, 131
Barnes, 68
Barras, Vicki, 66
Barrett-Jolly, Christopher, 42
Barrymore, Michael, 103–4
Bastin, Cliff ('Boy'), 221
BBC *see* British Broadcasting Corporation
BBC Choice, 172
BBC Four, 174

BBC Knowledge, 172
BBC One: popularity, 159, 172, 192; funding, 166, 171, 176; drama on, 171
BBC Radio Lancashire, Blackburn, 199
BBC Radio Leeds, 214
BBC Radio Shropshire, 25
BBC Scotland, 196
BBC Sport, 245, 247–8
BBC Technology: sold, 167
BBC Three, 174–5
BBC Two, 176
Beadle, Jeremy and Sue, 150–1
Beardsley, Peter, 229
Bennett, Jana: invests in drama, 171; doubts on unencrypted digital TV, 189; resists move out of London, 197; returns to BBC after US stay, 201; favours showing pictures of dead British soldiers, 250–1
Benson, Graham, 95
Berry, Nick, 99
Bertelsmann group, 137
Betty (TV drama), 113
Bhalla, Anita, 28
'Big Conversation, The' (discussion session), 218–19
Big Daddy (wrestler), 225–6
Bill (driver), 2, 9, 19
Bill, The (TV programme), 128, 137
Birt, John, Baron: at LWT, 56–7, 97; and GD's departure from LWT, 75; as Deputy Director-General of BBC, 97; plays in football match, 99–100; Bland on, 125; GD succeeds at BBC, 132, 139, 151–2; meets Hague with GD, 136; regime at BBC, 139, 144–5, 149; relations with GD, 142–4; opposes GD's appointment as successor, 143, 150; portrait, 144; leaves BBC and receives peerage, 152–3; management style, 156, 207; and BBC reorganization, 161–2, 168, 199; negotiates BBC licence fee, 166; champions online services, 177; introduces producer/broadcaster split, 192; insists on employing more women at BBC, 193; Scots hostility to, 195; unpopularity, 200; vision for BBC, 211; relations with Hussey, 232; and BBC's

Birt, John, Baron – *cont.*
  withdrawal from sports, 245; opposes Grade's
  appointment to BBC Chairmanship, 319–20;
  The Harder Path, 143
Black, Cilla, 62, 103
Blair, Cherie: friendship with Fiona Hillary, 10,
  15; asks for Manchester United shirt for son,
  243–4; at Wimbledon, 276
Blair, Euan, 244
Blair, Tony: on threat of Iraq weapons, 3, 251,
  292, 312–13; promises to call for no
  resignations from BBC, 7, 22–3; supported by
  Sun, 8; friendship with Fiona Hillary, 10, 15;
  and naming of Dr Kelly, 10; statement
  in Commons on Hutton report, 10; accused of
  cronyism, 14; popular antipathy to over Hutton
  report, 19; and GD's resignation from BBC, 32;
  and Millennium Dome, 132; GD supports
  financially, 135, 140, 147; supports BBC, 165;
  relations with Murdoch, 180, 182; complains of
  BBC reporting of Iraq war, 253–5, 257; and
  divisions over Iraq war, 253; Clare Short
  accuses of deceit over weapons of mass
  destruction, 267; protects Campbell, 268; and
  Campbell's attacks on BBC, 270, 272; Gavyn
  Davies meets, 273; threatens resignation if
  Gilligan story true, 274; BBC Governors deny
  accusations of lying by, 277; offers compromise
  to BBC, 278–9; applauded in Washington, 281;
  correspondence with GD on BBC independence,
  283–4; gives evidence at Hutton Inquiry, 285;
  accuses Gilligan of untruths, 288, 311, 325; on
  '45-minute' figure, 289, 303, 305; and decision
  to wage war in Iraq, 296–8, 303, 325, 330;
  visits Bush in Texas, 297; on availability and
  deployment of Saddam's weapons, 304–5;
  Scarlett's relations with, 311–12; and
  Campbell's methods, 314; public mistrust of,
  316, 319; and Scarlett's appointment to head
  SIS, 317; depicted in *The Deal*, 322; GD's
  disillusionment with, 324–7; justifies war in
  Iraq, 326
Blake, Juliet, 82, 84
Bland, Christopher: mistrusts Pauline Neville-
  Jones, 5; on BBC resignations after Hutton, 12;
  on Fiona Hillary, 15; and GD's dismissal from
  BBC, 16; on GD's attitude to Governors, 28;
  offers GD post of Director of Programmes at
  LWT, 97–9; and GD's promotion to Managing
  Director of LWT, 106; sends GD to Harvard
  Business School, 106, 107; and unions, 112;
  reforms LWT, 114–15; investment gains at
  LWT, 117; and successful auction bid for LWT,
  120; on Granada's attempted takeover of LWT,
  122, 124; addresses Royal Television Society,
  125; as BBC Chairman of Governors, 136, 139;
  and John Birt, 144, 146; cynicism over strategy,
  145; and GD's appointment as Director-
  General, 146, 149–52; and moving BBC's news
  time, 158; and GD's organizational changes at
  BBC, 164; and GD's absence during important
  story, 250
Blind Date (TV programme), 103
Blix, Hans, 261
Blue Peter (TV programme), 168

Booth, Mark, 239–43
Bottomley, Virginia, 166
Bough, Frank, 71
Boulton, Adam, 78, 147
Boxer, Charles, 52
Boyd, Alan, 99
Bragg, Catherine, Lady (Cate Haste), 31
Bragg, Melvyn, Baron: friendship with GD, 17,
  32; and GD's resignation, 20; efficacy on TV,
  76; predicts GD as BBC Director-General, 141;
  supports GD as BBC Director-General, 147
Breach, Warren, 102
Breakfast Time (BBC programme), 71
British Broadcasting Corporation (BBC):
  condemned by Hutton report, 1, 3, 7; GD's
  resignation from, 1, 15–20, 287, 318–19, 328,
  329–30; Governors' behaviour, 1, 7, 33; Exco
  (executive team), 10; Governors' meeting on
  Hutton report, 12–13; reports Hutton inquiry,
  12; composition of Governors, 13, 27–8; staff
  demonstrates support for GD, 23–6, 33, 328;
  GD joins as Director-General, 134, 135–6,
  139–40, 152–4; under Birt, 139, 144–5, 149;
  and Governors' appointment of Director-
  General, 145–6; online services, 145, 177–9;
  opposition to GD's appointment as Director-
  General, 146–8, 150; GD's manifesto on,
  148–9; report-writing at, 155–6; moves news
  time to 10 o'clock, 157–61; organizational
  structure reformed, 161–4; financial
  arrangements and reforms, 164–71, 173; licence
  fee, 165–6; commercial activities, 166; BSkyB's
  rivalry with, 172, 321; digital channels
  introduced and increased, 172–4; radio services,
  175–7; interactive TV, 179; develops Freeview,
  183–5; as equal opportunity employer, 192–5;
  and ratings, 192; national and regional
  coverage, 195–7; GD visits sections, 198–9;
  library service, 199–200; premises and
  buildings, 199; GD's management style at,
  200–5, 207–8; culture change initiatives,
  207–20; leadership training programme,
  217–18; values defined, 217; loses pre-eminence
  in sports, 245; football deals, 246–8; reporting
  of Iraq war, 251–8; Campbell attacks at
  Foreign Affairs Committee hearing, 269–71;
  Governors' meeting on Gilligan report, 275–7;
  reaction to Hutton report, 287; GD's optimism
  for future of, 318–19; strengthened by Hutton
  Report, 319; proposed changes to governance
  and regulation of, 320–1
British Satellite Broadcasting (BSB), 226–7
Broadcast Act (1992), 105
Bromley, John, 222–4, 227, 235
Brooke, Magnus, 3–4, 23–4, 26
Brooks, Richard, 153
Brown, Gordon: votes on tuition fees, 7; and BBC
  staff demonstration in support of GD, 23; and
  BBC licence fee, 165; depicted in *The Deal*, 322
Bruce Lockhart, Sally, 84
Bruno, Frank, 222, 224
BSkyB: bids for Channel Five, 131, 182; opposes
  BBC's proposed two-tier licence fee, 165;
  launched, 172; rivalry with BBC, 172, 321;
  interactive services, 179; Murdoch controls,

180, 183; and digital terrestrial television, 183–5; joins Freeview, 185–7; BBC pays for digital satellite platform, 187–8; deal with BBC for unencrypted service, 189–91; negotiates football rights, 231–2; failed attempt to buy Manchester United, 239–43; and sport, 245, 247, 249

Buerk, Michael, 159

Bugner, Joe, 24

Building One BBC (booklet), 162–3

Bull, Deborah, 27

Bush, George W., 281, 296–7, 306, 324–5

Butler, Robin, Baron: Inquiry and Report (2004), 279, 288, 293–5, 297–9, 308, 311

By the Seaside (TV programme), 83–4

Byford, Mark: as GD's deputy at BBC, 17–18, 29–30; GD recommends to staff on resignation, 21; accompanies Ryder while making apology statement, 22; Pauline Neville-Jones supports, 28–9; as acting Director-General after GD's departure, 30; as candidate to succeed Birt as Director-General, 146, 149–50; as potential successor to GD, 174; on shortage of women at BBC, 193

Caldecott, Andrew, QC, 6, 12–13, 309

Callaghan, James, Baron, 53

Campaign for Racial Equality, 193

Campbell, Alastair: suspected of leaking Hutton report, 8; complains to BBC, 22–4, 31, 32, 253–8, 265–6; vendetta against Gilligan, 169–70, 272–4, 279, 282; and Tessa Jowell, 175; and *The Sun*'s support for Labour, 182; GD avoids, 205; accused of 'sexing up' Iraq dossier, 259–60, 262, 265–8, 275, 282–3, 291–2, 316; dislikes Marsh, 261; appears before Commons Foreign Affairs Committee, 268–71, 310; attacks BBC, 269–72, 319; BBC Governors reject accusations, 277; cleared by Foreign Affairs Committee, 278; on Gilligan's describing Kelly as intelligence officer, 279; resignation, 284, 314, 317; accuses Gilligan and BBC of lying, 288, 311; redrafts September Dossier, 298, 301, 307, 310, 312–13; denies briefing press on Iraq weapons threat, 302; and 45-minute claim, 307; diary published, 310; and 'dodgy dossier' (February 2003), 313–14; power and tactics, 313–15, 328; manner, 316; and GD's resignation from BBC, 318

Can West (Canadian company), 130–1

Canetty-Clarke, Neil, 115

Carling, Will, 234–5

Carlton (TV company), 120–1, 183–5, 322

Carter, Phil, 227, 228, 230

Cassidy and Leigh (Guildford news agency), 47

Casualty (TV programme), 194

Catchphrase (TV game show), 95

Cayton, Bill, 222

Central Intelligence Agency (CIA), 306, 312

Central Religious Advisory Council, 105

Channel Five: bids for, 127, 130–1; BSkyB attempts to buy, 131, 182; launched, 132; retuning, 132; programmes, 137

Channel Four: coverage of Hutton inquiry, 12; launched, 174; commissioning policy, 192

Charles, Robert, 233

Checkland, Michael: as Director-General of BBC, 97–8, 146

Chidgey, David, 285

children's channels, 172–4

Chisholm, Sam, 231–2

Churchill, Sir Winston, 252

Claridge, David, 81–2

Clark, William, 252

Clifton, Val, 41

Cohen, Ben, 64

Cohen, Tony: works on *The Six O'Clock Show*, 63, 65, 67; as GD's strategist at LWT, 105, 164; and LWT franchise auction bid, 120; in international business, 128

Collins, Neil, 241

Common Agricultural Policy, 58–9

Communications Act (2003), 175, 182

Conlan, Tara, 6, 9

Connolly, Billy, 103

Conrad, Jess, 81

Conservative Party: attempts to prevent GD's appointment as BBC Director-General, 136; improved relations with BBC, 320

Cook, Robin, 260, 267, 304–5; *Point of Departure*, 304

Cooke, Stephen, 242

Cooper, John Kaye, 95, 104, 122

Coppock, Peter, 117

Cotton, Sir William, 138

Coutaz, Cecile Frot, 129

Cox, Barry: and Blairs, 10; interviews GD for LWT job, 56; and *The London Programme*, 57; and *Six O'Clock Show* mishap, 63; applies for Director of Programmes post at LWT, 99; and Blair's relations with Murdoch, 182; entertains GD, 323

Cox, David, 59, 75, 147

Cram, Steve, 99–100

Crown Castle, 186

Crozier, Adam, 246

Cummins, Brian, 45–7

Cutting It (TV programme), 196

Daily Mail: attacks GD and BBC, 9; and NHS organisation, 206

Daily Star, 82

Daily Telegraph: advertisement of support for GD, 1, 25–6, 177, 220, 319, 329; hostility to ethnic employees at BBC, 93; criticizes GD's policy at BBC, 156–7; on public reaction to Hutton Report, 316

Daltrey, Roger, 44

Damazer, Mark: reads Hutton report, 3–4; attempts to persuade Davies not to resign, 10; speech on GD's resignation, 21; at TV-am, 78; supports GD's appointment as BBC Director-General, 147; supports Jana Bennett showing dead British soldiers on TV, 250–1; responds to Campbell's attack on BBC, 272; resurrects *Newsnight* report on weapons of mass destruction, 273; reveals Kelly as BBC source, 281; concern for Gilligan, 282; hears Susan Watts's tape of Kelly interview, 282

Dando, Stephen, 13, 15, 209

Dartmouth, Devon, 127
Davies, Gavyn: reads Hutton report, 5–7, 28;
  resignation from BBC Chairmanship, 7–8,
  10–13, 18, 31, 287, 330; and GD's resignation
  from BBC, 16, 18, 22, 30–1; and GD's attitude
  to Governors, 28–9; and Byford's position as
  GD's deputy, 29; on funding of BBC, 165;
  criticizes BBC's narrow class appeal, 197; and
  culture change at BBC, 219; on Iraq war, 251;
  letter from Blair on reporting of Iraq war,
  253–4; and Campbell's attack on BBC, 272; on
  Campbell's excessive behaviour, 273; discusses
  Gilligan story with BBC Governors, 275–6;
  Blair offers compromise to, 278–9; and legality
  of Iraq war, 279–80; on government threat to
  BBC independence, 283; and Campbell's
  resignation, 284
Davies, Howard, 149
Davies, Michael, 96
Davis, Steve, 99
Deakin, Michael, 69, 70–2, 74, 78
Dearlove, Sir Richard, 266, 304
Deech, Ruth, 27
Defence, Ministry of: hounds David Kelly, 3; and
  Gilligan's broadcast, 262–4; and Kelly's
  admission to being source, 279; on Iraq's
  weapons, 306
Defence Select Committee (House of Commons),
  306
Dein, David, 226–30
Diamond, Anne, 79
digital radio, 175–7
digital terrestrial television (DTT), 183–5
Dingemans, James, 284–6
Dobson, Frank, 205
Dodgin, Bill, 221
'dodgy dossier' see February Dossier
Doherty, Moya, 84
Dolgen, John, 189
Dors, Diana, 79–81
Duncan, Andrew, 17, 185, 209
Duncan Smith, Iain, 267
Dunn, Richard, 121–2
Dyke, Alice (GD's daughter): and intrusive
  journalists, 2; birth, 96; and GD's out-of-work
  period, 126; provokes GD to shave off beard,
  141; on Mandela, 191
Dyke, Denise (GD's mother), 34–7, 39, 43–4,
  285
Dyke, Greg: resignation from BBC, 1, 15–21,
  30–3, 287, 318–19, 329–30; diet, 7, 18;
  statement on Hutton report, 11; e-mails BBC
  staff on resignation, 20–1; broadcast interviews
  after resignation, 27; attitude to BBC
  Governors, 28–30; public support for, 31–2;
  birth, background and upbringing, 34–41, 43;
  joins Labour Party, 39, 49; schooling, 39–40,
  43; works as paper boy, 41; sports, 43;
  Saturday work as youth, 44; as trainee manager
  at Marks & Spencer, 44–5; early journalistic
  work, 46–7, 51–2; joins National Union of
  Journalists, 47; political interests and views,
  47–8, 140, 323–7; attends York University,
  48–51; buys house in York, 50; sues York
  Evening Press, 50; works for Wandsworth

Community Relations Council, 52–3; contests
  and loses 1977 GLC election, 53–4; on
  limitations of political action, 53; joins current
  affairs department of London Weekend
  Television, 55–61; attends Harvard Business
  School, 56, 61, 67, 106–8, 201; marriage
  breakdown, 59–60, 328; trade union activities
  at LWT, 65–6; sets up home with Sue, 68; as
  Editor-in-Chief of TV-am, 69, 73, 76–80;
  declines initial offer of TV-am post, 70–1; joins
  board of TV-am Ltd, 86; investment in TV-am,
  88; leaves TV-am and joins TVS, 90, 92–3;
  relish for producing, 92; family and home life,
  96–7, 328; returns to LWT as Director of
  Programmes, 97–101; moves to Twickenham,
  98–9; plays in David Frost's football team,
  99–100; shareholding in LWT, 99, 115–17;
  management style and views, 106–10, 156,
  200–7; as Managing Director of LWT, 106,
  108, 109–10; views on management, 106–8,
  201, 206; and father's death, 110–11, 328;
  reforms at LWT, 113–14; as Chairman of ITV,
  122; and loss of LWT to Granada, 125–6;
  wealth, 125–6; buys property, 127; buys and
  sells international companies for Pearson,
  127–30; horse-riding, 127; joins Pearson, 128;
  leaves Pearson, 133–4; as BBC Director-
  General, 134, 135–6, 139–40, 151–4; criticized
  for supporting Labour, 135–6; delivers
  McTaggart lectures, 140, 157, 160, 167, 170,
  255, 322–3; shaves off beard, 140–1;
  opposition to appointment as Director-General,
  146–8, 150; manifesto on BBC, 148, 198; sells
  shares on appointment to BBC, 152–3; first
  visits BBC sections, 198; human relations with
  staff, 200, 202–3; supports Manchester United,
  222, 227, 328; on Board of Manchester United,
  237, 239–45; gives evidence to Hutton Inquiry,
  272, 285–6; questioned by BBC governors on
  Gilligan story, 276; buys significant
  numberplate, 280
Dyke, Howard (GD's brother): childhood, 34, 38,
  40; academic career, 42
Dyke, Ian (GD's brother), 34–5, 37–9, 42;
  sporting prowess, 221
Dyke, Joe (GD's son), 2, 9, 26, 97, 237
Dyke, Joseph (GD's father), 34–5, 37–9, 43, 222;
  death, 110–11, 328
Dyke, Len (GD's uncle), 44
Dyke, Leonard (GD's grandfather), 36
Dyke, Lil (née Silverton; GD's grandmother),
  37
Dylan, Bob, 328

Easby, Dennis, 235
East, Trevor, 226, 229, 231–2
Eddelson, Mike, 238
Eden, Anthony (1st Earl of Avon), 252, 255
Edinburgh Television Festival, 145, 257; see also
  McTaggart lectures
Edwards, Martin, 227, 236–7, 239–42
Eldridge, Roy, 47
Elizabeth II, Queen: Coronation, 38
Elizabeth the Queen Mother: death, 250
Elliot, Nick, 70, 99–101, 322

Elstein, David, 98, 131–2
Enron (US company), 164
Entwistle, George, 273
Eubank, Chris, 225
European Union: 'Code of Law' and constitution, 270
Evans, Jenny, 60
Evans, Nick: works on Newcastle *Evening Chronicle*, 52; encourages GD to apply for TV post, 55–6; as editor of *The London Programme*, 60–1; *The Horse Whisperer*, 52
Evening Mail (Slough newspaper), 47–8
Evening Standard, 302
Everett, Katharine, 210
Ewart, Keith, 83
Extending Choice (BBC document), 145
Eyre, Richard, 29, 220

Fair Game (TV programmes), 233–4, 236
Fairbairn, Carolyn, 20, 164, 184–5, 189, 321
Fairley, John, 101–2
Falklands war (1982), 252
Fallon, John, 135
Farrell, Terry, 71
Faure-Walker, Rupert, 240
February Dossier (2003; 'dodgy dossier'), 313
Ferguson, Sir Alex, 239
Fleet Holdings, 87
Flynn, Roger, 209
football: on TV, 225–34, 245–8
Football Association: BBC negotiates deal with, 190; and formation of Premier League, 230–1; administration, 236; and BBC's broadcast of FA Cup, 245–6
Football League, 227–8, 230, 246
Ford, Anna, 70, 76–7
Foreign Affairs Select Committee (House of Commons), 266–7, 269–70, 273–5, 277–8, 280–1, 295, 310, 326
Forrester, Andy, 65
Fox, Paul, 228
Fox News, 181
Francis, Dick, 252
Frears, Stephen, 322
Freeview, 183–7, 321
Frost, Carina, Lady, 27
Frost, Sir David: and GD's departure from BBC, 26–7; meets Marcus Sieff, 45; sets up consortium for TV-am, 69–70; replaced at TV-am, 72; on board of TV-am, 77, 88; presents Sunday morning show on TV-am, 80; on Marsh's removal from TV-am post, 88–9; offers football place to GD, 99–100; garden parties, 205
Frost on Sunday (TV programme), 80, 102
Fry, Anthony, 96

Gaitskell, Hugh, 252
Galley, Carol, 124
Gatward, James, 92–4
Geary, Marianne, 51, 282
George VI, King: death, 37
Giant Haystacks (wrestler), 225–6
Giggs, Ryan, 244

Gill, David, 241–2
Gilligan, Andrew: and publication of Hutton report, 3; works for *Today* programme, 24; articles in *Mail on Sunday*, 27, 265, 267; broadcasts on weapons of mass destruction, 250–1, 258, 262–4, 265–6, 273, 288, 316; reports from Iraq, 257–8; meets David Kelly and investigates Iraq dossiers, 258–62, 279, 289–90, 292–4, 308, 314; Campbell's vendetta against, 269–70, 272–4, 282; earlier criticisms of government actions, 270; testifies to Foreign Affairs Committee, 273, 280–1; style, 276; concern for state of mind, 282; vindicated by Susan Watts's tape, 282–3; gives evidence at Hutton Inquiry, 285, 290–1; mistakes, 287–8, 295–6, 317; accused of untruths, 288, 311, 325; record of *Today* broadcast, 288–90; on 45-minute figure, 296
Gladiators (TV programme), 103
Gleeson, Dermot, 318
Glencross, David and Elizabeth, 96
Glyndebourne, 96
GMTV: wins ITV breakfast franchise, 90, 119, 121
Goldsmith, Harvey, 125
Gordon, Dave, 216
Gould, Philip, 310
Grade, Michael: as Director of Programmes at LWT, 58, 62; and *The Six O'Clock Show*, 64; visits USA, 75; as Controller of BBC One, 92; Tesler appoints, 97; protests against Murdoch's bid for Channel Five, 131; offers BBC post to GD, 138; on Birt's BBC, 139; as Chairman of BBC, 207, 318–20; management style, 208; defends BBC Governors, 277; hostility with Birt, 319–20
Gran, Maurice, 129
Granada Television: effects takeover of LWT, 59, 122–5, 321; in franchise auction bid, 119–20; DG owns shares in, 153; and DTT, 183–5; merger with Carlton, 322
Greaves, Jimmy, 100
Green, Hugh, 61
Green, Michael, 120–1, 183, 322
Green, Noel, 84
Greene, Hugh Carleton, 146
Griffee, Andy, 194
Grobbelaar, Bruce, 229
Grundy, Joy and Reg, 128–9
Grundy Worldwide (company), 128–9, 236
Guardian, The (newspaper), 23, 75, 141, 276, 316
Gutteridge, Tom and Rosetta, 118
Gyngell, Bruce, 88–90, 112, 120–3

Hague, William, 135–6
Hale and Pace (comedians), 120
Hale and Pace (TV programme), 103
Hall, Tony, 149
Haran, Maeve, 73
Hardaker, Alan, 230
Harrison, Roger, 114
Harvard Business School: influence on GD, 56, 201; GD attends, 61, 67, 106–8; and BBC achievement, 220

Harvey, Andrew, 23–4
Haste, Cate *see* Bragg, Catherine, Lady
Hat Trick (production company), 114
Have I Got News for You (TV programme), 92, 114
Havers, Nigel, 147
Hayes, Middlesex, 34–5, 38
Hayes Grammar School, 40
Hayes, John, 41
Hearn, Barry, 224–5
Heartbeat (TV programme), 102–3
Heggessey, Lorraine, 171, 201, 247
Henderson, Chris, 32, 98
Hewitt, Gavin, 293
Hewland, Jane, 55
Heywood, Andrew, 181
Higgins, Mick, 41
Highfield, Ashley, 178–9
Hill, David, 23
Hillary, Fiona: and Hutton report, 9; told of GD's dismissal from BBC, 15; bids farewell to GD, 26; and documentary on Mandela, 191
Hillingdon, Middlesex, 39, 41
Hillingdon Mirror, 45–7
Hillsborough Castle, Northern Ireland, 141–2
Hinley, Peter, 41
Hird, Thora, 285
Hitchens, Peter, 50
Hodgson, Patricia, 158, 163, 166, 191
Hogan, James, 152
Hogg, Douglas, 14
Hogg, Sarah, 13–14, 18, 27, 29, 276
Holby City (TV programme), 194
Hollick, Clive, 129–32
Holmes, Jon, 235
Holt, Miranda, 260–1
Home, Anna, 95
Hoon, Geoff, 279, 295, 306, 317, 326
Hornby, Dave, 43
Horsman, Matthew, 142
Housego, Fred, 64
Howard, Michael, 10
Howes, Christine (Sue's daughter), 36, 68, 131
Howes, Matthew (Sue's son), 68, 98, 110, 141
Howes, Sue (GD's partner): and Hutton report crisis, 2, 9; urges Gavyn Davies to resign, 11; and GD's resignation from BBC, 16, 26–7; GD meets, 52; sets up home with GD, 68; works as probation officer, 68; and GD's appointment to TV-am, 74–5; good judgement of people, 75; pregnancy, 92; at Glyndebourne, 96; and GD's appointment as LWT Director of Programmes, 98; meets Michael Barrymore, 103; and effect of wealth, 126–7; and GD's appointment as BBC Director-General, 140; stays at Hillsborough Castle, 141–2; and GD's appointment to Board of Manchester United, 237; watches Wimbledon tennis, 248, 276; at Michael Pallett birthday party, 282; Peru holiday, 284; dislikes New Labour triumphalism, 324; on GD's manner of leaving organizations, 327
HSBC (bankers), 240–1, 243
Hughes, Janice, 240
Humphrys, John, 262, 264, 270, 288–9

Hurst, Peter, 46
Hussey, Marmaduke (Duke), 98, 232–3; *Chance Governs All*, 170
Hutchinson (publishing company), 115
Hutton, James Brian Edward, Baron: report published, 1–4, 286; findings, 4–5, 10–11, 33, 287, 291, 316, 330; report leaked to *Sun*, 4, 8–9; claims to be shocked at reaction to report, 23; on defective BBC editorial system, 264, 268; Campbell testifies to, 268–9; GD testifies to, 272, 285–6; Susan Watts testifies to, 273; sees drafts of September Dossier, 275; and Susan Watts's tapes of Kelly interview, 283; appointed to direct inquiry, 284; and conduct of inquiry, 284–5, 310–11, 316; disregards nature of weapons of mass destruction, 288; and law on media communication, 290–1; dismisses Gilligan's claim on 'sexing up' of dossier, 293; on term 'sexing up', 293–4; questions Brian Jones, 295; questions Dearlove on Iraq's weapons, 304; and Geoff Hoon, 306; and importance of 45-minute claim, 307–9; refuses to allow cross-examination of Blair, 310; on Scarlett, 312; findings dismissed by public, 316, 319

Illsley, Eric, 268
Independent, The, 12, 299
Independent Broadcasting Authority (IBA): and TV-am, 70–1, 80, 82; and TVS, 94
Independent on Sunday, The, 268
Independent Television Commission, 117–18, 130, 139, 188, 190–1; and Thames TV's losing franchise, 121
Ingram, Adam, 263–4
Intelligence and Security Committee (ISC), 267
Iraq: supposed weapons of mass destruction, 3, 251, 261–2, 267, 274, 289, 292, 294–9, 300, 303–5, 309, 312, 324–5; pictures of dead British soldiers in, 250–1; BBC reporting of war, 251–8; legal grounds for war in, 280, 296–8, 303, 324; *see also* September Dossier
Irvine, Ian, 89
ITN, 322
ITV: network and companies, 94; drama on, 101; and auction of franchises, 111–13, 117–19; union power curtailed, 112–13; GD's Chairmanship of, 122; evening news time, 158–9; advertising revenue falls, 171–2, 192; joins BSkyB digital platform, 188; and football rights, 228–9, 232; decline in importance, 321
ITV Digital (*earlier* On Digital), 184–5, 246–7, 321
ITV Network Centre, 322
ITV Sport, 222–3, 233

Jack, David, 221
Jackson, Michael, 141, 174
Jason, David, 102
Jay, Margaret, Baroness, 205–6
Jay, Peter, 57, 70–2, 76, 78
Joint Intelligence Committee (JIC): and Iraq dossier, 259, 264–5, 298, 302, 309
Jones, Brian, 295, 299–300

Jones, Clive: with GD at TV-am, 74, 77–80, 82; on improved TV-am ratings, 84; and TV-am's financial problems, 87; leaves TV-am, 89–90; at TVS, 95; joins Carlton, 126; and GD's candidature for BBC Director-General, 147
Jones, Gareth, 200–1
Jones, Merfyn, 28, 318
Jones, Roger, 150
Journal (Newcastle newspaper), 51–2, 78
Jowell, Tessa, 158, 175, 319–20
'Just Imagine' (discussion sessions), 215–19

Kane, John, 41
Kaufman, Gerald, 257
Keane, Roy, 244
Kearney, Martha, 142
Kee, Robert, 70
Kelly, David: suicide, 3, 59, 279, 281, 284; named by government, 10–11, 285, 309; claims government's 'sexing-up' dossier, 23, 275, 291–4, 308; Gilligan meets and interviews, 258–60, 285, 288, 290, 308, 314, 316; as Susan Watts's source, 273–4, 280–3, 285, 290, 292; admits to being Gilligan's source, 279, 280; testifies to Foreign Affairs Commitee, 280–1; role in drawing up dossier, 290–1; on 45-minute figure, 296, 308–9; knowledge of Iraq's weapons, 307
Kelly, Tom, 291
Kennedy, John F.: assassinated, 43, 329
Khan, Anvar, 193
King, Don, 222
King & Hutchings (newspaper group), 46
Kirsch (sports organization), 247
Kotter, John, 107, 216
Kwei-Armah, Kwame, 194

Labour Party: GD supports, 39, 49, 135–6, 140, 327; GD suggests new plans for, 107; hostility to BBC, 147; Murdoch's influence on, 165, 181–2; divisions over Iraq war, 253, 255; and 'spin', 314; return to power, 324; *see also* Blair, Tony; Campbell, Alastair
'Labour Years, The' (*Panorama* TV programme), 315
Larriman, Mr (of King & Hutchings), 46–7
Lawley, Sue, 208
Leach, Clive, 123
'Leading the Way' team, 216
Leeds, 214
Leicester, 199
Liddle, Rod, 250
Live from the Palladium (TV show), 101
Livingstone, Ken, 54, 64–5
London Independent Broadcasting, 118
London Programme, The, 56–8, 60–1
London Studios (company), 114
London Weekend Television: GD gives shares to Richard Webb, 43; GD joins current affairs department, 55–7; Granada effects takeover, 59, 122–5, 321; franchise renewed (1982) and broadcasting time extended, 61; management and unions at, 65–7, 112; women directors at, 66; GD leaves for TV-am, 75; GD returns to as Director of Programmes, 97–101; GD acquires

shares in, 99; drama programmes, 101; GD as Managing Director, 106, 108, 109–10; and auction of ITV franchise, 111, 118–20; financing and shareholding reforms, 115–17; buys stake in Yorkshire/Tyne Tees Television, 123; shows football matches, 228
London's Burning (TV programme), 101
Loughrey, Pat, 15, 17, 189, 195
Lynton, Michael, 149

McColgan, John, 84
Macdonald, Angus (Gus), Baron, 94, 118
McGovern, George, 49
McHugh, Peter: GD meets on Newcastle *Journal*, 52; at TV-am, 78, 89; supports GD's appointment to BBC Director-General, 147
McKeon, Alan, 129
McKinsey (management consultants): and reorganization of BBC, 161–2, 169, 204; and sport on BBC, 245
McTaggart lectures, Edinburgh, 139–40, 157, 160, 167, 170, 255, 320, 322–3
Mabuza, Lindiwe, 191
Mail on Sunday: interviews GD's ex-wife, 60; on BBC's ethnic imbalance, 193; Gilligan writes in, 265, 267; on Campbell, 268
Major, John, 131
'Making it Happen' (BBC culture change initiative), 210–11, 213–17, 219–20, 275
Manchester: BBC operations in, 196–7
Manchester Evening News Business Awards, 247
Manchester United Football Club: GD gives up directorship, 151, 244–5; GD supports, 222, 227, 328; GD invited onto Board, 237, 239; GD invests in, 238; BSkyB attempts to buy, 239–43; playing successes, 244
Mandela, Nelson, 191, 329
Mandelson, Peter, 107, 132–3, 145, 278, 282
Manning, Sir David, 273
Marks, Laurence, 129
Marks & Spencer: GD works for, 44–5
Marr, Andrew: on leak of Hutton report, 8; on Davies's resignation, 11; on Campbell's resignation, 284
Marsh, Kevin, 258, 260–4, 285
Marsh, Richard, 72, 77, 88–9
Marsh, Terry, 225
Match of the Day (TV programme), 228, 233, 245–8
Matthews, Cerys, 218
Maxwell, Robert, 174
Me and My Girl (TV comedy), 104
Mellor, David, 54, 117, 236
Men Behaving Badly (TV programme), 122
Mentorn (company), 118
Menuhin, Yehudi, Baron, 76
Mercury Asset Management, 124
Meridian Television, 127–9
Merrick, Ken, 244
Merrilees, Bob, 84
Merrill Lynch (stockbrokers), 242
Merseybeat (TV programme), 196
Mildred, Mark, 53

Millennium Dome, 132–3
Miller, Ron, 102–3, 117, 123
Millichip, Bert, 230
Milne, Alasdair, 98, 146
Milner, Simon, 12–13, 15–16, 30–1, 275–6
Mitchell, Al, 104
Mittal, Lakshmi, 315
Monds, Fabian, 28, 318
Moore, Adrian, 90
Morgan, Peter: *The Deal* (drama), 322
Motson, John, 247
Mowlam, Mo, 141–2, 150
Murdoch, James, 132
Murdoch, Rupert: reduces bid for Channel Five, 131; supports Iraq war, 147; New Labour's deference to, 165, 182; media dominance, 180–3, 321; hostility to BBC, 183; and football rights, 231–3; attempts to buy Manchester United, 239–43; Blair discusses with Prodi, 315; TV series on, 322
Murphy, Gerry, 185
Murphy, Mike, 129

National Health Service: GD observes and reports on, 205–7, 209
Neighbours (TV programme), 128
Neill, Ron, 71, 74, 139–40, 150
Neville-Jones, Pauline: reads Hutton report, 5–7; and proposed resignations from BBC, 8, 15; qualities, 14; and GD's resignation from BBC, 16–17, 28–31, 318; changes mind on GD's position, 28–31; supports Byford, 28–9; opposes GD's appointment to BBC, 154; attacks Iraq dossier, 267
Newbon, Gary, 235
News 24, 172
News International (company), 180
Newsnight (TV programme): on Hutton report, 12; Christopher Bland appears on, 16; presents Susan Watts's report on weapons of mass destruction, 273–4, 280, 293
Nield, Alison, 205
Niger: Saddam's supposed purchase of uranium from, 312, 324
Nixon, Richard M., 49, 314
Norridge, Julian, 56
Northern Ireland, 141, 275

Oborne, Peter and Simon Walters: *Alastair Campbell*, 272
Observer, The (newspaper), 267
Office, The (TV programme), 142
Omar, Rageh, 256
On Digital *see* ITV Digital
One BBC (document), 161
'One BBC Group': activities, 162, 164, 166, 170, 192, 200, 217–18
Only Fools and Horses (TV programme), 62
Orr, Marjorie, 58
Osman, Sally, 10
Ottaway, Richard, 280
Owen, Nick, 72

Packer, Kerry, 87–8
Page & Moy (travel company), 115

Pallett, Michael, 282
Panorama (TV programme), 315
Parkinson, Mary, 76–7
Parkinson, Michael, 70, 76–7
Parry, Rick, 231–2
Paxton, Robin, 119
pay TV: and sport, 248–9
Peacock, Alan, 111
Pearson Television, 105, 127–30, 133–4, 136–7, 236
Peretsman, Nancy, 128–9
Perry, Sydney, 105
Peru, 284
Pevensey Bay, East Sussex, 35
Phillips, Trevor, 147
Phillis, Bob, 143, 162
Pickard, Nigel, 95
Plantin, Marcus, 103–4
Plowman, Jon, 142
Poirot (TV programme), 101, 103
Pollard, Eve, 79
Polygram (music company), 118–19
Potter, Dennis, 139
Powell, Colin, 313
Powell, Enoch, 239, 276
Powell, Jonathan, 301–2, 303, 309
Premier League (football): established, 229–31; and TV rights, 230–3, 245–6, 249
Price, Andy, 64–5
Prodi, Romano, 315
Project, The (broadcast drama), 261
Public Adminstration Select Committee (parliamentary), 309
Putney: GLC election (1977), 53–4
Puttnam, David, 182

Question Time (TV programme), 256

Rabbatts, Heather, 150
Radio Four, 176
Radio Two, 177
RAI (Italian state broadcaster), 187
Rebuck, Gail, 108
Rees, Gordon, 6
Rees, John, 48, 51
Rees-Mogg, William, Baron: criticizes Hutton report, 4, 283; and GD's shareholdings, 153
Reid, John, 265
religion: on TV, 104–5
Reynolds defence ruling (2001), 290, 308
Rippon, Angela, 70, 76–7
Rixon, John, 222, 244
Robben Island, South Africa, 329–30
Robinson, Gerry, 123, 125
Roland Rat, 81–2, 84, 86, 92
Root, Jane, 144, 209
Ross, Jonathan, 177
Ross, Paul, 177
Rowan, Kathy, 89
Rowland, 'Tiny', 238
Royal Television Society, 32, 102, 125
RTL (Luxembourg company), 130, 133, 137
rugby football, 234–5, 249
Rusbridger, Alan, 141
Ruth Rendell Mysteries, The (TV series), 95

Ryder, Richard Andrew, Baron: reads Hutton report, 5–7; apologizes, 11, 22–3, 287; requests GD's resignation, 15–17; Mark Byford accompanies while making statement, 21; at Governors' meeting on Gilligan story, 276

Sacks, Jonathan, Chief Rabbi, 211
Saddam Hussein, 251, 289, 297–8, 301, 304, 309, 312, 325; see also Iraq
Salmon, Margaret, 151–2
Salmon, Peter, 17, 23, 189, 245, 247
Sambrook, Richard: reads Hutton report, 3–4; and leaked Hutton report, 8; and Byford's position at BBC, 30; government complains to over reporting of Iraq war, 253, 257; thanks Gilligan for staying in Baghdad, 258; Campbell complains to, 265–6, 271; GD discusses Gilligan story with, 265; responds to Campbell's attack on BBC, 271–2; questions Susan Watts on sources, 273, 281; questioned by BBC governors on Gilligan story, 276; and Mandelson's suggestion for compromise, 278; GD buys numberplate for, 280; on Kelly's disappearance and suicide, 281
Sarkis, Angela, 27
Scardino, Marjorie, 133–4
Scarlett, John: government influence on, 220; drafts dossier under Downing Street pressure, 264, 275, 296, 301, 302, 303, 309, 311–12, 317; disbelieves Saddam's possession of weapons of mass destruction, 304, 306–7; as head of SIS (MI6), 313, 317
Schierenberg, Tai-Shan, 144
Schlosser, Herb, 33
Schmeichel, Peter, 244
Scholar, Irving, 227, 231
Schummer, Dan, 225
Scotland: BBC in, 195–6
Scotsman, The, 269
Scott, Emma, 17, 23–4, 26, 155, 185, 198
Scott, Selina, 71
Scotti, Tony, 130
Scurfield, Ralph, 40
Secret Intelligence Service (SIS; MI6), 262, 279, 298, 300, 304, 307, 312, 317
SelecTV, 129
September Dossier (Iraq's Weapons of Mass Destruction), 59, 259–60, 264–6, 282–3, 291–2, 294–6, 298–303, 306–7, 310, 311–12, 316, 328
Sharman, Mark, 95
Shaw, Julie, 59
Shevas, Anne, 264
Shier, Jonathan, 103
Short, Clare, 262, 267
Shorthouse, Dominic, 130
Sieff, Marcus, 45
Sikora, Karol, 110
Silverton, Albert, 37
Simpson, John, 214, 252
Sissons, Peter, 250
Six O'Clock Show, The (TV programme), 61–5, 67, 73; scrapped, 101
Sixsmith, Martin, 315
Sky News, 181
Smith, Chris, 133, 150, 157–8, 165–6, 175

Smith, John (BBC's Finance and Property Director), 11, 19, 164, 166, 170, 212, 272
Smith, John (chairman of Liverpool FC), 227, 230
Smith, Jon, 272
Smith, Robert, 28, 318
Smith, Sir Roland, 237–42
Snoddy, Ray, 46, 119, 130, 147
Snow, Jon, 12, 207
Socialist Workers Party, 49
Solskjaer, Ole Gunnar, 238–9
Sondhi, Ranjit, 28, 318
South Africa: GD visits, 32, 329–30
South Bank Show, The (TV programme), 62, 103
Southall, Middlesex, 38–9
Southgate, Colin, 128
Southgate, Michael, 105, 114, 122, 236
'Spin Doctors' (Panorama TV programme), 315
Spindler, Susan, 210, 214–15
Springsteen, Bruce, 149
Stanton, Jane, 87
Stapleton, John, 27, 32, 79–80, 83, 85, 89, 147
'State of the Union' (TV programme), 235
Stevenson, Dennis, Baron, 149, 237, 243
Stevenson, Michael, 321
Stockbridge, Hampshire, 127
Stoke-on-Trent, 199
Stothard, Peter, 146–7, 154, 257
Straw, Jack, 268, 277
Street-Porter, Janet, 56, 63–4
Suez crisis (1956), 252, 255, 325
Sugar, Alan, 231–2
Sun, The (newspaper): reaction to Hutton report, 4–5, 8; receives leaked Hutton report, 4, 8–9; disparages GD, 81; supports New Labour, 182; on Campbell's attack on BBC, 269; on Iraq threat, 302
Sunday Telegraph, 239, 241–2, 266
Sunday Times, 141–2, 153
Sunrise consortium, 90
Swanmore, Hampshire, 93

Tarbuck, Jimmy, 99, 101
Tarrant, Chris, 83–4, 86
Tatnall, Jane, 40
Taylor, Christine (GD's ex-wife): at York, 50; trains and works as probation officer, 51–2; marriage breakdown, 59–60, 67–8
Taylor, Graham, 236
Taylor, Steve, 199
Teletubbies, the, 81
Television South West (TSW), 118, 120
Ten O'Clock News (BBC), 157–61
Tenet, George, 306
Tesler, Brian, 58, 97–9, 106, 115, 117, 120
Thames Television: as rival to LWT, 103; loses franchise, 121; bought by Pearson, 128
Thatcher, Margaret, Baroness: and appointment of BBC Governors, 14; Gyngell's friendship with, 89, 121; hatred of unions, 111; and TV franchise auctions, 113, 117–18; and Birt's term at BBC, 144; and appointment of Hussey as BBC Chairman, 232; style as Prime Minister, 326
Thomas, Ward, 123
Thompson, Daley, 99

Thompson, Mark: and BBC news time, 158; succeeds GD as Director-General of BBC, 162, 174, 319; and funding of BBC One, 171; leaves BBC for Channel Four, 174; turns down Freeview, 186; favours ethnic employees at BBC, 194; as Director of Television, 149, 195; and changes at BBC, 210, 212; and repeat broadcast of England football win over Germany, 247

Thomson, Caroline, 13, 17, 278

Time Warner (US company), 127

Times, The: opposes GD's appointment as BBC Director-General, 146-8, 150; on GD's property business, 153-4; on Campbell's accusations against BBC, 269; Baldwin at, 315

Titchmarsh, Alan, 137

Today programme: GD visits staff, 24; GD's interview on, 27; Gilligan broadcasts on weapons of mass destruction, 250-1, 258, 260, 262-3, 277, 317; editorial system, 258, 264, 268; Ingram appears on, 264; Reid attacks Gilligan's story on, 265; Campbell attacks, 269; and Newsnight report on weapons, 273-4

Tusa, John, 153-4

TV-am: launched, 69-70; financial and organizational problems, 71-3, 84-5; GD joins as Editor-in-Chief, 72-3, 76-7; disorder at, 76-8; relaunch and success, 79-86, 89; GD joins board, 86; investments increased, 87-8; staff rosters reorganized, 87-8; changes under Gyngell, 89-90; closes down (1992), 90; GD leaves, 90; union action at, 112; and franchise auction, 119-20

TVS: GD joins as Director of Programmes, 90, 92-3; business success, 93-4; programmes and management, 95-6; auction bid for franchise, 118

Twiggy, 113

Tyne Tees Television, 123

Tyson, Mike, 222

UKTV (consortium), 130

Ullman, Tracey, 129

United News and Media, 130, 136-7

United States of America: GD's interest and travel in, 49; dominance, 173-4; media companies ownership in ITV, 175; Murdoch operations in, 181; corporate culture in, 209-10; and Iraq war, 256; scepticism over Iraq's weapons, 306; media support for Iraq war, 321-2

Van Gelder, Roy, 66

Vaughan, Paul, 83

Vietnam war, 49

Virgin (consortium), 130-1

Waddell, Gavyn, 66

Wade, Rebekah, 5, 8

Wakeling, Viv, 95

Walden (TV programme), 101

Walden, Brian, 111

Walker, Roy, 95

Wandsworth Council for Community Relations, 52-3

Warburg Pincus (US finance house), 124, 130

Wark, Kirsty, 24

Warren, Frank, 225

Waterman, Dennis, 99

Watts, Susan, 273-4, 280-2, 285, 290, 292-3

weapons of mass destruction (WMD) see Iraq

Webb, Andy, 78, 89

Webb, Christine, 47

Webb, Martin, 42

Webb, Richard, 42-3, 238, 327

Webber, John, 77

Weekend World (TV programme), 55-9, 62, 70, 101

Weller, Keith, 41

Weller, Roger, 41

Wheldon, Sir Huw, 252

White City: BBC building, 212-13; BBC music centre planned, 271-2

White, Noel, 230

Whittle, Stephen, 264

Wiles, Danny, 63

Williams, Peter, 95

Willis, Wincy, 79

Wilson, Harold, Baron, 325

Wilson, Kate, 263

Windsor, Barbara, 81

Witley Park, Surrey, 270

Wogan, Terry, 64

women: directors at LWT, 66; at BBC, 192-3

Wood, Ann, 81-2

Wood, Dudley, 234-5

Wood, Lynn Faulds, 27, 78, 83, 86, 89

Wood, Victoria, 177

Woodward, Bob: Plan of Attack, 306

World at One, The (radio programme), 261

Wright, Jeff, 48, 51, 68, 235

Wyatt, Will, 150-1, 161; The Fun Factory, 143, 145

Wyndham Goldie, Grace: Facing the Nation: Television and Politics, 1936-1976, 255

Yates, Paula, 64

Yeading Junior school, 39

Yentob, Alan, 148, 209, 271-2

York Evening Press: GD wins libel suit against, 50-1

York University: GD attends, 48-51; GD elected Chancellor, 51

Yorke, Dwight, 238-9

Yorkshire Television, 101-2, 123, 233, 236

Young, Barbara, 29, 150

Young, Mal, 194l

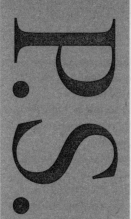

Ideas,
interviews
& features…

About the author

2   Leading by Example:
     Q and A with Greg Dyke

4   Life at a Glance

6   Top Ten Favourite Films

9   Top Ten Favourite Tracks

About the book

10   A Collective Failure? by Greg Dyke

15   A Day in the Life of Greg Dyke

Read on

16   If you loved this, you'll like…

17   Find Out More

Leading by Example

Louise Tucker talks to Greg Dyke

In your acknowledgments you start by mentioning that autobiographies were something that you used to believe shouldn't be taken too seriously, before you wrote one. Did writing your own have a valuable purpose for you?

Writing the first half was interesting, going back through my history and seeing patterns emerging, but I can't imagine writing another. It would be too hard. This one was in my head. Sue's question about why is it always a drama when I leave somewhere is probably the truest line in the book. Her remark implied that it was somehow my fault and I asked myself was it? Yeah I could have given the governors more regard but I thought they were wallies and I was quite happy with that. I am still quite happy with that. I'm not going to play the game. People like me because I am what I am, I say what I think. At the BBC I didn't understand the politics so I didn't have to get involved.

What's changed since you wrote it?

What *hasn't* changed in the whole time is that people still congratulate me for standing up to the government. Not just BBC people but when I go round Tesco's they come up to me and say 'you were dead right, well done' or 'someone had to stand up to them'. Blair thinks this is about Islington people disliking him but the hostility goes much deeper. But he'll get away with it.

Now that you've written the book, what's next?

I feel ready to do something else. Writing a book was interesting and worth doing but I think that I ought to go and do another full-time job, in fact I probably want to and ought to. I don't need the money but I can't stop working. I feel like I should be doing something. I've just bought a hotel in Sheffield and I'm planning to turn it around, like I did with a golf course. It's not about making the money but about making it work.

The public speaking pays the bills. I also draw pensions from Pearson and the BBC but I can't live off them: they don't pay for the horse. I'll never retire, I can't imagine it. Up till now I've turned down all the non-exec jobs that I've been offered but I might go back to do one of those.

The family is pissed off that I'm always around and yet it's such a special time: my son's about to go off, the last one, and it's sad to think that they won't ever be that close again. Alice is at Leeds University so when Joe goes it will be the end of an era.

It's interesting to read of the way your life boomerangs: you start off somewhere then go back, even down to where you live. It's a strong current in your life: why do you think that is?
Never lose your roots, they matter, never lose where you came from. At the age of 57 most of my friends come from at least two decades ago. If you're the boss you don't make friends because you're busy climbing through the organisation. My best friend I've known since we were kids together, some others from

6 I'm not going to play the game. People like me because I am what I am, I say what I think. 9

LIFE
at a Glance

BORN

May 1947 Hayes
Middlesex

EDUCATED

Yeading Junior School,
Hayes Grammar School
and York University

CAREER

From local journalism to
television, including stints
at London Weekend
Television, TVS, TV-am,
Channel Four, Channel
Five, Pearson Television
and the BBC.

FAMILY

Lives with his partner Sue
in Twickenham, Middlesex
and has four children.

HOBBIES

Sport, particularly
football, riding and skiing.

newspapers, some in recent years but most
are not from the media. Sue and I always had
another life. We had a rule: never invite
anyone to the house because of business, not
if you don't like them – we chose not to.

**How does it feel to write about so many of
your friends, colleagues and enemies and
how did you always find something good to
say about each and everyone, bar a few
exceptions?**
People are never all bad. Someone said to me
how many people have you lost since leaving
the BBC and I said nobody. People in our lives
were separate from them, from work. That's
what I don't understand about David Kelly:
why didn't he just go back into his family and
friends? His daughter was getting married a
few weeks later. The test of people is how they
cope with tough times. Leaving the Director-
Generalship was not as traumatic as leaving
LWT. Not many people leave an organisation
with staff on the street and since I would have
left anyway that was a good way to go.

How do you feel about the BBC now?
I think Mark Thompson is shocked because
he thought he was coming back to an
organisation where people didn't answer back
and now they are answering back. At the BBC
you're on the defensive, it's the only job in the
world where you're under attack all the time. I
was attacked for being commercial and my
response to that was 'no, I'm competitive'.

Do you have any regrets?
I have no aspiration to be anybody else – I've
made money, I've run the BBC – but I wish I'd
had a wider education, I wish I'd read more.

I'd like to understand classical music more. The books I read are either crap novels on planes or serious stuff but not great novels. My musical tastes are stuck in my twenties and thirties like most people's. The earliest stuff I like is Buddy Holly. When I went on the Ken Bruce Show I did add one Blur song: I asked my son 'what's that Blur song I like?' because it was so embarrassing that nothing I'd chosen was later than 1970. I included Neil Young and my brother said 'I hope you're not going to embarrass us all with this stuff'. In fact I've spent the last 18 months going to see all these guys again, like Fleetwood Mac and Dylan. I met Dylan after 40 years of being a fanatic. I don't often pull rank but Scorsese was making a film about him in London and I asked if I could meet him.

Did he know who you were?
I don't think he knew who anybody was!

You describe the age of your parents as 'the age of respect': how would you describe the early 21st century?
I come from a generation where we rejected parents' values completely. We were the aberration, kids are now much closer to their parents. We're now the parents and don't give a fuck what the neighbours think. My children say to me 'what are we supposed to rebel against?!'

I hope that it's an age of opportunity. I dislike tuition fees: they're based on a bogus concept that graduates earn more which is no longer the case 'cause there's so many of them. I passionately believe that children should carry on in education as long as possible, get as much education as possible.

> 〈The test of people is how they cope with tough times. 〉

Top Ten
Favourite Films

Oh! What a Lovely War

The Great Escape

The Producers

One Flew Over the Cuckoo's Nest

Cabaret

Butch Cassidy and the Sundance Kid

E.T.

City of God

All Quiet on the Western Front

A River Runs Through It

I know so many people who would have had more fulfilling lives if they hadn't left school at fifteen.

You're still a West Londoner, and your career and your book are very focused on the city: how do you feel about London as a city and what do you think it is about it that keeps people, despite all its drawbacks?
London is a great place because you can walk into a shop and meet all sorts of people from all sorts of backgrounds. I love the cosmopolitan nature of it.

Success, said Maeve Haran about you, resulted because 'you didn't have enough imagination to contemplate failure' and you said that there was some truth in that. But what do they each, success and failure, mean to you?
Some people go into things believing they're not going to work and if you go into things believing things will be fine then they will be but you're still shocked when they're not. When the Hutton report came out there was nothing further from my mind – that I might not be a Director-General – I was shocked when it happened. I think you get success if you like the world. It was as easy to get on with the bloke on the door as much as anybody else. I've always hated the status nature of society. I've been lucky: I've run organisations that weren't status conscious.

And what does leadership mean?
A good friend of mine is writing a book on leadership and he's identified four qualities of leadership: I have the highest results in the first three but no marks in the fourth. The

fourth is survival, watching your back but you can't do 1–3 if you spend all your time watching your back and being involved in politics. The single most important thing in an organisation is the stories that people tell about you: like soldiers, which officers are liked and which are not and why. The question to ask is would you go over the top with them? You have to lead by example. I was very impressed by Southwest Airlines who work on the basis of employing for attitude. Employ the positive people or make sure that you can turn the people you've got into positive people and give them confidence. Your job as a leader is to give people confidence. You have to believe that people perform better if they are valued: then they often perform better than you think they will.

You mention being asked to write a leadership book: would you do it now?
I thought about taking a chapter out and expanding it but I'm really not sure I want to write another book.

Is there a perfect job for you?
No, not really. What motivates me is that I think the job is difficult. I'm not motivated by money-making. Money in capitalism is a measure of success. If I made a lot of money now I might give it away. I gave some of my payoff from the BBC to York University, I give away a lot. Sue and I have a trust and we recently gave twenty thousand to Shelter to do work in prisons. Sue used to be a probation officer and we're both interested in penal policy. You can change lives with a small amount of money.

❝What motivates me is that I think the job is difficult. I'm not motivated by money-making.❞

What are your politics now?

I'm a left of centre libertarian now. I don't believe in politics anymore. Look at the recent ruling on terrorism. The Law Lords ruled that the idea of keeping people without trial was unlawful and the government seemed to ignore it. Our government is desperately illiberal, they don't care about democracy or freedom. I felt the public welcomed Tony Blair because he seemed different, straight, honest but events suggest he's not which makes him worse, because he promised difference. The other lot didn't, they didn't promise to be straight. Blair is the end result of the end of ideology, the end result of the wall coming down. Politics is now about consumerism so if a poll tells him it's good then he'll do that. This government stands for the *Daily Mail*, they stand for the media; there is no belief except for their need to win again. That's not to say that there aren't some good things that have been done because there have been. Schools look better, so do hospitals – but the staff aren't happier because the government don't think it's important to treat people well.

And what of your early ambitions to be a Labour MP?

Long gone, long gone. I wanted to be an MP for the same reasons that they did, as a career. I'd be much more use now. Government, whatever you want to say about it, is a system of patronage because there's nowhere else to go in politics so you've got to suck up. Believers in New Labour, who were expecting a caring society and got a capitalist one, are terribly disappointed by what we have.

❝ Never lose your roots, they matter, never lose where you came from. ❞

At university you were fascinated with Watergate, not surprisingly since it was as contemporary to you as a student as Iraq is to us. Do you think the government has now had its own version of Watergate?

In terms of the long-term impact of the whole affair, I think in twenty years we will see this as the beginning of the change of our democracy. We will have to change our democracy because as Butler discovered we have a presidential system in Britain but without the checks and balances. That's what we've seen with Thatcher and Blair: there is no one to say no to them. I'm happy for us to have a President but I want limited terms of governance and a Supreme Court. A friend of mine, who is high up in television, read the book and said that the Hutton chapter was devastating and that it will stand forever as a story of what the government did.

You've worked in TV for years: are there any programmes that are more significant than others?

I love *The Office*: when I was at the BBC I watched an episode, the appraisal episode, with about ten other senior staff at BBC and we all looked at each other during it and thought oh my God! And, in terms of class, if you come from a working-class background you spend your life thinking you're still Terry from the TV programme *The Likely Lads* when in fact you've become Bob. The programme wasn't really about the two of them: it was about Terry and Thelma because they represent the two ways for the working classes to progress. It takes you an age in your life to realise that you can be both, a little bit of Terry and a little bit of Bob. But don't be Thelma!

Top Ten
Favourite
Tracks

Whiter Shade of Pale
Procul Harum

Just Like a Woman
Bob Dylan

The Night They Drove Old Dixie Down
The Band

After the Goldrush
Neil Young

Rave On
Buddy Holly

Satisfaction
Rolling Stones

Summertime
Ella Fitzgerald

Born to Run
Bruce Springsteen

Always on My Mind
Elvis Presley

American Pie
Don McLean

9

A Collective Failure?

by Greg Dyke

LOOKING BACK A YEAR OR SO and knowing what we now know, the whole Dr Kelly saga has a rather unreal quality to it because, today, there is no doubt that the BBC story which led to my departure from the BBC was fundamentally right when it said that Downing Street had sexed up the case for going to war in Iraq.

So if this was true why did such a bizarre series of events happen, events which led to the departure of the two top players at the BBC? In particular why did Tony Blair and Alistair Campbell pursue such a vendetta against the BBC? The answer I suspect is that they had convinced themselves that they were right. They couldn't have known how much information would come out.

In fact it only became public because of two unforeseeable events: Dr Kelly killing himself which led to Blair setting up the Hutton Inquiry and George Bush establishing an inquiry into how the security services in the USA got their intelligence about Iraq so wrong, leaving Blair with no option but to do the same. Without these two inquiries – both of which were forced upon the Prime Minister by outside circumstances – we would know very little.

What is now clear is that the person who has suffered the most from Lord Hutton's report is Lord Hutton himself. He was a virtually unknown Law Lord when he was selected to chair the inquiry into the death of Dr David Kelly. So why was he picked? We now know his name was suggested because it was thought that Hutton was likely to support the establishment position.

But Hutton had the wrong impact. He delivered what Downing Street wanted but the public rejected his views almost immediately. Given that it was six months before the concrete evidence which destroyed Hutton's report was actually published, with Lord Butler's devastating critique of the way Blair runs Government, how did the public know so early that Hutton's was a deeply flawed report? The problem was that Lord Hutton's findings didn't line up with the evidence given to the inquiry, evidence which the British public had seen and heard for themselves, so they instinctively rejected his ridiculously one-sided findings.

Of course the BBC governors didn't take the same view as the public and decided to get rid of me as a result, even though up until then they had supported the position we had all taken collectively. If I was guilty so were they. But much more important is what impact has the whole affair had on the BBC?

Back in 2003 Michael Grade, now the chairman of the BBC, appeared on *Question Time* and praised the stand taken by the governors to support the story. Curiously since he became Chairman neither Grade nor his new Director-General, Mark Thompson, has said anything significant about the affair publicly. In particular neither Grade nor Thompson has said whether or not they support the abject apology which the acting chairman Lord Ryder gave on behalf of the

‘Why did Tony Blair and Alistair Campbell pursue such a vendetta against the BBC?’

governors the day after Hutton reported. Ryder apologised 'unreservedly' for everything, a statement we later discovered he had sent to, effectively clearing with, Downing Street before he gave it.

The reason all this matters is that the whole affair has compromised the reputation of the BBC and as a result its independence has been questioned, particularly overseas. Whenever I've travelled abroad in the past year I have found a very strong belief that it was Tony Blair personally who got rid of both Gavyn Davies and me as a means of pulling the BBC into line and to stop it challenging the Government in the future. The feeling abroad is that the BBC had gone along with this to preserve *its* future.

Until the new leaders of the BBC stand up and make their position clear on the Gilligan affair people won't know for certain the truth of the matter. There are also other executives inside the BBC who were both responsible for, and intimately involved in, the Kelly affair who have also gone remarkably quiet; it's time for them to speak out too.

And we certainly need to know if the current Board of Governors at the BBC – and particularly those who were there a year ago – think negotiating a decent Charter renewal settlement is more important than the BBC's independence from Government?

And then we come to Dr Kelly. I have never been a conspiracy theorist but too many questions have been asked and not answered about his death. An inquiry asking the simple question 'did he kill himself or not?' is needed if only to clear the matter up. Personally I suspect it would find that he did commit suicide but that does need to be established

❝ The whole affair has compromised the reputation of the BBC and as a result its independence has been questioned, particularly overseas. ❞

for certain. However the likelihood of this Government re-opening the whole affair is nil and as a result the conspiracy theorists will continue to gain credence.

And finally Blair, Campbell and the Downing Street machine. I understand why it is said that Gordon Brown finds it difficult to believe a word Tony Blair says, which is odd because I didn't feel that a year ago when I was forced out of the BBC. It was the publication of the Butler report which changed everything for me.

Butler showed without question that the famous dossier arguing the case for going to war in Iraq had been sexed up. It is now obvious that John Scarlett, the Chairman of the Joint Intelligence Committee, signed off on the September dossier when the supporting evidence was at best questionable. Unlike the head of the CIA who was forced to resign, Scarlett got his reward when he was appointed to run MI6, but his position is untenable. Who would buy a used car from this man let alone intelligence to justify going to war again?

What is interesting is that the public now believe, like Gordon Brown, that what Blair says is not to be trusted. His trust ratings have collapsed as a result of Iraq, Hutton and Butler, and outside of the Labour loyalists it is hard to find many who any longer believe or respect him, a dramatic turnaround in only two or three years. But Blair is still Prime Minister and is likely to remain so for some years after Labour is re-elected in May. So why has Blair not paid the price for misleading the nation?

I suspect what the whole sad tale tells us is that the public have given up on traditional

> ❮ The public now believe, like Gordon Brown, that what Blair says is not to be trusted. His trust ratings have collapsed as a result of Iraq, Hutton and Butler. ❯

> **❝The great loser in the whole story is public trust in the political process overall and in politicians in particular. ❞**

politics and particularly on politicians. They had great hopes in Blair in that he offered them a new form of politics, but in their eyes he has betrayed them. The problem they now face, however, is who to vote for. When I was promoting this book I addressed large meetings all over the country and the question people asked time after time was 'what's the alternative?' So the public's sense of betrayal is not only about Blair; the great loser in the whole story is public trust in the political process overall and in politicians in particular. That should worry us because our democracy has been undermined by this whole affair.

Of course in the end Lord Butler avoided the decision he should have taken. In his report he said that no one individual should take the blame and that what had happened was the result of a 'collective failure'. But only one person in Government can be responsible for a collective failure on that scale and that's the Prime Minister. In the end Lord Butler, having produced an insightful report, had a failure of nerve; he should have called on the Prime Minister to resign.

A Day in the Life of Greg Dyke

I'M ALWAYS UP FIRST IN OUR HOUSE. Even though I no longer have to be at a job every morning I haven't got out of the habit of waking up at seven. I make the tea and wake up everyone else just before eight. With only one of our four kids still at home the whole process of early morning is more relaxed than it used to be.

Most days start in my rather small study where I write my weekly column for the *Independent*, get involved in my various business interests (the latest being the acquisition of a hotel in Sheffield) and draft the countless speeches which I seem to do these days. I joke that they are virtually all about leadership or weapons of mass destruction.

I can't say I miss the series of tedious meetings that dominated my life at the BBC – looking back now I can't even remember what we used to discuss at such length. And I've discovered I can live happily without reading the press cuttings which used to be so important. I now know that most stories are read by virtually no one.

I have some interesting lunches, enjoy being back involved in the commercial world after four years in the public sector, and live a more relaxed life. But one question still dominates all: do I want to continue this eclectic life or do I want to be an executive again? At home I'm regularly asked 'got a job yet?' so maybe I haven't got a lot of choice.

> ❛We have a presidential system in Britain but without the checks and balances. That's what we've seen with Thatcher and Blair: there is no one to say no to them. ❜

If you loved this,
you'll like…

***Citizen Greg: The Extraordinary Story of
Greg Dyke and How He Captured the BBC***
Chris Horrie and Steve Clarke
An account of Greg Dyke's career from local
journalism to Director-General of the BBC.
Includes interviews and anecdotes from many
of Dyke's colleagues and friends.

Shooting History
Jon Snow
Another well-known and well-loved figure in
British broadcasting takes us through
political history and personal memoir from
the forties to the noughties.

***An Honourable Deception?: New Labour,
Iraq, and the Misuse of Power***
Clare Short
Labour MP Clare Short, who had served in
Tony Blair's government for almost two
terms, resigned from the Cabinet over the war
in Iraq in 2003. This is her account of why and
an insider's examination of what lies at the
heart of Blair's government.

***Uncertain Vision: Birt, Dyke and the
Reinvention of the BBC***
Georgina Born
An independent portrait of one of the biggest
and most well-known corporations in the
world. Based on the late 1990s, when John
Birt was Director-General, the author met
and interviewed people from all ranks within
the BBC in order to write a history of the
organisation and those who work in it.

Find Out More

SURF

www.the-hutton-inquiry.org.uk
All the information about the Hutton inquiry
into the death of Dr David Kelly.

www.butlerreview.org.uk
Information about the Butler Review of
Intelligence on Weapons of Mass
Destruction.

www.number-10.gov.uk
The official Downing Street website.

www.downingstreetsays.org
An unofficial website which lists all the PM's
Official Spokesman's daily press briefings to
political journalists.

WATCH

There is, as yet, no film of the Hutton or
WMD inquiries but other landmark political
films include:

All The President's Men (1976)
Film of the Bernstein/Woodward classic book
starring Dustin Hoffman and Robert
Redford. William Goldman won an Oscar for
the screenplay.

Three Days of the Condor (1975)
A bookish CIA researcher, played by Robert
Redford, comes back from his lunch break to
find all his colleagues shot dead. When he
tries to get help from his superiors, they send
someone to shoot him. For the next three
days, Joseph Turner (codename 'Condor')

must find out who is responsible before he is shot too.

The Manchurian Candidate (1962 and 2004)
A Korean War POW is brainwashed into becoming an assassin by Communists; another soldier and former POW Bennett Marco, played by Frank Sinatra, is sent to investigate. Originally made in 1962, the 2004 Jonathan Demme remake moves the action and political background to Iraq and the first Gulf War.

VISIT

Visit the sites of much of the Hutton/Butler drama; the BBC and the Houses of Parliament.

BBC Television Centre
Wood Lane,
London W12 7RJ
www.bbc.co.uk/tours
Bookable tours of the TV studios, newsroom and interactive studio.

House of Commons, London, SW1A 0AA
House of Lords, London, SW1A 0PW
www.parliament.uk
Tours of both houses are available, depending on the time of year.